RENEWALS 458-4574

DATE DUE

GAYLORD			PRINTED IN U.S.A.

Devolution and constitutional change in Northern Ireland

MANCHESTER
1824

Manchester University Press

DEVOLUTION series
series editor Charlie Jeffery

Devolution has established new political institutions in Scotland, Wales, Northern Ireland, London and the other English regions since 1997. These devolution reforms have far-reaching implications for the politics, policy and society of the UK. Radical institutional change, combined with a fuller capacity to express the UK's distinctive territorial identities, is reshaping the way the UK is governed and opening up new directions of public policy. These are the biggest changes to UK politics for at least 150 years.

The *Devolution* series brings together the best research in the UK on devolution and its implications. It draws together the best analysis from the Economic and Social Research Council's research programme on Devolution and Constitutional Change. The series will have three central themes, each of which are vital components in understanding the changes devolution has set in train.

1 **Delivering public policy after devolution**: **diverging from Westminster**: Does devolution result in the provision of different standards of public service in health or education, or in widening economic disparities from one part of the UK to another? If so, does it matter?

2 **The political institutions of devolution**: How well do the new devolved institutions work? How effectively are devolved and UK-level matters coordinated? How have political organisations which have traditionally operated UK-wide – political parties, interest groups – responded to multi-level politics?

3 **Public attitudes, devolution and national identity**: How do people in different parts of the UK assess the performance of the new devolved institutions? Do people identify themselves differently as a result of devolution? Does a common sense of Britishness still unite people from different parts of the UK?

Devolution and constitutional change in Northern Ireland

Edited by
Paul Carmichael, Colin Knox and
Robert Osborne

Manchester University Press

Manchester and New York

distributed exclusively in the USA by Palgrave

Published by Manchester University Press
Oxford Road, Manchester M13 9NR, UK
and Room 400, 175 Fifth Avenue, New York, NY 10010, USA
www.manchesteruniversitypress.co.uk

Distributed exclusively in the USA by
Palgrave, 175 Fifth Avenue, New York,
NY 10010, USA

Distributed exclusively in Canada by
UBC Press, University of British Columbia, 2029 West Mall,
Vancouver, BC, Canada V6T 1Z2

British Library Cataloguing-in-Publication Data
A catalogue record for this book is available from the British Library

Library of Congress Cataloging-in-Publication Data applied for

ISBN 978 0 7190 7388 5 *hardback*

First published 2007

16 15 14 13 12 11 10 09 08 07   10 9 8 7 6 5 4 3 2 1

Typeset by Servis Filmsetting Ltd, Manchester
Printed in Great Britain
by Biddles Ltd, King's Lynn

Contents

Figures

Tables

Abbreviations

AME	Annually managed expenditure
BIC	British–Irish Council
BIIC	British–Irish Intergovernmental Conference
C&AG	Comptroller and Auditor General
CAJ	Committee on the Administration of Justice
CoC	Committee of the Centre
CPA	Commissioner for Public Appointments
DED	Department of Economic Development
DEL	Departmental expenditure limit
DETI	Department of Enterprise Trade and Investment
DFM	Deputy First Minister
DPP	Director of Public Prosecutions
DUP	Democratic Unionist Party
ECHR	European Convention on/Court of Human Rights
EDF	Economic Development Forum
EOC	Equal Opportunities Commission
EPF	Executive Programme Funds
ESRC	Economic and Social Research Council
EU	European Union
FEA	Fair Employment Agency
FEC	Fair Employment Commission
FM	First Minister
FPC	Finance and Personnel Committee
GAA	Gaelic Athletic Association
GFA	Good Friday Agreement
IICD	Independent International Commission on Decommissioning
IMC	Independent Monitoring Commission
INI	Invest Northern Ireland
IRA	Irish Republican Army
MEP	Member of the European Parliament

MLA	Member of the Legislative Assembly
NATO	North Atlantic Treaty Organisation
NDPB	Non-departmental public body
NGO	Non-governmental organisation
NIA	Northern Ireland Act
NICS	Northern Ireland Civil Service
NIE	Northern Ireland Executive
NIHRC	Northern Ireland Human Rights Commission
NILGA	Northern Ireland Local Government Association
NIO	Northern Ireland Office
NIPB	Northern Ireland Policing Board
NIUP	Northern Ireland Unionist Party
NLA	National Liberation Army
NSMC	North/South Ministerial Council
OFMDFM	Office of the First Minister and Deputy First Minister
PAC	Public Accounts Committee
PAFT	Policy Appraisal and Fair Treatment
PESA	Public Expenditure Statistical Analysis
PfG	Programme for Government
PMB	Private Members Bill
PR	Proportional representation
PSNI	Police Service of Northern Ireland
RAB	Resource accounting and budgeting
RPA	Review of Public Administration
RUC	Royal Ulster Constabulary
SDLP	Social and Democratic Labour Party
SMP	Single member plurality
STV	Single transferable vote
TME	Total managed expenditure
UKUP	UK Unionist Party
UUP	Ulster Unionist Party

Contributors

Dominic Bryan is Director of the Institute of Irish Studies, Queen's University, Belfast; Chair of Democratic Dialogue, Ireland's first think tank; and has worked with the Northern Ireland Human Rights Commission and the Community Relations Council. He is an anthropologist researching political rituals, public space and identity in Northern Ireland.

Paul Carmichael is Head of School of Policy Studies at the University of Ulster. His research interests include UK and comparative public administration, including territorial governance, local government and the civil service, on which he has published widely. He has been a consultant to central government departments and agencies, local authorities, other public bodies and local media. In addition, Professor Carmichael is Honorary Secretary of the Political Studies Association and Vice-Chair of the Public Administration Committee of the Joint University Council.

John Coakley is a fellow at the Woodrow Wilson International Center for Scholars, Washington, DC, and an associate professor of politics in University College, Dublin. He has recently edited or co-edited *The Territorial Management of Ethnic Conflict* (2nd edition, Frank Cass, 2003), *Politics in the Republic of Ireland* (4th edition, Routledge, 2004), *From Political Violence to Negotiated Settlement: The Winding Path to Peace in Twentieth-Century Ireland* (University College Dublin Press, 2004) and *Renovation or Revolution? New Territorial Politics in Ireland and the United Kingdom* (University College Dublin Press, 2005).

Brice Dickson has been Professor of International and Comparative Law at Queen's University, Belfast, since 2005. From 1999 to 2005 he served as the first Chief Commissioner of the Northern Ireland Human Rights Commission, a statutory body created as a result of the Belfast (Good Friday) Agreement, and in the 1990s he was for five years a member of the Equal

Opportunities Commission for Northern Ireland. From 1991 to 1999 he was the foundation Professor of Law at the University of Ulster. He has published extensively on the legal system of Northern Ireland, civil liberties and human rights, the role of judges and French and German law.

Oonagh Gay has worked in the House of Commons Library for over 20 years. She is currently Head of the Parliament and Constitution Centre, responding to queries from MPs, research assistants, academics and journalists. She has specialised in several aspects of parliamentary reform, parliamentary standards, electoral law, public administration and devolution, and has produced a series of briefing papers available on the parliamentary website and also published a number of articles in specialist journals. She is a member of the Study of Parliament Group, and council member of the Hansard Society. She completed an 18-month secondment to the Constitution Unit, University College London, where she has published comparative work on the regulation of parliamentary standards, the parliamentary audit function and Officers of Parliament.

Mark Goodwin is Professor of Human Geography at the University of Exeter. His research has centred on an analysis of the structures and processes of sub-national government, and he was co-director of a recent ESRC project on 'Constitutional change and economic governance: territories and institutions' (L219252013). His publications include over fifty refereed papers and chapters, and he has written or edited eight books, including *The Local State and Uneven Development* (Polity Press, 1998), *Introducing Human Geographies* (Arnold, 1999), *Practising Human Geography* (Sage, 2002) and *Envisioning Human Geographies* (Arnold, 2004).

Martin Jones is Professor of Human and Director of the Institute of Geography and Earth Sciences at the University of Wales, Aberystwyth. He researches in the general field of political and economic geography and is author of *New Institutional Spaces* (Routledge, 1999), co-editor of *State/Space: A Reader* (Blackwell, 2003), and co-author of *An Introduction to Political Geography* (Routledge, 2004).

Rhys Jones is Senior Lecturer in Human Geography in the Institute of Geography and Earth Sciences at the University of Wales, Aberystwyth. His research interests focus on the geographies of the state and nationalism. In particular, he is interested in the 'peopling of the state' or, in other words, the active role played by state personnel in reproducing state organisations and territories.

Eric Kaufmann is Lecturer in Politics and Sociology at Birkbeck College, University of London. He is the author of *The Rise and Fall of Anglo-America: The Decline of Dominant Ethnicity in the United States* (Harvard, 2004), editor of *Rethinking Ethnicity: Majority Groups and Dominant Minorities* (Routledge, 2004) and has written numerous journal articles in the field of nationalism and ethnic conflict. He is currently working on a book on the Orange Order in Northern Ireland since 1950. He is also an editor of the journal *Nations & Nationalism*.

Michael Keating is Professor of Regional Studies at the European University Institute, Florence; and Professor of Scottish Politics at the University of Aberdeen. He has published widely on urban and regional politics and nationalism. His most recent book is *The Government of Scotland. Public Policy Making after Devolution* (Edinburgh University Press, 2005).

Colin Knox is Professor of Comparative Public Policy in the School of Policy Studies at the University of Ulster. His research interests include public administration reform and local government. He was a joint researcher with Professor Paul Carmichael on the recent ESRC Devolution and Constitutional Change programme.

Roger Mac Ginty is a lecturer at the Department of Politics, University of York. His research focus is on political violence, conflict and peacemaking. His latest book is *No War, No Peace: The Rejuvenation of Stalled Peace Processes and Peace Accords* (Palgrave, 2006).

John McGarry is Professor of Political Studies and Canada Research Chair in Nationalism and Democracy at Queen's University, Kingston, Ontario, Canada. His latest books include *The Northern Ireland Conflict: Consociational Engagements* (Oxford University Press, 2004), co-authored with Brendan O'Leary; *The Future of Kurdistan in Iraq* (University of Pennsylvania Press, 2005), co-edited with Brendan O'Leary and Khaled Salih; and *European Integration and the Nationalities Question* (Routledge, 2006), co-edited with Michael Keating.

Lee McGowan is Senior Lecturer in the School of Politics, International Studies and Philosophy at Queen's University, Belfast. His research interests focus particularly on European competition policy and Northern Ireland in the EU. He has published widely in journals, including the *Journal of Common Market Studies, Journal of Contemporary European Studies, European Journal of Political Research, Governance, Irish Political Studies,*

Journal of European Public Policy, Public Administration and *Regional and Federal Studies*. He is currently working on a new book for Palgrave on competition policy in the EU.

Gillian McIntosh is a research fellow in the Institute of Irish Studies, Queen's University, Belfast. Her main interests are in Irish history, and centre around the themes of ritual, symbolism and commemoration. Her publications include *The Force of Culture. Unionist Identities in Twentieth-Century Ireland* (Cork University Press, 1999) and *Belfast City Hall. One Hundred Years* (Blackstaff Press, 2006).

Arthur Midwinter is a visiting professor in the Institute for Public Sector Accounting Research at the University of Edinburgh. He was formerly Dean of the Faculty of Arts and Social Science at the University of Strathclyde. His research interests are in devolution finance and local government finance, and he has advised the London Assembly, the Northern Ireland Assembly and the Scottish Parliament.

James Mitchell is Professor of Politics at Strathclyde University. His chapter draws on research completed under his project, 'Devolution and the centre', part of the ESRC Devolution and Constitutional Change programme.

Paul Mitchell teaches political science and research methods in the Department of Government and the Methodology Institute at the London School of Economics and Political Science. He is a co-principal investigator of the ESRC-funded Northern Ireland Election Study, and his most recent book (with Michael Gallagher) is *The Politics of Electoral Systems* (Oxford University Press, 2005).

John Morison is Professor of Jurisprudence and Head of the School of Law at Queen's University, Belfast. With the late Professor Stephen Livingstone he was holder of a grant within the ESRC Devolution and Constitutional Change programme for a project titled 'The role of law and Litigation in articulating Northern Ireland's emerging constitutional framework' (L219252114). Professor Morison is a member of the Board of Directors of the European Public Law Centre based in Athens, and in 2005 was appointed as a member of the Judicial Appointments Commission for Northern Ireland.

Brendan O'Leary, an Irish citizen, is Director of the Solomon Asch Center and Lauder Professor of Political Science at the University of Pennsylvania.

He was educated at Oxford and the London School of Economics and Political Science, where he was a professor and chaired its Department of Government. He is the author, co-author or co-editor of 15 books and over a hundred articles and chapters in refereed journals and university press volumes. *The Northern Ireland Conflict: Consociational Engagements* (with J. McGarry; Oxford University Press) was published in 2004, and *The Future of Kurdistan in Iraq*, (co-edited with J. McGarry and K. Salih; University of Pennsylvania Press) in 2005. He has been a constitutional advisor in Iraq, Northern Ireland, Somalia, and South Africa.

Robert Osborne is Director of the Social and Policy Research Institute at the University of Ulster. His previous publications include *Higher Education in Ireland: North and South* (Jessica Kingsley, 1996), *Fair Employment in Northern Ireland: A Generation On* (co-editor; Blackstaff, 2004) and *Devolution and Pluralism in Education in Northern Ireland* (co-editor; Manchester University Press, 2005). His current research interests lie in equality policy, education and devolution.

Henry Patterson's most recent book is *Ireland since 1939* (Oxford University Press, 2002). He was currently completed a book on popular unionism and Orangeism since 1945 with Eric Kaufmann for Manchester University Press.

Jonathan Tonge is Professor of Politics at the University of Salford. Recent books include *The New Northern Irish Politics* (Palgrave, 2005) *Northern Ireland* (Polity, 1995) *Sinn Féin and the SDLP* (with Gerard Murray; Hurst/O'Brien, 2005) *Northern Ireland: Conflict and Change* (2002, Pearson). Co-editor of *Irish Political Studies*, he has recently published articles on Northern Ireland in *Political Studies*, *Party Politics* and *Contemporary British History*, and has completed three ESRC projects on Northern Ireland's political parties.

Margaret Ward is Director of the Women's Resource and Development Agency. Her former work has included Assistant Director of Democratic Dialogue, research fellow at Bath Spa University College and women's officer for the Department of Community Services, Belfast City Council. Her publications include *Unmanageable Revolutionaries: Women and Irish Nationalism* (Pluto Press, 1983); biographies of Maud Gonne and Hanna Sheehy Skeffington, and a co-edited book (with Louise Ryan) *Irish Women and Nationalism: Soldiers, New Women and Wicked Hags* (Irish Academic Press, 2004).

Rick Wilford is Professor of Politics at Queen's University, Belfast. He has written extensively on Northern Ireland politics and, with Robin Wilson, leads the Northern Ireland devolution monitoring project which is co-funded by the ESRC and the Leverhulme Foundation and coordinated by the Constitution Unit, University College, London.

Robin Wilson has been Director of the think tank Democratic Dialogue since its foundation in 1995. Along with Professor Rick Wilford of Queen's University, Berfast, he is co-leader of the Northern Ireland team in the devolution monitoring project coordinated by the Constitution Unit, of which they are both honorary senior research fellows. He chairs the policy committee of the Northern Ireland Community Relations Council and is an adviser to the Council of Europe project on intercultural dialogue and conflict prevention. He is a member of the advisory council of the Dublin-based think tank TASC, with which Democratic Dialogue was partnered in sponsorship of the island-wide Democracy Commission. He is a former editor of *Fortnight* magazine and a frequent contributor to the British, Irish and international media on Northern Ireland affairs.

Acknowledgements

We are very grateful for the support of Charlie Jeffrey who, as Director of the ESRC's Devolution and Constitutional Change Programme, ensured that research on Northern Ireland was fully represented in the Programme as the contributions to this book testify. We would also like to thank Sharon Corcoran for preparing the index. Above all, however, we would like to express our gratitude to Hazel Henderson. Hazel played a pivotal role in assisting in the editing of chapters, chasing contributors about queries and generally ensuring the smooth preparation of the book. As editors, however, we must take responsibility for any errors or omissions.

Paul Carmichael
Colin Knox
Robert Osborne
December 2006

1
Introduction

Paul Carmichael, Colin Knox and Robert Osborne

Background

The establishment of devolved institutions in Scotland, Wales and Northern Ireland from 1999–2000 onwards, during which powers were transferred from Westminster to the regions, witnessed a significant landmark in the politics of the United Kingdom. As Hazell (2000: 1) noted: 'the United Kingdom entered the year 2000 with four governments instead of one. It had replaced a unitary system of government with a quasi-federal system.' Early indications of the likely outcomes ranged from one in which devolution was seen as unstable, likely to produce conflict between different parts of the UK and end in the disintegration of the UK union, through to the emergence of new territorial politics which would revitalise and strengthen democracy in a union whose structures were outdated and moribund (Jeffery, 2002).

To track the emergence and development of devolution the Economic and Social Research Council (ESRC) funded a major (in excess of £5 million) research programme in 2000 to explore the series of devolution reforms in Scotland, Wales, Northern Ireland, London and the English regions since 1997. Entitled 'Devolution and Constitutional Change', the programme was designed to build a critical mass of research capacity, capable of providing rigorous and balanced analysis of the impact and outcomes of devolution.

The programme sought to address questions broadly around three key themes:

- *Nationalism and national identity.* How do people in different parts of the UK understand and participate in the new institutions? Do they identify themselves differently as a result of devolution?
- *Governance and constitutional matters.* How well do the new devolved institutions work? How far is the UK 'centre' in Westminster and Whitehall having to change the way it works as a result of devolution?

- *Economic and social policy.* Does devolution result in the provision of different strands of public service or in growing differentials in economic performance from one part of the UK to another?

Some 35 projects were chosen to address these and related questions. The projects were selected to meet two challenges, according to the Programme Director, Professor Charlie Jeffery. The first was to mobilise and develop insights from across the social science disciplines, providing a fuller understanding of the devolution dynamic and its implications for the UK. The second challenge was to feed the research into policy debates by identifying potential pitfalls and problem areas, setting out alternative options, and creating opportunities for policy learning through comparison with experience elsewhere.

Treatment of the particular circumstances which have surrounded devolved government in Northern Ireland has featured in a number of the ESRC research projects. Devolution followed directly from the 1998 Belfast (Good Friday) Agreement, which provided, *inter alia*, for a democratically elected Assembly 'inclusive in its membership, capable of exercising executive and legislative authority, and, subject to safeguards, to protect the rights and interests of all sides of the community' (NIO, 1998: 5) Commenting on the importance of the Agreement, Bogdanor noted:

> The Agreement has a double significance for the government of the United Kingdom since it proposes not only a solution to the Irish problem, but also recognition of the process of devolution to the non-English parts of the United Kingdom. (Bogdanor, 2001: 109)

This demanded a great deal of the Agreement. The conjunction of devolution and the implementation of the Agreement, where the former is wholly dependent on the vagaries of the latter, have resulted in intermittent attempts at devolved government in Northern Ireland. The latest suspension of the Northern Ireland Assembly since October 2002 has further embedded direct rule from Westminster, with limited short-term prospects at the time of writing (early 2006) of re-establishing a power-sharing Executive and devolved Assembly.

Structure of the book

This edited volume brings together researchers from the ESRC Devolution and Constitutional Change programme, whose projects examined Northern Ireland either exclusively or as part of a comparative project, and other experts. As such, it does not look specifically at the Northern Ireland experience of devolution during the 1921–72 period. Rather, the concentration is on the post-1998 Belfast Agreement era, and readers seeking an evaluation of the earlier experience of devolution are pointed towards, among others, the substantial analyses of the period such as Lawrence (1965), Birrell and Murie (1980), Buckland (1979) and Wilson (1989). For those who also need a perspective on the long years of direct rule, Cunningham (2001) can be recommended as a starting point.

This book aims to assess the Northern Ireland experience from four key perspectives. First, it considers the inextricable link between devolution and constitutional developments, to which Bogdanor refers. Second, it examines how the main political parties responded to devolution and the major challenges faced by society in moving beyond conflict (such as political symbolism, the role of women, equality and human rights issues). Third, it attempts to assess some of the outworkings of devolved government in its short-lived form, or those seeded in devolution and carried on by direct rule ministers. Finally, Northern Ireland devolved government and associated institutions are located within the wider relationships with Westminster, the Republic of Ireland and Europe.

Robin Wilson's chapter (Chapter 2) considers various efforts of successive UK (and Irish) governments, among others, to create a durable and acceptable arrangement for resolving Northern Ireland's longstanding constitutional imbroglio. Wilson notes how the 'Sunningdale Agreement' was an elite-negotiated 'consociationalist' design in which there is an 'unthought-through elision' between individuals, communities and the political domain. Recalling Brian Barry's remarks, this approach was rooted in what amounted to a misapplication of Arend Lijphart's work. In the meantime, suggests Wilson, Lijphartian analysis has itself been transformed – Lijphart himself now accepts that his classic text rested on outdated primordialist assumptions. For Northern Ireland meanwhile, longevity and associated sense of intractability has had a perverse, perpetuating effect on the Northern Ireland conflict. Indeed, ironically, if the later Belfast (Good Friday) Agreement was 'Sunningdale for slow learners', it has brought with it a collapse of the 'moderate middle'. In moving beyond consociationalism, Wilson calls for an alternative integrationist perspective in which a coalition of the 'moderate middle' is more realistic than an inclusive executive. Most militant 'ethno-nationalists' tend to operate on assimilationist assumptions that lead to indefinite zero-sum conflict and the reification of identities. The ensuing mutual veto arrangements must be avoided, with a move instead to more cross-community (but not all party) coalitions – 'secular weighted majority decision making'. As a 'deeply divided society', consociationalism has been tried in Northern Ireland but found wanting – integrationism offers a better way, involving government by the 'moderate middle' rather than grand coalitions; weighted majorities and minority rights safeguards, not mutual veto; intercultural dialogue, not segmented autonomy; and equality of life-chances throughout, not proportionate allocation of public sector posts. A virtuous cycle must be fostered based on increasing inter-communal trust and diminution of old enmities that transcend the zero-sum battle of unionist/nationalist, rather than institutionalising it. In short, 'both/and' rather than 'either/or'. Wilson laments how 'too much policy focus has attended to paramilitaries and their future, and too little to politics and constitutional design'.

In Chapter 3, Roger Mac Ginty draws on time series data from the Northern Ireland Life and Times Survey. Despite a period of political flux in which there were repeated suspensions of the devolved institutions, Mac Ginty manages to produce some clear conclusions based on an extensive survey of public opinion. Mac Ginty indicates that, in one sense, there is no discernible devolution effect, inasmuch as Catholic and Protestant attitudes to Northern Ireland's constitutional status remain largely unchanged. However, given that such 'pure' choices are unrealistic, given the complexity of contemporary multi-level governance arrangements both within the UK and Europe, a more subtle and nuanced approach to discerning public attitudes is required. The former dyadic choice of 'United Ireland' or 'Northern Ireland as part of the UK' has been challenged by additional devolved constitutional permutations and possibilities. The most popular constitutional option for Northern Ireland is entrenched devolution, whereby Northern Ireland remains in the UK but with its own elected parliament, which has law-making and tax-raising powers, albeit with differential attitudes forthcoming from Protestants and Catholics. For Mac Ginty, nonetheless, there is a discernible 'devolution effect', with support for devolved options diluting that for the 'pure' constitutional goals. The Belfast Agreement is a form of 'enhanced consociationalism', leaving both nationalists and unionists in 'the uncomfortable Janus-faced position of having to cooperate together on functional devolved matters in the power-sharing Assembly, while working against each other to secure constitutional objectives'. Interestingly, neither Protestant nor Catholic respondents shared much enthusiasm for a constitutional referendum (on Northern Ireland's future). Equally revealing, irrespective of their 'preferred' fate for Northern Ireland, small and declining minorities of both Protestants and Catholics would 'happily accept' the will of the majority, suggesting that both communities have internalised the principle of consent. However, with the fitful experience of devolution thus far, we are left to ponder whether devolution will be regarded as desirable but unworkable and hence will citizens retrench to type?

John Morison (Chapter 4) explores the extent to which the Belfast Agreement and the ensuing Northern Ireland Act 1998 are novel in constitutional terms. Based on interviews with leading politicians, civil servants and lawyers, he considers the possible existence of a new constitutional paradigm that arises in respect of the making of the Agreement itself (and the subsequent Act), the operation of executive government, and the detail of the litigation arising from the Act and its impact. Morison's research suggests that law played a fairly minor role, due in large part to the very traditional perceptions of law held by most of the participants to the process. In short, the law followed the politics. However, he asks whether the Agreement and Act are undervalued as matters of constitutional law, for they cannot be accommodated into traditional accounts of UK constitutionalism as an act of the Westminster Parliament, making provision for devolved government in one part of the Kingdom for the settlement is now backed by an international treaty and dual referendum. Second, the Executive in Northern Ireland was based on the idea of a coalition. However, with some ministers (Democratic Unionist Party – DUP) refusing to sit in the cabinet, it suggests the need for a more formal structure on which to organise government, as the normal Westminster model and its conventions do not apply. Third, most politicians instinctively disliked reporting to the courts to resolve what they regarded as essentially political issues. Most litigation was for tactical reasons (short-term), albeit while espousing fairly traditional approaches to legal interpretation. Few politicians seemed interested in getting the courts to adopt a particular interpretation of the constitution, which might be significant in guiding future conduct. Overall, the 1998 settlement did not transform the constitutional landscape directly or immediately. Law in the courts had a role in regulating unstable relationships, but that role was always secondary, Morison contends. Nonetheless, law remains central to the Agreement and though, in the view of James Hamilton, founding father of the US constitution, the courts are the 'weakest branch' of the constitution, the courts can play a useful role, should a new constitutional paradigm be allowed to develop.

Chapter 5, by John McGarry and Brendan O'Leary, is reprinted here from an earlier publication (*Political Quarterly*, 2004) together with a short postscript which enables the authors to address recent developments. They write from an unashamedly pro-Agreement perspective and their chapter is designed to explore how the procedures of the Assembly and Executive, including the rules governing the operation of the Office of First Minister and Deputy First Minister, elections, ministerial positions, and voting in the Assembly, might be reformed/revised within the letter and spirit of the Agreement, so as to enhance the stability of the institutions. They consider from where the challenges to the Agreement and institutions have come, that is, who has been responsible for the succession of crises that have prevented full implementation of the Agreement, while also considering who must yet fulfil their obligations to ensure compliance. McGarry and O'Leary speculate on the prospects for the proposed changes outlined in the subsequently 'Comprehensive Agreement' almost concluded between the DUP, Sinn Féin and the two governments in December 2004. However, they contend that the changes would have created even more institutional obstacles to executive formation, instead preferring their own original suggestions for modifying the procedures. They add that, though this Comprehensive Agreement foundered over the issue of photographic evidence of decommissioning, they believe Sinn Féin and the British government are now meeting their obligations under the Belfast Agreement. Equally, while the loyalist paramilitary groups have not yet reciprocated republican moves on decommissioning, their activities (such as the rioting of September 2005) do not threaten the peace process. The DUP's refusal to share power with Sinn Féin is the biggest impediment to restoration and operation of the political institutions. Interestingly, McGarry and O'Leary argue that while some steps can be taken to address the DUP's concerns, both governments must act in the absence of DUP engagement. For instance, the British–Irish Intergovernmental Conference should revert to the functions and capacities enjoyed by its predecessor (under the Anglo-Irish Agreement), alongside incremental promotion of the cross-border dimension and all-island cooperation. The latter, in particular, would provide a strong impetus for those opposed to the Agreement, such as the DUP. Equally, they contend, that it is in Sinn Féin's own interest to make devolution work, rather than let the Agreement fall in abeyance. Overall, while accepting that the institutions are flawed, they contend that these flaws can be addressed without destroying the institutions altogether.

Henry Patterson and Eric Kaufman (Chapter 6) provide a convincing explanation of the shifting sentiments within popular unionism, with a detailed analysis of grassroots opinion within both the Ulster Unionist Party (UUP) and the Orange Order: two 'highly democratic, decentralised institutions' which, until recently, were closely related with, and supportive of, one another. Drawing parallels with modernisation processes that have challenged status hierarchies around the western world since the Second World War, they chart the steady substitution of the old unionist 'squirearchy' by 'self-made populists'. Consequently, almost irrespective of some important but arguably short-term factors such as popular discontent over delays in Irish Republican Army (IRA) decommissioning, they contend that a 'tipping point' has been passed in which there has been a major electoral realignment within unionism since the late 1990s, manifest in the decline of the UUP and rise of the DUP. The DUP is held to be much better placed to articulate the aspirations and fears of ordinary unionists. Unlike their forebears, grassroots unionists (be they in the UUP itself, the Orange Order or simply the population at large) have become much less deferential towards the social elite. As that elite flirted with reform moves in the 1960s and sought an accommodation with nationalists in the 1970s and again in the 1990s, so its legitimacy has waned. Such developments have made elite accommodation – the precursor to durable power sharing – that much less likely. Pessimistically, Patterson and Kaufman contend that, under unionism's new leadership, the prospects for securing an accommodation with Sinn Féin appear remote, leaving devolution marooned as a governing mechanism for Northern Ireland.

Jonathan Tonge considers the changing approaches and electoral fortunes of the Social Democratic and Labour Party (SDLP) and Sinn Féin in his chapter on nationalism and republicanism (Chapter 7). Tonge contends that both (Northern) Irish nationalism and republicanism have experienced change. For a variety of reasons both endogenous and exogenous, Sinn Féin's ideological stance has undoubtedly mellowed, enabling it to brook decisions considered unthinkable less than a generation ago – and yet the effect on its electoral performance has been electrifying. Ironically, in contrast, in achieving (all that) it had strived for over almost 30 years, with the Belfast Agreement, the SDLP has experienced a dramatic reversal in its electoral fortunes. Sinn Féin is now more focused on the 'equality agenda'. The old notion of 'liberty' being the precursor to 'equality' has been subordinated to its acceptance of political pluralism. It is not the sole representative of Irish nationalism. As a minority within a minority, the SDLP is left to search for a new role, albeit one that may prove elusive. Unlike Sinn Féin which is all-Ireland, the SDLP remains an exclusively northern-based nationalist force (for the time being) that faces an acute dilemma. Does it fight on the same ground as Sinn Féin or seek a new centre ground accommodation with the UUP? Tonge's analysis begs the question of whether there has been a blurring of the fault line between nationalists and republicans and whether Northern Ireland's nationalist/republican community needs two communal parties.

Paul Mitchell's contribution (Chapter 8) on party competition and voting behaviour since the Belfast Agreement describes how the 'old guard', in the shape of the SDLP and UUP, have been 'outflanked' by Sinn Féin and the DUP respectively. He points to the 1994 IRA cessation of its armed campaign as the catalyst for Sinn Féin's renewed electoral advances. The party's electoral growth in the 1980s and 1990s, he argues, can be explained by mobilising nationalist non-voters and new-age cohorts, rather than directly winning SDLP voters. This changed after the Belfast Agreement – the peace process 'has been the handmaiden of Sinn Féin's electoral growth'. Recent Sinn Féin's electoral growth is explained at the SDLP's expense. On the unionist side, the DUP's success is linked to the 1998 Agreement and its implementation, which became a major electoral liability for the UUP. Mitchell's analysis explains the shift to the DUP as its success in taking advantage of the UUP's internal difficulties after 1998 and its own moderation in policy position. He concludes that the once 'extreme' parties have successfully outflanked and partially replaced their more moderate intra-ethnic rivals. This would entitle the DUP to the post of First Minister in a new coalition, and four other Executive members (with two each from the UUP, Sinn Féin and the SDLP). Whether the DUP will use its electoral strength to become Northern Ireland's leading party of government in a power-sharing Executive is another question.

Dominic Bryan and Gillian McIntosh's contribution (Chapter 9) on symbols and identity examines how the Belfast (Good Friday) Agreement has, under the banner of encouraging plurality, entrenched the main communities through its recognition of two cultural blocs and, at the same time, tried to find what they describe as 'a hyphenated British–Irish form around a common Northern Irishness'. Bryan and McIntosh illustrate the potency of symbolism in Northern Ireland with examples such as controversies over flags, the symbols of the Assembly, the new badge for the Police Service of Northern Ireland, royal visits to the province, the Saint Patrick's Day parade and Remembrance Day. They conclude that devolution and the Northern Ireland Assembly have not heralded the reduction in symbolic conflict. Rather, Westminster-derived policies and legislation have influenced the most changes, in the form of a draft Bill of Rights, equality and fair employment legislation and proposals in the *Shared Future* policy document. In short, symbolism remains strong in the Northern Ireland context and strategies to defuse its impact have been exerted from above (through direct rule ministers) rather than within political interest groups in Northern Ireland.

Margaret Ward's chapter on the changing role of women in the context of devolution (Chapter 10) provides evidence that although gender has not been a particularly decisive force in the Northern Ireland Assembly, female representatives have articulated issues for the marginalised and excluded in society. Despite the fact that more women were elected to the 2003 Assembly (18), the loss of political representation by the Women's Coalition was explained 'more as a reassertion of sectarian voting patterns rather than as a vote against women'. Ward describes the problems in redressing gender-based discrimination within public bodies such as the Police Service of Northern Ireland(PSNI), the appointment of independent members of the Northern

Ireland Policing Board, non-departmental public bodies and the judiciary. More positively, she commends gender representation on district policing partnerships and the way in which the appointment process was completed. In the same vein she outlines the role played by women in the voluntary and community sector, both in countering the gender deficit in decision making and in the cross-community peace building, albeit with an inadequate and declining resource base. The voluntary and community sector is an area within which Ward concludes women can play a full part in decision making and which will 'go some way towards redressing the democratic deficit contingent on the lack of a devolved institution and the lack of gender parity in political and public life'.

Brice Dickson and Robert Osborne's chapter on equality and human rights since the Agreement catalogues the developments in both fields (Chapter 11). These include the creation of the Equality Commission, the implementation of section 75 (Northern Ireland Act), establishing the Human Rights Commission and the production of a draft Bill of Rights for Northern Ireland. Formative evaluations are offered by the authors on these developments. They judge the Equality Commission to be a 'fairly cohesive body' by the end of its first five years, but are less impressed by the implementation of section 75, which is seen as a 'diligent but generally unambitious approach from the public services'. This contrasts with the field of fair employment, which has witnessed a marked improvement of Catholics in employment, especially in the public sector. Such improvements in employment practises, however, sit uneasily among the Protestant community, with the 50:50 recruitment quota system now in place for those applying to join the PSNI. The Belfast Agreement committed the British government to create a Northern Ireland Human Rights Commission, but may have 'oversold the concept of human rights by not being specific enough on which rights would be better protected . . . or in what manner those protections would be guaranteed'. Hence the government is 'unhappy' about having a comprehensive Bill of Rights for Northern Ireland where others in the UK would not enjoy such protections as the Bill affords. Instead, it is the Human Rights Act 1998, which came into force throughout the UK in 2000, more than the Belfast Agreement that has alerted 'every public authority in Northern Ireland to the need to operate strictly in accordance with the European Convention on Human Rights'. While the authors describe the picture regarding human rights as 'rosier than it was but not as bright as it could be', they call for them to be depoliticised and urge a greater sense of urgency on the part of government in addressing issues of equality and human rights.

Rick Wilford's chapter on the Northern Ireland Assembly and Executive provides an overview of the workings of the devolved institutions at Stormont

(Chapter 12). The convention of collective responsibility did not feature in the Executive: individual ministerial responsibility, rather than cabinet government, was the norm. This led to governing parties treating their departments as party fiefdoms. Wilford concludes that the achievements of devolution were, perhaps, 'rather modest but they are noteworthy given that there were additional constraints that affected the activities of the Assembly and the Executive'. These constraints he outlines as structural, arising from the consociational template (inclusive power sharing, the proportionality principle, the unanimity rule) and operational (the wide remit of the statutory committees). The proposed changes to the workings of the institutions (the process of Executive formation, procedures to achieve collective responsibility and measures to enhance the scrutiny of the Executive) could lead to more durable political arrangements. Wilford argues, however, that these changes must be underpinned by improvements in community relations, and ways of countering perceptions that the Agreement has brought disproportionate advantages to the nationalist over unionist communities.

In Chapter 13 Arthur Midwinter considers the vexed matter of finance. Finance is central to the fate of devolution. However, there remains much confusion as to the nature of the financial relationship between London and the devolved administrations, as well as to the possible effects of recalculating the current manner in which financial entitlements are determined. Midwinter notes that the financial arrangements for devolved government largely continue the block-and-formula approach that evolved after the Barnett Formula was introduced in 1980. Much of the confusion revolves around a belief that Northern Ireland 'does badly' under Barnett, relative to its needs. However, such assertions overlook the fact the Barnett Formula applies only to the annual change in spending, thereby protecting the historic baseline; that large elements of expenditure are determined outwith the Barnett Formula; and, that convergence may be offset or accelerated by relative population change. Add in the effects of rapid real-terms budgetary growth nationally under New Labour (the principal driver of spending in the devolved territories) in a period of low inflation, and the picture becomes still more complicated. Moreover, there continue to be significant differences between individual spending programmes. One area of controversy has been the extent to which an infrastructure deficit existed in Northern Ireland (variously estimated at £6 billion) and, if so, how it might be tackled. However, set against calls for radical surgery on or even abandoning of the Barnett Formula through a new needs-assessment review is the fact that Northern Ireland's needs relative to England (and Great Britain) have fallen. Tampering with the Barnett Formula may well yield unintended – and uncomfortable – results for Northern Ireland. Another complication is that of local taxation.

While the debate rages over the introduction of water charges in Northern Ireland, local taxpayers would appear to fare favourably with their counterparts in Great Britain. Midwinter concludes that there is insufficient evidence to demonstrate that Northern Ireland has been disadvantaged by the application of the Barnett Formula since devolution, and cautions against hasty calls for a needs assessment review.

Knox and Carmichael, in Chapter 14, examine the most fundamental review of sub-regional governance in Northern Ireland in a generation – the Review of Public Administration. Many of the structures which emerged with direct rule in the early 1970s were regarded as temporary, while renewed devolution was awaited. With the Belfast Agreement of 1998 a consensus existed that sub-regional structures were ripe for review. Knox and Carmichael examine the processes involved in the Review, the reactions of the key organisations to the process of the Review and, finally, the outcomes of the Review and the likely impact on public services. They note that although the Review was started under devolution, as a result of the suspension of the Assembly, local politicians will have little input to its implementation. Arguments made by direct rule ministers that the cornerstone of the new structures will be 'strong local government' are not believed, since there is only a marginal increase in powers. In part this limited change arose from the unwillingness of the parties to argue for a significant increase in council powers. Knox and Carmichael conclude by noting that the government's claims that all savings will be redirected to 'front-line services' will be difficult to track.

In Chapter 15 Goodwin, Jones and Jones track some of the main developments under devolution to the institutional structure for economic governance. They note the centrality of economic concerns for all three of the devolved regions, but also highlight the extra dimension of creating additional economic opportunities to help heal Northern Ireland's divisions, outlined in the Northern Ireland Executive's first Programme for Government. By far the most significant developments related to the creation of Invest Northern Ireland, to replace existing bodies and the advisory Northern Ireland Economic Development Forum. The authors highlight the dynamic of the processes which take place after devolution, which is a 'dynamic process' rather than a static event.

Michael Keating (Chapter 16) locates the distinctive devolution settlement in Northern Ireland both in the wider processes of devolution in the UK and the 'new regionalism' in Europe. He examines a range of literature, and especially Scottish experience, to consider 'the ability of the devolved institutions to make policy and the various constraints they face'. He notes that 'in Scotland the UK government has devolved in order to keep the state together', whereas 'the province has the right to secede in order join the Republic' – a difference that means that Whitehall and Westminster 'are less likely to be concerned, should Northern Ireland move in its own distinct policy direction'. Devolved administrations lack the think tanks and policy forums available in London, and much policy divergence arises from 'not always following England all the way, rather than striking out on their own'. Policy divergence is tolerated by London as long as it does not upset the agenda in England. Keating characterises the attitude from London towards the devolved regions as being 'little interested in what they do, and spurns the idea that it might learn from them'. In the face of the overwhelming resource advantage in London, Keating suggests that the devolved regions should forge their own policy networks in order to challenge London dominance.

One of the least analysed aspects of the Northern Ireland situation relates to the role of Northern Ireland MPs at Westminster. Gay and Mitchell in Chapter 17 examine the situation in some detail. They argue that Westminster is a 'distant' place for MPs from Northern Ireland. The separateness of the party structures in Northern Ireland compared with the rest of the UK, together with the small numbers and patterns of attendance, reinforces the limited role the parties play outside Northern Ireland issues. The nationalist parties, moreover, play an even more limited role, either because of abstention, as in the case of Sinn Féin, or by limited attendance or participation in divisions, as with the SDLP. The work of the Northern Ireland Affairs Committee is also assessed, and it is noted that the Committee has taken on a tougher range of issues in more recent times.

John Coakley in Chapter 18 examines the relationships between Britain and Ireland and the 'Strand 2' relationships arising from the Belfast Agreement. The North–South dimension has operated 'only with some difficulty' as a result of difficulties within the UUP and the refusal to cooperate by the DUP when devolution was operating, and the complete suspension of the work of the North/South Ministerial Council (NSMC) after the devolved institutions were suspended in October 2002. However, while developments at the political level have been limited, administrative activity, particularly in relation to the six implementation bodies (plus Tourism Ireland), has progressed under the direction of a team of civil servants seconded from the Irish and Northern Irish civil services and based in Armagh. Moreover, East–West relationships (Strand 3) through the British–Irish Council have continued to develop, with a schedule of administrative activities around two areas: the environment and misuse of drugs being especially noteworthy. Coakley concludes by noting that North–South developments will be limited until the devolved institutions are restored, but also notes that the British–Irish relationship, so long a major political difficulty, no longer requires continuous and careful attention.

In Chapter 19 Lee McGowan examines devolution and relations with the European Union (EU). In many ways McGowan argues that the relationship with Europe was one of the forgotten parts of the devolution experience between 1999 and 2002. He documents how both Members of the Legislative Assembly (MLAs) and the Northern Ireland Executive sought both to overcome their own lack of knowledge of European institutions but set out to put those relationships on a systematic basis. The creation of the Office of the Northern Ireland Executive symbolised the serious way the devolved institutions set about developing relations with Brussels. Moreover, both bodies 'had rapidly adjusted to the impact of the EU on a host of salient public policy issues of direct concern to the devolved bodies . . . from agriculture and fisheries to the environment and the euro'. Alongside these matters McGowan notes that among the cross-border or Strand 2 parts of the Agreement, the creation of the North/South Ministerial Council involved a specific mandate to consider 'the European dimension of relevant matters, including the implementation of EU policies and proposals under consideration in the EU framework', and that its views on these matters are 'represented appropriately at relevant EU meetings'. He observes that 'no clear explanation has yet emerged as to how the views of a body made up of the government of one member state and the executive of a region of another might be "represented appropriately" at EU meetings, nor what weight any such views might have'. He concludes that when devolution is returned there will be much to do to build on the early work on relationships with the EU.

Conclusions

What can we say about the Northern Ireland experience of devolution from the contributions of key researchers in the field? It would be trite to draw any definitive conclusions, given the fleeting experience Northern Ireland has had with devolution. Charlie Jeffery, reporting on the interim findings of the Devolution and Constitutional Change programme, notes that 'devolution has bedded in remarkably smoothly but it remains a fractured project, a collection of separate initiatives which lacks an overarching sense of purpose' (Jeffery, 2004). These comments are apposite when considering Northern Ireland. While Northern Ireland could hardly be described as a region where 'devolution has bedded in remarkably smoothly', its short-lived experience offers some cause for optimism. Wilson and Wilford, addressing the specific question of whether devolution has made a difference, conclude:

That tangible improvements have been made to the lives of many is testament to the persistence of regional politicians in what at times has been a decidedly inauspicious context. In addition, during the latest and most protracted suspension the expanded team of direct-rule Ministers has been active, expediting legislative proposals bequeathed by their devolved predecessors and taking forward new, though well-flagged, policy initiatives. (Wilson and Wilford, 2004: 80)

The longer direct rule continues, however, the more bullish English ministers become in their pursuit of unpopular policy decisions – the abolition of education selection, introduction of water charges and the reform of public administration, to name but a few. In 2003 a public opinion survey (Northern Ireland Life and Times Survey) found that over half those responding (53.8 per cent – excluding 'don't knows') 'wouldn't mind either way' if the Assembly was to be abolished and direct rule maintained indefinitely. This, despite the fact that the majority of people (59 per cent) believed that devolved government had achieved either 'a lot' (12 per cent) or 'a little' (47 per cent), (Knox and Carmichael, 2005). As the list of more controversial policy decisions grows, the public is becoming increasingly frustrated with local politicians who continue to receive (part) payment as MLAs, yet refuse to broker an agreement on the restoration of devolution. Direct rule ministers are equally unimpressed with criticisms of their policies by local representatives. Lord Rooker's most recent acerbic reaction to complaints about his proposals to reform public administration was that if MLAs didn't like them, they knew what to do!

The ongoing devolution agenda is dominated, once again, by the wider political/constitutional issues as Northern Ireland struggles with the formation of a power-sharing Executive comprising its two key political antagonists (Sinn Féin and the DUP). Wilson and Wilford (2004: 84) set out four useful criteria against which the potential for devolution 'to make a difference' could be judged. Has devolution: engendered political stability; facilitated policy innovation; enhanced accountability; and improved community relations (to which we would add human rights and equality)? Political stability remains the *sine qua non* for the potential of devolution to be maximised. Without it, the other factors cannot be fully achieved.

The contributors to this edited collection have provided independent retrospective and prospective analyses of both the problems of devolution and its future possibilities. Without the assistance of the Devolution and Constitutional Change ESRC programme this detailed research would have been impossible. In particular, Charlie Jeffery showed imagination in his support for a strong Northern Ireland component in the overall ESRC programme (sometimes seen as the backwater of UK-wide research initiatives). The output from the authors in this edited volume vindicates the wisdom of his endorsement. The editors would like to thank Professor Jeffery for the enthusiasm with which he embraced the Northern Ireland devolution agenda and for his frequent appearances in Belfast to support the ongoing work. Oh, for such tenacity among our local politicians!

References

Birrell, D and Murie, A. (1980) *Policy and Government in Northern Ireland: Lessons of Devolution*. Dublin: Gill and Macmillan.

Bogdanor, V. (2001) *Devolution in the United Kingdom*. Oxford: Oxford University Press.

Buckland, P. (1979) *The Factory of Grievances – Devolved Government in Northern Ireland*. Dublin: Gill and Macmillan.

Cunningham, M. (2001) *British Government Policy in Northern Ireland, 1969–2000*. Manchester: Manchester University Press.

Hazell, R. (2000) 'Introduction: the first year of devolution' in R. Hazell (ed.) *The State of the Nations: The First Year of Devolution in the United Kingdom*. Thorverton: Imprint Academic.

Jeffery, C. (2002) *Devolution and Constitutional Change*. ESRC research programme.

Jeffery, C. (2004) *Devolution: What Difference Has it Made?* ESRC policy briefing.

Knox, C. and Carmichael, P. (2005) 'Devolution – the Northern Ireland way: an exercise in "creative ambiguity" ', *Environment and Planning C: Government and Policy*, 23 (1), 63–83.

Lawrence, R. (1965) *The Government of Northern Ireland*. Oxford: Clarendon Press.

NIO (Northern Ireland Office) (1998) *The Agreement. Agreement Reached in the Multi-Party Negotiations*. Belfast: NIO.

Wilson, T. (1989) *Ulster: Conflict and Consent*. Oxford: Blackwell.

Wilson, R. and Wilford, R. (2004) 'Northern Ireland: renascent?' in A. Trench (ed.) *Has Devolution Made a Difference? The State of the Nations 2004*. Thorverton: Imprint Academic.

2

Constitutional innovation since 1972: where next?

Robin Wilson

The first time as tragedy . . .

The cartoonist Martyn Turner, asked to design a cover for a twenty-first anniversary anthology of articles from Belfast's *Fortnight* magazine, founded in 1970, came up with an Esher drawing, in which caricatured politicians and paramilitaries – who were later to morph into paramilitary politicians – marched constantly up stairs suggestive of steady progress, only to travel around in a repetitive circle.

Ever since the British government assumed direct rule over Northern Ireland, abolishing the unionist-monopoly regime at Stormont in 1972, it has assumed – regardless of the party in power – the task of trying to establish a stable 'power-sharing' alternative. In 1975–76 this task was handed over (*faute de mieux*) to the regional politicians, via the Constitutional Convention; in 1982–85 the strategy was progressively to entice them into (shared) power, via a consultative assembly and 'rolling devolution'. In 1980 desultory talks between the parties were brokered by the UK government; in 1991 and 1992 this was essayed with more commitment. But only in 1973 and 1998 did that government, in association with the government of the Republic of Ireland, shoehorn the parties into arrangements which realised – if only temporarily – the power-sharing goal (Elliott and Flackes, 1999: 609–620).

In 1972 the newly established Northern Ireland Office (NIO) reviewed the experience of devolution in Northern Ireland over the prior half century. In a Green Paper it analysed the problem through a Westminsterist filter and a communalist lens:

> The alternation of governing parties which has for so long been a characteristic of the British political system, and which has undoubtedly contributed in a marked degree to the stability of Parliamentary Government in Great Britain, accordingly did not exist in Northern Ireland . . . The special feature of the Northern Ireland situation was that the great divide was not between different

viewpoints on such matters as the allocation of resources and the determination of priorities, but between *two whole communities*. (NIO, 1972: 4; my emphasis)

In a subsequent White Paper, setting out proposals, the Northern Ireland Office (NIO, 1973: 13) thus presented the aim as one of 'binding *the minority* to the support of new political arrangements' (again my emphasis) via the proposed power-sharing system. In the run-up to the implementing Northern Ireland Constitution Act of 1973, elections were held by single-transferable vote for an assembly. This electoral system, originally applied to the old Stormont Parliament before the unionist government abolished it in the 1920s, was resurrected to ensure fair Catholic representation, but did nothing to encourage inter-ethnic conciliation. The then unionist leader, Brian Faulkner, proved unable to 'deliver' the Protestant electorate, and indeed had to split from his own party shortly after the power-sharing Executive came into office.

The Executive was appointed by the Northern Ireland Secretary, William Whitelaw, its voting members comprising six unionists and four from the SDLP, as well as one from Alliance. While this was an elite-driven approach, it did depend on cooperation between the Chief Executive, Brian Faulkner, and his Deputy, the SDLP leader, Gerry Fitt. The Secretary to the Executive, Ken Bloomfield, in a private interview years later on his retirement, was to speak warmly of the chemistry they had established.

A border poll in March 1973, boycotted overwhelmingly by Catholics, had confirmed Northern Ireland's constitutional status as part of the UK. Though it was envisaged this would be revisited every ten years, in 1983 the then Secretary of State, James Prior (wisely) declined to repeat the exercise, anticipating a meaningless sectarian head count, and the notion appears to have been forgotten by 1993. This did not, however, stop the idea being resurrected in 1998, with this time potentially only a seven-year interval between these highly destabilising events.

In compensation, the SDLP sought and gained, at a conference in Sunningdale in December 1973, potentially powerful North–South arrangements which could be represented as a vehicle for progressively realising – or, as one party figure unfortunately put it, 'trundling the unionists into' – a united Ireland, a construction facilitated by the refusal of the then coalition government in Dublin to agree to the rescinding of the republic's territorial claim over the North (Bew and Gillespie, 1999; Elliott and Flackes, 1999). The by then Lord Whitelaw reflected a decade and a half later that this 'proposition' had gone 'too far' (Wilson, 1989).

It was this, elite-negotiated, aspect of the arrangements which was to become a misnomer for the overall package and which, unlike the remainder – legislated on foot of the Green and White Papers and wider public debate – was to prove its Achilles heel.

Faulkner was politically assassinated by a 70 per cent defeat when he tried to get the Sunningdale Agreement past his ruling Ulster Unionist Council the following month. And the fundamentalist opponent of power sharing, Ian Paisley, leader of the DUP, was able to mobilise opposition on the basis of the slogan 'Dublin is just a Sunningdale away'.

Remarkably, the then Cabinet Secretary in Dublin, Dermot Nally, later confided that the Taoiseach, Liam Cosgrave, would have subsequently acceded – had it not been too late – to the request from Faulkner that the Executive be saved by suspending the Council of Ireland. Officials had calculated that the Council, until then discussed entirely in ideological terms, could end up employing civil servants numbered in the tens of thousands.

What is distinctive about this constitutional design, underpinning what have come to be known as 'consociationalist' approaches to power sharing, is an unthought-through elision between (diverse) individuals, the (homogeneous) political 'communities' ('unionist' and 'nationalist') into which they are hoovered up, and the political parties that are deemed simply to express (rather than at least in part to constitute) them. In this flattened perspective, democratic politics is thus reduced to elite deals between those who present themselves as communal representatives – rather than a process of public dialogue to address divisive issues, allied to protection of the rule of law and human rights and the fostering of inter-ethnic integration in society at large.

Few people had heard of consociationalism in 1973: the work that put Arend Lijphart's thinking into general circulation, *Democracy in Plural Societies*, was only published four years later. Lijphart (1977) set out, on the basis of his interpretation of governance arrangements in Belgium, Switzerland, the Netherlands and Austria, the four common characteristics which came to define his model: 'segmental autonomy' (communal apartheid), a grand coalition of all 'segments', mutual-veto arrangements between communal elites and proportional distribution of public appointments.

Yet a 1975 journal article diagnosed the Northern Ireland power-sharing experiment explicitly as an exercise in consociationalism. Indeed, it precisely warned that 'attempts to apply the "consociational model" outside its original areas (especially in divided societies such as Northern Ireland or Canada) may make things worse'(Barry, 1975).

But in 1971 the Queen's University political scientist John Whyte had published a pamphlet based on Lijphart's thinking which was taken up by the then Home Secretary, Reginald Maudling.[1] And in the elisions made between individuals, 'communities' and the political domain, the NIO's subsequent thinking reflected the essentialist conception of identity Lijphart assumed from anthropologists like Geertz and Furnivall. These figures he interpreted as perceiving 'communal attachments' as 'primordial' and 'plural' societies as places where people 'mix but do not combine' (Lijphart, 1977). In popular parlance, as widely applied to Northern Ireland – and the Balkans (Glenny, 1999) – this is the 'ancient hatreds' view.

Fast forward to 1998 and the Belfast Agreement (Ruane and Todd, 1999; Wilford, 2001), by which time this consociationalist 'common sense' had become deeply engrained. The 'inclusive' governmental arrangement, with seats in government distributed by the d'Hondt rule, was a Lijphartian 'grand coalition' *par excellence*: even in Belgium, for example, the xenophobic Flemish Interest (formerly Vlaams Blok) party is conventionally treated as a pariah, despite its strong support in that 'community', when it comes to government formation.

The arrangements for securing 'cross-community support' for 'key decisions', such as the election of the First Minister and Deputy First Minister, requiring as they did the registration of Assembly members as 'unionist', 'nationalist' or 'other', consolidated the 'mutual veto' only implicit in 1974 – though, critically, played out on the North–South level – at the expense of the quality of the relationship between the two principals.

The electoral system was once again STV (single transferable vote), this time with six (rather than five) member constituencies. Candidates thus had to secure just one seventh of the vote for a quota, incentivising mobilisation of core communal support rather than broader public appeal, in a context in which elections in Northern Ireland were becoming even more bifurcated affairs with further erosion of the centre ground (Ruohomaki, 2001).

This highly complex package was entirely the product of secret negotiations, with the public only allocated a rubber-stamping role in the subsequent referenda rather than any access to the arguments. And so it proved much more difficult to set in train than in 1974, with an impasse of 18 months following the referenda, as yet more negotiations took place. This time, the weak link on which sectarian opponents of power-sharing could focus was not the North–South-structures: the discrete, technocratic institutions (with only around 700 staff) established by the Agreement, allied to the removal of the territorial claim in the Republic's constitution, have defused that issue (if a quarter of a century belatedly).

Rather, it was the broadening of the governmental coalition to include not only the 'traditional' communal elites but also, in effect, paramilitary warlords, normally – as in the post-Yugoslav administrations – excluded from democratic political power at the behest of the international community because of their competing loyalty to illegal networks. This led to the obvious contradiction that the Republic's government was insisting on the inclusion in government of a party – Sinn Féin – which no party in the Republic was itself willing to countenance in the government of the state, given its allegiance to the IRA represented a standing affront to Article 15(6) of Bunreacht na hEireann.

While power was eventually devolved in December 1999, the arrangements became progressively more unstable, with successive suspensions in February 2000 and in August and September 2001, before the final collapse in October 2002. The second Assembly election, due in May 2003, was postponed twice by the Prime Minister, Tony Blair, in the knowledge that no further power-sharing government would be possible given the growing polarisation – but then held anyway that November, despite the availability of the alternative option of pursuing the Agreement's four-year review as a route to engendering more stable arrangements. As anticipated, the DUP emerged the victor, as to a lesser extent did Sinn Féin (Wilford and Wilson, 2004).

The review of the Agreement, when it finally began in February 2004, was allowed to degenerate into another private political arm-wrestle, at some remove from the deliberative connotations of the term. Months of unproductive exchanges and summitry led to a document agreed by the Prime Minister and the Taoiseach, Bertie Ahern, which they released in December 2004, unfortunately without the support of any of the parties. This putative agreement (Wilford and Wilson, 2005) would have introduced even more rigidly consociational elements – with the effective removal altogether of the partnership between First and Deputy First minister – and abandoned any remaining pretence to reconciliation as a goal.

The December document could be reactivated following the statement by the IRA leadership of July 2005, calling a halt to its continuing activities. These included the £26-million robbery of the Northern Bank in Belfast city centre within weeks of the document appearing, and the brutal murder of Robert McCartney in a nearby bar the following month. A spirited campaign by the sisters of McCartney greatly embarrassed the republican leadership internationally, highlighting its continued association with paramilitarism and criminality. And the statement was followed in September 2005 by the pathbreaking announcement by the Independent International Commission on Decommissioning (IICD) that the IRA's arsenal had been decommissioned.

The statement did not commit the IRA as a whole to a 'final' end to its campaign – that requires an 'army convention' of volunteers – still less to the disbandment of an organisation, membership of which (under the Terrorism Act 2000 and older legislation in the Republic) remains illegal. And it was widely recognised that the IICD report would have to be followed by a 'clean bill of health' in successive reports from the separate Independent Monitoring Commission, vis-à-vis criminal activity by the IRA, if Sinn Féin were to be seen to have transformed itself from a Leninist organisation into one compatible with liberal democracy.

In any event, however, the DUP remained hostile to sharing power with Sinn Féin, suggesting after the July statement that at minimum such a move would be two years away. Even this was with an eye to the same 'blame game' as the republican movement was playing. Given the DUP has never shared power *with the SDLP* in any of the council chambers it dominates, since the current local government system was established alongside the Assembly in 1973 – and the party recently rejected a pointed invitation to do so from the SDLP in three such councils – it can safely be said it will not do so with Sinn Féin at the level of regional government any time soon. The only arrangements it might countenance, as with its acceptance of ministries under the Agreement but refusal to sit in the power-sharing Executive, would be a Balkanised government which would represent the antithesis of the very notion of a sharing of power across the sectarian divide for wider conciliatory purposes.

Forces for inertia

It was also in 1974, the year the power-sharing Executive collapsed, that there was the failed *enosis* bid by the Greek officer Nicos Sampson and the reprisal Turkish invasion issued in the long period of constitutional stand-off which, uniquely in Europe, Cyprus has shared with Northern Ireland. Repeated efforts under the auspices of the United Nations to establish a 'bizonal, bicommunal federation' have failed, most recently with the referendum defeat for the Annan plan in April 2004.

Horowitz (2002) points out how this very longevity and associated sense of intractability has had a perverse, perpetuating effect in both cases. In the face of successive failures, far from adopting a reflexive and self-critical stance, talks negotiators have tended to cling to any ideas, however problematic, that they have not driven off the table in previous rounds, and to accept uncontested diagnoses of failure, however unpersuasive, as they try once more to craft political arrangements. These forces for inertia are enhanced by third-party brokers with a high stake in the outcome – in these two cases respectively the UN and the London and Dublin governments – anxious to go with the flow of the parties' thinking and to talk up any progress they have made.

At the August 2005 funeral of Lord Fitt, Austin Currie, a fellow SDLP minister in the 1974 Executive, said that although it had only lasted five months, 'it established for the future the necessary architecture for a lasting agreement' (*Irish Times*, 1 September 2005). And the Belfast Agreement was famously described in its euphoric aftermath by Séamus Mallon – who went on to play a creditable role as Deputy First Minister – as 'Sunningdale for slow learners'. Mallon not only thus expressed complacency about the validity of that model but also implicitly rehearsed the conventional wisdom on the reason for its failure: the fact that the more extreme forces in Northern Ireland, including the 'republican movement', were not on board.

Yet since then the 'moderate middle', far from being boosted by the Agreement, has collapsed. In his valedictory speech as departing Member of Parliament in April 2005, Mallon fumed at the Prime Minister and the Taoiseach for indulging Sinn Féin (*Belfast Telegraph*, 16 April 2005): 'The more often they ask, the more often they get. It's a remarkable feat to wipe out the centre ground of unionism and nationalism in the middle of a peace process. I haven't spoken to either of them since.' Yet while the Prime Minister and the Taoiseach have indeed allowed a wholly perverse system of incentives – an 'auction mentality' (Horowitz, 2001: 341) – to take hold, this is only part of the explanation.

As the vertiginous growth of the DUP, compared with the plateau secured by Sinn Féin, has shown, it is in fact particularly moderate Protestant opinion, as in 1974, that has been eviscerated. Moreover, not only has the Agreement failed to sponsor the reconciliation many envisaged, but the 'peace process' has not even brought peace as it would normally be understood – that is to say, the rule of law, with the state exercising a monopoly of legitimate force.

The unilateral ceasefires by the main paramilitaries in 1994 represented a belated recognition by their leaders that their organised, offensive campaigns had become politically unsustainable – a reality subsequently underscored by 9/11, 11/3 and 7/7. Yet not only did the incidence of violence subsequently begin to rise again, it continued to rise after the Belfast Agreement – and only began to fall after the demise of the institutions in 2002 (PSNI, 2005). What has changed is the pattern: rather than lethal, 'disciplined', organised violence in pursuit of recognisable political goals, we have mostly non-fatal but diffuse violence, symptomatic of a deeply embedded culture of intolerance – indeed, the reported incidence of some hate crimes has risen alarmingly (Jarman, 2005).

Missing the point

The dynamic towards political inertia over the period since direct rule was first introduced has been paralleled by an intellectual incuriousness – among policy makers and the parties to the Northern Ireland conflict – about three relevant and interconnected international debates: on nationalism, power-sharing and 'identity politics'.

The debate on nationalism, to which in the 1980s such texts as Gellner (1983), Anderson (1983) and Smith (1986) gave rise, has pitted 'primordialists' and 'perennialists' against 'instrumentalists' and 'modernists', while the debate on power-sharing models has contrasted consociationalist and integrationist approaches. Those who support consociationalist forms of power sharing tend to adopt the former, taken-for-granted, understanding of nationalism or indeed more generally of 'identity', while integrationists tend to adopt the latter, in which identity is seen as a social construct.

Lijphart (1977 and 2002) would identify consociationalism with power sharing *tout court*. But this has come under increasing challenge: Van Schendelen (1984) found Lijphart's concepts slippery, Halpern (1986) showed his cases did not conform to the model, Pappalardo (1981) demonstrated that the factors he claimed favoured consociationalism were mostly causally and empirically dubious, and Bogaards (1998) added that they had shifted over time. It has been variously suggested that consociationalism only works where it is not necessary, and where it is (by Lijphart's lights) it can be associated with widening ethnic division – in Belgium, for example (Cartrite, 2002). Academic interest in the theory has been in decline since the mid-1980s (Lustick, 1997).

But alternative power-sharing models have been thin in policy terms. In contrast with the standard, four-element, consociationalist 'tool box', they have mainly been associated to date with incentivised cross-communal vote-pooling (Horowitz, 1985; Reilly, 2001).

The third debate helps provide some answers. Here what is at stake is whether one understands 'identity' in essentialist (Taylor, 1992) or anti-essentialist (Benhabib, 2002) terms – whether one thinks, respectively, of society embodying 'a variety of cultures' (a mosaic of discrete elements) or 'cultural variety' (a *mélange* of individual expressions) (Bauman, 2002). Essentialist conceptions of ethnic identity are linked to a 'politics of recognition', which is associated with consociationalist propositions via the premise that 'high fences make good neighbours'. Critics represent identity as plastic and complex, and so advocate measures which privilege intercultural dialogue in the hope that divided societies might, over time, become 'normal' civic societies.

Political scientists reading Lijphart tended not to appreciate the extent to which an older generation of anthropologists underpinned his conception of the 'segments' in ethnically divided societies. Allen and Eade (1999) describe modern thinking in the discipline thus: 'Anthropologists do not view corporate identities as springing from primordial motivations, but rather as a product of social interaction, embedded in particular historical, political and economic contexts.' In fact, there is some frustration among anthropologists about what the dust jacket of that volume describes as the 'prevalent simplistic primordialism of most media coverage and political analysis'.

Within the study of ethnic politics, Chandra (2001) also bewails 'a puzzling step backward' in which the cumulative findings of what she calls the 'constructivist' approach 'are being conspicuously and consciously ignored' – such as in the work of Kymlicka (1995). In the face of this, Lijphart (2001) now accepts that his classic 1977 text rested on outdated, primordialist assumptions.

Lijphart claims that his preference for 'self-determined' rather than 'pre-determined' group affiliation saves the theory nevertheless. In Northern Ireland, the 'segments' are 'self-determined' – though, by the by, the December 2004 document, by requiring candidates for election to designate *at that point* would have substituted pre-determination. But, however the segments are constituted, the risk with consociationalist arrangements is that they do not merely recognise but entrench communal division (O'Flynn and Russell, 2005).

Beyond consociationalism

The aims of all four of the policy 'tools' of consociationalism can be effected with more sharply honed instruments in an integrationist perspective. The trick is to recognise that the fear of ethnic 'lock-in' to which consociationalism attends can be otherwise assuaged.

On the composition of power-sharing government, once one takes account of intra-ethnic party competition – never mind non- or inter-ethnic parties – a coalition of the 'moderate middle' is actually *more* realistic than an inclusive executive. As Horowitz pointed out at a seminar in London on electoral systems for Northern Ireland in early 2004, to expect all significant parties to come together in government in the wake of a power-sharing agreement would imply that that the latter could instantly magic away decades of division – a Herculean assumption.

The best that can be hoped for is incremental progress in reducing division, starting from a realisable coalition embracing the more moderate 'communal contenders', as against more militant 'ethno-nationalists' – to use the phraseology developed by Eide (1993). For if the former do recognise to varying degrees that persons affiliating to different ethnic communities have to rub along together in a shared polity, the latter operate on assimilationist assumptions, which can only be a recipe for an indefinite zero-sum conflict with their equal-and-opposite antagonists.

A cross-communal but not all-party coalition will in itself be one guarantee against ethnic oppression, as the 'minority' component – if the 'majority' is divided by intra-ethnic tension and the ethnic outbidding party is not included in government – may well be critical to government formation. In any event, mutual-veto arrangements can be supplanted by mechanisms that prevent lock-in without reifying identities. Thus power-sharing accords may make provision for secular weighted-majority decision making on controversial issues, without requirement of communal registration.

The international minority-rights declarations promulgated in the 1990s by the United Nations, the Organisation for Security and Co-operation in Europe and the Council of Europe – largely in response to conflicts in central and eastern Europe – represent a supportive set of external standards for the integrationist approach. The Bill of Rights envisaged in the Belfast Agreement could have been of value in this regard, giving such standards a justiciable status as well as having educational value, but the debate around the Bill has been captured by the ethno-nationalist protagonists and turned into yet another site of struggle for 'parity of esteem'.

Proportional representation in public – and indeed private – employment should be the product of equal-opportunity legislation, including scope for affirmative action as required, in *any* society. But this in sharp contrast to communal patronage. The latter is not only inefficient but in the case of the *Proporz* system in Austria (one of Lijphart's original cases) gave Jörg Haider's xenophobic Freedom Party an easy stick with which to beat the 'red-black' establishment during his political ascendancy (Fallend, 2004).

Finally, in a divided society, segregation is highly likely to be the starting point for reconciliation. Yet high fences do not make good, but rather mistrustful, neighbours.

The security offered by segregation is illusory, as stereotyped enemy images merely perpetuate antagonism and ethno-political entrepreneurs maintain their dominance by sustaining an ever-present sense of insecurity. While 'community' has a comforting connotation, what Bauman (2001) drily calls the 'really existing community', will always disappoint those who seek its solace: 'Security is the enemy of walled-up and fenced-off community' (Bauman, 2001). That is why mixed Ballynafeigh in Belfast is peaceful, while segregated Ballymena is not.

Genuine security comes from the cultivation of cross-communal civic networks, whether these are business relationships, trade-union or other voluntary organisations or ecumenical connections. On the basis of his comparative research on cities in India more or less prone to Hindu–Muslim riots, Varshney (2002) concludes: 'Vigorous associational life, if inter-communal, acts as a serious constraint on the polarizing strategies of political elites.'

As Habermas (2004) argues, tolerance is not 'a *one-way street* to cultural self-assertion by groups with their own collective identities'. He goes on: 'The coexistence of different life forms as equals must not be allowed to prompt segregation. Instead, it requires the integration of all citizens – and their mutual recognition across cultural divisions as citizens – within the framework of a shared political culture.'

Where next?

Northern Ireland has long been, and remains (Wolff, 2002), a 'deeply divided society'. While violence has irregularly declined since the early 1970s, stable democratic institutions have remained a receding horizon. Consociationalist models have been tried by policy makers, particularly in the early 1970s and, with the Belfast Agreement (Wilford, 2001), in the late 1990s. The collapses, in 1974, 2000, 2001 and 2002, call for a rethink.

Integrationism does offer another policy tool-kit:

- government by the 'moderate middle', supported by vote-pooling incentives, rather than grand coalition;
- weighted-majority and minority-rights safeguards, rather than mutual veto;
- intercultural dialogue in the pursuit of tolerance, rather than segmental autonomy;
- equality of life-chances throughout, rather than proportionate allocation of public-sector posts.

Northern Ireland already has fair-employment arrangements in place, including now critically in the police. Since March 2005 it has also had in place a policy framework to tackle intolerance and associated segregation – *A Shared Future* (OFMDFM, 2005) – though its aims and objectives are significantly more robust than the commitments made by individual departments as to how integrationist government is willing to be. The second element above could be introduced, after proper public debate across these islands, via modifications to the Belfast Agreement and enactment of the long-awaited Bill of Rights.

The first element, however, is a long way off. The cavalier attitude of London and Dublin to political polarisation in Northern Ireland has left an inauspicious climate. Nowhere in the world does power sharing operate on the basis of cooperation between two ethno-nationalist parties (though in the wake of the 2001 Ohrid Agreement in Macedonia the Social Democrats have provided a moderate Slav partner for the ethnic-Albanian group formerly aligned to the secessionist National Liberation Army (NLA), albeit after the prompt handover of NLA weapons to the North Atlantic Treaty Organisation (NATO) in front of the TV cameras).

An agreed, rather than involuntary, power-sharing government could however subsist as a 'minimum winning coalition', given the minority safeguards recommended above. This has fallen victim to the law of the excluded middle, as unionists have supported a voluntary coalition, excluding Sinn Féin, which offends (mainly Catholic) aspirations to political equality as citizens. Nationalists, meanwhile, have remained wedded to government formation by an automatic mechanism, which offends (mainly Protestant) concerns about democratic accountability.

In reality, political equality and popular control are internationally recognised as *twin* features of democratic societies (IDEA, 2002). What is needed is a project for an egalitarian, agreed coalition – one that would be accountable to an assembly but would not be weighted towards ethnic dominance on either side, and where inter-ethnic partnership and collective responsibility would cement the centre ground.

It is possible to establish a virtuous circle of accommodation and stability, with increasing intercommunal trust and a diminution of old enmities, by transcending the zero-sum constitutional battle between unionism and nationalism, rather than institutionalising it. In today's globalised environment, particularly in the context of the engagement of these islands in decades of European integration since 1973, it is possible to pursue a 'both/and' rather than 'either/or' approach to Northern Ireland's constitutional position – to turn a threat into an opportunity. Indeed, it is essential that such a cosmopolitan perspective be adopted if the region is to cope confidently with the challenges of the twenty-first century.

Moving towards an alternative electoral system such as the alternative vote (with a proportionality top-up) or the additional member system would favour cross-communal vote pooling and magnetise parties to compete around the centre, rather than as now with communal parties merely competing intracommunally. Such a decision could be determined by an expert independent commission, again after extensive public consultation, to assuage concerns about partisan bias.

This does not require the abandonment of the Agreement but it does entail reforms which can draw the sting from the unionist–nationalist antagonism, incentivise conciliatory rather than confrontational behaviour, and promote a more outward-looking rather than ideological perspective. Fortunately, in large measure such reforms go with the grain of public opinion, as evidenced by sustained evidence from the Northern Ireland Life and Times Survey.

The reforms could be introduced by amendments to the Northern Ireland Act. They would not require further prolonged inter-party negotiations. They would also not depend on (though they would accelerate) any decisions by paramilitaries to accept democratic norms, and they would not be subsequently vulnerable to walk-outs by any individual party.

It would, however, add legitimacy to the new arrangements if the package were, like the Belfast Agreement, to be subject to a referendum in Northern Ireland. Because of the wording of the section of the Republic of Ireland's constitution on North–South arrangements in the aftermath of the Agreement, a referendum to make a further constitutional adjustment might well also be necessary there.

Conclusion

Discussion of the reasons for persistent political failure in Northern Ireland tends to be confined to the short-term cycles of the media and ministers and officials dealing with short-term crisis management. This is matched by a lack of any serious reflection on the deeper questions of constitutional engineering required to effect power-sharing arrangements which can progressively reduce inter-ethnic tensions and see democratic institutions stabilised, rather than those which entrench communal division and so dig their own political grave.

In this sense, too much policy focus has attended to paramilitaries and their future, and too little to politics and constitutional design. Even if the IRA were finally to renounce violence and abandon criminal activity, 'loyalist' paramilitaries were to do likewise and the DUP were to agree to take part in governmental arrangements with Sinn Féin – *in toto* fairly heroic assumptions – such arrangements could represent a sectarian carve-up of power rather than a harbinger of reconciliation.

Note

1 I am indebted to Bill Smith for this information.

References

Allen, T. and Eade, J. (1999) 'Understanding ethnicity', in T. Allen and J. Eade (eds) *Divided Europeans: Understanding Ethnicities in Conflict*. The Hague: Kluwer Law International.

Anderson, B. (1983) *Imagined Communities*. London: Verso.

Barry, B. (1975) 'The consociational model and its dangers', *European Journal of Political Research*, 3, 393–412.

Bauman, Z. (2001) *Community*. Cambridge: Polity Press.

Bauman, Z. (2002) 'Cultural variety or variety of cultures?' in Siniša Malešević and Mark Haugaard (eds), *Making Sense of Collectivity*. London: Pluto Press.

Benhabib, S. (2002) *The Claims of Culture: Equality and Diversity in the Global Era*. Princeton, NJ: Princeton University Press.

Bew, P. and Gillespie, G. (1999) *Northern Ireland: A Chronology of the Troubles 1968–1999*. Dublin: Gill and Macmillan.

Bogaards, M. (1998) 'The favourable factors for consociational democracy: a review', *European Journal of Political Research* 33, 475–496.

Cartrite, B. (2002) 'Contemporary ethnopolitical identity and the future of the Belgian state', *Nationalism and Ethnic Politics* 8 (3), 43–71.

Chandra, K. (2001) 'Introduction: constructivist findings and their non-incorporation', *Newsletter of the American Political Science Association Organized Section in Comparative Politics*, 12 (1), 7–11.

Eide, A. (1993) *New Approaches to Minority Protection*. London: Minority Rights Group.

Elliott, S. and Flackes, W.D. (1999) *Northern Ireland: A Political Directory*. Belfast: Blackstaff Press.

Fallend, F. (2004) 'Are right-wing populism and government participation incompatible? The case of the Freedom Party of Austria', *Representation*, 40 (2), 115–130.

Gellner, E. (1983) *Nations and Nationalism*. Oxford: Blackwell.

Glenny, M. (1999) *The Balkans 1804–1999: Nationalism, War and the Great Powers*. London: Granta Books.

Habermas, J. (2004) 'Religious tolerance – the pacemaker for cultural rights', *Philosophy*, 79, 5–18.

Halpern, S. (1986) 'The disorderly universe of consociational democracy', *West European Politics*, 9 (2), 181–197.

Horowitz, D.L. (1985) *Ethnic Groups in Conflict*. Berkeley: University of California Press.

Horowitz, D.L. (2001) *The Deadly Ethnic Riot*. Berkeley: University of California Press.

Horowitz, D.L. (2002) 'Eating leftovers: making peace from scraps off the negotiating table' in Günther Baechler and Andreas Wenger (eds), *Conflict and Cooperation: The Individual Between Ideal and Reality*. Zürich: Neue Zürcher Zeitung, 293–309.

IDEA (International Debate Education Association) (2002) *Handbook on Democracy Assessment*. The Hague: Kluwer Law International.

Jarman, N. (2005) *No Longer a Problem? Sectarian Violence in Northern Ireland*. Belfast: Institute for Conflict Research.

Kymlicka, W. (1995) *Multicultural Citizenship*. Oxford: Clarendon Press.

Lijphart, A. (1977) *Democracy in Plural Societies*. New Haven, CT: Yale University Press.

Lustick, I. (1997) 'Lijphart, Lakatos and consociationalism', *World Politics*, 50 (1), 88–117.

Lijphart, A. (2001) 'Constructivism and consociational theory', *Newsletter of the American Political Science Association Organized Section in Comparative Politics*, 12 (1), 11–13.

Lijphart, A. (2002) 'The wave of power-sharing democracy' in Andrew Reynolds (ed.) *The Architecture of Democracy: Constitutional Design, Conflict Management, and Democracy*. Oxford: Oxford University Press.

NIO (Northern Ireland Office) (1972) *The Future of Northern Ireland: A Paper for Discussion*. Belfast and London: NIO.

NIO (Northern Ireland Office) (1973) *Northern Ireland Constitutional Proposals*. Belfast and London: NIO.

O'Flynn, I. and Russell, D. (2005) *Power Sharing: New Challenges for Divided Societies*. London: Pluto Press.

OFMDFM (Office of the First Minister and Deputy First Minister) (2005) *A Shared Future: Policy and Strategic Framework for Good Relations in Northern Ireland*. Belfast: OFMDFM; also available at www.asharedfutureni.gov.uk.

Pappalardo, A. (1981) 'The conditions for consociational democracy: a logical and empirical critique', *European Journal of Political Research*, 9, 365–390.

PSNI (Police Service of Northern Ireland) (2005) *Security-Related Incidents, 1990/01–2005/06*. Available at www.psni.police.uk/security_related_incidents_fy-18.doc (accessed 2 September 2005).

Reilly, B. (2001) *Democracy in Divided Societies: Electoral Engineering for Conflict Management*. Cambridge: Cambridge University Press.

Ruane, J. and Todd, J. (eds) (1999) *After the Good Friday Agreement: Analysing Political Change in Northern Ireland*. Dublin: University College Dublin Press.

Ruohomaki, J. (2001) *Two Elections: Two Contests – The June 2001 Elections in Northern Ireland*. Belfast: Democratic Dialogue; also available at www.democraticdialogue.org/working/Elect.htm.

Smith, Anthony D. (1986) *The Ethnic Origins of Nations*. Oxford: Blackwell.

Taylor, C. (1992). *Multiculturalism and the Politics of Recognition*. Princeton, NJ: Princeton University Press.

Van Schendelen, M. P. C. M. (1984) 'The views of Arend Lijphart and collected criticisms', in M. P. C. M. van Schendelen (ed.) *Consociationalism, Pillarization and Conflict Management in the Low Countries*. Amsterdam: Uitgeverij Boom.

Varshney, A. (2002) *Ethnic Conflict and Civic Life: Hindus and Muslims in India*. New Haven: Yale University Press.

Wilson, R. (1989) 'A proconsul remembers', *Fortnight*, 271, 6–8.

Wilford, R. (ed.) (2001) *Aspects of the Belfast Agreement*. Oxford: Oxford University Press.

Wilford, R. and Wilson, R. (2004) 'The virtual election: the Northern Ireland Assembly election of 2003', *Representation*, 40 (4), 250–255.

Wilford, R. and Wilson, R. (2005) 'Northern Ireland; while you take the high road' in Alan Trench (ed.) *The Dynamics of Devolution: The State of the Nations 2005*. Thorveton: Imprint Academic.

Wolff, S. (2002) 'Conclusion: the peace process in Northern Ireland since 1998' in S. Wolff and J. Neuheiser (eds) *Peace at Last? The Impact of the Good Friday Agreement in Northern Ireland*. New York: Berghahn Books.

3
Public attitudes to constitutional options in the context of devolution

Roger Mac Ginty

Introduction

The Northern Ireland conflict, like other chronic conflicts, displays a multitude of symptoms and manifestations that often mask the essential causes and maintenance factors behind it. To a large extent, the daily hubbub of contemporary Northern Ireland politics (arguments over police reform, politico-religious marches and sectarian resource competitions etc.) are merely symptomatic of the deeper constitutional clash. Constitutional preferences have become suffused with a powerful mix of politico-social and politico-religious identity clashes, to the extent that traditional pro-united Ireland versus pro-UK arguments are often difficult to disaggregate from other events and processes connected with the conflict. However, division over Northern Ireland's constitutional status is rarely far from the surface.

This chapter examines the extent to which devolution, and the attendant peace process and Belfast Agreement, impacted on attitudes towards constitutional issues. The chapter uses public attitudes survey data to capture and chart constitutional preferences during one of the most significant periods in Northern Ireland's contemporary political history. The survey results show significant attachment to traditional constitutional goals (a united Ireland or Northern Ireland to remain within the UK). Yet when survey respondents are presented with a wider range of constitutional choices, a 'devolution effect' is discernible, with support for devolved options diluting support for the 'pure' constitutional goals.

There is a danger that observers are over-generous in investing retrospective wisdom into the strategies of key actors in Northern Ireland's peace process. Policies couched in legalese or that make conscious connections with ideological tropes may – in fact – be the product of guesswork and *ad hoc* policy making. Thus, to say that a key peace-process aim of the British and Irish governments was to encourage Northern Ireland's political parties to put constitutional claims on hold and cooperate over functional issues may be to over-interpret the coherence of intergovernmental policy (Arthur, 2000). Nevertheless, by chance or design, both governments saw the advantages of encouraging local political actors to cooperate on the day-to-day governance of Northern Ireland, while parking competing constitutional claims. Nationalist–unionist collaboration on functional issues would transmit a powerful message to those committed to political violence and, in the long-term, would have the capacity to help break down images of 'the other' as untrustworthy. In the best-case scenario, the rigidity of constitutional politics could be eroded as a by-product of functional cooperation. Networks of cross-community collaboration and partnership would form an effective counter to the dynamic for separation.

A key feature of consociational arrangements, and the Belfast Agreement can be regarded as enhanced consociationalism (O'Leary, 2001), is that they rest on a meta-level bargain beneath which lie a series of local or adjunct compromises that enable the operation of a *modus vivendi* (Lijphart, 1977: 25–31). Sometimes these local compromises take the form of unspoken agreements. In consociational arrangements in Belgium and Switzerland, the practice has been that grand coalitions rest on the often unspoken acknowledgement that key sticking points or sensitive issues are best left to one side lest they spark the collapse of the entire edifice. In other words, successful consociational political arrangements depend as much on a favourable political culture as they do on institutional mechanisms. A common criticism of power sharing and consociational arrangements is that they only work when divisions are relatively benign and thus are unsuited to deeply divided societies in which divisions are fundamental or inflamed to the point of violent conflict. They also risk reinforcing and institutionalising the segmentation of a deeply divided society by affirming inter-communal boundaries (Sisk, 1996: 39). A particular problem relates to the durability of power-sharing arrangements. As Sisk notes:

> A key feature of powersharing – the mutual veto, whereby decisions are only taken with the widest possible consent and only with a near consensus – often leads to the use of 'political blackmail'. Unable to get consensus, governance stagnates and policy-making drifts; the result is a 'cold peace', in which the parties do not continue to employ violence but neither have they embarked on a serious process of reconciliation. When powersharing arrangements lead to such political immobilism . . . frustration emerges and tensions rise; one or more parties defect from the accord. (Sisk, 2003: 140)

Northern Ireland has provided power sharing with a peculiarly unpropitious environment. Pro-Belfast Agreement unionists sold the peace accord to their constituency as a means of securing Northern Ireland's place within the UK. The UUP reassured the electorate that as a result of the Belfast Agreement:

The Union has been strengthened because it is in our hands alone. Not one word of the Act of Union has changed. The Republic's illegal claim to Ulster will go. Even Dublin now recognises that the British people of Ulster must decide their own future, and accepts the status of Northern Ireland as part of the United Kingdom. (UUP, 1998)

Sinn Féin, on the other hand, interpreted the same document in a radically different way, emphasising the federalising and all-island aspects of the Agreement. For republicans, the Agreement was a transition point on the journey to Irish unity; it was 'a work in progress' (Sinn Féin, 2005: 7).

In sum, the pro-UK and pro-united Ireland constitutional objectives of key antagonists remained intact, despite the agreement of a major peace accord and the endorsement of that accord by 70 per cent of the electorate in the May 1998 referendum. Nationalists and unionists were in the uncomfortable Janus-faced position of having to cooperate together on functional devolved matters in the power-sharing Assembly, while working against each other to secure constitutional objectives. For republicans this meant simultaneously undermining the state of Northern Ireland while discharging their ministerial portfolios. For unionists this meant simultaneously maintaining a position that republicans were enemies of Northern Ireland while cooperating with them in a power-sharing government.

About the survey

The time series data used in this chapter comes from the Northern Ireland Life and Times Survey, which contains an annual political attitudes module, funded in 2000, 2001 and 2003 by the ESRC under its Devolution and Constitutional Change programme.[1] The survey is a joint initiative from the University of Ulster and the Queen's University of Belfast, and the fieldwork is conducted in the autumn of each year. 1,800 adults are interviewed face-to-face and issued with an additional self-completion questionnaire. Response rates have averaged at 67 per cent in the 1998–2003 period, a figure that compares well with similar attitudinal surveys in England, Scotland and Wales. Addresses (a simple random sample) are selected from the postcode address file. Interviewers select one adult for interview at each address via a Kish Grid method. Interviews are carried out using computer-assisted personal interviewing. A pilot survey is conducted prior to the main survey to assist questionnaire design.[2]

The independent variables used during this chapter are 'Protestant' and 'Catholic' rather than unionist and nationalist. The survey shows a strong equivalence between self-identification as Protestant and unionist (over

70 per cent), and Catholic and nationalist (over 60 per cent). Since substantial numbers of Catholic and Protestant respondents refuse to identify themselves as nationalists or unionists, the use of the religious labels yields a higher sample. Indeed, the use of religious identity as a virtual proxy for political identity is further legitimised as the survey repeatedly reveals the salience of Northern Ireland's sectarian differential as the key fault-line in society. Survey respondents are allowed to identify themselves as 'no religion'. Research in deeply divided societies is often attended by ethical and practical problems (Smyth and Robinson, 2001). Devolution's troubled infant years in Northern Ireland presented the survey research with peculiar practical problems. The initial delay in the establishment of the Northern Ireland Assembly, followed by its repeated suspension, complicated the task of questionnaire compilation, the timing of fieldwork and the development of a time series based on the same questions being asked on an annual basis. The suspension of the Assembly had serious implications for survey questions on Assembly performance rather than questions on constitutional preferences, though it is worth noting nonetheless that the survey was conducted during a period of political flux.

Constitutional preferences

The 'What do you think the long-term policy for Northern Ireland should be?' question has been used by the Northern Ireland Life and Times Survey over many years as a way of ascertaining support for the basic dyadic constitutional choice: Northern Ireland as part of a united Ireland or the UK? Responses to this question crystallise the extent of division in Northern Ireland and the intractability of the constitutional dispute. As Table 3.1 shows, the vast majority of Protestant survey respondents (averaging at 83 per cent over the 1998–2004 time period) regard Northern Ireland's continued presence within the UK as their preferred constitutional arrangement. Yet only a fifth of Catholics (on average) share this preference. In other words, Northern Ireland by virtue of forming part of the UK, faces a massive legitimacy deficit among the minority community. On average 49 per cent of Catholics (just short of a simple majority) regard Irish unity as their long-term constitutional preference. Responses to this question record little change in attitudes to constitutional preference over the lifetime of the time series. While there are year-on-year changes and signs of volatility in the 1999–2001 period, perhaps the most striking feature of the responses is that Catholic and Protestant attitudes to Northern Ireland's constitutional status remain largely unchanged. In a sense, there is no discernible 'devolution effect', or devolution does not seem to have had a significant impact on public attitudes to Northern Ireland's constitutional future.

Table 3.1. Constitutional preferences, 1998–2004 (%)

	1998			1999			2000			2001			2002			2003			2004		
	Cath.	Prot.	All	Cath.	Prot.	All	Cath.	Prot.	All	Cath.	Prot.	All	Cath.	Prot.	All	Cath.	Prot.	All	Cath.	Prot.	All
Remain part of the UK	19	85	57	16	87	56	20	83	60	15	79	50	22	83	55	21	82	55	24	85	59
Reunify with the rest of Ireland	49	4	22	48	3	21	42	4	17	59	5	28	46	3	22	49	5	24	47	5	22
Independent state	10	4	6	18	4	11	15	6	9	6	5	6	9	4	7	10	5	7	15	6	11
Other answer	4	2	3	2	2	3	4	2	3	3	2	2	3	2	3	1	2	2	3	1	2
Don't know	20	7	13	16	4	9	19	6	11	17	10	14	20	7	14	19	7	12	12	3	7

Survey question: What do you think the long-term policy for Northern Ireland should be?

It is worth noting that the survey records a modest yet persistent public interest in an independent Northern Ireland. This option was not given to survey respondents in the question, but has been suggested by them. On average 8 per cent of respondents favour independence for Northern Ireland during the 1998–2004 period, a constitutional option not promoted by any major political party or pressure group. Also noticeable is the significant proportion of survey respondents who record themselves as 'don't knows'. Catholic levels of uncertainty have regularly outstripped those of their Protestant counterparts. This may reflect a reticence to articulate an opinion on such a sensitive issue. It may also reflect, however, genuine confusion on behalf of Northern Ireland citizens in the context of wider political change.

Table 3.1 is useful in recording attitudes towards the basic dyadic 'either/or' constitutional choice (either a United Kingdom or a united Ireland). Yet such 'pure' choices are unrealistic in the contemporary complex constitutional and governance environment. The establishment of supranational bodies (namely the EU) and UK-wide devolution mean that Northern Ireland's citizens have experienced multi-level governance, with different institutions operating simultaneously and possessing different competencies and responsibilities. With this in mind, the 2001 and 2003 surveys presented respondents with a more complex set of constitutional options. The simple united Ireland and United Kingdom choices were augmented with a broader range of options, including independence for Northern Ireland and variations in the nature of devolution available.

What becomes clear is that, given the choice, many survey respondents are willing to express a preference for constitutional options other than the traditional either/or formula. Indeed, a distinct 'devolution effect' is on view, with a plurality of all respondents in 2001 (43 per cent) and a slight majority in 2003 (52 per cent) opting for a devolved constitutional arrangement. Overall, the largest number of respondents in 2001 (31 per cent) and 2003 (30 per cent) opted for Northern Ireland to remain part of the UK but to enjoy enhanced devolution. In many respects this is a remarkable finding since the observed evidence of 'devolution lite' in operation (especially by 2003) was one of repeated suspensions, chronic inter-communal mistrust and legislative timidity. In sum, by the time the 2003 survey was in the field, devolution as formulated under the Belfast Agreement had failed. Many survey respondents seemed to be operating on the basis of hope and faith rather than actual experience of 'devolution plus' as an effective form of government.

There was, however, a sectarian differential in the appetite for an extension of the powers devolved to Northern Ireland. Protestant survey respondents (by a margin of 2:1 in 2003) were more favourable than their Catholic counterparts to the notion of enhanced devolution. Doubtless, the formulation of

Table 3.2. Constitutional preferences from enhanced list of options, 2001 and 2003 (%)

	2001			2003		
	All	Catholic	Protestant	All	Catholic	Protestant
Northern Ireland should become independent: separate from UK and EU	3	4	2	2	2	1
Northern Ireland should become independent: separate from UK, but part of EU	7	9	6	7	10	5
Northern Ireland should remain part of the UK, with its own elected parliament which has law-making and taxation powers	31	14	47	30	18	37
Northern Ireland should remain part of the UK, with its own elected Assembly which has limited law-making powers only	12	4	18	22	9	31
Northern Ireland should remain part of the UK without an elected Assembly	13	7	17	12	7	17
Northern Ireland should unify with the Republic of Ireland	21	49	1	17	38	2
Don't know	13	13	9	11	15	7

Survey question: Which of these statements comes closest to your view?

the survey question (that 'Northern Ireland should remain part of the UK' as part of devolution) reassured many Protestants on their meta-constitutional aim. Support for the status quo, or that Northern Ireland should remain within the UK but with its elected Assembly with limited law-making powers, was particularly low among Catholic survey respondents. In 2001 only 4 per cent of Catholics favoured this option, growing to 9 per cent by 2003. When offered alongside a more extensive range of constitutional options, support for Irish unity falls from 28 per cent overall in 2001 (Table 3.1) to 21 per cent (Table 3.2). Among Catholics, support for Irish unification falls back to under 50 per cent. By 2003, Catholic support for a straightforward united Ireland had further receded to 38 per cent, while support for both 'devolution lite' and 'devolution plus' had increased. Irish unity, though, remains by far the most popular choice among Catholics, even if support for minimalist or enhanced forms of devolution are combined. It is also worth noting that substantial numbers of Catholics opted for the 'don't know' category in 2001 (13 per cent) and 2003 (15 per cent), possibly reflecting a lack of certainty in a changing constitutional environment. Responses to this question illustrate the intractability of the Northern Ireland conflict and the inability of any one constitutional option to secure majority support within one ethno-sectarian community, let alone across both communities. Any constitutional option recommended by the British and Irish governments therefore could only hope to secure a plurality of support if offered alongside a menu of extensive constitutional choices.

The plurality in favour of devolution shown in Table 3.2 is reinforced by other survey evidence. In 2001 and 2003 survey respondents were asked to indicate which level of government they thought ought to have most influence on how Northern Ireland was run (Table 3.3). Respondents were only invited to identify already existing tiers of government; therefore possible preferences, such as Irish unity, were not on offer. Nevertheless, the responses to this question were interesting in revealing the Northern Ireland Assembly to be, by far, the most popular layer of government.

In 2001 65 per cent of all respondents opted for the Northern Ireland Assembly as the tier of government they thought ought to hold most power. By 2003 this figure had fallen to 50 per cent (presumably reflecting the serial collapse of the Assembly), but it still represented a strong plurality among respondents. The relatively strong levels of support for the devolved option seem somewhat counterintuitive given the patent failure of devolution to survive chronic nationalist–unionist mistrust. A strong sectarian differential is noticeable though, with Catholic respondents more favourable to devolution than their Protestant counterparts. In 2001 74 per cent of Catholic respondents favoured the Northern Ireland Assembly as the primary tier of govern-

Table 3.3. Preferred tier of government in a multi-level governance environment, 2001 and 2003 (%)

	2001			2003		
	All	Catholic	Protestant	All	Catholic	Protestant
Northern Ireland Assembly	65	74	61	50	55	46
UK government at Westminster	17	7	24	18	8	27
Local councils	7	8	6	15	15	16
European Union	2	3	1	4	7	1
Other	2	1	2	1	2	1
Don't know	8	7	6	11	14	10

Survey question: Who do you think ought to have most influence over how Northern Ireland is run?

ment, as against 61 per cent of Protestants who felt likewise. In the absence of a united Ireland option, many Catholics may regard devolution as an opportunity to dilute the 'Britishness' of the Northern Ireland state. They may also share the Sinn Féin view that a devolved Northern Ireland could act as a vehicle that could deliver Irish unity at a later stage.

The survey shows low levels of faith in the 'mother of all parliaments' as the most appropriate body to govern Northern Ireland. In 2001 17 per cent of all respondents opted for the UK government at Westminster as their preferred primary governing body, with this figure rising marginally to 18 per cent in 2003. The 2003 figures comprises of a mere 8 per cent of Catholics and less than a third of Protestants (27 per cent).

The principle of consent

The record of referendums as mechanisms to 'solve' ethno national disputes has been poor. While referendums bring advantages of directness and clarity, they are a blunt tool in situations usually marked by their complexity. Reducing a multifaceted conflict to a simple 'yes' or 'no' choice is highly problematic, not least because referendums risk producing new grievances and minorities (Gallagher, 1996; Mac Ginty, 2003; Reilly, 2003). Despite warnings from other conflict situations, a key feature of the Belfast Agreement was the 'principle of consent' or the notion that Northern Ireland's constitutional future would be decided by its citizens in a referendum. The principle of consent took practical form through a clause in the Agreement enabling the Secretary of State to call a referendum 'if at any time it appears likely to him that a majority of those voting would express a wish that Northern Ireland should cease to be part of the United Kingdom and form part of a united Ireland' (NIO, 1998: 3). Moreover, the Agreement compelled the British and Irish governments not only to respect, but to facilitate, the wishes of the majority. Once the first referendum had been held, a referendum had to be held every seven years, thus establishing a 'conveyor belt' of constitutional battles.

At one level, allowing Northern Ireland's citizens to be the ultimate constitutional arbiters via a referendum is an attractive option: it democratises the dispute, empowers the antagonists through the ballot box, and prevents the British and Irish governments from reaching an elite *fait accompli* behind closed doors. At another level, however, the Agreement made permanent Northern Ireland's conditional status within the Union and legitimised political interest in the nationalist versus unionist demographic balance. This seemed to contradict a key aim of the Belfast Agreement: to reach a comprehensive peace settlement that would put constitutional issues to bed and allow local parties to cooperate on functional matters. The Agreement had billed itself as a 'truly historic opportunity for a new beginning', yet it risked condemning Northern Ireland to a repetition of past constitutional wrangles (NIO, 1998: 1).

Northern Ireland's politicians required little encouragement to maintain an interest in constitutional issues, despite the existence of new power-sharing political institutions created under the Agreement. There was much speculation on the possibility of the nationalist minority overtaking the unionist majority in the medium term. Both nationalist and unionist political leaders eagerly awaited the publication of the 2001 Census results to see if there had been any significant shifts in the sectarian demographic balance. Republicans urged the Secretary of State to hold a referendum and thus start – as they saw it – the 'countdown to a united Ireland' (McLaughlin, 2002). The then leader of the UUP, David Trimble, also joined the calls for a referendum, believing that a pro-Union majority would puncture nationalist optimism that Irish unity by consent was an achievable goal. 'Let's call the republican's bluff', Trimble said. 'Let's put the issue to bed for another generation. Let's make it clear that for the next generation the United Kingdom is here to stay' (Trimble, 2002).

In this context, the Northern Ireland Life and Times Survey sought to ascertain if there was support for a constitutional referendum, and if citizens would respect the principle of consent upon which the Belfast Agreement rested. In 2002 the survey asked respondents whether they thought that a constitutional referendum should take place within the next six months. As Table 3.4 shows, there was strong opposition to such a proposal: overall 64 per cent of respondents opposed the proposal, which breaks down to 53 per cent of Catholic respondents and 72 per cent of Protestants. That a majority of Protestants were opposed to a constitutional referendum is unsurprising:

Table 3.4. Attitudes towards a referendum on Northern Ireland's constitutional position, 2002 (%)

	All	Catholic	Protestant
Yes	22	26	18
No	64	53	72
Other answer	1	1	0
Don't know	14	20	9

Survey question: Do you think that there should be a referendum within the next six months on whether Northern Ireland should unify with the Republic of Ireland?

such a referendum threatened the status quo of Northern Ireland's place within the Union. Catholic rejection of the proposal, albeit by a slender majority, is more surprising. Only 26 per cent of Catholic survey respondents were in favour of a referendum within six months. This may have been due to calculations that the inter-communal demographic balance had yet to reach a favourable position. Alternatively, however, it may have reflected a diminishing appetite for Irish unity among Catholics, with devolution serving to satisfy nationalists' traditional grievances and aspirations. Whatever the reason, the enthusiasm shown by some political leaders for a constitutional referendum was not shared by substantial numbers of electors, and the Secretary of State did not sanction a referendum.

While the Belfast Agreement compels the British and Irish governments to become facilitators of constitutional change should the people of Northern Ireland vote for it as part of a referendum, the consent principle partially rests on the losing side in any referendum respecting the wishes of the majority. The survey sought to ascertain public reactions to the result of a constitutional referendum. Respondents in favour of constitutional options other than Northern Ireland remaining within the UK (Irish unification, an independent Northern Ireland, other answer or don't know) were asked how they would react to if a majority of people in Northern Ireland never voted for Northern Ireland to become part of a united Ireland. In other words, this question was largely answered by non-unionists. As Table 3.5 shows, non-unionists showed a strong respect for the principle of consent, with an average of 64 per cent of respondents saying they would 'happily accept' the will of the majority over the 1998–2004 time series. An average of 26 per cent said they could live with such an outcome. In each year, 4 per cent or less said that they would find such a decision impossible to accept. There was little significant variation in responses to this question over the life of the time series.

Survey respondents who identified themselves as non-nationalists were asked to identify their response should the majority of people in Northern

Table 3.5. Support or rejection of the principle of consent among non-unionists, 1998–2004 (%)

	1998	1999	2000	2001	2002	2003	2004
Impossible to accept	4	2	3	4	2	2	2
Could live with it	26	24	29	23	27	27	29
Happily accept	64	68	61	64	66	64	64
Don't know	6	6	6	10	6	7	5

Survey question: If the majority of people in Northern Ireland never voted to become part of a united Ireland, do you think you would . . .

(Asked to respondents who had answered 'Reunify with the rest of Ireland', 'Independent state', 'Other answer' or 'Don't know' to the question 'What do you think the long-term policy of Northern Ireland should be?'(Table 3.1)).

Ireland ever vote to become part of a united Ireland (Table 3.6). An average of 40 per cent of non-nationalist survey respondents over the 1998–2004 period said that they would 'happily accept' the wishes of the majority of the people if they ever voted for Northern Ireland to unify with the rest of Ireland. An average of 39 per cent said that they 'could live with' such a proposition, while an average of 16 per cent said that it would be 'impossible to accept'. The survey showed a sharp decline in the proportion of respondents adopting the rejectionist position between 2002 and 2004.

The survey reveals that both communities have internalised the principle of consent – a key feature of the Belfast Agreement and the mechanism through which Northern Ireland's constitutional future rests. Clearly there is a difference between asking such a question as part of a political attitudes survey and actual reactions should an acute constitutional crisis arise. Nevertheless, the survey shows a widespread respect for constitutional change or the status quo if such positions are validated through a referendum. It is worth noting, however, that nationalist acceptance of the principle of consent is stronger than that of unionists. While an outright majority of non-unionist survey respondents would 'happily accept' the wishes of the majority, non-nationalist acceptance is less fulsome. The proportion of non-nationalists who say that they would find a united Ireland 'impossible to accept' by far outstrips the proportion of non-unionists who would find a permanent rejection of a united Ireland impossible to accept. In part this may reflect the reality of Northern Ireland's current position within the UK and demographic evidence that suggests that a pro-united Ireland majority is unlikely for the foreseeable future.

Given that the consent principle institutionalises constitutional uncertainty, the Northern Ireland Life and Times Survey sought to gauge public expectation of a united Ireland within 20 years. A number of republican leaders, including Sinn Féin President Gerry Adams, have predicted a united

Table 3.6. Support or rejection of the principle of consent among non-nationalists, 1998–2004 (%)

	1998	1999	2000	2001	2002	2003	2004
Impossible to accept	16	19	17	18	19	13	11
Could live with it	38	35	41	36	35	45	46
Happily accept	41	42	37	39	42	37	40
Don't know	5	5	5	8	5	5	3

Survey question: If the majority of people in Northern Ireland ever voted to become part of a united Ireland, do you think you would . . .

(Asked to respondents who had answered 'Remain part of the UK', 'Independent state', 'Other answer' or 'Don't know' to the question 'What do you think the long-term policy of Northern Ireland should be?' (Table 3.1)).

Ireland within a 20 year timeframe. As Table 3.7 shows, public expectations of Irish unity within 20 years have declined since the Belfast Agreement was reached. In 1998 42 per cent of survey respondents thought that a united Ireland was either very or quite likely within 20 years. By 2003 that figure had reduced to 29 per cent. The decline is discernible within both communities, falling from 45 to 26 per cent among Catholic respondents and 42 to 32 per cent among Protestant respondents. The proportion believing that a united Ireland was quite or very unlikely rose from 42 per cent overall in 1998 to a majority position (52 per cent) in 2003. Interestingly, from 2002 onwards, Catholic pessimism on the likelihood of Irish unity has outstripped that of Protestants. It is worth noting that there has been considerable instability in Protestant attitudes towards the likelihood of Irish unity within a generation. In 2000 49 per cent of Protestant survey respondents thought that Irish unity was quite or very unlikely. By the following year that figure had fallen to 39 per cent, only to rise again to 49 per cent by 2002. Overall though, Protestant fears of Irish unity have eased, perhaps indicating that Protestant survey respondents are becoming increasingly assured that the Belfast Agreement and the devolved political environment (or what is left of it) will not deliver them into Irish unity in anything but the long term.

Concluding discussion

On reviewing the Northern Ireland Life and Times Survey evidence, it can be argued that devolution has let a constitutional genie out of the bottle. Nationalist and unionist public attitudes that (since the collapse of Sunningdale at any rate) had been largely restricted to the either/or dyadic choice of a united Ireland or Northern Ireland as part of the UK have been

Table 3.7. Likelihood of a united Ireland within 20 years, 1998–2003 (%)

	1998			1999			2000			2001			2002			2003		
	Cath.	Prot.	All	Cath.	Prot.	All	Cath.	Prot.	All	Cath.	Prot.	All	Cath.	Prot.	All	Cath.	Prot.	All
Very likely	10	11	10	11	8	9	10	7	8	15	13	14	8	7	7	5	6	6
Quite likely	35	31	32	33	30	31	25	28	27	29	31	29	20	27	24	21	26	23
Quite unlikely	22	21	22	25	23	23	25	19	21	18	18	18	21	20	21	24	25	25
Very unlikely	17	22	20	15	27	21	21	30	27	19	21	20	34	29	31	32	24	27
Even chance	9	8	8	8	7	8	5	5	5	6	6	6	7	8	7	7	10	9
Don't know	7	7	8	8	6	7	14	11	12	13	11	14	9	9	10	10	9	10

Survey question: At any time in the next 20 years, do you think it is likely or unlikely that there will be a united Ireland?

challenged by additional devolved constitutional permutations. Support for devolved political options has eroded support for traditional or 'pure' nationalist and unionist constitutional goals. This is somewhat surprising since the observed evidence of devolution in action has been one of mutual acrimony and distrust, ultimately leading to collapse. In short, post-Belfast Agreement devolution has failed to become self-sustaining and failed to deliver inter-group cooperation. The consociational architecture has been unable to deliver a situation whereby inter-group partnership on functional matters relegates conflicting meta-constitutional goals into the background. Yet despite this obvious failure, the survey shows significant public support for devolved constitutional options. More than this, the survey shows support for an extension of devolution beyond the reserved levels initially granted through the Belfast Agreement. According to the survey, the most popular constitutional option for Northern Ireland would be enhanced devolution, or for Northern Ireland to remain in the UK but with its own elected parliament which has law-making and tax-raising powers. We must assume that many survey respondents recognised that any devolved option would involve an element of nationalist–unionist power sharing.

The enhanced devolution outcome may owe its relative popularity to its ability partially to satisfy both nationalists and unionists. For unionists, Northern Ireland remains inside the UK under this formulation. For nationalists, Northern Ireland has substantial autonomy, perhaps space in which citizens who do not primarily identify themselves as British may imagine they would be more comfortable. But a question remains: what will happen to the constitutional genie of devolution given the failure of devolution to take root? Will it flourish or wither? In one reading, the demand for devolution may grow as citizens become frustrated at the return to direct rule. Having tasted the possibilities of devolved rule, citizens may direct their politicians to re-engage in political process that would facilitate enhanced devolved arrangements, perhaps arrangements more able to withstand the shocks that fatally undermined the 1998–2002 variant of devolution. But there is another reading of the situation. Citizens may view devolution as unworkable: notionally a good idea but one that was unable to find sufficient nationalist–unionist commonality to survive. Having observed this political model fail, citizens may retrench and return to the old certainties of the either/or constitutional positions.

Notes

1 ESRC projects 'Political attitudes to devolution and institutional change in Northern Ireland' (L327253045) and 'Public attitudes to devolution and national identity in Northern Ireland' (L219252024).

2 Discussion of the sensitivities of conducting public attitudes research in deeply divided societies can be found at Mac Ginty et al. (2001: 482–484) and Brown and Mac Ginty (2003: 87–88).

References

Arthur, P. (2000) *Special Relationships: Britain, Ireland and the Northern Ireland Problem*. Belfast: Blackstaff Press.

Brown, K. and Mac Ginty, R. (2003) 'Public attitudes towards partisan and neutral symbols in post-Agreement Northern Ireland', *Identities: Global studies in culture and power*, 10, 83–108.

Gallagher, M. (1996) 'Conclusion' in M. Gallagher and P.V. Uleri (eds), *The Referendum Experience in Europe*. Basingstoke: Macmillan.

Lijphart, A. (1977) *Democracy in Plural Societies: A Comparative Exploration*. New Haven and Yale: Yale University Press.

Mac Ginty, R. (2003) 'Constitutional referendums and ethnonational conflict: the case of Northern Ireland', *Nationalism and Ethnic Politics*, 9 (2), 1–22.

Mac Ginty, R., Wilford, R., Dowds, L. and Robinson, G. (2001)'Consenting Adults: the principle of consent and Northern Ireland's constitutional future', *Government and Opposition*, 36 (4), 472–92.

McLaughlin, M. (March 2002) 'Countdown to a united Ireland', Sinn Féin press release.

NIO (Northern Ireland Office) (1998) *The Agreement. Agreement Reached in the Multi-Party Negotiations*. Belfast: NIO.

O'Leary, B. (2001) 'Comparative political science and the British Irish Agreement' in J. McGarry (ed.), *Northern Ireland and the Divided World: Post-Agreement Northern Ireland in Comparative Perspective*. Oxford: Oxford University Press, 53–88.

Reilly, B. (2003) 'Democratic validation' in J. Darby and R. Mac Ginty (eds) *Contemporary Peacemaking: Conflict, Violence and Peace Processes*. Basingstoke: Palgrave, 174–183.

Sinn Féin, (2005) *A Green Paper on Irish Unity: Sinn Féin Discussion Paper*. Dublin: Sinn Féin.

Sisk, T. (1996) *Powersharing and International Mediation in Ethnic Conflicts*. Washington DC: United States Institute of Peace Press.

Sisk, T. (2003) 'Power-sharing after civil wars: matching problems to solutions' in J. Darby and R. Mac Ginty (eds) *Contemporary Peacemaking: Conflict, Violence and Peace processes*. Basingstoke: Palgrave, 139–150.

Smyth, M. and G. Robinson (eds) (2001) *Researching Violently Divided Societies: Ethical and Methodological issues*. Tokyo/London: United Nations University Press/Pluto.

Trimble, D. (March 2002) 'Speech to the Ulster Unionist Party AGM by Rt. Hon. David Trimble MP, MLA'.

UUP (Ulster Unionist Party) (1998) 'Say YES for the Union', referendum communication from the Ulster Unionist Party. Belfast: UUP.

4

Towards a new constitutional doctrine for Northern Ireland? The Agreement, the litigation and the constitutional future

John Morison

Introduction

This chapter asks whether the settlement provided by the Belfast Agreement and the Northern Ireland Act 1998 is really something new in UK constitutional terms. It seeks to begin to provide an answer by looking at three themes that came out of an ESRC-funded research project which involved an extensive series of interviews with politicians, civil servants and lawyers from Belfast, London and Dublin.[1] These interviews were undertaken with the objective of discovering:

- the background to the drafting of the Agreement and its subsequent translation into the Northern Ireland Act 1998;
- some further details about the operation of executive government since 1998;
- the approach of the parties and lawyers in a series of legal cases that arose from the Act and its wider impact.

Exploring these themes across some 50 interviews with leading figures from the political, governmental and legal world who were closely involved in the creation and outworking of the Agreement, the project findings provide some additional insights into the important issue of what the settlement in Northern Ireland was about in constitutional terms and whether it represented the sort of paradigmatic shift that some have seen.

There are a variety of people who are prepared to describe the settlement provided by the Belfast Agreement and the Northern Ireland Act 1998 as something new and different. Prime Minister Tony Blair famously felt the 'hand of history' on his shoulder, and those involved in producing the Agreement declared that 'we, the participants in the multi-party negotiations, believe that the agreement we have negotiated offers a truly historic opportunity for a new beginning . . . a fresh start'. The long title of the Northern Ireland Act 1998 describes it ambitiously as 'An Act to make new provision for the government of Northern Ireland' and indeed this theme is picked up in much of the academic commentary with, for example, books and articles carrying references in their titles to ideas of a 'new beginning' (Harvey, 2001), a 'constitutional moment' (McEvoy and Morison, 2003), and a 'new territorial politics in the British Isles' (Todd, 2005). References to 'democratic renewal' (e.g. Harvey (ed.), 2001) also appear, as do notions of 'political transformation' (McEvoy, 2000). There is also much reference to the Northern Ireland arrangements in comparative terms with settlements in South Africa (e.g. McGarry, 1988) and elsewhere (e.g. Bell, 2000; McGarry (ed.), 2001; O'Leary and McGarry, 2003). Campbell, Ní Aoláin, and Harvey (2000) refer to the settlement as being at the 'frontiers of legal analysis' and McCrudden (2004), too, sees the experience in Northern Ireland 'raising issues at the heart of the British constitutional tradition, as it was and as it might become'.

Notwithstanding the current setbacks to devolution, this continuing willingness to see the Agreement as in some way constitutive, as standing above ordinary politics or regular law in a way that successfully moves on from the past to redefine the future through a single 'constitutional moment', stands in contrast to constitutional traditions within the UK more generally. There, constitutionalism tends to mean a gradual process of accretional change to traditional forms, punctuated by the occasional bout of constitutional modernisation, of which the Blair Government's reform programme is the most spectacular instance (Oliver, 2003; Morison, 1998). In particular the reaction to the Northern Ireland settlement raises the question of whether it might be better to see the Agreement as representing not simply the high-water mark of the traditional Westminster style constitutionalism – as it is operated in the slightly alien context of Northern Ireland (see Morison and Livingstone, 1995) – but as amounting to something new.

It might be possible to fit the Northern Ireland constitutional experience into, for example, the wider project of reform, devolution and modernisation in the UK, as some commentators have attempted (e.g. Barnett, 2002; Bradley and Ewing, 2003). Alternatively, and particularly in relation to any new role for the judges, it may be thought that 'red light v. green light arguments' (see Harlow and Rawlings, 1997) can be developed to explain the situation, or that the now rather tired debate about ultra vires can be stretched to cover the new dispensation (e.g. Craig, 2003: Forsyth and Elliot, 2003) or even that emerging ideas of 'constitutional legislation' can accommodate the change. (Elliot, 2003)

Alternatively, it may be thought that a wholly new approach is required. For example, we may wish to consider that the Northern Ireland settlement represents what Teitel (2000) describes as 'transitional constitutionalism'. Whereas traditionally constitutionalism is viewed as foundational and forward looking, transitional constitutionalism looks back to undoing problems of the past as well as laying foundations for the future. It is also provisional, subject to revision, and contested, where the boundary between 'ordinary' and 'constitutional' politics becomes blurred. Such a description may seem to resonate in Northern Ireland and require both a new constitutional practice and theory. In particular it may require judges to use their power creatively 'not to "block" democracy but to make it more deliberative' (Sunstein, 2001). Alternatively, we may try to fit the Northern Ireland experience into ideas generated in North America. These may involve reference to a general process of constitutional history, involving a series of constitutional moments occurring within a narrative of continuing 'normal politics' (Ackerman, 1991; 1998), notions of a constitutional revolution occurring through the agency of a particular coalition of forces taking control (Balkin and Levinson, 2001), or gradual processes of change and consolidation across dominant sets of institutions or ideology (Tushnet, 2004).

Whether we would prefer to attempt to develop existing accounts or import a constitutional paradigm directly from elsewhere still leaves open the question of how we might evaluate the impact on wider British constitutionalism of the 'new beginning' that is represented by the Belfast Agreement and the Northern Ireland Act 1998. It was precisely this task that our ESRC project attempted. In particular we attempted to explore:

- the extent to which the new dispensation produced a 'new politics' or at least a new form in the operation of government;
- whether judicial activism increases in response to the new constitutional arrangements;
- the degree to which courts develop overtly or otherwise a new constitutional theory underlying the new constitutional arrangements;
- whether or not judicial intervention produces changes in the practices or strategies of other public institutions;
- the extent to which developments in Northern Ireland reflect more general trends in a changing judicial role and the explanation of that role throughout the UK;
- any spillover whereby changes in the practices of the courts influence debates about changes in the appointments procedure of judges and the composition of the Northern Ireland judiciary.

Clearly there is not space here to detail how all these issues played out in the research (see further Morrison and Lynch, 2007). Instead this chapter attempts to address the particular issue of the possible existence of a new constitutional paradigm by reporting briefly on the three areas that reflect the themes that were explored in the ESRC research project. The first relates to the making of the Agreement itself and its subsequent translation into the Northern Ireland Act 1998 (NIA). The second is the phenomenon of executive government, an area which became of increasing interest as the research developed, and the third relates directly to the detail of the litigation arising from the Act and its impact.

Making the Agreement

The basic story of how the Agreement came about has been told extensively in other places. This project focused particularly on the extent to which considerations about law and litigation played a role in its formulation. The overall impression was that it was very limited. Politicians and officials on all sides stressed that the emphasis was very much on getting political agreement and that in the highly pressurised context of the negotiations there was insufficient time to go into what they perceived as the 'fine detail' of law. The parties did not seem to seek legal advice to any significant degree. Lawyers we spoke to suggested they had been consulted by politicians on some specific institutional details – more to do with prisoner release and policing than with the structure of government – but not on the overall structure of the settlement. Several of the parties, notably Alliance, SDLP and UUP, had a number of practicing or academic lawyers among their negotiating teams and appeared to turn to them to examine draft proposals, but not in any particularly systematic or legalistic way. On more than one occasion indeed it was suggested the UUP leader's background in law had inhibited negotiations, as matters of detail were pursued to the detriment of broader principles. Among those interviewed it seemed that Sinn Féin had made the broadest use of legal advice, and indeed they indicated that they had received a large amount of unsolicited legal advice. Again much of this focused on issues around policing and human rights and perhaps proved more significant at the stage of converting the Agreement to an Act than at the stage of negotiating the Agreement itself.

The position of the two governments was especially interesting. The UK, which appeared to be in receipt of considerable legal advice from both Home Office and Foreign Office lawyers (the latter in respect of Strands 2 and 3) adopted much the same approach as the parties. The emphasis was very much on getting the political deal sorted out, with the idea that this could all be translated into law once agreed. The possibility of subsequent legal challenges was forseen, but officials appeared to be confident that the courts would not wish to become too embroiled in political controversy, and that even if they did things could always be fixed by subsequent legislation. It was also interesting that as the negotiations spanned across the remit of several UK departments, the legal advice was drawn from different sources and used from a variety of perspectives. This differed from the Irish government approach, which was markedly more holistic, perhaps as a consequence of the tradition of a written constitution. The Irish government, though again stressing the need to deal with things at the political level and not to become too preoccupied with legal technicalities, appeared rather more concerned with the legal form, at least in respect of Strand 2. Several of those who worked on the Irish government side during the negotiations indicated to us an awareness of the development of constitutional review by the Irish courts in general, and of challenges to the Anglo-Irish Agreement and Nice Treaty in particular. The advice of the Attorney General was sought on these matters and Irish officials obviously spent considerable time identifying a formulation for the repeal of Articles 2 and 3 of the Irish constitution which would satisfy the Irish courts as well as the political parties to the negotiations. Officials also seemed well aware of the broader implications of these constitutional changes, especially for the issue of Irish citizenship and immigration law, which subsequently became apparent in litigation. On the other hand, Irish officials seemed much less interested in the likely impact of these changes in UK constitutional law. This was especially true in respect of the Strand 1 aspects, discussion of which the Irish government did not formally take part in.

The approach to law evident during the negotiations continued with the translation of the Agreement into the NIA 1998. Formal input into this was confined to those parties who actively participated in the Westminster Parliament, and therefore excluded the Irish government and abstentionist Sinn Féin. However, it was clear that both, especially the latter, made their views well known to the UK government and contributed to the shaping of the legislation. Again, discussions about law, both from within and without Parliament, focused on matters of technical detail, even if several of these, such as the scope of the powers of the Human Rights Commission and the Equality Commission, were of considerable wider significance. Some comment was made to us regarding the unusual nature of the Agreement as the basis for legislation and how this departed from the type of briefing papers those drafting legislation would normally rely upon. Previous constitutional legislation, such as the Government of Ireland Act 1920 and the Northern Ireland Constitution Act 1973, was drawn on to shape the legislation, as was some of the devolution legislation for Scotland and Wales. However, the template remained very much the Agreement, and the task focused on the giving effect to the Agreement in UK law, as is reflected in the preamble to the NIA.

Even so, few of those we spoke to seemed in any way aware of the constitutional significance of drafting a statute to delineate the basis for the government of part of the UK on the basis of a broad-ranging agreement endorsed by Northern Ireland's political parties, the Irish government and referendums in Northern Ireland and Ireland. While the basis for legislation may be regarded as significantly different from usual, it was still looked upon as essentially a normal set of policy instructions for the drafting of a statute.

Overall therefore the impression obtained during the research of the role of law during the negotiations leading to the Agreement and the NIA 1998 was that it played a fairly minor role, due in large part to the very traditional perceptions of law held by most of the participants. Law was envisaged as simply whatever set of rules the parties to Agreement could be made to agree upon. At most, law and litigation was seen as a potential irritant, something one official suggested legally minded ministers had to be discouraged from relying on. The focus was very firmly on getting a political deal and then reducing it to some sort of legal form. It was clearly hoped that if this was done competently then the opportunities for one of the parties to challenge the workings of the deal would be few. Even if someone was minded to do so, it was hoped that they could be persuaded from this by political means, but if that proved unsuccessful most felt the courts would be unwilling to become involved. Even if the courts did become involved, it was felt that fresh legislation could always be passed to set things right again. There was little sense that anyone saw the law in a more positive sense, as a repository of values and norms that could be drawn upon to help construct and sustain whatever agreement was reached. This is of course one of the functions constitutional law plays in most countries, where the constitution is not simply a set of rules but also a set of values and principles on which the society is founded and around which the institutions of the society are structured. Contrary to the UK, where traditionally constitutional law has been seen as no different from any other law – with the Act of Union having the same status as the Dentists Act – in most countries the constitution is seen as having a 'higher' status and as a text whose content is reflective of broader ideas about the relationship of citizens to each other and to the state.

At first sight it may not seem surprising that those involved in negotiations about Northern Ireland's constitution operated on the basis of traditional notions of constitutional law. However there are perhaps three reasons why this might have been otherwise.

First, a number of commentators have suggested that traditional British notions of constitutional law, where the law is simply the reflection of the wishes of those who have gained political power, may be particularly inappropriate in the context of a divided society such as Northern Ireland. In such a society law can become a tool for instability and oppression, as those who find themselves in a political minority at least fear that political defeat may lead to a diminishing of their citizenship and may indeed find this to be the case. At the level of institutional detail the Agreement, with its provisions for weighted voting and entrenched human rights guarantees, marks a move away from this type of constitution, but it might be argued that the shift needs to go further to reflect ideas about the purpose of the constitution itself.

Second, even at the time of the Agreement, and perhaps more so subsequently, there were signs of a change within UK constitutional discourse itself. The recognition of the supremacy of European Union (EU) law, the incorporation of the European Convention on Human Rights (ECHR), devolution legislation and the widening scope of judicial review have led judges and other commentators to begin to re-evaluate the nature of UK law and the constitutional relationship of the courts to other branches of government. Most graphically in *Thoburn* v. *Sunderland City Council* [2002] 3 WLR 247 the courts were seen as developing the idea of 'constitutional statutes' which have a different status than ordinary statutes. In time this may lead to the courts developing a more extensive articulation of the structure and norms of the constitution, one which develops more clearly the scope of their role in a way which goes beyond the mere checking of whether conduct conforms to clear rules.

A third reason why this approach to law may not have been appropriate is that it is predicated on a view of the constitution and of constitutional relationships which results very much from constitutional characteristics historically present in the British constitution but which were never likely to be true of the new situation in Northern Ireland. These characteristics include strong parliamentary government (where the winning political party will always be able to claim a high level of democratic support for its actions), collective responsibility of ministers to the cabinet and strong traditions of ministerial accountability to Parliament. Where these characteristics are present, as Guarnieri and Pederzoli (2003) observe, courts will largely be deferential to the Executive and will be reluctant to enter the political fray. However in Northern Ireland the arrangements provided by the Agreement and NIA meant there was always likely to be a weak Executive, with high potential for conflict among its members and a limit on the extent to which members of the Executive were likely to be accountable to the Assembly. In addition power was fragmented away from both the Assembly and Executive by the possibility of legislation being subjected to judicial review on a range of competence grounds – notably those relating to human rights and equality – and by the creation of various quangos and independent commissions. Such conditions, as in federal constitutions, create the opportunity for more extensive conflict between, rather than within, power centres and a greater opportunity for courts to intervene, especially as the democratic legitimacy of other branches of government is not quite as overwhelming as in a strong parliamentary system. It says something for the limited constitutional thinking which took place at the time of the Agreement that the parties appeared to believe they could make significant changes in the nature of the legislature and executive from that which prevailed in the traditional Westminster model, but largely leave the judicial branch untouched. What thinking there was, which fed into the commitment to the Criminal Justice Review, focused largely on the issue of whether the judiciary were 'representative' of community decisions. While this is an important issue in itself, it might be thought likely that this had the potential only to deteriorate into an unsatisfactory squabble about politicising the judiciary and undermining judicial independence if broader questions about the role and structure of the courts in the type of democracy that the Agreement envisages are not addressed.

This study is not the first to comment on the extent to which the significance of the Agreement and the NIA has been undervalued as a matter of constitutional law. Campbell, Ní Aoláin and Harvey (2003) point out that they cannot simply be accommodated into traditional accounts of UK constitutionalism as an act of the Westminster Parliament making provision for devolved government of one part of the Kingdom. The basis for governing Northern Ireland has shifted from simply being whatever the Westminster Parliament decrees, to relying on an Agreement backed by an international treaty and underpinned by the dual referendums (Morison, 2001; McEvoy and Morison, 2003). It is unclear whether as a matter of politics or law the UK government could simply ignore this, though constitutional scholarship in the UK has yet to accommodate the significance of this.

The particular understanding of constitutional law which those who negotiated the Agreement proceeded on may seem an esoteric point of somewhat limited interest. However, it is significant because, as the study found, important litigation resulting from the Agreement and the Act has depended on what approach to the constitution the courts hold. This is especially clear in *Robinson* [2002] UKHL 32 where, ironically, the court's willingness to depart from traditional understandings of constitutional law proved highly beneficial for the government's case. This is explored in more detail below, where it is argued that a more explicit articulation of such a different constitutional approach might be most beneficial for the development of a more satisfactory constitutional regime for Northern Ireland. Before moving to this, however, it is important to highlight some of the findings about the specific experience of cabinet government in Northern Ireland's devolved administration and the constitutional problems which this posed.

The operation of cabinet government

The approach taken to the formation and operation of the Executive was one of the constitutional innovations of the Agreement and the NIA. In UK constitutional law the rules governing the formation and operation of the Executive have largely been a matter of constitutional convention. Appointment is made by the Prime Minister and the convention of collective responsibility requires the cabinet to speak with one voice. The power of the Prime Minister to dismiss a cabinet minister for speaking or acting in a way which is out of line with an agreed collective decision provides an effective means of ensuring such decisions are respected. As ministers have, with few exceptions, been drawn from the same political party as the Prime Minister, difficulties with regard to inter-Executive disputes are rare. This form of cabinet government also facilitates a free flow of information between officials as, whatever their department, all are ultimately working for the same government.

Such a system of Executive formation is of course closely tied to the simple majority voting system, and the corollary of this system is that usually one political party will have a majority in the House of Commons. The adoption of proportional representation (PR) systems in Scotland and Wales raised the possibility that this would not always be the case in the devolved Assemblies, and indeed coalition rather than single party governments have become the norm. In Northern Ireland, the combination of PR and the use of the d'Hondt system for the appointment of the Executive made it not merely likely but indeed inevitable that the Executive would be made up of parties which had opposed each other in the election. In such circumstances the possibility of establishing collective responsibility on the traditional Westminster model were slim, and disappeared when election results produced the outcome that two of the ministers would be drawn from the DUP, which refused to sit in the Executive in protest at the inclusion of Sinn Féin.

These circumstances suggested the need for a more formal structure on which to organise government. The NIA said relatively little about such issues, beyond specifying the formal circumstances in which ministers could be appointed and dismissed. More extensive detail was provided in the Agreement itself and in a subsequent ministerial code agreed between the parties and later approved by the Assembly in 2000. The Agreement clearly envisaged that each minister was to be given a high degree of autonomy. Paragraph 24 indicates that 'Ministers will have full executive authority in their respective areas of responsibility, within any broad programme agreed by the Executive Committee and endorsed by the Assembly as a whole'. The Executive Committee is stated, in paragraph 19, to be 'a forum for the discussion of, and agreement on, issues which cut across the responsibilities of two or more Ministers, for prioritising executive and legislative proposals and for recommending a common position where necessary (e.g. in dealing with external relationships)'. The one collective responsibility of ministers is to 'agree each year, and review as necessary, a programme incorporating an agreed budget linked to policies and programmes, subject to approval by the Assembly, after scrutiny in Assembly Committees, on a cross-community basis'.

This leads to issues about how well the Executive worked and, particularly, it connects to the litigation about nominations to the North/South Ministerial Council (*In the matter of applications by De Brún and Martin McGuiness for judicial review* [2002] NI 442) and litigation about refusing the release of ministerial papers to non-participating ministers (*In the matter of an application by Maurice Morrow and Gregory Campbell for judicial review* [2002] NI 261). It also raises important issues about how civil servants operate in such circumstances and give advice, as well as constitutional issues about the funding of such cases between different government departments from departmental budgets.

Litigation on the Agreement

The Agreement has thrown up a number of cases. Most but not all of these touch on the interpretation of the NIA, but others raise aspects of the Agreement, such as the policing provisions, which were given effect to in other legislation. One might also argue that the many human rights cases which have come before the courts in Northern Ireland in recent years are related to the emphasis placed in the Agreement on human rights. Most of the cases followed up in detail by the project were cases brought by politicians, indeed sometimes by members of the government against each other – something unusual in UK constitutional law but not in many other parts of the world. Although the number of cases is relatively small, they do raise a number of interesting points. The research focused on particular cases where extensive interviews were carried out with the parties involved:

- *Re Williamson's application for judicial review* CA [2000] NI 281.
- *In re an application by Seamus Treacy and Barry MacDonald for judicial Review* 6 January 2000; *Re Treacy's and another's application for judicial Review* QB [2000] NI 330.
- *In the matter of an application by Bairbre de Brún and Martin McGuinness for judicial review* 2001 NIQB 3; *In the matter of applications by Bairbre de Brún and Martin McGuinness for judicial review* 2001 NICA 43.

- *In the matter of an application by Conor Murphy for judicial review* 2001 NIQB 34.
- *In the matter of an application by Maurice Morrow and Gregory Campbell for leave to apply for judicial review* 2001 NIQB 13; *In the matter of an application by Maurice Morrow and Gregory Campbell for judicial review* 2002 NIQB 4.
- *Re Northern Ireland Human Rights Commission's application for judicial review* CA [2001] NI 271; *In Re Northern Ireland Human Rights Commission (Northern Ireland)* [2002] UKHL 25.
- *In the matter of an application by Peter Robinson for leave to apply for judicial review* 2001 NIQB 39; *In the matter of an application by Peter Robinson for leave to apply for judicial review* 2001 NIQB 42; *In the matter of an application by Peter Robinson for judicial review* 2001 NIQB 49; *In the matter of an application by Peter Robinson for judicial review* 2002 NICA 18A; *Robinson* v. *Secretary of State for Northern Ireland and Others (Northern Ireland)* [2002] UKHL 32 [2002] NI 390.
- *In the matter of an application by Mark Parsons for judicial review* 2002 NIQB 46; *In the matter of an application by Mark William John Parsons for judicial review* 2003 NICA 20.
- *In the matter of an application by Damien McComb for judicial review* 2003 NIQB 47.

There are a number of general issues arising from this litigation (see Anthony, 2002). First, the volume of cases is fairly low. Civil servants to whom we spoke suggested that they had expected more, but also that more often there is a threat of litigation than actual resort to it. Several factors appear to be responsible for this. First, the influence of individuals should not be underestimated. Clearly some parties had politicians or advisers who were more legally minded than others, and who were therefore more likely to be analysing developments with a view to potential litigation. A second factor relates to resources. Some politicians, for example, claimed that they could not justify the use of party funds to explore speculative legal points and looked enviously at the ability of those in government to use public money to pursue disputes between the parties. Also there was a general view that the courts would not be willing to become involved in difficult matters of political controversy. This view was reinforced by decisions of the courts, such as that in the *Williamson* case where the invocation of 'soft-edged review' suggested a judicial reluctance to become involved in high-profile political disputes. The signals given in this decision were referred to as one reason why some of the most controversial issues, such as the extent to which decommissioning had taken place and whether this constituted a breach of the Agreement, have not been taken before the courts. However, the most prominent reason overall appeared to be that most politicians instinctively disliked resorting to the courts to resolve what they saw as essentially political issues. Moreover, unlike in many political systems where points of constitutional impasse can be resolved only by the courts, there was another outlet via a reference to the British or Irish government to put pressure on one side or the other. Indeed it is perhaps no accident that two of the most high-profile cases were brought by the anti-Agreement DUP, which did not previously have a reputation for using the courts, but which lacked the possibility of resort to either government to enforce their view of the Agreement.

Those cases which did come before the courts therefore tended to be pursued for tactical reasons, where other options were unavailable or unattractive. At least one case, *De Brún* relating to nominations to the North/South Ministerial Council (NSMC), appeared to have arisen for purely tactical reasons, where the First Minister needed to be seen for political reasons to be taking a firm stand against Sinn Féin, although it proceeded on what was always likely to be rather thin legal ground. Another, the *Robinson* case, was also pursued as a more tactically effective way of getting the UK government to agree to an election where other routes, such as vetoing the budget, might have produced the same result but with greater political difficulties. In carrying out the research we were struck by the degree to which both politicians and lawyers involved in these cases pursued generally short-term tactical gains and espoused fairly traditional approaches to legal interpretation. There was little evidence of any emphasis on a strategic focus whereby those involved in the litigation were seeking to persuade the courts to adopt a particular interpretation of the constitution, one which might be significant in guiding future conduct and shaping future litigation. Instead the emphasis was very much on particular gains, such as appointment to the NSMC or having an election called. Moreover the litigation did not appear to impact significantly on the day-to-day conduct of politics. Although the resort to the courts by politicians indicated a breakdown of trust, and an inability to deal with issues politically, there was little evidence that distrust was increased by the use of the courts by one side or another. Indeed, with the exception of those politicians who were also lawyers, we found evidence of only limited knowledge of politicians about cases with which they were not directly involved.

By and large the settled understandings of politicians and officials have been reflected in the cases which have come before the courts. There has been a marked judicial reluctance to move beyond deciding cases on anything but the most narrow grounds. One issue of particular interest is the status of the Agreement. In most cases it is fair to say that neither judges nor the lawyers who appeared before them have given great weight to any arguments of this nature. In some early cases, such as *Murphy* or *De Brún and McGuinness*, the court indicated a general view that the actions of the Secretary of State were not inconsistent with the Agreement, but did not spend a significant amount of time on the interpretation of its status or content. The House of Lords decision in *Robinson* suggested that the Agreement was relevant at least to the interpretation of the 1998 Act and that its relevance flowed more from the sense of overall purpose it gave to that Act, rather than specific commitments contained or not contained within it (see Lynch, 2003). Since then Kerr J has suggested in the *McComb* case a wider application where it may be relevant to the interpretation and application not just of the NIA but also of other legislation passed under its 'aegis'. In that case it was the sentence review legislation, but the same observations could apply at least to policing, criminal justice and victim legislation, as these all flow from explicit provisions in the Agreement. Whether it might eventually be argued that all legislation passed in Northern Ireland post 1998 is really under the 'aegis' of the Agreement is a moot point. If this were to be the case, then the Agreement would clearly have attained the 'constitutional status' Lord Hoffman suggests in *Robinson*. However, as in *Robinson*, this would only be the beginning of a judicial process of distilling the key aspects of the Agreement as the text itself is too prolix and diffuse to serve as a constitution.

Conclusion

The research does not suggest the 1998 settlement transformed the constitutional landscape directly or immediately. Considerations about the law were not to the fore during the negotiation of the Agreement. While law in the courts was used to 'regulate' some of the unstable relationships within the Executive, its role was always secondary. However, law remains central to the Agreement and the role of the courts in articulating a new constitutional framework is of abiding importance. This is not to suggest that if people had resorted to the courts more often or if the courts had done a different job this would have saved the Agreement and that Northern Ireland's constitutional politics would now be flourishing. As James Hamilton, founding father of the US constituition, famously observed, the courts are the 'weakest branch' of the constitution and struggle always to impose their will on the legislature or executive. Courts may interpret or develop a constitution, but they cannot make it by themselves. Nevertheless the research does suggest that the courts can play a useful role and one that can be built on as a new constitutional paradigm is developed – if the opportunity returns.

Note

1   As with some other contributions to this volume, the background for this chapter lies with a project carried out under the ESRC programme on Devolution and Constitutional Change. This project, titled 'The role of law and litigation in articulating Northern Ireland's emerging constitutional framework' (L219252114), was begun in March 2002 by the author and Professor Stephen Livingstone, with the valuable research assistance of Marie Lynch. Following the premature death of Professor Livingstone the findings of the project were reported to the ESRC by the author alone in June 2004. The loss of Stephen, who was the finest colleague and friend, is felt in many ways in almost every aspect of the work of the School of Law. However, it is in this final project where Stephen's direct influence is still very discernable as his incomplete contribution simultaneously shows both the huge intelluctual strength of the input that he did make and the gap that his passing leaves.

References

Ackerman, B. (1991) *We the People: Foundations.* Cambridge MA: Cambridge University Press.

Ackerman, B. (1998) *We the People: Transformations.* Cambridge MA: Cambridge University Press.

Anthony, G. (2002) 'Public law litigation and the Belfast Agreement', *European Public Law*, 8, 401.

Balkin, J. and Levinson, S. (2001) 'Understanding the constitutional revolution', *Virginia Law Review*, 87, 1045.

Barnett, H. (2002) *Constitutional and Administrative Law* 4th edition. London: Cavendish.

Bradley, A.W. and Ewing, K.D. (2003) *Constitutional and Administrative Law* 14th edition. Harlow: Longman.

Bell, C. (2000) *Peace Agreements and Human Rights.* Oxford: Oxford University Press.

Campbell, C., Ní Aoláin, F. and Harvey, C. (2003) 'The frontiers of legal analysis: reframing the transition in Northern Ireland', *Modern Law Review*, 68, 317.

Craig, P.P. (2003) 'Constitutional foundations: the rule of law and judicial review', *Public Law*, 92.

Elliot, M. (2003) 'Embracing "constitutional" legislation: towards fundamental law?', *Northern Ireland Legal Quarterly*, 54, 25.

Forsyth, C. and Elliot, M. (2003) 'The legitimacy of judicial review', *Public Law*, 286.

Guarnieri, C. and Pederzoli, P. (2003) *The Power of Judges.* Oxford: Oxford University Press.

Harlow, C. and Rawlings, R. (1997) *Law and Administration* 2nd edition. London: Butterworths, Law in Context series.

Harvey, C. (2001) 'The new beginning: reconstruction constitutional law and democracy in Northern Ireland' in C. Harvey (ed.) *Human Rights, Equality and Democratic Renewal in Northern Ireland.* Oxford: Hart Publishing, 9–52.

Harvey, C. (ed.) (2001) *Human Rights, Equality and Democratic Renewal in Northern Ireland*. Oxford: Hart Publishing.

Lynch, M. (2003) 'Robinson v. Secretary of State for NI: interpreting constitutional legislation', *Public Law*, 640.

McCrudden, C. (2004) 'Northern Ireland, The Belfast Agreement, and the British constitution' in J. Jowell and D. Oliver (eds) *The Changing Constitution* 5th edition. Oxford: Oxford University Press.

McEvoy, K. (2000) 'Law, struggle and political transformation in Northern Ireland', *Journal of Law and Society*, 27, 542.

McEvoy, K. and Morison, J. (2003) 'Beyond the "constitutional moment": law, transition, and peacemaking in Northern Ireland', *Fordham International Law Review*, 26 (4), 961–995.

McGarry, J. (1998) 'Political settlements in Northern Ireland and South Africa', *Political Studies*, 46 (5), 853–870.

McGarry, J. (ed.) (2001) *Northern Ireland and the Divided Worlds: Post-Agreement Northern Ireland in Comparative Perspective*. Oxford: Oxford University Press.

Morison, J. (1998) 'The case against constitutional reform', *Journal of Law and Society*, 25, 510–535.

Morison, J. (2001) 'Democracy, governance and governmentality: civic public space and constitutional renewal in Northern Ireland', *Oxford Journal of Legal Studies*, 21, 287.

Morison, J. and Livingstone, S. (1995) *Reshaping Public Power: Northern Ireland and the British Constitutional Crisis*. London: Sweet and Maxwell, Modern Legal Studies series.

Morison, J. and Lynch, M. (2007) 'Ligtigating the Agreement: towards a new judicial constitutionalism for the UK from Northern Ireland?' in J. Morison, K. McEvoy and G. Anthony (eds) *Judges, Transition and Human Rights: Essays in Memory of Stephen Livingstone*. Oxford: Oxford University Press.

O'Leary, B. and McGarry, J. (2004) *The Northern Ireland Conflict: Consociational Engagements*. Oxford: Oxford University Press.

Oliver, D. (2003) *Constitutional Reform in the UK*. Oxford: Oxford University Press. 2003

Sunstein, C. (2001) *Designing Democracy: What Constitutions Do*. New York: Oxford University Press.

Teitel, R. (2000) *Transitional Justice*. Oxford: Oxford University Press.

Todd, J. (2005) 'A new territorial politics in the British Isles?' in J. Coakley, B. Laffan and J. Todd (eds) *Renovation or Revolution? New Territorial Politics in Ireland and the United Kingdom*. Dublin: University College Dublin Press.

Tushnet, M. (2004) *The New Constitutional Order*. Princeton: Princeton University Press.

5

Stabilising the Northern Ireland Agreement

John McGarry and Brendan O'Leary

Introduction

As critical admirers of Northern Ireland's Agreement, we consider here how it may be best stabilised following the uncertainty of the first phase in efforts to implement it (1998–2003) and the new challenges offered by the results of the 2003 Assembly election (see McGarry and O'Leary, 2004). Appropriate default options must be considered if the Agreement is ineradicably ruined, but that moment has not yet materialised. The Agreement will, of course, work best if all parties and governments fulfil their obligations on its implementation. We begin by outlining these responsibilities. We then detail ways in which the Agreement's rules, for electing the First Minister and Deputy First Minister, and for passing key measures, could legitimately be changed under the Agreement's review process. Our goals here are to enhance the stability of the political institutions, and to address the concerns of those who see the current rules as unfair.

Parties to the conflict: responsibilities and incentives

The considerations we address here are both normative and strategic, implying courses of action that are both morally appropriate and potentially politically advantageous. These may be considered separately for the two main national communities and for their respective patron states.

Under the Agreement Sinn Féin (and the loyalist political parties) are obliged to use their good offices to ensure the comprehensive decommissioning and disarmament of the paramilitary organisations respectively associated with them. This expectation was implicit in the entire negotiating process. It was understood, however, both in the timetable attached to the implementation of the Agreement and its negotiation (which prompted Jeffrey Donaldson's withdrawal from the UUP negotiating team), that the starting date for decommissioning was not specified. And, as importantly, that its completion, two years after the referendum which endorsed the Agreement, would not occur until all other parties to the Agreement, particularly the UK government, had fulfilled their obligations, especially by bringing the new institutions into being and executing the reforms and confidence-building measures that are an integral part of the peace process (particularly the reform of policing, the administration of justice and the new human rights protections). In the security field it was rightly understood that decommissioning would have to apply to loyalists as well as republicans, and that decommissioning would be matched by extensive demilitarisation.

In this chapter we are not concerned to establish which parties are to blame for the failures of fully reciprocal action in these matters to date. We observe, impartially, that in the first two years after the referendum, republicans, loyalists and the UK government were all in default of the spirit and sometimes the letter of their obligations under the relevant provisions of the Agreement. The UK government looked as if it would deliberately fail to fulfil its own commitments on policing reform, and had been tardy in its approach to the reform of the administration of justice and in encouraging a new human rights system. Aside from the Loyalist Volunteer Force's one act of compulsory decommissioning when one of its members was caught in flagrante with weapons, no loyalist organisation has engaged in any decommissioning. The IRA's position in this period was widely seen as conditional, equivocal and ambiguous. But, that said, it is reasonable to argue that when all major aspects of the Agreement for which it is responsible are fully implemented by the UK government (including the repeal of the suspension power it granted itself outside the framework of the Agreement), it would be fair to have provisions enabling the exclusion from ministerial office in the Assembly of parties which maintain links with paramilitary organisations, or which are judged not to have repudiated such organisations' maintenance of their military capacities. Such provisions should be developed within the existing provisions of the Agreement, if at all possible.

So, what should be done as regards Sinn Féin and the IRA and their relationships? Much the best thing that could be done should be done by the two organisations themselves: the IRA should unambiguously declare its war to be over, decommission its weapons in cooperation with the international commission, and unambiguously dissolve its organisation; Sinn Féin should welcome all such announcements and declare current membership of the IRA, or any offshoots of the IRA, incompatible with party membership. But what if these paths continue to be refused *after* the UK government has fulfilled all its obligations on confidence-building and repealed its statute with the power of suspension?

One path is a legal one: the courts could be left to determine whether parties have associations or conduct activities in breach of their ministerial oath of office, and be empowered to suspend such parties' entitlements to ministerial office until such time as their conduct is deemed fully democratic. This would probably require fresh primary legislation at Westminster, passed outside the Agreement's procedures, and would therefore be open to the valid objection that it is 'extra-Agreement' (in the same way as the Northern Ireland Act 2000, which provides the government's suspension power). 'Juridification' is, moreover, a difficult road. Once judges start extensively to regulate political parties there may be undesirable repercussions. It is not evident that Spanish judges' decisions to proscribe Basque political parties are either democratic or productive. Juridification might be a less pressing issue if judges were widely regarded as impartial in Northern Ireland, but in fact they are not widely representative, and making such decisions might place them in unenviable positions.

The second path is the internal political one. It is embedded in the Agreement. It provides for the Assembly to determine whether a party entitled to ministerial nominations is in breach of its oath of office – which incorporates commitments to exclusively democratic means. But, complain unionists, this provision operates under the constraint that it requires cross-community consent. And so, they correctly maintain, in the 1998–2003 Assembly Sinn Féin was protected from the possibility of suspension from the Executive by the decision of the SDLP to support inclusive government (as long as the Agreement was not fully implemented). As a result of the 2003 Assembly elections, Sinn Féin now has this protection mechanism within its own hands: it can veto any attempt to exclude its ministers from office.

It may well be, however, that the political route is still the best way to handle republican decommissioning. If the rest of the Agreement is unambiguously implemented while the IRA remains in existence, maintains its organisational capacity, and engages in punishment beatings and self-styled policing operations, then Sinn Féin will eventually pay an electoral price, North and South – perhaps a more extensive price in the South than in the North, but a price nonetheless. We believe that as long as it is interested in expanding its electoral base there will be strong incentives for Sinn Féin to repudiate the present case for the existence of the IRA, and for the SDLP to vote for Sinn Féin's suspension from office until such time as the IRA decommissions and dissolves itself, even if that vote has no immediate consequence. We think, and have regularly argued, that the electoral process creates strong incentives for Sinn Féin to deliver the IRA's final dissolution or to disassociate itself from its twin (O'Leary, 2001a, 2001b, 2001c). We still think that is the case, and believe that the party's successes in 2003, especially its overhauling of the SDLP, owed much to significant decommissioning by the IRA.

The third path is inter-governmental, and is the one that has recently been accepted by the two governments. It is the establishment of an independent and international commission (the Independent Monitoring Commission) to determine, after due deliberation, whether a party is in breach of (Mitchell's) democratic principles. We believe that such a commission has merits, though there must be some possibility that a four-member commission might be stale-mated 2–2 in making an appropriate and convincing determination. That said, we believe that this political mode of deciding on the merits of finding a party in breach of the Mitchell principles is better than the juridical route – though it too suffers from the fact that it has not yet been agreed inside the procedures for review within the Agreement. We would expect, however, that the SDLP, although presently reluctant, will embrace this idea even if the republican movement remains recalcitrant. We would commend one important change to the existing proposed measures if they are progressed: any future suspension of a party's entitlement to office, and the duration of that suspension, which would be triggered by the determination of the international commission, should require ratification by the two sovereign governments in the British–Irish Intergovernmental Conference (BIIC).

The loyalist parties which made the Agreement have proven electorally brittle. One, the Ulster Democratic Party, has dissolved itself; the other, the Progressive Unionist Party, has a tough future, having seen its representation in the Assembly halved, to one MLA, in 2003. Loyalists have no immediate prospects of ministerial office; in consequence, the Agreement's incentives do not affect their conduct in the same way as republicans. Electoral imperatives encouraged the start of republican decommissioning; loyalists do not have such incentives with anything like the requisite intensity. Their paramilitary organisations have merely committed themselves to decommission on receipt of confirmation of the IRA's dissolution. We believe there will be some loyalist decommissioning after the completion of IRA decommissioning, but also that loyalist – and republican – organisations which reject the Agreement, or which fail to implement decommissioning, must be dealt with by the new police service, fairly, impartially and effectively. The ambiguous status of the loyalist organisations that are on formal ceasefire should be reviewed by the new police service in conjunction with the two governments. We believe that the firm and impartial handling of current crimes by loyalists will con-siderably strengthen the IRA's disposition to dissolve.

The unionist community was divided by the negotiation and the making of the Agreement. It remained divided in the referendum over its adoption. And public support for the Agreement has wavered significantly within the unionist community. As we write it is low, outweighed by those disappointed by or hostile towards the Agreement. But sufficient support to make the

Agreement work has been there when progress has been evident. Unionists, according to surveys we have conducted, are and consider themselves likely to be supportive of the Agreement if it generates both peace and prosperity (Evans and O'Leary, 2000). For reasons that we have made clear elsewhere we think that it remains possible to vindicate this belief (McGarry and O'Leary, 2004).

The unionist community's political allegiances are largely divided between two parties. One of these, the formally pro-Agreement UUP, has been deeply internally divided. To manage the rejectionists within his party, its leader, Trimble, at regular intervals, has breached the Agreement, both in principle and in spirit. He delayed Executive formation even though according to the terms of the Agreement that process did not require prior decommissioning of weapons by the IRA. He rejected outright the recommendations of the Patten Commission on policing – established under the terms of reference of the Agreement. He refused to nominate ministers to attend and carry out their functions on the North/South Ministerial Council (NSMC) – and was found before the courts to have acted unlawfully in doing so. He helped persuade Secretary of State Mandelson embark on the disastrous path of diluting the Patten Commission's recommendations – which, of course, made attaining republican decommissioning of their weapons less rather than more likely (McGarry and O' Leary, 2004: ch. 13). He encouraged him to pass the Northern Ireland Act 2000, which was in breach of the UK's treaty obligations with the Irish government, and with both the letter and spirit of the Agreement, and which has subsequently been used to suspend both the institutions of the Agreement and legally scheduled elections – against the express wishes of the Irish government. This was a pro-Agreement leader with some difficulties in being whole-heartedly pro-Agreement.

When due allowance is made for Trimble's difficulties in managing his party, two thoughts should be uppermost in the minds of those who want to be clear-eyed about the Agreement. First, it is not sensible to provide incentives for politicians who are in difficulties with their own party to play institutional havoc. The UK government has finally promised that it will, in principle, remove the suspension power it gave itself in contravention of the Agreement. Well and good, and the sooner the better. Its decision to suspend the institutions and then to postpone elections for the Assembly in the cause of 'saving David' worked against its other objective: to ensure that republicans delivered on their commitments. In addition, it cannot be democratic for the UK government to determine electoral processes on its judgement calls on how the Northern Irish will vote: Westminster-determination is, after all, supposed to have been superseded by self-determination under the

Agreement. Second: we will only know the Agreement's institutions are secure when their offices are held and tested by those most initially opposed to or suspicious of them. In the immediate aftermath of the Assembly elections in which the DUP and Sinn Féin achieved majority status within their respective blocs, there has been considerable pessimism about the Agreement's prospects. However, we think there is a reasonable prospect that the DUP's leaders will think twice about utterly wrecking the Agreement – although it will be vital that other appropriate incentives are in place to clarify the leaders' minds. For representative unionist politicians, including the secondary leadership of the DUP, to work the Agreement they need demonstrable evidence that the Agreement will benefit them, and that it will guarantee the dissolution of the IRA.

We indicate below where the two governments might encourage the full liberalisation of the Agreement's consociational institutions (as regards designation; the rules for passing key measures; and the rules for electing the First and Deputy First Minster). We emphasise, however, that the British government's completion of policing reform is crucial in consolidating the Agreement. Without it, the IRA is most unlikely to fulfil its necessary acts of completion, and there will not be political stability. In the joint declaration of May 2003, the UK government provided a framework for settling policing questions. It has, in effect, repudiated Secretary of State Mandelson's disastrous handling of the Patten Commission's recommendations in 2000–01. It is committed, in the context of a peaceful settlement, to a robust Policing Board; a representative police service; effective cooperation between the new Police Service of Northern Ireland(PSNI) and Ireland's Garda Síochana; the reform of the Special Branch; normalised and community policing; and the devolution of policing and criminal justice. The devolution of responsibility for policing will be the final proof that the settlement has taken root. It is to take place in the next Assembly provided it is 'broadly supported' by the local parties. There is no possibility of such support unless the IRA decommissions fully – it may be calculating that it would be prudent not to do so until it has a deal which trades decommissioning in return for the devolution of policing. There is, however, little possibility of such support if policing were to become the preserve of either nationalist or unionist ministers. We recommend therefore that policing become a joint responsibility of the two first ministers, who could also take a justice portfolio, and organise their joint office to have these two jurisdictions, justice and policing, separated within their offices but reporting to both of them. We find this a better idea than the most obvious alternative: a single justice department, headed by one minister; a justice department rotated between different parties; and separate justice and policing departments, each headed by a minister from a different tradition. We think it would be correct and prudent politics on the part of Sinn Féin to propose a Deputy First Minister (or a junior minister with responsibility for policing within the Office of the First and Deputy First Ministers) who has no record of involvement in the IRA.

The May 2003 Joint Document, together with previous proposals on the administration of justice, and developments in the pipeline on human rights, prefigure a transformation of the administration of justice along the lines we have supported elsewhere (McGarry and O'Leary, 2004: ch. 12). It remains regrettable, however, that under-resourcing has slowed the work of the new human rights commission; and more unsettling that the appointment process has led to the over-representation of persons opposed to the spirit and letter of the Agreement. But it remains the case that on balance both policing and justice reforms look primed to fulfil the promise of the Agreement. Public inquiries, present and promised, may partially redress the grievances of the relatives of the victims of unlawful state-sanctioned killings by the police and army or through collusion between public officials and paramilitaries.[1] The merits of a truth and justice commission to achieve reconciliation lies beyond our fields of research competence: we are not opposed to such a commission, but note that it is not required by the Agreement. Nevertheless, republicans and nationalists have taken some satisfaction from the fact that a series of inquiries and investigations by the UK authorities have demonstrated to international satisfaction the partial and defective nature of the unreformed RUC.

What if the local parties cannot agree on the implementation of the Agreement? What if the Review process leads to an impasse? These questions are on everyone's minds, and must be addressed by the officials and ministers of the two sovereign governments. The governments of Ireland and the UK are the key guarantors of the Agreement. It is a legal fact that if the Assembly and the NSMC – which are mutually interdependent – cannot function, then the BIIC reverts to the functions and capacities its predecessor enjoyed under the Anglo-Irish Agreement (O'Lear, 1999). It is worth publicly highlighting this fact, if only to concentrate the minds of the DUP's leadership. Destroying the local Northern Ireland dimension of the Agreement and the NSMC will merely restore the institutional content of the 1985 Anglo-Irish Agreement, albeit with two important qualifications. The first is that the transformation of Ireland's constitution is now entrenched – though there is nothing to stop the Irish government proposing new amendments to the constitution that would reflect the demise of the Agreement. The second is that the failure of the Agreement's Assembly will not, and should not, preclude the UK and Irish governments from deepening their cross-border and all-island cooperation, through or outside the BIIC. All reasonable readings of the Anglo-Irish Agreement (1985) and subsequent inter-governmental documents, declarations and treaties, especially the Downing Street Declaration (1993), the Framework Documents (1995), the Agreement (1998) and the British–Irish Agreement (1999), places duties on both two governments to promote and extend cross-border and all-island cooperation. Such cooperation would be better than an immediate shift towards full joint sovereignty arrangements – though it would have the character of functionally de-limited de facto joint sovereignty arrangements. Such cooperation should, in the interests of legitimacy, operate most evidently in the functions agreed for North–South and East–West cooperation in the 1998 Agreement. The Irish government would be right to emphasise these possibilities if the Agreement were to break down, both to temper possible hubris within the ranks of the DUP, and to shield the parties of government in Ireland from electoral competition from Sinn Féin.

The incentives of this default scenario would be clear. The pro-devolution DUP would face the fact that no effective working of the Agreement's institutions by the Assembly would mean no devolution, period, and the growth in the scope and influence of the BIIC. This default scenario is not just one with negative incentives for unionists. Sinn Féin has proven, contrary to the suppositions of many, to like devolution, albeit as 'a transitional arrangement' in its political discourse. Its leaders know it will flourish best within the framework of a working Agreement, rather than one in default.

But we think these incentives of a well-presented default scenario are not enough. The governments must also bind themselves.

The Agreement of 1998 recognised the right of the Irish people to national self-determination, although it qualified the classical interpretation of this right, namely that it be exercised within a single all-Ireland unit on a majoritarian basis. Nonetheless, according to the Agreement, and the presently correct reading of Ireland's laws and constitution, the partition of Ireland now rests on a decision of the people of Ireland, North and South. And any decision to end partition will be taken on the same basis, i.e. it will require concurrent endorsement, South and North. The institutions of the Agreement are a product of Irish choices, North and South, and not the choices of Great Britain's Parliament or people. So in a formal legalist understanding of the present situation, all that separates formerly militant Irish republicans and the British state on the question of self-determination are therefore questions of trust. The UK government has agreed that as part of the full implementation of the Agreement it is willing to repeal the Northern Ireland Act 2000 (the 'Suspension Act'). But, it is not enough that this Act be repealed, as and when the rest of the Agreement is implemented by all parties. It would not be enough because the Act was proof that the UK's understanding of the

Agreement did not, as promised, respect the right of the Irish people, North and South, to self-determination – as expressed in their respective endorsements of the institutions of the Agreement. In Westminster's eyes every element of the Agreement – including the portions unionists strongly like – is revisable and alterable, according to the current will of the current UK Parliament. There is nothing in the UK's constitutional arrangements to stop a future Parliament behaving as Minister Mandelson persuaded it to do.

It is therefore desirable to have the full Agreement with any outcomes of an agreed review – but without the UK Northern Ireland 2000 Act (the Suspension Act) – entrenched in a treaty, which would be attached as a joint and justiciable protocol to whatever new European constitution may be proposed and agreed in the immediate future. This is the sole easy means to constitutionalise the Agreement which cannot be otherwise constitutionalised in the UK's constitution-free system. Each member state's constitution has to be compatible with the EU's new constitution and this would be the best way of ensuring no clash of laws between the UK and Irish states. This proposal would constitutionalise the Agreement so that a unilateral suspension of any of the Agreement's institutions by the UK or Ireland would be regarded as a breach of the EU constitution by the appropriate court. If these ideas were followed and implemented, then as a matter of legal fact it would be true that the partition of Ireland (if it continued indefinitely) and its reunification (if that happened in the future) would both be the products of Irish national self-determination, north and south. The Agreement would be constitutionalised – and protected from the unilateral actions of either the UK or Irish Parliaments. It would also, arguably, be consistent with the volitions of two types of nationalist, Irish nationalists and British unionists.

Assembly procedures: the case for revision

There is a strong case for reviewing the Assembly's rules for electing the First Minister (FM) and Deputy First Minister (DFM), and for passing key measures. Under current rules, the election of the FM and DFM requires concurrent majorities of nationalist and unionist members of the Assembly. The passage of key measures requires 40 per cent support within each of the two major blocs (nationalist, unionist) and 60 per cent overall. To render the rules operable, members must 'designate' themselves as 'unionist' or 'nationalist', though they may also opt out and designate themselves 'other'. As liberal critics of the Agreement point out, the rules have unfair elements. They privilege nationalism and unionism over other forms of identity. We do not think, however, that these incentives, or their removal, are of significant empirical consequence in explaining the distributions of support across nationalists, unionists and others. While Northern Ireland's voters have overwhelmingly supported nationalist and unionist parties for over a century, the rules arguably create disincentives for them to change their behaviour in the future. That is because there is an incentive for voters to choose nationalists or unionists, as members from these groups will, *ceteris paribus*, count more than 'others' or be more pivotal. The rules have the effect of pre-determining, in advance of election results, that nationalists and unionists are to be better protected than 'others'. The 'others', if they were to become a majority, would be pivotal in the passage of all normal legislation, but nationalists and unionists would have a more pivotal role in any key decision requiring cross-community support.

Moreover, the rules help to explain Northern Ireland's recurring crises over Executive formation and maintenance. These have stemmed largely from machinations over the institution of the dual premiership. So far these positions have been held by three moderates: David Trimble of the UUP, and Seamus Mallon and Mark Durkan of the SDLP. Mallon, the (first) DFM used the threat of resignation from his post in 1999 before the Executive was even formed (Mallon, 1999). The unilateral suspension of the Agreement's institutions by the Westminster Parliament in 2000, 2001 and 2002 arose from threatened resignations by FM Trimble. The UK felt politically bound to act because the posts of FM and DFM are tightly interdependent: the resignation or death of one triggers the other's formal departure from office and requires fresh elections within six weeks. The UK government consistently calculated with each threat – or manifestation – of a resignation by Trimble that he might not be able to secure his re-election, either before or after Assembly elections. This prompted the UK government to suspend the Agreement's institutions, in breach of the Agreement.

The impasse that has existed since the Assembly elections of November 2003 can also be traced to the dual premiership. The DUP, which won a majority of unionist seats in the Assembly, now has a veto on the election of a joint FM/DFM team. It is ironic that the dual premiership, elected by cross-community procedures, and supposedly a moderating 'integrative' institution, has been the lightning rod for deep tensions between blocs, as much as it has been a mechanism for joint coordination and creation of calm by moderate leaders.

The rule for electing the FM and DFM was primarily designed to assure nationalists that there would be no return to the simple majority procedures of the old Stormont Parliament. However, on two occasions, it has been used by unionist opponents of the Agreement to prevent the establishment of a government supported by around 70 per cent of the Members of the

Assembly (MLAs). The first occurred on 2 November 2001, when David Trimble and Mark Durkan failed to be elected. They were rescued only because a sufficient number of members of the Alliance Party and Women's Coalition redesignated from 'others' to 'unionists', permitting them to win a second vote, but allowing critics of the Agreement a good laugh at the nature of the 'designation' rules. The second occurred in the wake of the November 2003 Assembly elections. The rule allowed the DUP to declare that the elections, which reflected high, indeed unchanged, levels of support for pro-Agreement parties, meant the death of the Agreement, or at least its renegotiation.

How might the rules be changed under the Agreement's provisions for review, so that they are more fair and less destabilising?

Everyone should be aware that all voting rules are manipulable in some respect (there is a theorem to this effect in political science), and that there are no universally acknowledged voting procedures which meet all reasonable tests of fairness, consistency and efficiency when there are more than three voters and three options (the Arrow theorem). Constitutional designers and rule makers should, however, be open about their preferences. We believe that a review could proceed in the spirit of an Agreement that was plainly intended to create binational institutions in Northern Ireland, with incentives for inclusive Executive power sharing, and strong protections for minorities. In practice, that means that supporters of the Agreement should be happy with rules that make it difficult for the 'no unionists' to wreck the Agreement, but grant them a fair share in its institutions, and help 'yes nationalists', 'yes unionists' and 'others' to govern Northern Ireland with significant consensus. But since the Agreement was endorsed in double referendums, and is an outcome of Irish national self-determination, it is vital that any proposed changes be minimal, and within the spirit of the Agreement.

The concurrent majority rule for the election of the premiers is problematic but it also has legitimacy. It is in the Agreement, and it would be an undesirable precedent if it were to be replaced. It ensures that the FM/DFM team has substantial support among the two primary blocs that have been in conflict. For these reasons, there is an argument that it should be kept as the rule of first resort. But we do think that there are several default rules which could be used if, as on 2 November 2001 or in the wake of the 2003 Assembly elections, concurrent majorities cannot be achieved. It would be within the spirit of the Agreement to have such a default rule, provided that this rule was consistent with the design of the Agreement. We also believe that the default rule we propose below is better than the existing rule.

We assume that a default of simple majority rule (50 per cent plus 1) is a non-starter. This could lead to a FM/DFM team that was exclusively unionist or, in the future, exclusively nationalist. And its logic is not within the spirit of the Agreement.

We also assume that it would be unreasonable to require concurrent majorities, not just of unionists and nationalists, but also of the 'others'. While that default rule would rectify the complaint of the 'others' that their votes are less important under parallel consent, this change would unjustifiably inflate their importance. It would make them the most pivotal or decisive group. Given that the 'others' are likely to be currently and for the foreseeable future a very small group, this change would correct their current grievance, that the present rule discriminates against them, with a rule that discriminates even more heavily against nationalists and unionists.

One obvious default is a voting rule that is also in the Agreement and designed to protect minorities, but that requires a lower threshold of support. This is the Agreement's 'weighted majority' rule: 60 per cent of the MLAs voting, including 40 per cent of both nationalists and unionists. Trimble and Durkan would have been comfortably elected by this rule on 2 November 2001. They secured over 70 per cent support in the Assembly, 100 per cent of nationalist votes and 49 per cent of unionist votes. If this rule had been used after the elections of November 2003 (and the defection of three MLAs from the UUP to the DUP in January 2004), it might narrowly have allowed both nationalist parties to team up with the UUP to elect a FM/DFM team, or for both unionist parties to team up with the SDLP. This default rule would make it likely that parties would try to use it, i.e. both unionist parties and both nationalist parties would avoid electing a FM/DFM team under the concurrent majority rule, in the expectation that they could find more 'reasonable' partners under the default rule.

Some may find this option attractive. We think it is arguably undemocratic and potentially counterproductive. An overriding principle of the Agreement is inclusion. As Sinn Féin and the DUP are the largest parties in their blocs, there is a sound democratic case that they should have the opportunity to take up the positions of FM/DFM. This would be prudent as well as principled. If Sinn Féin and the DUP did take the positions of FM/DFM, it would bind them to the institutions of the Agreement. It would further consolidate republican support for constitutional politics, and it would make the DUP think twice about the advantages of destructive behaviour.

The other difficulty with this possible default rule is that it requires members to designate as nationalists, unionists, or 'others' – a requirement that Alliance thinks institutionalises differences. Like the parallel consent rule, it discriminates against the 'others', as their votes are less pivotal.

Alternatively, the FM/DFM team could be elected by 'simple weighted majority'. In this case, it would need to win the support of more than a simple majority, say two-thirds. This is the favoured rule of Alliance, which has pushed for the review (APNI, 2004). It likes it because it does not require designation and it treats all MLAs as equals. It is also relatively straightforward, and echoes similar rules in other countries' constitutions. Trimble and Durkan would have been elected under this rule on 2 November 2001, and might have been narrowly re-elected after November 2003.

But a weighted majority of two-thirds would not ensure stability. The number of votes required to block the election of a FM/DFM team would be a relatively low 36, not much higher than the 30 that rejectionists mustered in November 2001, or the minimum number of 34 (33 DUP, 1 UKUP) that they could muster after November 2003. It might also appear unreasonable, as it would mean that a FM and DFM could not be elected even if they could command as much as 66 per cent support in the Assembly.

This problem could be addressed by dropping the threshold to 60 per cent. The repercussions of lowering the threshold would be to raise the salience of the 'others', and to make it easier to exclude the DUP or Sinn Féin. For the reasons given above we believe that for the positions of FM and DFM this logic is problematic – though as we argue below there is a case for applying this rule in the Assembly for almost all other key decisions.

Decision by d'Hondt

The d'Hondt rule is also in the Agreement, and is currently used for allocating all the other ministers in the Executive. If it became the default rule for the election of the premiers, then, in the absence of parallel consent, the FM and DFM would go to the two largest parties in the Assembly. We believe it would be best to have this as the rule, but also consider it the best default rule. After the November 2003 Assembly elections, the DUP, as the largest party, would get the FM position under the d'Hondt process. The DFM would go to the second largest party. But, which party is that? After the defection of the three UUP MLAs to the UUP, the UUP and Sinn Féin are now each tied on 24 MLAs in joint second place. The Agreement solves such ties by granting precedence to the party with the higher share of first preference votes, in this case Sinn Féin.

The advantage of d'Hondt is that it is decisive. It tells us which parties get the positions in the absence of inter-party agreement. No protracted bargaining or designation shifts are required to resolve an impasse. The Assembly's current rules even cover the difficulty that might arise if the two parties have the same number of MLAs – the relevant position would go to the party with the highest first-preference vote share.

Using d'Hondt as the default for the election of the FM/DFM enhances the prospect of the positions being filled – rather than being used for bargaining to break or renegotiate the Agreement (the DUP's current tactic). If one party refused to take its position, or resigned from it, the post would go to the next largest party which did not hold the other post.

The use of d'Hondt to allocate other ministries in the Executive helps explain why the DUP was not been able to do with the cabinet what both David Trimble and Seamus Mallon were able to do with the dual premiership. The DUP was not able to threaten boycotts or resignation in the hope of extracting concessions or provoking a review because the DUP knew that under the d'Hondt allocation process its ministries would simply go to other parties.

Of course, simple d'Hondt would create the possibility of a FM/DFM team that was exclusively unionist or, particularly if unionism were to fragment, an exclusively nationalist dual premiership.

Two possible provisos might be devised to prevent this undesirable scenario. One, similar to the logic of the Agreement, would have the default rule specify that the FM and DFM must come from the largest parties in each of the nationalist and unionist blocs, with the FM being from the party with the largest number of MLAs. This proviso would, however, not be regarded as fair by the others. A second proviso might be better. It would specify that the dual premiers cannot be from one bloc, but would come from the two largest parties allowing for this proviso. That would mean that if the 'others' grew in size then they might be able to win one of the top two positions, and that it could not be the case that the top two posts are held by one bloc. (A supplemental rule for the election of the premiers only would stop parties changing the designations they proclaimed to the electorate to take any strategic advantage a second-placed unionist or nationalist party might gain from declaring itself to be other.)

If d'Hondt, as we envisage it, was the current rule or default rule for the election of the premiers, it would entitle the DUP, as the largest party in the unionist bloc and largest party in the Assembly, to the position of FM. Likewise, it would entitle Sinn Féin, as the largest party in the nationalist bloc, to the position of DFM. But, if the DUP refused to partner Sinn Féin, then it would presumably forfeit its opportunity for one of the premierships to the UUP. It is possible that the UUP would consider the premiership, in some scenarios, as a poisoned chalice. However, it may well be prepared to take up the offer in return for transparent decommissioning and effective disbandment by the IRA, particularly if the alternative is government by a strengthened BIIC.

Separately, but relatedly, we believe that the rule which requires that the resignation of one premier must trigger the other's loss of office might be reconsidered. This was not in the original text of the Agreement – though we concede that it is consistent with its spirit. We have all seen that this power is a most destructive bargaining chip.

We believe the review might consider a revision, namely, that the resignation of a premier leads to the immediate fresh allocation of the two posts according to the d'Hondt process, plus our favoured second proviso specified above. So, for example, if Peter Robinson resigned, the DUP could nominate Nigel Dodds to replace him, or vacate the position – in which case, on our proviso, it would go to the UUP, and if the UUP declined the offer it would go to the Alliance party and so on. This rule would create a small incentive for Executive maintenance, and weaken the incentive to behave destructively. It cannot guarantee Executive maintenance, but rules can never do that.

This proposal is motivated by a simple calculation: the dual premiership has been the most vulnerable institution to date. All crises have flowed through it, and each premier or party leader with a majority in either bloc has possessed a nuclear institutional weapon. They have used the weapon. We may want to disarm the leaders from having too much destructive power.

An alternative way to disarm the premiers' power to manufacture crises would be for the UK to repeal its extra-Agreement and treaty-breaking Northern Ireland Act 2000 (the Suspension Act). If that happened then it would be clear that the resignation of a premier, and the failure to elect a new team of premiers within six weeks, would generate fresh elections. That would make any premier think very carefully before using the resignation threat.

The election of the FM and the DFM is the only activity which requires the use of the parallel consent rule – and it has no default rule for resolving a crisis. That is why we have spent such time on it. The other weighted majority rule, 40 per cent support within each of the two major blocs (nationalist, unionist) and 60 per cent overall, is available for all other decisions. It, too, has merits because it was negotiated as part of the Agreement, but is it the best rule available?

We must reiterate that any proposal of change to make all blocs (nationalist, unionist and 'other') equal, i.e. that a measure would require 40 per cent support among each of three blocs as well as 60 per cent overall, would generate two problems. One: it would make the 'others', when they are small, much more pivotal than their numbers warrant. Two: it would retain the designation principle, which some reject.

We believe it is worth considering having a simple weighted majority, i.e. 60 per cent support overall among MLAs for any key decision other than the election of the premiers (and one other matter that we shall specify below). This change would address the designation issue. Cross-community confidence is, however, the key question, and was at the heart of the Agreement's design. We must ask several questions before considering such a change.

First, is there likely to be a majority of 60 per cent willing to consider and capable of imposing its will in an undesirable way on a minority?

Nationalists now consistently have over 40 per cent of the popular vote in recent elections, and the Catholic share of the population, which normally votes nationalist, is increasing. In most Assembly elections, these electoral and demographic facts will translate into nationalists winning over 40 per cent of the seats (or 44 out of 108). In the 1998 and 2003 elections, nationalists fell just short of this mark, winning only 42 seats. But even in these circumstances, which are unlikely to be repeated into the future, nationalists could only be outvoted on key measures if virtually all 'others' voted with the unionist bloc. As the 'others' stand on a platform of impartiality between unionism and nationalism, this is an unlikely scenario. If some 'others' consistently voted with unionists against all nationalists, the offending 'others' would have difficulty retaining their seats in the next elections. Effectively, then, a 60 per cent weighted majority rule will protect nationalists, now and later. Nationalists, and nationalists and 'others', by contrast, fall short of 60 per cent, so they could not coerce all unionists in the foreseeable future. But, under such a rule change 'no unionists' would be unlikely to command 40 per cent support in Northern Ireland – and the Assembly – as a whole, and therefore could not block measures which enjoyed substantial support across nationalists, unionists and 'others'. For these reasons, among others, we believe this rule change might be considered.

We add, however, one important proviso. The Bill of Rights envisaged under the Agreement, to be effective, must have the support of a majority of the Assembly, and at least 40 per cent of nationalist and unionist MLAs. If the Bill of Rights is to be effective and not hi-jacked by a coalition of unionists and the 'others' it must receive the protection envisaged for its passage by the Assembly in the Agreement (i.e. either parallel consent or weighted consent). We strongly believe that the Bill of Rights must pass the Assembly with the requisite levels of support demanded under the Agreement – indeed it would be better to have no distinct Bill of Rights than to have a Bill of Rights dictated by a 60 per cent majority of the Assembly that excluded the assent of nationalist MLAs. This is not an unprincipled argument on our part. It suggests the retention of the original rules of the Agreement for the implementation of the key features of the Agreement, while suggesting appropriate rule changes for making the fully implemented Agreement work effectively.

Conclusion

It is a common and fundamental criticism of consociational institutions, like Northern Ireland's Assembly and Executive, that they are unworkable. Critics of such institutions feel vindicated by the unfolding of events since 1998. However, much of the instability has not been related to the consociational institutions themselves. It has largely been a result of the failure of republicans and the British government to reach agreement on how to settle, and sequence, related steps on decommissioning, policing reform, justice reform, and demilitarisation. We have outlined here in brief, how we think these issues should be addressed.

The institutions are also flawed, but it is possible, and desirable, to address these flaws without destroying the institutions. We have argued that the institutions should be entrenched, so that they can no longer be suspended to suit the narrow interests of particular parties. We have also recommended changes to the institutions' decision-making rules that would make them fairer and more stable. And we have recommended changes to the office of the FM and DFM that would enhance its durability. Some of these changes require measures by the British government that are consistent with the spirit and letter of its obligations under the Agreement. The others can be addressed by the Northern Ireland parties themselves, under the Agreement's provisions for review. Our proposed rule changes will not guarantee that the institutions will work, but they will make matters more difficult for those intent on wrecking them, and they can be made within the letter and spirit of an appropriately conducted review.

Postscript

Our chapter was written in the summer of 2004. Two years later in 2006, the Agreement's institutions remain suspended; Sinn Féin and the DUP remain the largest parties in the nationalist and unionist blocs, respectively; and the DUP's leader remains publicly unprepared to share power with Sinn Féin. But there have been important developments which bear on our analysis.

The DUP and Sinn Féin came very close to a comprehensive bargain in late 2004. It fell apart, according to the dominant speculation, because the DUP insisted that the decommissioning of IRA weapons be photographed. It is possible the DUP may have used this demand for symbolic surrender as cover for more substantive objections; perhaps its leaders had cold feet; and they had been floating a trial balloon designed to test their supporters' receptivity to compromise. The governments subsequently published the details of what they were prepared to term a 'Comprehensive Agreement' (DFA, 2004). Among its provisions were proposed changes to the rules for Executive formation, including the positions of FM and DFM. Under these, the FM/DFM and rest of the Executive would have been elected, as previously, under the concurrent majority and d'Hondt rules respectively, but before the government could take office the entire slate of ministers would have required the Assembly's approval under the concurrent majority rule. The effect of this change would have been to extend the high threshold of support required to elect the FM/DFM to the entire slate of ministers. While the DUP and Sinn Féin's support for these proposals would have guaranteed their initial success, the changes, in our view, would create even more institutional obstacles to Executive formation. A party commanding a majority in either bloc would be able to prevent the formation of an Executive, not only if it objected to the FM and/or DFM, but also if it objected to the allocation of a ministerial portfolio to a particular party, or to any of its ministers. The proposed changes would also increase the privileges that nationalists and unionists enjoy in the Assembly at the expense of others, reinforcing the corporate aspects of Northern Ireland's consociation. We believe that our proposed changes to the rules for Executive composition, as set forth in this chapter, are therefore better than those apparently agreed by the DUP and Sinn Féin in late 2004.

Second, comprehensive IRA decommissioning took place at last. The Independent International Commission on Decommissioning (IICD) announced on 26 September 2005 that the IRA had destroyed the 'totality' of its arsenal, in line with estimates provided by both the British and Irish security forces. This event followed an IRA statement on 28 July in which a spokesman announced that it had ended its armed campaign, and instructed its volunteers to 'assist the development of purely political and democratic programmes through exclusively peaceful means'. This breakthrough opened the way back to changes supported by the Joint Declaration of May 2003, and reaffirmed in the Comprehensive Agreement: the removal of the suspension power, further substantive demilitarisation, and legislation to devolve policing and criminal justice, to take effect as soon as there was agreement among the local parties. By January 2006, Sinn Féin appeared prepared to sit on the Policing Board, in the context of devolution (*UTV Internet*, 2005).

The two governments welcomed the IICD's statement, and promised that if the Independent Monitoring Commission (IMC) certified in its two reports of October 2005 and January 2006 that the IRA was refraining from paramilitary and criminal activity, that they would expect the local parties to re-engage in negotiations. We may now say that both Sinn Féin and the British government are meeting their obligations under the Agreement, albeit belatedly.

Decommissioning, let alone disbanding, has yet to take place among loyalist paramilitaries. Since they have always proclaimed that their violence is defensive, it can hardly be considered unthinkable that they will follow suit before long. For all the mayhem that has resulted from intra-loyalist feuds and notwithstanding continuing sectarian attacks on nationalist civilians, loyalist paramilitaries have been fairly disciplined in avoiding lethal inter-community violence. They do not appear to be a threat to the peace process.

So, the major obstacle to the restoration and operation of the Agreement's political institutions is the DUP's opposition to sharing power with Sinn Féin. In January 2006 the party stated that there was 'no possibility of an executive including Sinn Féin/IRA for the foreseeable future', and appeared to offer as an alternative the option of rolling devolution, during the initial stages of which there would be no Executive but the Assembly would have a legislative role (DUP, 2006).[2] The DUP did not welcome the IICD's statement on decommissioning, or even claim credit for it, as it might have done. Instead it expressed concern over its lack of transparency, and feared that it would precede more concessions to republicans. The determination of some unionist politicians to portray their community as serial losers continued, and was one of the factors that led to violent loyalist riots in Belfast in mid-September 2005.

To facilitate progress, the UK government should deal with legitimate DUP concerns, including taking steps to deal with paramilitary racketeering, and the seizure of illegally gained assets. The Assets Recovery Agency has been employed to go after IRA money-laundering, and launched a raid in Manchester in early October 2005, aimed at the recovery of £9 million in IRA equity (*Irish Independent*, 2005). The DUP's proposals, included in the Comprehensive Agreement, which are aimed at making ministers more accountable to the Executive and the Executive to the Assembly, can be accepted – they pose no fundamental threat to the Agreement. There are limits, however, to how far the governments can go to placate the DUP. It would be deeply unwise to row back on demilitarisation, or to renege on vital parts of the Patten Report on policing, which was mandated by the Agreement.[3] The increasing acceptance by nationalists of Northern Ireland's police is a prize that should not be lost.

We have said what we think should be done in the event of a continuing impasse among the local parties. Failure to operate Executive power-sharing should not prevent progress on those parts of the Agreement (reaffirmed in the Joint Declaration) that do not require devolution. Nor should it preclude the UK and Irish governments deepening their cross-border and all-island cooperation, through or outside the BIGC. Publicly highlighting this fact may concentrate the minds of unionist hardliners. Saying no to power-sharing, they should be told, means saying yes to the BIGC.

This intergovernmental approach is considered undemocratic, because it does not involve local politicians. The SDLP's proposals for direct rule ministers to be replaced by unelected technocrats, even if the latter are subject to the Northern Ireland Assembly, are no better in this respect. Better, in our view, to proceed along the lines unveiled by the Secretary of State in November 2005, namely to give increasing powers to a smaller number of larger local authorities (NIO, 2005). Where this results in heterogeneous jurisdictions, proportionality and power-sharing principles will need to be applied, with a proportion of the bloc grant, or an extension of powers, being made conditional on such arrangements.[4] Local governments are subject to all the human rights and equality provisions that apply to the public sector. Intergovernmental cooperation combined with robust and accountable local governments is the best substitute for a failure to agree consociation at the Northern Ireland level. It also has merit even if there is a functioning consociation. The prospects for such a consociation are by no means in the coroner's court.

Notes

1 For a comprehensive analysis of these cases, see Ní Aoláin (2000).
2 In fact, the DUP did not provide any outline of the way forward, but stated that details would be forthcoming later.
3 An end to the 50:50 requirement for police recruitment, before the police has become representative, and before republicans have accepted the PSNI, would, in our view, be a dangerous step.
4 See our recommendations in McGarry and O'Leary (1995: 376).

References

APNI (Alliance Party of Northern Ireland) (2004) *Agenda for Democracy: Alliance Party Proposals for the Review of the Agreement*, 7 January. Belfast: APNI.

DFA (Department of Foreign Affairs) (2004) *Proposals by the British and Irish Governments for a Comprehensive Agreement*. Available at http://news.bbc.co.uk/nol/shared/bsp/hi/pdfs/08_12_04_british_irish_proposals.pdf (accessed 16 January 2006).

DUP (Democratic Unionist Party) (2006) 'DUP outlines the best way forward', press release, 16 January 2006. Available at www.dup.org.uk/articles.asp?Article_ID=1928 (accessed 18 January 2006).

Evans, G. and O'Leary, B. (2000) 'Northern Irish voters and the British–Irish Agreement: foundations of a stable consociational settlement?' *Political Quarterly* 71 (1), 78–101. *Irish Independent* (2005) 'Uncovering of Provo wealth will cause trouble for peace process', 7 October.

Mallon, S. (1999) 'Statement by the Deputy First Minister (Designate), Northern Ireland Assembly', 15 July, 325.

McGarry, J. and O'Leary, B. (1995) *Explaining Northern Ireland: Broken Images*. Oxford: Blackwell.

McGarry, J. and O'Leary, B. (2004) *The Northern Ireland Conflict: Consociational Engagements*. Oxford: Oxford University Press.

Ní Aoláin, F. (2000) *The Politics of Force: Conflict Management and State Violence in Northern Ireland*. Belfast: Blackstaff Press.

NIO (Northern Ireland Office) (2005) 'Speech by Secretary of State on Outcome of Review of Public Administration', Hilton Hotel, Belfast, 22 November. Available at www.nio.gov.uk/speech_by_secretary_of_state_on_outcome_of_review_of_public_administration_22_november_2005.pdf (accessed 18 January 2006).

O'Leary, B. (1999) 'The nature of the Agreement' *Fordham Journal of International Law*, 22 (4), 1628–1667.

O'Leary, B. (2001a) 'Personal view: ignore the prophets of doom', *Financial Times*, 11 June.

O'Leary, B. (2001b) 'Elections, not suspensions', *The Guardian*, 13 July.

O'Leary, B. (2001c) 'Reid should not allow a new Unionist boycott', *Irish Times*, 4 October.

UTV Internet (2005) 'Sinn Féin signals end to police boycott', 15 January. Available at www.u.tv/newsroom/indepth.asp?pt=n&id=69249 (accessed 18 January 2005).

6

From deference to defiance: popular unionism and the decline of elite accommodation in Northern Ireland

Henry Patterson and Eric Kaufman

Introduction

On 29 November 2003 the UUP, the party that had governed Northern Ireland from partition in 1921 to the imposition of direct rule by Edward Heath in 1972, lost its primary position as the leading unionist party in the Northern Ireland Assembly to the DUP of Reverend Ian Paisley. On 5 May 2005 the electoral revolution was completed when the DUP trounced the UUP in the Westminster elections, netting twice the UUP's popular vote, ousting David Trimble and reducing the UUP to just one Westminster seat. In March 2005 the Orange Order, which had helped to found the UUP exactly a century before, cut its links to this ailing party.

What explains this political earthquake? The press and most Northern Ireland watchers place a large amount of stress on short-term policy shifts and events. The failure of the IRA to show 'final acts' of decommissioning of weapons is fingered as the main stumbling block which prevented a re-establishment of the Northern Ireland Assembly and, with it, the credibility of David Trimble and his pro-Agreement wing of the UUP. This was accompanied by a series of incidents which demonstrated that the IRA, while it may have given up on the 'armed struggle' against the security forces, was still involved in intelligence gathering, the violent suppression of its opponents and a range of sophisticated criminal activities culminating in the robbery of £26 million from the Northern Bank in Belfast in December 2004.

However, our analysis suggests that longer-term factors are at work within unionism which severely limit the scope for moderates to achieve a lasting power-sharing deal. To understand these processes, we must look at the history of two key unionist institutions, the UUP and the Orange Order. First, it is important to note that both the UUP and Orange Order are highly democratic, decentralised institutions. Within the UUP, constituency associations have a high degree of local autonomy from the party centre.[1] In the Orange Order, a system of elections elevates leaders from local lodges through district, county and then Grand Lodge levels. All of this theoretically allows the grass-roots to keep their leaders close to the centre of popular opinion.

Yet, despite their democratic structure, both institutions were dominated for a long time by small cliques drawn from the Ulster–Protestant social elite. This socio-political system held until the mid-twentieth century. The UUP was formed a century ago, well before partition, and was dominated by an elite of merchants, industrialists and large landowners (Gibbon, 1975). It organised the pan-class mobilisation of Ulster Protestants against the Asquith government's Home Rule Bill of 1912 and formed the government which took power in the new state of Northern Ireland in 1921. The Orange Order, formed in 1795, is a fraternity whose network of some 800 lodges reaches into almost every unionist community in Northern Ireland. The Order provided the UUP with support and acted as a mobilising agent for the UUP machine. From the formation of the UUP in 1905, the Order was entitled to a significant representation of the delegates to its ruling Ulster Unionist Council. The upper echelon of the Order, focused on the 40-odd members of the Central Committee of the Grand Lodge, was dominated by the same social class as the UUP elite. Meanwhile, private lodges were mostly working class. Within the UUP, a similar discrepancy ensured that the party leadership was far more socially elite than its footsoldiers at branch level.

Social revolution

However, during the twentieth century the Orange Order underwent major social changes. In 1954, for example, the Order's Grand Master was former Northern Ireland Prime Minister John Millar Andrews. Its 35-member Central Committee was dominated by grandees: just nine lacked a title and there were 16 JPs and five OBEs. In 1995 the Order's Grand Master was Martin Smyth, a Presbyterian preacher of middling Belfast origins. In that year, the 41-members of Central Committee contained just ten titled delegates, with only five JPs (GOLI, 1954, 1995).

The UUP mirrors this shift: in the 42 years from the formation of Northern Ireland it had only three leaders: James Craig, John Andrews and Basil Brooke, Lord Boorkeborough. All came from either the bourgeoisie or landlord class. Brookeborough's successor, Captain Terence O'Neill, although he became associated with the modernisation of Ulster economy and society, was part of the traditional landed elite (Mulholland, 2000:12), as was his successor and cousin, James Chichester-Clark. The last unionist Prime

Minister, Brian Faulkner, although despised by some of the Ulster landed gentry, still came from a modest bourgeois background. Things changed in the 1970s, when Faulkner was replaced by the bluff Fermanagh farmer, Harry West who in turn gave way in 1979 to James Molyneaux, a farmer's son, who served as UUP leader until 1995. Molyneaux and Smyth both took office in the 1970s and exemplify the decline of deference within unionism and the rise of a more self-confident, populist grassroots.[2]

This social revolution went well beyond the pinnacle of these organisations to encompass a wider elite down to the level of the hundred-odd Orange districts. In 1901 a majority of district lodge officers worked in white-collar occupations and were more socially elite than local lodge officers and the unionist population. By 2001 MOSAIC postal code analysis shows that there was no status difference between the top and bottom of the Orange Order, while its class composition slipped *vis-à-vis* the wider unionist population (GOLI, 1901, 2001).

Political revolution

The social revolution within Orangeism, and, to a lesser extent, the UUP, was linked with a major political revolution in which the rank and file gained the confidence to challenge their 'betters'. Things began to change in the period after the Second World War when the unionist government was forced by the fear of defection of working-class Protestants to the Northern Ireland Labour Party to accept the welfare state, despite the instinctive reaction within the party that it was an alien and 'socialistic' importation. In the post-war period the Prime Minister, Lord Brookeborough, chose to pursue a path of increasing financial dependence on the Treasury to stave off loss of support because of the province's economic difficulties and high level of unemployment (Bew, Gibbon and Patterson, 2002: 86–99). Many grassroots loyalists were concerned that the welfare state and new factories in areas like Londonderry would upset the demographic balance and undermine unionist control of border counties like Fermanagh and Tyrone where Catholics were a majority of the population (Patterson, 2002: 130–131). The Prime Minister was also aware that the new international situation with the creation of the United Nations and the Universal Declaration of Human Rights left the regime open to new forms of criticism from its nationalist and labour opponents (Patterson, 1999). This encouraged him to try and ensure that the government did not do anything which would allow it to be presented as 'sectarian' and discriminatory. The result was a chorus of criticism that his government was 'appeasing' the Catholic Church and other 'enemies of Ulster'. Thus even before the pressures of the civil rights movement in the 1960s, the traditional unionist and Orange elites were under pressure from both dissident loyalists and also from increasing numbers of working-class Protestants in Belfast, who seemed to be prioritising material interests over ethno-national loyalties.

Prior to the 1960s, despite these instances of challenges from the grass-roots, dissidence was held in check by the norms of deference expressed so well by a Tyrone district Orange lodge as late as November 1967:

> In view of the vacancy for Grand Master, this lodge recommends the Marquis of Hamilton, MP . . . it would be an honour for County Tyrone to have such a worthy brother in this high office. He would bring grace and dignity to this office [and this would] mean much goodwill for the Orange Institution in Ireland. (Fintona District Lodge 8, 1967)

However, the political reforms of the 1960s began under Terence O'Neill's leadership and maintained during the tenure of reformist leaders Chichester-Clark and Faulkner, alienated many unionists from their political class. O'Neill's decision to have an historic meeting with the Irish Taoiseach, Sean Lemass, in January 1965, and his rhetoric of communal bridge-building aroused the ire of evangelical Protestants led by the Reverend Ian Paisley. The opposition of Paisley's Free Presbyterian Church to the emerging ecumenical movement was also reflected in the Orange Order, where the relatively moderate Grand Master, Sir George Clark, became the butt of rank-and-file criticism for being too close to the government, and resigned in 1967 (Mulholland, 2000: 127). The formation of the Northern Ireland Civil Rights Association in 1967 and the onset of protest marches both aimed at forcing British government pressure on O'Neill for reform of the local government franchise, of the mechanisms for the allocation of public employment and housing, and of policing (Purdie, 1990). Many rank-and-file unionists saw the civil rights movement as simply a new tactic adopted by nationalists and republicans to destroy the state.

What emerges from meetings and resolutions of both the UUP and the Orange Order is the increasing hostility between the Orange Order as well as many ordinary UUP supporters and reformist Prime Ministers. Populist leaders like the Reverend Martin Smyth, James Molyneaux who (was from 1970 unionist MP for South Antrim), the Reverend John Brown from county Antrim and William Douglas from county Londonderry, had emerged within the Order's Central Committee from the mid-1960s. These figures challenged the patrician leadership of the Order and opposed any concessions to the nationalist minority – even if this put the Stormont administration's life in danger. The British were equally adamant that the unionist-led government pursue reform, and forced these administrations to change or face fiscal and political sanctions. As the unionist regimes of 1969–72 haltingly embraced reform, they incurred the wrath of the Orange Order and many within the unionist party branches. Whereas even in the 1960s it would have been considered shocking to chastise the Prime Minister, this was no longer the case. In the words of Antrim Orange leader the Reverend John Brown: 'The P.M. [James Chichester Clark] is at heart an Englishman . . . keen to obey the generals' (GOLI, 1970a) and 'The man [Prime Minister James Chichester Clark] is stupid, unreliable, and depends on his blind acceptance of the "advice" of his "professional advisers" ' (GOLI, 1970b).

As the unionist governments came under ever more obvious supervision and pressure for change from London, they were also faced with an intensifying campaign of shootings and bombings by the Provisional IRA which had emerged in 1970. Issues of security and law-and-order came to dominate intra-unionist debate, with the unionist elite being charged with failure to respond effectively to the IRA. British-imposed reforms of the security forces – the abolition of the 'B' Special Constabulary and the reform and disarming of the Royal Ulster Constabulary – further enraged the Orange and unionist rank and file. The UUP began to splinter into reformist and right-wing tendencies, with the former largely located in the middle-class suburbs of Belfast and predominantly Protestant constituencies like North Down. By the time Edward Heath imposed direct rule in March 1972, the UUP faced serious challenges from Paisley's DUP and the right-wing Vanguard movement of former cabinet minister, William Craig. The right wing finally took over the party in 1974 when Brian Faulkner attempted to form a power-sharing administration with the nationalist SDLP. Though there was a solid bloc of pro-power-sharing unionists, ranging from 30–50 percent of the total unionist population, these tended to be disproportionately better educated and resident in greater Belfast. Thus they were largely absent (or passive) within the rank and file of Orangeism, though some did play a role in the UUP and its liberal offshoots like the Faulkner's short lived Unionist Party of Northern Ireland (UPNI) or the Alliance Party.

From the mid-1970s the UUP managed to reassert its leading position in Protestant politics by projecting itself as the moderate and 'sensible' centre of gravity of pro-union politics, in contrast to the 'extremism' of Paisley's DUP. Although the DUP was able to establish a substantial base of support in traditional working-class areas of Belfast on top of its core original rural and evangelical base, it failed to overtake the UUP. This was, in large part, because of the fear of many Protestants that DUP dominance would provoke a major crisis in relations with the UK government. James Molyneaux's leadership of the UUP moved it towards a policy of low-key integrationism. This was opposed by a strong devolutionist wing of the party, in which border unionists like Harry West played a central role. However, the problem for the devolutionists was their unwillingness to accept the only terms on which self-government for the province was likely to be made available: power sharing with the SDLP, and some sort of North–South institutions to accommodate Northern Catholics' Irish identity (Walker, 2004: 222–223).

Molyneaux's crypto-integrationist strategy suffered a major blow when Margaret Thatcher signed the Anglo-Irish Agreement with the Irish Taoiseach, Garret FitzGerald, in 1985. The Agreement gave the Irish state an unprecedented degree of institutionalised influence on the governance of Northern Ireland and was met by a massive wave of unionist opposition (Aughey, 1989: 62–98). However, the DUP was unable to capitalise on Molyneaux's discomfiture, in part because the Agreement could be seen as a response to DUP extremism and also because unionist grassroots pressure for a united response was bound to favour the dominant party in the unionist bloc.

The IRA's declaration of a 'complete cessation of military activities' in August 1994 heralded a radical shift in the balance of forces which finally undermined Molyneaux's leadership. His emphasis on winning influence at Westminster appeared increasingly ineffectual when John Major's government agreed the Joint Framework Documents with the Irish government in 1995. These contained provisions for North–South institutions which caused acute unionist alarm, and internal pressure forced Molyneaux to resign as leader. His replacement was David Trimble, the MP for Upper Bann, who had won the support of many Orangemen in the party because of his role in the confrontation between Portadown Orangemen and the police over a banned Orange procession at Drumcree (Godson, 2004: 123–145). However, Trimble, a long-time critic of Molyneaux, was soon to become associated with a more pro-active style of leadership, centred on the belief that the IRA cessation had created a situation where unionists would be further marginalised if they did not engage in negotiations with nationalists and republicans. This was particularly be the case, he believed, when Tony Blair won a landslide victory in the 1997 general election.

It was Trimble's decision to enter all-party talks which included Sinn Féin in the autumn of 1997 that created the conditions for the Belfast Agreement. The DUP remained outside the talks process, accusing the UUP leader of compromising with the political representatives of terrorism. It was clear from the referendum on the Agreement that little more than a half of Protestants supported it, while in the subsequent elections for the Northern Ireland Assembly the UUP received its lowest ever share of the vote and anti-Agreement unionist parties, led by the DUP, outpolled Trimble's party (Mitchell, 2001: 33). Although Trimble had won the support of 70 per cent of the party's ruling Ulster Unionist Council for the Agreement, his margin of support soon fell as unionist discontent on a range of issues, including the Patten Report on Policing, the early release of paramilitary offenders and the delay in decommissioning IRA weapons, increased rapidly (Patterson, 2004).

North-East v. border

Another important facet of popular Ulster unionism is region. North-East Ulster (Antrim, Belfast, north Down) has a very different unionist tradition than border counties. In the North-East, there are few Catholics, and most Protestants are Presbyterians or Methodists. There is a long tradition of tenants rights or working-class populism which has bred a more 'rebel' mindset that is suspicious of authority (including that of the Crown). In border areas, Catholics are often a majority, and more Protestants are members of traditional institutions like the Church of Ireland, UUP and Orange Order. Their mindset is more 'traditional' and less willing to challenge the continuities of loyalty to the Crown, party and government. In this curious way, 'tradition' is more moderate than rebellion.

Border Protestants – exemplified by figures like Harry West, the critic of O'Neill and subsequent leader of the UUP (1974–79) – initially opposed reforms in local government and housing. As late as 1980, surveys showed Protestants in border areas to be more hostile to power-sharing than in Belfast. However, this was grounded more in a 'rational' fear of losing local government control than in militant Protestantism. 'Loyal' border unionists were more likely to stick with the UUP (as 'our party') than their northeast Ulster counterparts. Today, in interviews, border respondents stress their need to work with the Catholic majority in their areas. Thus James Cooper, a prominent Fermanagh unionist who was also a party officer and supporter of the Agreement: 'My perception of Fermanagh Unionism is that it has always been very realistic . . . the workings of Unionism on the ground were very pragmatic and that derives from the fact that the population in Fermanagh was split 50:50'.[3]

Border constituency associations were thus more likely to support the Good Friday Agreement (GFA) after 1998.

Thus, by the 1990s, border unionists' staunch opposition to power sharing had turned to moderation – especially in southern Armagh, Tyrone and Fermanagh. This is illustrated by the maps in Figures 6.1, 6.2 and 6.3. Figure 6.1 show that the UUP vote amongst Protestants at local level in 1993 was weakest in North Antrim and greater Belfast, and strongest along the southern border and County Londonderry. Figure 6.2 examines the inclinations of UUP constituency associations in 2003. Notice that unlike Londonderry, southern-border associations are solidly behind Trimble and the GFA. Thus border areas

Figure 6.1 UUP share of Protestant vote at local government level, 1993

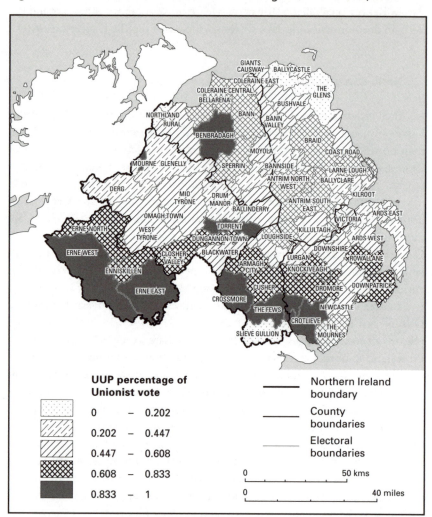

are generally the only places where voters solidly backed the UUP and the UUP solidly backed the Agreement.

This is especially pronounced within the Orange Order, and this 'Orange divide' is highly statistically significant when it comes to explaining voting patterns within the UUC. The map in Figure 6.3 shows the difference between two groups of delegates from the same constituencies: Orange delegates and UUP constituency association delegates. Note that in northeast Ulster, Orange UUC delegates are 'rebels' who stand out from their non-Orange constituents as militantly anti-Agreement: they are 63 to 80 percentage points

Figure 6.2 Support for the Good Friday Agreement, UUC Constituency
Association Delegates, 2003

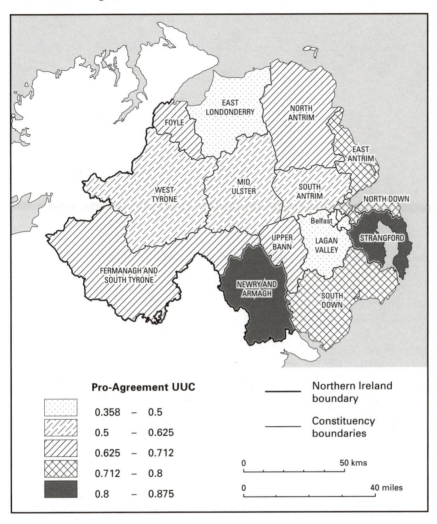

more anti-Agreement than their non-Orange counterparts. In border counties, by contrast, Orangemen are more 'traditionalist' and differ a great deal
less in their views from their non-Orange neighbours. In four areas, Orange
delegates were actually more pro-Agreement than non-Orange delegates!

Looking more broadly at patterns within the UUC in 2003, delegates'
gender, class and education made little difference to their vote. Instead,
delegates' constituency association or, if Orangemen, their county lodge,
was statistically most significant in explaining their stance toward the Good

Figure 6.3 Difference between Orange and non-Orange (UUC Delegate) support for the Good Friday Agreement, by Constituency Association, 2003

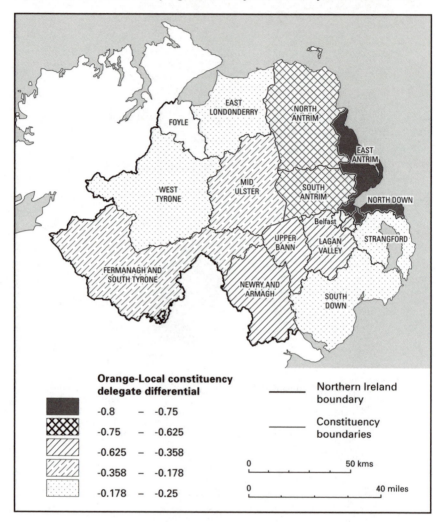

Friday Agreement. Moreover, Orange delegates and Young Unionists tended to oppose the Agreement, while the 17 MLAs (who stood to lose status and salary if the Assembly was suspended) were almost unanimously pro-Agreement. In effect, local networks mattered more than individual characteristics when it came to a vote on the UUC floor.

What of the wider swath of the unionist population and the rise of the DUP? In 2001, when the UUP still held an electoral advantage over the DUP, long-term signs pointed toward an in-built DUP demographic advantage.

Figure 6.4 Predictors of support for the UUP in the 2001 election (Protestants only), by Wald Test statistic

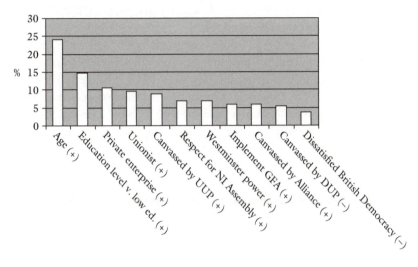

This is because, as Figure 6.4 shows, age was by far the most important predictor of a DUP vote. Education and support for private enterprise were also very important, though class and gender were not significant (NB insignificant factors are excluded from the graph). Recent research on the Orange Order undertaken by Jocelyn Evans and Jon Tonge (2002) confirms this finding: younger Orangemen are significantly more likely to vote DUP than their older counterparts. It seems that 'rebel' unionism has transcended its roots in North Antrim and Belfast and is being carried by less deferential new generations throughout Northern Ireland.

Conclusions

The period since 1998 has been one of electoral realignment within unionism. Unquestionably, this is linked to short-term shifts in public opinion revolving around issues like decommissioning. But beneath the surface, a longer-term cultural shift has been taking place from 'loyalty' to 'rebellion', which made a UUP–DUP 'tipping point' increasingly likely. The unionist population has become less willing to defer to its social elite, and newer generations are expressing this new 'defiance' by voting increasingly for the DUP. This shift in attitude is partly due to a modernisation process that has swept through the western world and challenged status hierarchies of all kinds since the 1950s. In Northern Ireland it is also related to the decline of the

Stormont majoritarian system. Unionist elites were pressured by the British to reach an accommodation with the Catholic minority. As unionist leaders acceded to reform in the 1965–74 period, they lost legitimacy in the eyes of unionist working and rural people.

Within the Orange Order, a new generation of 'self-made' populists replaced the old 'squirearchy' in leadership roles by the early 1970s. In the UUP populists made important inroads after 1975. The grass roots were rising, and in the 1975–95 period their sentiments were expressed by Martin Smyth, the Orange Grand Master, and James Molyneaux, the UUP leader. More recently, modernisers under David Trimble regained control of the UUP and engineered a compromise with nationalists which took the form of the historic Belfast Agreement. This accommodation ultimately ensured that Trimble met the same fate as Faulkner did in 1973–74. In short, a more anti-elitist unionism is in the ascendant, rendering elite accommodation (which is key to all power-sharing systems) difficult.

Martin Smyth, James Molyneaux and Ian Paisley emerged from the grass roots, have histories of populist activism and thus identify with their anti-establishment origins. Their biographies are hence quite different from previous unionist leaders and from David Trimble. Given this pattern, it is unlikely that Paisley's DUP will reach an accommodation with Sinn Féin that will relaunch devolved government in Northern Ireland. It is even arguable that the unionist population must, like the Iranian people, experience and tire of militancy in order to bring forth more liberal generations committed to compromise.

Notes

1 On the structure of the party, see Harbinson (1973: 35–60).
2 For a detailed account of the West-Molyneaux years, see Walker (2004: 221–248).
3 Interview with James Cooper, 17 January 2003.

References

Aughey, A. (1989) *Under Siege: Ulster Unionism and the Anglo-Irish Agreement* Belfast: Blackstaff Press.

Bew, P., Gibbon, P. and Patterson, H. (2002) *Northern Ireland 1921–2001: Political Forces and Social Classes.* London: Serif.

Fintona District Lodge 8 (1967) 'Resolution in County Tyrone', *Grand Lodge Minute Book*, November.

Gibbon, P. (1975) *The Origins of Ulster Unionism*. Manchester: Manchester University Press.

Godson, D. (2004) *Himself Alone: David Trimble and the Ordeal of Ulster Unionism* London: Harper Perennial.

GOLI (Grand Orange Lodge of Ireland) (1901) *Reports of Proceedings*. Belfast: Archives of GOLI, Schomberg House.

GOLI (Grand Orange Lodge of Ireland) (1954) *Reports of Proceedings*. Belfast: Archives of GOLI, Schomberg House.

GOLI (Grand Orange Lodge of Ireland) (1970a) *Central Committee Minutes*, August. Belfast: Archives of GOLI, Schomberg House.

GOLI (Grand Orange Lodge of Ireland) (1970b) *Central Committee Minutes*, November. Belfast: Archives of GOLI, Schomberg House.

GOLI (Grand Orange Lodge of Ireland) (1995) *Reports of Proceedings*. Belfast: Archives of GOLI, Schomberg House.

GOLI (Grand Orange Lodge of Ireland) (2001) *Returns*. Belfast: Archives of GOLI, Schomberg House.

Harbinson, J.F. (1973) *The Ulster Unionist Party, 1882–1973. Its Development and Organisation*. Belfast: Blackstaff Press.

Mitchell, P. (2001) 'Transcending an ethnic party system? The impact of consociational governance on electoral dynamics and the party system' in R. Wilford (ed.) *Aspects of the Belfast Agreement*. Oxford: Oxford University Press.

Mulholland, M. (2000) *Northern Ireland at the Crossroads: Ulster Unionism in the O'Neill Years, 1960–9*. London: Palgrave Macmillan.

Patterson, H. (1999) 'Party versus order: Ulster Unionism and the Flags and Emblems Act', *Contemporary British History*, 13 (4), 110–114.

Patterson, H. (2002) *Ireland Since 1939*. Oxford: Oxford University Press.

Patterson, H. (2004) 'The Limits of "New Unionism": David Trimble and the Ulster Unionist Party', *Eire/Ireland*, 39 (1/2), Spring/Summer, 164–168.

Purdie, B. (1990) *Politics in the Streets: The Origins of the Civil Rights Movement in Northern Ireland*. Belfast: Blackstaff Press.

Tonge, J. and Evans, J. (2002) 'For God and Ulster? Religion, politics and Orangeism in the Ulster Unionist Council', paper presented to the Political Studies Association of Ireland Annual Conference.

Walker, G. (2004) *A History of the Ulster Unionist Party: Protest, Pragmatism and Pessimism*. Manchester: Manchester University Press.

7

Nationalism and republicanism

Jonathan Tonge

Introduction

Regardless of its ultimate fate, the 1998 Good Friday Agreement (GFA) has elicited considerable change within Irish nationalism and republicanism. Some of the most important developments occurred within the Irish Republic, where the government, supported by the vast majority of voters in a referendum, transformed its constitutional claim to Northern Ireland to a mere aspiration of Irish unification. In Northern Ireland, developments were even more dramatic. The longstanding representative of Irish republicanism, Sinn Féin, downgraded its political demand for British withdrawal from Northern Ireland, while the IRA abandoned its 'armed struggle' for a similar goal. The divisions between constitutional nationalism, as espoused by the SDLP since its formation in 1970, and republicanism, as represented by Sinn Féin, were increasingly blurred, as the traditional faultline of violence versus constitutionalism was eroded.

Sinn Féin's emergence as the main representative of nationalists in Northern Ireland has occurred despite an apparent stealing of the SDLP's political clothes. Sinn Féin appears reconciled to the 'agreed Ireland' promoted by the SDLP, a retreat from enforced unity. Sinn Féin entered a 'partitionist' Northern Ireland Assembly at Stormont, accepted only modest all-Ireland executive bodies, ended the IRA's campaign and prepared to support eventually the Police Service of Northern Ireland. Republicanism's primary concern appeared to be less with the abstract, far-reaching goal of Irish reunification than with the immediate gains of an 'equality agenda' designed to enhance the daily lives of northern nationalists (and boost Sinn Féin). The question was whether significant differences remained between nationalism and republicanism. In addressing this question, this chapter assesses post-GFA political developments within Sinn Féin and the SDLP, and the electoral ramifications of the partial erosion of difference.

The slow and partial convergence of nationalism and republicanism

The SDLP's origins in the civil rights movement conditioned its political outlook. From its formation in 1970, it operated within the parameters of constitutional nationalism, advocating a united Ireland through consent and non-violent means. Republicans concluded that the loyalist backlash against civil rights campaigns merely indicated the need for the immediate destruction of Northern Ireland. Sinn Féin offered support for the maintenance of the republican 'physical force tradition' in removing British rule from Northern Ireland, backing an IRA armed struggle evident only episodically until the organisation's rebirth in 1970.

Within these broad ideological frameworks, both parties trimmed policy according to circumstances. The SDLP offered socialist credentials and attempted to reorientate anti-partitionist nationalism towards an equality agenda. The party supported power sharing with unionists, allied to an Irish dimension, as a satisfactory interim arrangement. Nonetheless the SDLP also demanded from the British government 'an immediate declaration that she believes it would be in the best interests of all sections of the communities in both islands, if Ireland were to become united on terms which would be acceptable to all the people of Ireland' (SDLP, 1972). The party's interest in power-sharing dwindled after the collapse of Sunningdale in 1974, and in 1976 the SDLP briefly committed itself to unequivocal demands for British withdrawal from Northern Ireland (Murray, 1998; Murray and Tonge, 2005). This 'greening' of the SDLP continued in terms of the type of member recruited after the failure of Sunningdale, generally much more nationalist than socialist (Evans, Tonge and Murray, 2000). However, the party retreated from its brief 'Brits out' phase and insisted, under the leadership of John Hume for over two decades from 1979 onwards, that a united Ireland was subject to unionist consent.

During the 1970s, Sinn Féin's Eire Nua strategy offered a federal Ireland of four Irish provinces, a policy displaced by demands for a unitary Irish state, with 'no concessions to loyalism' in the 1980s. Unionist consent for change was viewed as a useful, but non-essential, component of the move towards unification; it could not be elevated to a veto. With the IRA's armed campaign incapable of achieving victory, the republican second front, electoral politics, was opened from 1981 onwards, and began with the election victories of imprisoned republican hunger strikers. Like the armed campaign, electoralism reached a ceiling in terms of achievement, the rise of Sinn Féin checked by a combination of IRA activity and the 1985 intergovernmental Anglo-Irish Agreement.

Possible convergence of nationalist and republican politics was aired during the public discussions between the two parties commenced in 1988.

'Hume–Adams' was perhaps of less importance than the private initiatives undertaken by the Sinn Féin President, Gerry Adams, during the 1980s, in creating a formula for Irish self-determination which might not necessarily yield a united Ireland (Moloney, 2002). By the 1990s there were clear signs of a changing approach by Sinn Féin. Juxtaposed with a stepping up of the IRA's campaign prior to the 1994 ceasefire, the alterations in policy did not merit huge attention, but marked a significant departure from fundamental-ist to pragmatic republicanism, which began in 1986 with Sinn Féin's deci-sion to no longer boycott Dail Eireann. Entry to a hitherto 'partitionist' parliament was followed by new thinking unveiled in the 1992 document *Towards a Lasting Peace in Ireland* (Sinn Féin, 1992). The consent and alle-giance of unionists for a united Ireland were acknowledged as vital, although not necessarily a prerequisite. The British government was urged to act as a persuader to unionists to accept unity, a more positive role for the British now envisaged than under the previous 'Brits out' call. In 1993 Sinn Féin declined to reject outright the Downing Street Declaration, although its assertion that self-determination would be exercised on a North *and* South basis (i.e. sepa-rately) made clear that partition would remain. The late 1980s and early 1990s marked a process of Sinn Féin movement from its territorial republi-canism towards the people-based unity of the SDLP.

Various explanations have been offered for the changes in republicanism. Endogenous factors included the lack of commitment to republican theology of Provisional republicanism, grounded in the Catholic defenderism of 1969 and vulnerability to British state strategies (McIntyre, 1995, 2001); the inability of the IRA to win the war (cf. Coogan, 2000; Mallie and McKittrick, 1996; O'Brien, 1999); electoral failure in the Irish Republic (Ryan, 1994); the backlash from loyalists (Taylor, 2000); and the political ambitions of the party leader (Moloney, 2002). Exogenous explanations included the ending of the Cold War, diminishing British interest in Ireland (Cox, 1998; Cox et al., 2001) and, at an already advanced stage of republican change, the unac-ceptability of terrorism after '9/11'. Palpably, many unionists are uncon-vinced by the depth of change; others argue that Sinn Féin has not necessarily changed greatly and remains a party committed to egalitarian and transfor-mationist principles (cf. Maillot, 2004; Ruane and Todd, 1999).

Nationalism, republicanism and devolution

The three strands of the GFA addressed the sets of relationships which, according to the SDLP, needed harmonising in new political arrangements: those between the communities in (a) the North, (b) between North and

South, and (c) between Britain and Ireland (Hume, 1997). Given the weakness of the nationalist negotiating position in constitutional terms (an indecisive, albeit dangerous, IRA campaign and an Irish government lukewarm on unification) the main focus of the GFA lay upon internal changes within Northern Ireland, many of which enraged unionists.

Sinn Féin converged on the SDLP position that an agreed method of Irish self-determination was more important than its immediate outcome. The SDLP position was that the dual referendum on the GFA, North and South, was the 'most fundamental embodiment of parity of esteem' (Mallon, 1997). The SDLP acknowledged that the dual referendum amounted to an exercise in 'co-determination', given that the North would retain a veto, irrespective of how the Irish Republic voted (Mallon, 1997). Sinn Féin also rejected the idea that the dual referendum was a genuine exercise in national self-determination, but supported a 'yes' vote in both polities. Traditional republicans, those who had defected to the small ultra groups of Republican Sinn Féin and the 32 County Sovereignty Committee, scorned the idea that separate North–South referenda on a single constitutional option, with the alternative of a united Ireland omitted from the ballot paper, could constitute anything approaching 'national self-determination'. What the SDLP had labelled 'parallel consent' (SDLP, 1998) was perceived by republican ultras as the 'unionist veto' rewritten.

The delicate internal politics of the Provisional republican movement led to denial over imminent tactical direction, epitomised as late as 1997 by Sinn Féin's 'no return to Stormont' slogan. However, Sinn Féin had given a guarded welcome to the 1995 British–Irish Framework Documents, despite their proposal for a Northern Ireland Assembly. Sinn Féin's denial over entry to an Assembly, even though the Adams–McGuiness leadership privately accepted its inevitability at least one year before its actuality, meant that the SDLP did most of the nationalist bargaining in respect of the GFA (Hennessey, 2000). The most notable exceptions were the non-negotiable demand for IRA prisoner releases and the decoupling of IRA decommissioning from the timetable for institutional arrangements (*An Phoblacht/Republican News*, 1997: 1, 1998a: 21). Much of the GFA's constitutional architecture reflected SDLP thinking in terms of broad outline of its three strands, although the all-Ireland aspects of the deal amounted to less than the original aspirations of constitutional nationalists, let alone republicans.

Predictably, the GFA applied the northern 'consent principle' to constitutional change. For nationalists, the main constitutional negotiating positions concerned the all-Ireland architecture. Here there was retreat not merely from the Framework Documents, but also from the Heads of Agreement propositions of the British and Irish governments offered at the start of multi-party negotiations. Although six new cross-border executive bodies were established, they were mainly anodyne, and the creation of more was conditional upon approval of the Northern Ireland Assembly. The North/South Ministerial Council (NSMC) was bereft of executive power. Sinn Féin's rhetoric of transition (not all of which was believed by the party leadership) was set against the reality of a deal largely devoid of a serious shift to Irish unity. Despite this, the GFA was hugely popular with nationalists and republicans, the overwhelming majority (99 per cent) of Catholic voters backing the Agreement in 1998 (Hayes and McAllister, 2001). Later surveys indicated strong continuing support (Irwin, 2002). Given this, Sinn Féin's support for the deal was based on electoral logic.

This popularity reflected the equality agenda offered by the GFA, promoted enthusiastically within and beyond the Assembly and Executive by Sinn Féin and SDLP ministers, several of whom were praised (quietly) by opponents, although Sinn Féin's were also criticised for supposedly sectarian decision making. The advantage of the equality agenda for nationalists was that many of the institutions with which it was associated – the Equality, Human Rights and Parades Commissions, plus some changes to policing – were not dependent upon the maintenance of devolution. As such, nationalist momentum could be maintained, and it was unsurprising that nationalists and republicans placed great emphasis upon internal change within Northern Ireland.

The new republicanism of Sinn Féin: the equality agenda

Sinn Féin's promotion of an equality agenda is indicative of how the party has reinvented its republicanism to suit electoral circumstances. While republicans have always claimed equality, liberty and fraternity as the key components of their ideology, the Irish variant of the creed traditionally stressed how liberty was a necessary precursor for equality. The Wolfe Tone adage of the need to sever the link with England was regularly articulated as justification for emphasis upon the national 'liberation struggle' from which equality would result. As late as the mid-1990s, Gerry Adams was still insisting that republicans could not be equal in a six-county state (Adams, 1995). The reordering of republican priorities assumes that economic (and presumably political) equality within Northern Ireland is attainable, rather than the mere rainbow-chasing of old, through republican influence at Stormont (see for example, *An Phoblacht/Republican News*, 1998b: 5).

The new approach is embodied in Sinn Féin's (2004) document *Rights for All*, which links the eradication of inequality to the promotion of Irish unity. Demands for a dedicated Department of Equality, with a remit across all departments, are accompanied by an opening assertion that the people of Ireland have a 'right to national self-determination'. This claim is followed by calls for all-Ireland health and education provision. Republicans are anxious to avoid the charge of being mere defenders of a (Catholic) minority in the North. The equality agenda of Sinn Féin has been associated by critics with a particularistic community defence, at odds with universal republican principles. The Sinn Féin Health Minister in the Northern Ireland Executive of 1999–2002, Bairbre de Bruin, was accused by unionists of sectarian decision making in relocating maternity services to nationalist west Belfast. Martin McGuinness (Sinn Féin) was accused of an anti-unionist agenda due to his opposition to the 11-plus transfer test; although this was a stance based upon ending class inequality and, as such, was supported by the working-class loyalists of the Progressive Unionist Party (McAuley and Tonge, 2003).

It is unclear how economic progress and full equality for northern nationalists will heighten desire for inclusion in an all-Ireland Republic. Sinn Féin's short-term demands in this respect are rights-oriented, centred upon allowing citizens in the North to vote in Irish presidential elections, and for elected representatives to be awarded speaking rights in Dail Eireann. Set against a backdrop of growing electoral successes, the overarching goal of unification is a lesser priority. The claim of Adams that the GFA marked a 'transitional phase in our struggle' could be interpreted in a variety of ways, while his assertion that the Agreement 'could and would have been a more decisive phase had we greater political strength North and South' recognised the weakness of republicanism (*An Phoblacht/Republican News*, 1999: 5). Sinn Féin urges the creation of a dedicated minister for Irish unity within the Irish Republic and demands the publication of a Green Paper outlining how the Irish government intends to progress towards this goal – calls met by a tepid response from the Fianna Fail government.

The second aspect of revisionist republicanism is its political pluralism. Whereas Irish republicanism was once marked by fixed, universal principles, its modern manifestation does not claim absolute truth. Instead, republicanism is seen as one competing ideology among others (Bean, 1995). Politically, this is manifested in the demand for respect for Sinn Féin's mandate, as one political actor among others, whose votes must be equally respected. This is far removed from the old insistence that the IRA Army Council is the one legitimate government of Ireland. Political rights are linked to economic rights in an inclusive agenda, in which 'equality becomes the key concept to facilitate the "all-Ireland architecture" of the future' (McGovern, 2004). Sinn Féin has mobilised in recent years under the slogan, 'An Ireland of equals', even if its precise meaning is unclear. Under republican orthodoxy, political equality is unattainable for one section of the population. If republicans have their nation state, unionists are presumably denied their nationhood, and vice-versa.

Consociationalism and the electoral rise of Sinn Féin

As Table 7.1 shows, Sinn Féin's support has soared since the IRA ceasefire in 1994, having been marooned at 10 per cent – less than one-third of the Catholic vote and insufficient to re-elect Gerry Adams as MP for west Belfast – in the early 1990s.

While always capable of attracting a solid working-class vote, even during the IRA's armed struggle, Sinn Féin has demonstrated an ability to mobilise votes from two particular sources: young electors and former non-voters (McAllister, 2004). The percentage of Sinn Féin supporters among 18–24 year olds is more than double that found in any other age category (Northern Ireland Life and Times Survey, 2004). Since overtaking the SDLP in 2001, Sinn Féin has consolidated its lead. The SDLP's 24–18 advantage in Assembly seats in 1998 was reversed exactly five years later, while Sinn Féin enjoys greater representation in the Westminster and European Parliaments (the SDLP lost its seat in the latter in 2004) and on local councils. Sinn Féin benefits from the greater modern propensity of SDLP supporters to offer lower preference vote transfers to the party, three-quarters of which now go to Sinn Féin, whereas transfers to Alliance or non-transfers were more common until the mid-1990s.

For critics of the consociational architecture of the GFA, Sinn Féin's electoral position as a nationalist bloc defender was bound to be consolidated (Horowitz, 2001; Wilford, 2001). Sinn Féin's status as a nationalist bloc defender followed the self-ascribed role of the Provisional IRA for several decades. The endorsement of the supposed extremes of Sinn Féin and the

Table 7.1. Sinn Féin and SDLP vote share, 1992–2005 (%)

Election	Sinn Féin	SDLP	Election	Sinn Féin	SDLP
1992 Westminster	10.0	23.5	1999 European	17.4	28.2
1993 Council	12.4	22.0	2001 Westminster	21.7	21.0
1994 European	9.0	28.9	2001 Council	20.7	19.4
1996 Forum	15.5	21.4	2003 Assembly	23.5	17.0
1997 Westminster	16.1	24.1	2004 European	26.3	15.9
1997 Council	16.9	20.7	2005 Westminster	24.3	17.5
1998 Assembly	17.6	22.0	2005 Council	23.2	17.4

Source: Tonge, J. (2005) *The New Northern Irish Politics?* Basingstoke: Palgrave.

DUP has occurred under the alleged deepening of sectarianism under the GFA. Its consociational features are criticised by sceptics as exacerbating division and denying a common humanity, exemplified by the requirement for Assembly members to designate as unionist, nationalist, or 'other', with the votes of 'others', under certain circumstances being of less value. At Executive level, the carving of a supposed collective into party ministerial fiefdoms worsened the sectarian faultline.

Although a superficially attractive critique with substance in terms of some institutional arrangements, the attack upon consociationalism is an inadequate explanation of the growth of Sinn Féin. The party's electoral growth predates and postdates the GFA, having commenced upon the IRA's ceasefire rather than a particular institutional arrangement, and has continued apace as the GFA and Stormont were mothballed. The growth of Sinn Féin accompanied an increase in the numbers of Catholics identifying as (a) Irish and (b) nationalist. A consociational deal like the GFA has played a part in the legitimation of 'rival' identities, but these identities have been developed alongside and outside consociational political arrangements. What is true is that the peace process has been concerned with the diversion of political questions surrounding territory, self-determination and anti-colonialism into issues of identity, which represent political cul-de-sacs (Gilligan, 2002). Again, however, the growth of 'Irish' identifiers among Catholics (and 'British' among Protestants) predates the GFA, while the growth of 'nationalist' identifiers may reflect the new 'respectability' accruing to such a label as it has become less associated with violence. Moreover, the growth of 'Irish' and 'nationalist' labels among Catholics has not diminished the sizeable section of the population adopting the hybrid label 'Northern Irish' or rejecting the labels 'unionist' or 'nationalist': 27 per cent and 37 per cent respectively in the 2004 Northern Ireland Life and Times Survey.

Having removed the electoral ceiling produced by IRA violence, Sinn Féin's structural and tactical advantages over the SDLP may offer more convincing explanations of electoral growth. As an all-Ireland party, Sinn Féin has scope to grow across the island, while portraying the SDLP as a sectional, northern nationalist party. The danger has been recognised by the SDLP, which examined, but rejected, the possibility of linkages with a party across the border. The post-GFA calls by sections of the Irish Labour Party for a merger were ignored, despite the appeals of some senior figures within the SDLP to form such a link and develop the party in an all-Ireland republican tradition, in which '1798 is central to the fundamental principles of the party' (Stephenson, 1999). The SDLP's advocacy of institutional all-Ireland linkages appears at odds with its own organisation, which remains grounded in northern nationalism with little room for expansion beyond the modest rise in the Catholic population in the North. Only 22 per cent of members supported merger with the Irish Labour Party, these drawn mainly from the socialist wing of the SDLP, a disappearing minority composed mainly of early joiners (Evans, Tonge and Murray, 2000). By the 1990s, motions to SDLP conferences urged that the party's constitution be rewritten to include formally the term 'nationalist party' in its constitution, the party having omitted the label at its mildly socialist birth (e.g. motion 93, Newry Branch, SDLP Annual Conference, Newry, 13–15 November 1998).

The nationalism of the SDLP

The SDLP's post-GFA dilemma has been to avoid portrayal as a party with its main achievement now completed. Having apparently won the arguments with Sinn Féin over (a) the utility of violence in furtherance of a united Ireland, (b) the acceptability of power-sharing with an Irish dimension, and (c) the possibility of reform and equality within a northern state, the SDLP faced the difficulty of convincing the nationalist electorate that it was better placed to defend the gains accruing from the GFA. Among party members, only half of whom believe that a united Ireland is 'the best solution', there was a sense of 'job done', with 82 per cent believing that the party had 'achieved the bulk of its objectives through the GFA', 68 per cent believing the GFA would 'lead to real power-sharing in the Belfast Assembly' and a similar percentage believing it would give Irish nationalism equal status to unionism (Evans, Tonge and Murray, 2000, Tonge and Evans, 2002).

Despite the strength of the SDLP's political leadership, recruitment had dwindled during the years of direct rule and the party had not developed replacements for its leaders, who had emerged during the civil rights era. Moreover, Hume's 'statesman' role and political altruism in dealing with Sinn Féin had been at the expense of the organisation of his own party (Murray, 1998). While elements within the party were anxious to develop communication and organisational skills, notably through the National Democratic Institute in the USA, others took little interest, particularly as the electoral threat from Sinn Féin dwindled temporarily in the late 1980s.

The post-GFA polity offered two potential roles for the SDLP: the first was as an ethnic nationalist party, promoting similar policies to Sinn Féin. This loose 'pan-nationalism', while developed around the principle of self-determination during the early peace process, could be extended in terms of human rights, equality, policing and justice. The alternative was to drive forward a coalition of the moderate centre with the UUP and embark on a risky (given the propensity of voters in ethnic bloc systems with two parties in each bloc to favour the stouter bloc defender) enterprise of marginalising Sinn Féin. It is an exaggeration to state that the decision for the SDLP lay starkly between pan-nationalism or cross-community centrism, but clearly there was a broad strategic choice. To some extent, the SDLP embarked on a 'pick-and-mix' role, strongly endorsing and defending the equality and human rights agenda of the GFA, which it claimed as its own, notwithstanding the rival ownership bid from Sinn Féin. The main difference between the parties lay on policing, the SDLP endorsing post-Patten arrangements, while Sinn Féin held out for greater change before taking seats on the Policing Board. The SDLP's nationalism has veered between 'post' and 'pan' versions. In the 'pan' version, the SDLP risked being 'out-greened' by Sinn Féin in a communal political system. This did not inhibit the SDLP Deputy First Minister in the Executive, Seamus Mallon, urging Sinn Féin supporters to foster nationalist unity and 'have faith in the ability of us all together to deliver change through the new politics' (Mallon, 1999).

The SDLP contemplated a centrist alliance with the UUP, but was thwarted by the internal instability within unionism, which prevented the pro-GFA wing of the UUP becoming sufficiently secure to consolidate such a pact. The SDLP was reluctant to support sanctions, such as exclusion from the Executive or Assembly, against Sinn Féin, despite continued IRA activity. As such, the SDLP was perceived as too close to republicans by the UUP and the anticipated First Minister (UUP)–Deputy First Minister (SDLP) duopoly never materialised, prior to suspension of the Assembly and Executive in 2002 and the electoral collapse of the SDLP and UUP one year later.

The rights-based nationalism of the SDLP stresses that nationalists and unionists are entitled to 'effective political, symbolic and administrative expression of their identity' to ensure full parity of esteem and equality of treatment (SDLP, 1997a). The cross-border linkages of the GFA, rather than parliamentary rights for northern nationalists in the Irish Republic, remain the SDLP's preferred route. This greater emphasis on economic unity as a route to political unification was reinforced by the party leadership. The party acknowledged that 'recognising and acknowledging two sets of rights as legitimate does not automatically reconcile them' (Farren, 1996).

The consistency of the SDLP's arguments in respect of the constitutional architecture of the GFA has not always been replicated in other spheres. The party has oscillated between bi-national approaches to conflict resolution and those which place Northern Ireland within a European context, as part of a Europe of the Regions. The European approach perhaps reached its height in the early 1990s, when the party advocated a direct role for the EU Commission in the governance of Northern Ireland. This position was quickly dropped by the party in the run up to the GFA, the party's position altering to a less specific acknowledgement that EU evolution will 'have the most pro-found implications for the political future of this island' (SDLP, 1997b). The SDLP was not alone in changing policy on the EU, Sinn Féin undergoing a rapid conversion from an anti-EU party to one that advocated 'critical engagement' and then support for an extension of the euro to Northern Ireland (Sinn Féin, 1999, 2003).

The SDLP fought Hume's final elections in 2001 on a post-nationalist vision. It was attacked by Sinn Féin, Adams insisting that the nation-state, in an Irish and other contexts, was far from dead. The post-nationalist aspirations of the SDLP envisaged a Europe in which territorial boundaries diminished in salience and support for supra-national institutions grew. EU involvement in Ireland has nonetheless recognised the border, even though the PEACE I and II programmes straddle the territorial boundary. As an election campaigning vehicle, however, the wider visions offered by Europeanism resonated less with the nationalist electorate than the immediate focus upon gains from an 'equality agenda'.

Conclusion

The pragmatic version of republicanism offered by Sinn Féin since the GFA is a very different entity from the absolutist form prior to the Agreement. Sinn Féin's leadership was cognisant of the lack of insistence upon a united Ireland from most nationalists and republicans. Only 3 per cent of Catholics in Northern Ireland declare that if the majority in Northern Ireland never voted to become part of a united Ireland they would find this 'almost impossible to accept' (Northern Ireland Life and Times Survey, 2004; Bric and Coakley, 2004). The variety of republicanism on offer is, first, more concerned with process than the 'end of history'; second, it is more pluralist in tone, advocating respect for electoral mandates rather than vanguardism; and, third, it emphasises the equality aspects of republicanism rather than universal territorial prescriptions. Sinn Féin continues to reiterate its support for a united Ireland as a necessary outcome; in this respect ideological failure may continue to accompany electoral success. Election triumphs have increased as the party has broadened its appeal to attract a 'softer' nationalist constituency of those aspiring to Irish unity, but who are reluctant to support armed struggle as the means of leverage and are concerned more with economic progress.

The softening of Sinn Féin's policy has moved the party closer to the SDLP, to the extent that the politics offered by both in representing their national community 'looks very like other left of centre political parties in Europe' (Harvey, 2005). Yet, as a 32-county party, Sinn Féin holds significant structural advantages over its nationalist rival in the North and its main electoral and ideological rival in the South, Fianna Fail. Growth across both jurisdictions will help defuse the charges of 'sell-out' offered by traditional republicans, as Sinn Féin can point out that all-Ireland, as distinct from 26-county or six-county constitutionalism, has never been attempted in pursuit of unity. The party could exercise considerable leverage in coalition government, North and South. This might represent the climax of the Adams' project. The default position in the North, 'greener' direct rule and small nudges towards British–Irish joint authority, might not harm Sinn Féin.

The new constitutionalism of republicanism is a tacit acceptance of the SDLP's arguments concerning the lack of utility of violence in the realisation of territorial and electoral goals, although internal changes in Northern Ireland may have been created through the IRA campaign. For the SDLP, winning the argument has been followed by losing the elections. The SDLP's insistence upon any solution addressing different sets of relationships and its consistent rejection of any internal solution has not been replicated in terms of its own organisation. A nationalist party based solely within the North has little room to expand and its existence may contradict the political dispensation it advocates, and fail to represent fully the ethno-national community it represents. As the party's then Deputy Leader remarked after the GFA, 'when I say our country, I don't just mean Northern Ireland' (Mallon, 1998). The leverage that can be exercised by the third or fourth party in Northern Ireland – the minority of a minority that Sinn Féin once represented – appears slight and diminishing, irrespective of the quality of argument. The question then is whether Northern Ireland's nationalists and republicans need two communal parties.

References

Adams, G. (1995) *Free Ireland: Towards a Lasting Peace*. Dingle: Brandon.

An Phoblacht/Republican News (1997) 'No releases, no deal', 4 December.

An Phoblacht/Republican News (1998a) 'Initial overview of the Agreement: Sinn Féin Ard Fheis 1998', 23 April

An Phoblacht/Republican News (1998b) Equality-SF opens up Stormont', 3 December.

An Phoblacht/Republican News (1999) 'Establishing the Republic', 16 December.

Bean, K. (1995) 'The new departure? Recent developments in republican strategy and ideology', *Irish Studies Review*, 10, 2–6.

Bric, M. and Coakley, J. (2004) 'The roots of militant politics in Ireland' in M. Bric and J. Coakley (eds) *From Political Violence to Negotiated Settlement*. Dublin: University College Dublin Press, 1–12.

Coogan, T.P. (2000) *The IRA*. London: Fontana.

Cox, M. (1998) 'Northern Ireland: the war that came in from the cold', *Irish Studies in International Affairs*, 9, 73–84.

Cox, M., Guelke, A. and Stephen, F. (eds) (2001) *A Farewell to Arms? From 'Long War' to 'Long Peace' in Northern Ireland*. Manchester: Manchester University Press.

Evans, J., Tonge, J. and Murray, G. (2000) 'Constitutional nationalism and socialism in Northern Ireland: the greening of the SDLP', in P. Cowley, D. Denver, A. Russell and L. Harrison (eds) (2000) *British Elections and Parties Review 10*, London: Frank Cass, 117–32.

Farren, S. (1996) 'Northern Ireland: towards a solution: principles, structures and process', Understanding the Peace Process in Northern Ireland seminar series, University of Salford, 23 March.

Gilligan, C. (2002) 'Identity as a concept for understanding the peace process', unpublished PhD thesis, University of Salford.

Harvey, C. (2005) 'Nationalism: a good cause', *Fortnight*, April/May, 425.

Hayes, B. and McAllister, I. (2001) 'Who voted for peace? Public support for the 1998 Northern Ireland Agreement', *Irish Political Studies*, 16, 73–94.

Hennessey, T. (2000) *The Northern Ireland Peace Process: Ending the Troubles?* Dublin: Irish Academic Press.

Horowitz, D. (2001) 'The Northern Ireland Agreement: clear, consociational and risky', in J. McGarry (ed.) *Northern Ireland and the Divided World*. Oxford: Oxford University Press.

Hume, J. (1997) Opening statement at the launch of Strand 1 talks, 7 October. Belfast: SDLP.

Irwin, C. (2002) *The People's Peace Process in Northern Ireland*. Basingstoke: Palgrave.

Maillot, A. (2004) *New Sinn Féin*. London: Routledge.

Mallie, E. and McKittrick, D. (1996) *The Fight for Peace*. London: Heinemann.

Mallon, S. (1997) Statement on the opening of Strand 2 negotiations, 7 October. Belfast: SDLP.

Mallon, S. (1998) Speech to SDLP Annual Conference, Canal Court Hotel, Newry, 13 November.

Mallon, S. (1999) Speech to SDLP Annual Conference, Wellington Park Hotel, Belfast, 5 November.

McAllister, I. (2004) 'The Armalite and the ballot box. Sinn Fein's electoral strategy in Northern Ireland', *Electoral Studies*, 23 (1), 123–142.

McAuley, J. and Tonge, J. (2003) 'Over the rainbow? Republican and loyalist cooperation in Northern Ireland since the Good Friday Agreement', *Etudes Irlandaises*, 28 (1), 177–196.

McGovern, M. (2004) 'The old days are over: Irish republicanism, the peace process and the discourse of equality', *Terrorism and Political Violence*, 16 (3), 622–45.

McIntyre, A. (1995) 'Modern Irish republicanism: the product of British state strategies', *Irish Political Studies*, 10, 95–110.

McIntyre, A. (2001) 'Modern Irish republicanism and the Belfast Agreement: chickens coming home to roost or turkeys celebrating Christmas?' in R. Wilford (ed.) *Aspects of the Belfast Agreement*. Oxford: Oxford University Press.

Moloney, E. (2002) *A Secret History of the IRA*. London: Penguin.

Murray, G. (1998) *John Hume and the SDLP*. Dublin: Irish Academic Press.

Murray, G. and Tonge, J. (2005) *Sinn Féin and the SDLP: From Alienation to Participation*. London: Hurst.

Northern Ireland Life and Times Survey (2004). Available at www.ark.ac.uk.

O'Brien, B. (1999) *The Long War: the IRA and Sinn Féin*. Dublin: O'Brien.

Ruane, J. and Todd, J. (eds) (1999) *After the Good Friday Agreement: Analysing Political Change in Northern Ireland*. Dublin: University College Dublin Press.

Ryan, M. (1994) *War and Peace in Ireland: Britain and the IRA in the New World Order*. London: Pluto.

SDLP (Social Democratic and Labour Party) (1972) *Towards a New Ireland*. Belfast: SDLP.

SDLP (Social Democratic and Labour Party) (1997a) *SDLP Submissions to Multi-Party Talks*. Belfast: SDLP.

SDLP (Social Democratic and Labour Party) (1997b) *Principles and Requirements: Strand 1: Agenda Item 1, Submission to Multi-Party Talks*. Belfast: SDLP.

SDLP (Social Democratic and Labour Party) (1998) *Building a New Agreed Ireland*. Belfast: SDLP.

Sinn Féin (1992) *Towards a Lasting Peace in Ireland*. Dublin: Sinn Féin.

Sinn Féin (1999) *Sinn Féin and the European Union*. Dublin: Sinn Féin Ard Chomhairle.

Sinn Féin (2003) *Sinn Féin and the European Union*. Dublin: Sinn Féin.

Sinn Féin (2004) *Rights for All*. Dublin: Sinn Féin.

Stephenson, J. (1999) Speech to SDLP Annual Conference, Wellington Park Hotel, Berfast, 5 November.

Taylor, P. (2000) *Loyalists*. London: Bloomsbury.

Tonge, J. and Evans, J. (2002) 'Party Members and the Good Friday Agreement', *Irish Political Studies*, 17 (2), 59–73.

Wilford, R. (ed.) (2001) *Aspects of the Belfast Agreement*. Oxford: Oxford University Press.

8
Party competition and voting behaviour since the Agreement

Paul Mitchell

Overview: the old guard out-flanked

The institutions created by the Belfast Agreement have spent more time in suspension than on active duty and thus (to date) have largely failed to transform Northern Ireland government and society in the manner hoped for during the spring and summer of 1998. It may be that verified IRA decommissioning during the summer of 2005 will eventually help create the conditions in which stable power-sharing governments can be created and sustained. There is no doubt, however, that the 'peace process' and Agreement have already transformed Northern Ireland's party system and voting behaviour. The party system of 2005 is virtually a mirror image of the pattern of competition in 1992.

It is well known that Northern Ireland has a dual party system in which each community effectively holds its own election to decide who will be its pre-eminent tribunes (Mitchell, 1999; Mitchell, O'Leary and Evans, 2001). Winning seats from the other communal bloc happens occasionally, but is effectively a bonus; the more serious party competition takes place within each segmented community. Some things, such as the overall size of the unionist bloc, have changed very little: the average vote share of the unionist bloc was 50.5 per cent during the 1990s (average of all eight elections) and has been 49.9 per cent since then (average of six elections during 2001–5). The nationalist bloc expanded from an average of 38.4 per cent in the 1990s to 41.3 since the new millennium, reflecting the electoral surge of Sinn Féin since the middle of the 1990s. Thus while the relative balance of the two main communal blocs is slowly changing, the real transformation of Northern Ireland electoral politics is primarily within rather than across these blocs.

The transformation is most dramatically highlighted by reviewing relative party fortunes at Westminster elections. For example, in 1992 (the last election before the 'peace process' was officially launched via the paramilitary ceasefires of 1994), the long dominant UUP had 9 of its members elected as

MPs and the DUP had 3 (from a total of 17 seats in Northern Ireland). In 2005 the UUP finally became a victim of the distorting single-member plurality (SMP) electoral system from which it had always previously been the principal beneficiary (see Mitchell and Gillespie, 1999).[1] The UUP, which as recently as 1997 controlled 10 of Northern Ireland's Westminster seats, was virtually wiped out in 2005 and managed to hold on to only a single seat; by contrast Ian Paisley's DUP won 9 seats (from a total of 18). The UUP's share of the vote was not of course quite as bad as a simple 'head count' of the MPs elected suggests. Still, the fact that SMP greatly exaggerates a party's losses is likely to be of little comfort to the UUP: its share of the vote in 2005 at 17.7 per cent is roughly half its total in 1992 (34.5 per cent). On the nationalist side the SDLP won 4 Westminster seats in 1992 and 3 in 2005. Meanwhile Sinn Féin went from no seats in 1992 to 5 in 2005.

While each party's number of Westminster MPs is a symbolically important means of 'signalling the score' in intra-bloc electoral competition, the sheer scale of the transformation in voting behaviour is revealed by the raw vote totals displayed in Figure 8.1 for the last four Westminster elections. In 1992 the UUP was by far the largest party and attracted just over 270,000 votes. By 2005 the party attracted less than half this number (47 per cent of the 1992 total).[2] By contrast, the DUP has grown from about 100,000 voters in 1992 to just under a quarter of a million in 2005 (see the fourth column of each party's votes of Figure 8.1 to compare the 2005 results). Over the same time period Sinn Féin has more than doubled its raw vote total, while the number of people voting for the SDLP in 2005 is only 68 per cent of the number of those willing to do so in 1992, immediately prior to the ceasefires. If we look at the shape of Figure 8.1 (and especially the fourth column of each party's votes which shows the 2005 results) it can be seen that the much-touted centre ground of Northern Ireland politics, which began sinking in 2001, has now sunk even further. The Alliance Party is increasingly in danger of not existing at all (in anything other than local government elections), while the long-dominant UUP and SDLP have been successfully outflanked by their more militant rivals in their respective communal blocs.

The timing of the electoral surges by Sinn Féin and the DUP are related but not identical. Following its first electoral contest in 1982 Sinn Féin's vote was essentially flat-lining at around 11 per cent, its average performance during the ten elections between 1982 and 1994. The 1994 IRA cessation of its armed campaign was clearly the catalyst for Sinn Féin's renewed electoral advances. The ceasefire, Sinn Féin's de facto acceptance of the consent principle (i.e. that Irish unification requires the consent of majorities in both Irish jurisdictions), and later its enthusiastic participation in all of the Agreement's institutions, has rendered the party much more acceptable and attractive to

Figure 8.1 Westminster elections, 1992–2005

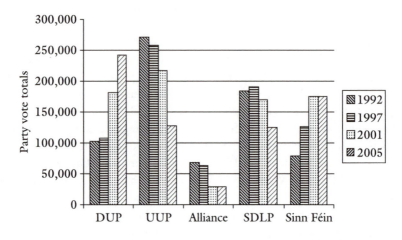

wider groups of nationalist voters. Figure 8.2 shows that the Sinn Féin vote immediately jumped at the first post-ceasefire election in 1996, and has followed a consistently upward trajectory ever since.[3] While there is evidence that much of Sinn Féin's early electoral growth (in the 1980s and even 1990s) was achieved by mobilising nationalist non-voters and new-age cohorts rather than by directly winning over SDLP partisans (Mitchell, 1999; McAllister, 2004), this has began to change in the elections after the Agreement (see discussion below). The peace process has clearly been the handmaiden of Sinn Féin's electoral growth; its incorporation into 'ordinary politics' has undermined the distinctiveness of the SDLP's strategic position as the 'acceptable face' of nationalist politics, and its principal bargaining actor. Especially for many younger nationalist voters, the question increasingly arises: why not vote for the fresher and more assertive brand of nationalism?

By contrast, the DUP's electoral surge came later and has been even more dramatic. The DUP had long been the leading proponent of what can be characterised as the 'Ulster says no' policy position: 'no' to virtually any policy initiative by the UK government which involved concessions to nationalists. The DUP was of course vociferously opposed to the Anglo-Irish Agreement of 1985, the Downing Street Declaration of December 1993, and the Framework Documents of 1995. All these were portrayed as 'betrayals' and 'capitulations' to the 'pan-nationalist front'. But almost three decades of stridently oppositional politics delivered only modest electoral growth for the DUP. The key event in explaining the DUP electoral surge has clearly been the 1998 Agreement: the implementation difficulties in the following years became a major electoral liability for the UUP and a great opportunity for the DUP – an opportunity that has been seized with relish.

Figure 8.2 Changing party fortunes before and after the 'peace process' and the Agreement: Westminster and Assembly elections

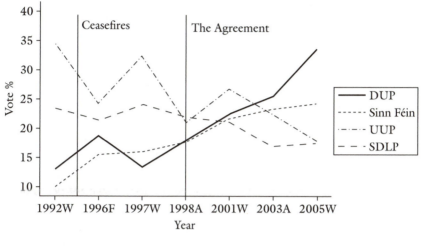

W = Westminster
A = Assembly
D = Forum for pene reconciliation

The average DUP vote before the Agreement (1973–97) was 15 per cent, whereas after the Agreement (1998–2005) it has been 25 per cent.[4] The DUP successfully took advantage of the UUP's internal difficulties after 1998 and received electoral benefits by moderating its policy position (Mitchell, O'Leary and Evans, 2001). Far from calling for the Belfast Agreement to be scrapped, the DUP called for its renegotiation. The DUP's best-known rallying cries of 'no surrender' and absolute opposition to any 'Dublin interference' in Northern Ireland had morphed by 2001 into a demand that any North–South institutional relationships be rendered more palatable by requiring that they be made more fully accountable to the devolved administration in Belfast.

This more nuanced opposition to another Anglo-Irish initiative repositioned the party more competitively, especially in relation to the disaffected supporters of an openly fractious UUP. The DUP had a long history as a party that favoured devolution, and neither the party nor many of its potential supporters wanted to bring down the new Assembly, they just wanted it run in a different manner, without Sinn Féin in government. The DUP was greatly aided by the plight of the UUP leader, David Trimble, continually trying to persuade his party to continue supporting the Agreement despite the failure of the IRA to start and then complete the decommissioning of its weapons.

While the latter eventually occurred in late 2005, it all came too late for Trimble. In short, Figure 8.2 shows that since 1998 the DUP vote has steadily and sharply risen, whereas since 2003 the UUP vote has gone into a tail spin.

In the next sections we will examine changing voter behaviour, first briefly on the question of the Agreement itself, and then more extensively on the fortunes of the parties.

Voting behaviour and the Belfast Agreement

Although the referendum approving the Agreement was passed with a 'yes' vote of 71 per cent on 22 May 1998,[5] it is well known that this high overall support masks a sharp difference of opinion between nationalists and unionists. The 1998 Referendum and Election Study found that 99 per cent of Catholics voted for the Agreement, but only 57 per cent of Protestants did so (Hayes and McAllister, 2001). Thus nationalist voters are almost unanimously in favour of the Agreement while support among unionists has always been precarious, not least since both communities believe that nationalists have been the principal beneficiaries of the Agreement and its institutions.

Of course the overall support figures for Protestants also masks a sharp party political difference of opinion within the unionist community. The DUP had, after all, walked out of the negotiations that produced the Agreement and campaigned against it during the referendum and subsequent 1998 Assembly elections. The UUP delegation to the negotiations agreed to accept the Agreement, but only by a majority vote, which prompted several of its

Table 8.1. Vote on the Belfast Agreement by party classification, 1998 and 2003 (%)

	UUP		DUP		APNI		SDLP		SF		Total	
	1998	2003	1998	2003	1998	2003	1998	2003	1998	2003	1998	2003
Yes	76	58	18	12	95	86	99	96	97	97	78	65
No	24	42	82	88	5	14	1	4	3	3	22	35

Notes. Estimates are the percentage of respondents who say they would vote 'yes' or 'no', and exclude non-voters, the unregistered and 'don't knows'. The 2003 survey question was 'If the vote on the Good Friday Agreement was held again today, how would you vote?'. The classification by party is based on party identification. The 1998 figures are based on a question in the 1999 survey asking respondents how they voted in the actual 1998 referendum.

Source: Northern Ireland Life and Times Survey 1999 and 2003.

Table 8.2. Change in vote on the Belfast Agreement by party,
1998–2003 (%)

	UUP	DUP	APNI	SDLP	SF	Total
Consistent Yes	60	8	88	97	95	59
Consistent No	15	60	12	1	1	23
Yes to No	24	30	–	2	4	18
No to Yes	1	2	–	–	–	1
(N)	(151)	(155)	(24)	(107)	(81)	(543)

Notes: The survey question for 2003 as in Table 8.1 and party classification is based on voting
at the 2003 Northern Ireland Assembly election and excludes non-voters and 'don't knows'.
For 1998 the question was: 'And how did you vote in 1998 when the referendum on the
Agreement was held?'.

Source: Northern Ireland Life and Times Survey 2003.

members also to walk out of the talks and to campaign openly for the
Agreement's rejection in the referendum.[6] Table 8.1 shows that 82 per cent
of DUP supporters say they voted against the Agreement in 1998, and their
opposition has since grown. The biggest change appears to be among UUP
voters: while 76 of them recall voting for the Agreement in 1998, their
support for a new 'yes' vote had dropped to 58 per cent by 2003.[7] Table 8.1
reports contemporaneous views concerning the Agreement: how the respondents say they would vote at the point in time at which they were asked. But
in order to track changing voting behaviour over time, it is useful to ask the
same respondents how they voted in 1998 and whether they would now
change their vote. For example if they were 'yes' voters in 1998, would they
now vote 'yes' or 'no'? This is precisely what Table 8.2 does.[8]

In short, what we see is that 60 per cent of UUP voters have consistently
supported the Agreement, and an equal number of DUP voters have consistently opposed it. The data confirm that substantial numbers of the 1998 'yes'
voters of both unionist parties report that they would change their vote if a
new referendum on the Agreement was held. Of those unionists who voted
'yes' in 1998, 24 per cent of UUP voters and 30 per cent of DUP voters say
they would now vote 'no'.

The demographics of party support

Despite pervasive electoral change, some things remain the same. Probably
the single most 'stable' feature of Northern Ireland electoral politics is that
the four main parties remain ethnically exclusive. Of those claiming to have

Table 8.3. Patterns of party support, 2003

	Total	*UUP*	*DUP*	*SDLP*	*SF*	*APNI*
Catholic	35	1	1	90	94	17
Protestant	61	95	97	8	–	55
No religion	4	4	2	2	6	28
18–44	42	32	44	39	58	30
45–65	39	39	37	44	36	47
65+	19	29	19	17	6	23
Male	47	50	46	43	55	53
Female	53	50	54	57	45	47
A level or higher	23	29	12	27	19	44
No formal qualifications	46	38	58	43	55	16
Professional/ managerial/ skilled non-manual	56	68	51	58	33	70
Manual (skilled, partly skilled and non-skilled)	44	32	49	42	67	30
Church attendance:						
Once a month or more	58	49	49	84	73	37
Less than once a month or ever	42	51	51	16	27	63
Reduce income differentials:						
Strongly agree/agree	53	41	50	63	71	31
Strongly disagree/ disagree	15	29	15	20	10	35

Note: The party support question was 'Which party did you vote for as your first preference in the recent [2003] Northern Ireland Assembly elections'. Non-voters and 'don't knows' are excluded. The income differential question was: 'It is the responsibility of the government to reduce the differences in income between people with high incomes and those with low incomes'. Response categories were a five-point scale, ranging from 'strongly agree' to 'strongly disagree'.

Source: Northern Ireland Life and Times Survey 2003.

voted in the 2003 Assembly elections, UUP and DUP partisans were almost entirely Protestant, while SDLP and Sinn Féin voters were overwhelmingly Catholic (see Table 8.3). Only the Alliance Party attracts voters from both communities, though as we have seen, the party is of diminishing size and importance. While observers of Northern Ireland politics understandably tend to focus on the 'big constitutional and governance questions', there is greater social and attitudinal patterning to party support than is often realised (see Evans and Duffy, 1997). In the nationalist party system, Sinn Féin voters are clearly much younger than SDLP partisans. Fifty-eight per cent of Sinn Féin voters are under 45, compared to less than 40 per cent of SDLP voters (see Table 8.3). Sinn Féin voters are also more likely (than SDLP voters) to be male, to be less educated, less religious and are much more likely to be manual workers.

On the unionist side the patterns are similar, with DUP voters tending to be younger than their UUP rivals. However, although the DUP and Sinn Féin are more attractive to younger voters, younger people as a group are much less likely to vote. In the 2003 survey 37 per cent of those under 45 said they did not vote in the 2003 Assembly election, compared with 28 per cent across all age groups. DUP voters are much less likely to be educated, with 58 per cent having no formal qualifications, compared to 38 per cent among UUP voters. It is not surprising then that UUP voters are much more likely to be from professional and managerial occupations. Finally, there is one question at the bottom of Table 8.3 which relates to one aspect of a socio-economic left–right dimension (whether governments should be tasked with reducing income differentials). This suggests that both nationalist parties take a more 'left-wing' position than the unionist parties, and that among unionists the DUP are to the left of the UUP (see also Evans and Duffy, 1997: 65).

Voting behaviour and changing party fortunes

Largely because it feared victories by the DUP and Sinn Féin in their respective blocs, the UK government twice postponed the 2003 Assembly election which should have been held by June (which marked the end of the Assembly's regular term). After no breakthrough in negotiations, the government eventually allowed the elections to be held on 26 November, after which it expected a quite different bargaining context to emerge. The election took place during a period in which the peace process was clearly stalled. The optimism of 1998 was either gone, or severely dented – given that durable power-sharing had not been established during the intervening five years. Also since the Assembly and its Executive had been suspended for over a year before the election, there was little prospect of further development of the pro-Agreement versus anti-Agreement division, which might encourage electoral cooperation between the UUP, SDLP and Sinn Féin. Partly because the innovative inter-ethnic pro-Agreement coalition had collapsed, it was always likely that the 2003 contest would revert to the traditional mould of Northern Ireland elections: a fierce intra-ethnic battle within the main blocs, with the rival parties mainly focused on emerging as their communities pre-eminent party.

Table 8.4. Assembly elections, 2003 and 1998

Party	2003 % votes	1998 % votes	2003 Seats (n)	1998 Seats (n)
DUP	25.6 (+7.5)	18.1	30 (+10)	20
Sinn Féin	23.5 (+5.8)	17.7	24 (+6)	18
UUP	22.7 (+1.4)	21.3	27 (–1)	28
SDLP	17.0 (–5.0)	22.0	18 (–6)	24
APNI	3.7 (–2.8)	6.5	6 (0)	6
PUP	1.2 (–1.4)	2.5	1 (–1)	2
NIWC	0.8 (–0.8)	1.6	0 (–2)	2
UKUP	0.7 (–3.8)	4.5	1 (–4)	5
Others	4.8	5.9	1 (–2)	3
Total	100	100	108	108
Turnout	64.0%	69.9%		

Source: Constructed from data at www.ark.ac.uk/elections.

There was indeed a very significant alteration in party fortunes between the first and second Assembly elections. The aggregate results are summarised in Table 8.4. Thus in 2003 the British governments recurring nightmare came to pass: the two 'extremist' parties, the DUP and Sinn Féin, came to dominate their respective communities. The DUP became the biggest party in Northern Ireland by gaining 7.5 per cent, a 42 per cent increase on its 1998 vote. The UUP slipped to third position, although its first preference vote was not as bad as widely expected, and even increased slightly. Nevertheless, the ratio of DUP to UUP voters was 53:47, the first time that the DUP had overtaken its rival in anything other than the unrepresentative European Parliament elections. The DUP won 30 seats in the Assembly, the number required to invoke the 'minority veto' provision of the consociational architecture – 'the petition of concern'. In reality of course, reaching this threshold would not now be so important since no government could be formed without the DUP's participation. Indeed, the election results underestimate the extent of the DUP's current dominance because following the election three anti-Agreement candidates (Norah Beare, Jeffrey Donaldson and Arlene Foster), who had just been elected on the UUP ticket, resigned and joined the DUP. Thus the DUP now had 33 MLA to the UUP's 24.

Given this reversal of fortunes in the unionist party system, a key question emerges: where did all these new DUP voters come from, and why did the UUP vote not correspondingly decline? The answer is that of those who voted for the UUP in 1998, just over one-fifth of them defected in 2003 to the DUP (Hayes, McAllister and Dowds, 2005; Mitchell, Evans and O'Leary, n.d.). The UUP managed to maintain its first preference vote in 2003, despite these direct losses to the DUP, because it gained 16 per cent of its 2003 vote from those who had supported the 'other' small unionist parties in 1998, especially the United Kingdom Unionist Party (UKUP) and the Ulster Democratic Party (UDP). All these smaller parties declined in 2003 (with the UDP even failing to contest the election), as reflected in the index of the effective number of elective parties (ENEP) declining from 6.1 in 1998 to 4.9 in 2003. Given that these minor unionist parties no longer have any electoral strength (for example the strongest of them, the Progressive Unionist Party, managed only 0.7 per cent in the 2005 local government elections), the electoral lifeline they provided for the UUP in 2003 was a one-time shift in support that cannot be repeated. Thus, while there was much discussion in 1996 of a 'splintering of the unionist vote', by 2003 it had consolidated with the DUP as its leading voice.

Sinn Féin marginally overhauled the SDLP in both the Westminster and local government elections of 2001, when the ratio between the two parties was 51:49 (Mitchell, O'Leary and Evans, 2001). Among nationalists, Sinn Féin was clearly the party with the electoral wind in its sails and it sought to confirm its dominance in 2003. Sinn Féin surpassed expectations by gaining 23.5 per cent of the first preference vote (a 33 per cent increase on its 1998 Assembly vote), while the SDLP vote declined by 23 per cent (compared to its 1998 vote) to produce a new two-party ratio of 58:42 in Sinn Féin's favour. While it has long been shown that much of Sinn Féin's electoral growth prior to the Agreement was achieved by mobilising prior non-voters and new voters, rather than directly attracting SDLP partisans, the scale of the apparent 'swing in the two-party vote' in 2003 renders this explanation much less credible for the most recent elections.[9] Sinn Féin must have won over prior SDLP partisans in order to fuel an electoral surge of this magnitude.[10] Survey evidence demonstrates that this is indeed what happened. Of those who voted for the SDLP in the 1998 Assembly election, almost one-fifth defected to Sinn Féin in 2003. By contrast, 94 per cent of those who voted for Sinn Féin in 1998 continued to do so in 2003. Another way of looking at this is to consider the composition of the Sinn Féin vote in 2003, which contained 28 per cent who had been SDLP voters in 1998 (Mitchell, Evans and O'Leary, n.d.). There is no question that recent Sinn Féin electoral growth has been principally at the SDLP's expense.

Party political attitudes to the Agreement and its institutions

These changes in voting behaviour, mostly in favour of the DUP and Sinn Féin (and which have continued since the election of 2003), would be much less likely if voters did not perceive that the parties in each bloc are adopting distinctive policy positions. Table 8.5 reviews voters attitudes to the

Table 8.5. Political attitudes to the Agreement, 2003

	Total	UUP	DUP	SDLP	SF
1 *Overall, the last Northern Ireland Assembly achieved . . .*					
A lot or a little	63	66	50	68	75
Nothing at all	34	31	47	31	22
2 *How good a job did the Assembly and Executive do in the ordinary day-to-day running of Northern Ireland?*					
A good job	27	22	11	41	53
A bad job	22	16	40	19	10
3 *What should be done about the Agreement?*					
Basically right and just needs to be implemented in full	23	14	1	35	62
Basically right but the specifics need to be renegotiated	38	50	23	50	27
Basically wrong and should be renegotiated	19	21	36	2	2
Basically wrong and should be abandoned	13	8	36	2	2
4 *Any Northern Ireland government should have to ensure that Protestants and Catholics share power.*					
Strongly agree/agree	81	85	62	95	89
Disagree	8	5	19	2	5
5 *Should parties linked to paramilitaries still involved in violence be allowed in any future Northern Ireland Executive?*					
No	77	93	95	63	36
6 *Do you think that reform of the police has . . .*					
Gone too far	44	64	81	3	2
Not gone far enough	25	9	5	41	76
About right	24	25	11	44	15
7 *Trust in the UK government to work in Northern Ireland's long-term interest.*					
Always/most of the time	25	27	11	45	10
Only some of the time	45	53	46	39	36
Almost never	29	20	41	12	50

Table 8.5. (continued)

	Total	UUP	DUP	SDLP	SF
8 *To what extent should the Republic of Ireland be involved in Northern Ireland affairs?*					
A lot	17	2	1	24	69
A little	38	47	16	65	28
Not at all	42	50	82	6	3

Note: Party classification is by voters in the Northern Ireland Assembly election 2003.

Source: Northern Ireland Life and Times Survey 2003.

Agreement and its institutions classified by partisan affiliation (based on the most recent evidence, which is from 2003).[11] Some quite clear patterns emerge.

When asked to rate the overall achievements of the last Northern Ireland Assembly, between two-thirds and three-quarters of the voters of the three principal pro-Agreement parties believed that such achievements were evident. Sinn Féin voters are the most enthusiastic about the Assembly, but by contrast almost half of DUP voters believed that it had achieved nothing at all. There is strong (81 per cent) overall and cross-party support for mandatory power-sharing between Catholics and Protestants: even 62 per cent of DUP voters agreed with this (see question 5 in Table 8.5). There continues to be less consensus on North–South relationships. Faced with the question 'to what extent should the Republic of Ireland be involved in Northern Ireland's affairs', 82 per cent of DUP voters in 2003 replied 'not at all'. UUP voters were evenly divided on the subject (see question 9 in Table 8.5), while, as expected, virtually all nationalists feel that Dublin should have a role, with Sinn Féin voters feeling it should have a much bigger role than SDLP voters. Policing is well known to be a contentious issue and most unionists feel that reform of the police has 'gone too far', while of course Sinn Féin supporters argue that it has not gone far enough. Overall, voters of the DUP and Sinn Féin are the most likely to believe that the UK government cannot be trusted to work in Northern Ireland's long-term interest.

Some interesting patterns emerge when voters were effectively asked 'what should be done about the Agreement?' (question 3 in Table 8.5). The answers suggest a close congruence between the respective parties', current policy positions and the views of their voters. Surely the mantra of Sinn Féin leaders in recent years has been that the Agreement is basically right and 'just needs to be implemented'. Sixty-two per cent of Sinn Féin voters picked this option when faced with the survey question: more than double the number of SDLP voters who thought likewise, whereas very few unionists thought this was the solution to the impasse. SDLP voters certainly think that the Agreement is 'basically right', but half of them thought that some of its specifics need to be renegotiated. There is a dramatic contrast between the two unionist parties: 64 per cent of UUP voters believe that the Agreement is 'basically right', while only 24 per cent of DUP supporters share that opinion. Indeed, 72 per cent of DUP voters said that the Agreement was 'basically wrong', with a large proportion believing that it should be abandoned altogether. Nevertheless, if one wanted to attempt to distil some optimism, although 36 per cent of DUP voters opted for abolition, 60 per cent of DUP voters thought that the best course of action was to renegotiate either the Agreement or some of its specifics. 'Renegotiate' is a significantly different policy position from the DUP's pre-Agreement mantra of simply 'Ulster says no'.

Conclusion

The elections of 2003 and 2005 confirm quite decisively that the DUP and Sinn Féin are now the leading parties representing the unionist and nationalist communities. For now, the electoral verdict 'is in': the once 'extreme' parties have successfully out-flanked and partially replaced their more moderate intra-ethnic rivals. For two years following the 2003 Assembly election, the DUP was able to avoid the tough question of whether it would lead a new government containing Sinn Féin, because of the IRA's failure to decommission its weapons. The IRA's announcement of the end of its armed campaign in July 2005, followed by the judgement of the Independent International Commission on Decommissioning in September that the IRA had decommissioned 'the totality of the IRA's arsenal', will make it progressively more difficult for the DUP to avoid negotiations on forming a new government and/or renegotiation of the Agreement. Based on current electoral strength, the DUP has some substantial incentives to lead a new coalition. In addition to selecting the First Minister, the d'Hondt portfolio allocation procedure means that the DUP would be entitled to four other Executive members (with two each for the UUP, Sinn Féin and the SDLP). Elections are not just about representing opinion; they are intrinsically about acquiring bargaining strength to be deployed during government formation, so that ultimately party policies can be implemented. It remains to be seen whether the DUP is willing to use its new-found electoral strength to become Northern Ireland's leading party of government.

Notes

1 The Gallagher index of disproportionality reveal that the 2005 results were 'typically disproportional' with a least squares (LSQ) index score of 14.9, following the aberration of the 2001 results, which were surprisingly proportional for a Northern Ireland SMP election (7.3 in 2001). The 1983–2005 average level of disproportionality is 16.2. For an explanation of the index see Gallagher and Mitchell (2005: Appendix B).

2 This kind of raw comparison can of course be affected by different levels of turnout. However, during the 1992, 1997 and 2001 elections roughly similar numbers of votes were cast (785, 123, 790, 889, and 810, 833 respectively). The only large decline was in 2005 when only 717, 502 votes were cast. Nevertheless, even *if* a sizeable proportion of non-voters are disillusioned former UUP supporters, the fact remains that they did not vote for the UUP in 2005.

3 Sinn Féin's average pre-1994 vote was 11 per cent (with a standard deviation of only 1.2), whereas its average post-1994 is 20 per cent (standard deviation of 3.4).

4 All figures exclude European Parliament elections, which are a very misleading measure of relative party strengths.

5 On a turnout of 81 per cent, the highest ever for a UK referendum.

6 In an early warning of worse things to come, the acrimony within the UUP was such that some of its leading anti-Agreement members, such as Jeffrey Donaldson, were prevented from standing as official UUP candidates in the 1998 Assembly elections (Wilford 1999).

7 Among Protestants as a whole (rather than just DUP and UUP supporters), only 40 per cent in 2003 said they would now vote for the Agreement (source: Northern Ireland Life and Times Survey 2003).

8 The table is of a similar format to a table first used in Hayes, McAllister and Dowds (2005), although the classification there is by religion rather than party voting.

9 Especially since there were no minor nationalist parties from which the SDLP might seek to offset any losses of its partisans to Sinn Féin.

10 Assuming that significant numbers of unionists had not suddenly found the SDLP attractive! This is a safe assumption, confirmed by the data.

11 The fieldwork for the 2003 Northern Ireland Life and Times Survey was carried out from October 2003 until February 2004.

References

Evans, G. and Duffy, M. (1997) 'Beyond the sectarian divide: the social bases and political consequences of nationalist and unionist party competition in Northern Ireland', *British Journal of Political Science*, 27, 47–81.

Gallagher, M. and Mitchell, P. (2005) *The Politics of Electoral Systems*. Oxford: Oxford University Press.

Hayes, B.C. and McAllister, I. (2001) 'Who voted for peace? Public support for the 1998 Northern Ireland Peace Agreement', *Irish Political Studies*, 16, 73–94.

Hayes, B.C., McAllister, I. and Dowds, L. (2005) ' The erosion of consent: Protestant disillusionment with the 1998 Northern Ireland Agreement', *Journal of Elections, Public Opinion and Parties*, 15 (2), 147–167.

Mitchell, P. (1999) 'The party system and party competition', in P. Mitchell and R. Wilford (eds) *Politics in Northern Ireland*. Boulder, Co: Westview Press.

Mitchell, P. and Gillespie, G. (1999) 'The Electoral Systems', in P. Mitchell and R. Wilford (eds) *Politics in Northern Ireland*. Boulder, CO: Westview Press, 66–90.

Mitchell, P., O'Leary, B. and Evans, G. (2001) 'Northern Ireland: flanking extremists bite the moderates and emerge in their clothes', *Parliamentary Affairs*, 54(4), 725–742.

Mitchell, P., Evans, G. and O'Leary, B. (typescript), 'Extremist outbidding in ethnic party systems is not inevitable: tribune parties in Northern Ireland'.

McAllister, I. (2004) ' "The Armalite and the ballot box": Sinn Fein's electoral strategy in Northern Ireland', *Electoral Studies* 23, 123–142.

Wilford, R. (1999) 'Epilogue' in P. Mitchell and R. Wilford (eds) *Politics in Northern Ireland*. Boulder, CO: Westview Press.

9
Symbols and identity in the 'new' Northern Ireland

Dominic Bryan and Gillian McIntosh

The 1998 Agreement set a new political context by affirming the current position of Northern Ireland as part of the new devolved context within the UK and, at the same time, recognising the particular circumstances of Northern Ireland within the island of Ireland. It did this by creating a unique set of political institutions governing power-sharing within Northern Ireland and the relationship between the UK and the Republic of Ireland.

> The participants . . . will:
> . . . (v) affirm that whatever choice is freely exercised by a majority of the people of Northern Ireland, the power of the sovereign government with jurisdiction there shall be exercised with rigorous impartiality on behalf of *all the people in the diversity of their identities and traditions* and shall be founded on the principles of full respect for, and equality of, civil, political, social and cultural rights, of freedom from discrimination for all citizens, and of *parity of esteem* and of just and equal treatment for the identity, ethos, and aspirations of *both communities.* (NIO, 1998: 2; our italics)

While the Agreement uses the language of plurality, it is essentially a political agreement designed to regulate two political blocs, unionism and nationalism, which broadly represent the Protestant and Catholic communities. This is intended to ensure 'that all sections of the community are protected', although only two communities are named, thus replicating communal politics in Northern Ireland. As such, within the Agreement there is a double bind. The concept of 'parity of esteem' involves the recognition of two cultural blocs and the Agreement suggests that the integrity of these cultural blocs should be acknowledged through the development of a Bill of Rights for Northern Ireland (Bryan, 2004). Yet it also looks to plurality in the hope that more inclusive forms of belonging can be found, possibly a hyphenated British–Irish form around a common Northern Irishness.

This double bind is perhaps revealed most acutely in the cultural aspects of the Agreement, in particular the way that rituals and symbols are dealt with in order to develop identities within the new context. Northern Ireland has a long history of conflict over rituals and symbols, with particular intensity being reserved for parades and flags (Loftus, 1990, 1994; Feldman, 1991; Rolston, 1991, 1992, 1995, 1999; Jarman, 1993, 1997; Bryson and McCartney, 1994; Buckley and Kenny, 1995; Bryan, 2000; Santino, 2001; Mac Ginty and Darby, 2002; Nic Craith, 2002; Brown and Mac Ginty, 2003; McCormick and Jarman, 2005; Bryan and Gillespie, 2005). Indeed, the Agreement cautiously refers to symbols:

> All participants acknowledge the sensitivity of the use of symbols and emblems for public purposes, and the need in particular in creating new institutions to ensure that such symbols and emblems are used in a manner which promotes mutual respect rather than division. Arrangements will be made to monitor this issue and consider what action might be required. (NIO, 1998: 20)

This chapter has two objectives. First to look at the influence, if any, this section of the Agreement has had on how symbols are dealt with either by political parties or by public bodies, in other words, to see how sensitive the participants to the Agreement have been in the use of symbols. Second, to see what attempts have been made to symbolise the new political status of Northern Ireland after the Agreement. This will be done by taking an overview of a number of case studies and be guided by a model developed by Harrison that argues that strategically symbols are (a) invented, (b) ranked in value, (c) appropriated by different groups and (d) destroyed or suppressed (Harrison, 1995). This is based on the simple premise that the use of symbols is a dynamic process reflecting changes in political circumstances and, moreover, that political strategies over the use of symbols will adjust to these circumstances. Perhaps the most famous recent example of this, from another peace process, was when Nelson Mandela put on a South African Springbok rugby shirt, an emblem of white South Africa, during the final of the 1995 Rugby World Cup Final.

Of course the political context in Northern Ireland since 1998 has not been one of stability. The Assembly operated for periods totalling less than two and a half years between 1998 and 2005. This, and the general political conditions, clearly influenced the likelihood of local political actors undertaking new symbolic strategies. Despite this, new strategies were developed by the British government, local policy makers and occasionally by political parties and representatives. In addition, legislation introduced at Westminster, as part of the Agreement, also influenced a range of public agencies and local councils.

Conflict on a landscape of symbols

It is instructive when looking at the conflict in Northern Ireland to see how much political time and legislation is spent debating and controlling symbols.

For example, public order legislation in the rest of the UK was originally developed to deal with fascist demonstrations in the 1930s and has since been routinely used and altered over labour disputes, to restrict neo-Nazi groups and their opposition, and most recently in the name of counter-acting terrorism. In Northern Ireland public order legislation was introduced in 1951, revised in 1970, 1971 and 1981, and then again in 1987, 1997 and 2005 (Hadden and Donnelly, 1997: 19–21). While it bears resemblance to the UK legislation, it was driven by particular local circumstances. It was a reflection of fundamental conflict over public spaces initiated by both civil rights demonstrations and a range of loyal order and loyalist parades. The Party Processions Act 1997 introduced a quite different public order regime to the rest of the UK, with a Parades Commission empowered to make determinations on disputed parades. The legislation on the control of parades pre-dated the Agreement but it was also introduced in recognition that the difficult political talks taking place leading up to the 1998 Agreement would have been made considerably more difficult if parades had been discussed. In the Agreement the only recognition of the tensions over parades is the paragraph on symbols quoted above.

The use of flags tells a similar story. The Flags and Emblems Act 1954 was specifically introduced to place public order controls on the popular use of flags, particularly, of course, displays of the flag of the Republic of Ireland, the Tricolour (Patterson, 1999). This Act was only repealed under the 1987 public order legislation. In addition, Irish nationalists have long complained about the over use of the Union flag on government and local council buildings. The Agreement offered no direct guidance on the use of flags, except the paragraph on symbols. Once the Assembly was up and running, the flying of flags on government buildings became an immediate issue. Unionists demanded that the Union flag be flown at all times. Sinn Féin called for both Union flag and Tricolour to be flown, but in practice their two ministers permitted no flags to be flown outside their departmental buildings. The lack of a Union flag outside the office building of the Department of Education, where Sinn Féin's Martin McGuinness was minister, led to a proliferation of Union flags being placed on surrounding lamp posts. Such was the contention that the then Secretary of State, Peter Mandelson, introduced The Flags (Northern Ireland) Order 2000. This designated particular days on which the Union flag should fly on designated government buildings. In October 2001 Sinn Féin requested a judicial review, arguing the legislation was 'not in keeping with the Good Friday Agreement'. The judgement found for the Secretary of State and argued that restricting the flying days to those practised in the rest of the UK struck a balance between acknowledging the constitutional position of Northern Ireland and those who opposed it (Bryan and Gillespie, 2005:18). A committee was set up by the new Assembly in

September 2000 to discuss the issue, but the collapse of the institutions meant there was little progress. The Alliance Party called for a new flag for Northern Ireland in January 2003, but none of the four larger political parties supported this strategy.

In contrast, Parliament Buildings, Stormont (in which the Assembly met) was an example of a new symbolic strategy working. In post-devolution Northern Ireland, public space, buildings and events offered the opportunity of sites that could provide for a shared sense of local identity. Not only is Stormont in east Belfast, a unionist-dominated area, but the building's history, architecture and the grounds it sits in are representative of Ulster unionism. For nationalists the very name 'Stormont' was synonymous with the inequities of unionist rule. Northern Ireland's first Prime Minister, Lord Craigavon, at Stormont's opening in 1932 expressed what it represented then: 'It is indeed a noble building, and will stand on its base of granite from the Mountains of Mourne, as a symbol of the link between Great Britain and Northern Ireland.' A building redolent of unionist supremacy, its reputation from the early years of the recent Troubles in the 1970s was as a heavily protected site, within which British ministers took shelter. As such, Parliament Buildings, Stormont was a problematic site as the home of the new Assembly, and was identified as such at an early stage by senior politicians.

The decision to keep it as the location of the new Assembly was both pragmatic and symbolic; the prohibitive cost of commissioning a new building combined with the fact that, following a fire there in 1995 (and the subsequent refitting), Parliament Buildings was a suitable and ready-made option. Mo Mowlam, Secretary of State for Northern Ireland (1997–2000), was the chief instigator of attempts to 'rebrand' the Stormont site (Mowlam, 2002: 57). For Linda Brown, in 1997 head of the government's Developing Stormont Committee, the symbolic importance of the site was even more basic; if Northern Ireland's politicians could not deal with the past and work together in Stormont, then it did not bode well for the future success of devolution. The Committee came up with a range of suggestions: tours by the public, function facilities for VIPs, charities and public bodies, a history exhibition, art exhibitions, public exhibitions, classical and popular music events, a children's playground, a visitors' car park, a gate-lodge coffee shop, an educational resource centre, revised security systems, facilities for sporting events, and parkland improvements. Mowlam was drawn to the concept of Stormont as a venue for popular concerts. Elton John performed at Stormont days after the passing of the referendum on the Agreement. It was described in the following celebratory terms in the *Irish Times*:

For the best part of a century, Sir Edward Carson has ruled the roost at Stormont Castle. A huge statue of the former Unionist leader, fist raised in the air, sits defiantly at the top of the hill. But last night, Stormont belonged to everyone . . . There wasn't a politician, flag or sectarian banner in sight. (28 May 1998)

This was a carefully managed media event, which placed Parliament Buildings centre-stage for the world's press. Indeed, this is literally true; members of the Developing Stormont Committee walked the grounds of the estate prior to the concert to work out logistically the optimum position for the stage, so that the building would dominate any photographs or camera shots.

Through a series of concerts, exhibitions and redevelopment of the estate, Parliament Buildings and the estate were effectively rebranded (Bryan and McIntosh, 2005). So in spite of Carson's statue, which still stands defiant in front of the building, Stormont has largely been reappropriated as a site for both nationalists and unionists. Indeed, since the Assembly being up and running has been linked to the success of the Agreement, a 'return to Stormont' has been heard more from nationalists than unionists. There were, however, conflicts over the use of symbols inside the building, such as a display of lilies in the lobby of the building in April 2001 to commemorate the republican dead.

For some of the new institutions it was relatively uncontroversial to develop new symbols, but reform of longer-standing institutions was harder. The new Assembly has a flax plant as its emblem, and the 11 new government departments have a representation of the Giants Causeway rock formation in County Antrim as their logo. The lack of controversy over these was probably not due to the unproblematic nature of these historical and geological emblems but because the institutions they represented were new. Far more problematic was the need for a new badge for the Police Service of Northern Ireland (PSNI). The issue of policing and security was central to the nature of the conflict in Northern Ireland. As such, police reform was one of the most controversial aspects of the Agreement. For unionists the Patten Report, *A New Beginning: Policing in Northern Ireland* (1999), was seen as a negation of Prime Minister Tony Blair's promise that the Royal Ulster Constabulary (RUC) would not be abolished. For nationalists the proposed reforms did not go far enough. Implicit in both attitudes were the conflicting unionist and nationalist views of the role of the RUC in the Troubles. During the debates an enormous amount of time was spent discussing issues of symbolism, particularly the RUC badge: a crown above a harp. The final decision over the new badge was left to the new Police Board, which included representatives of the main political parties, except Sinn Féin. The design which finally emerged was, in many ways, a reflection of the wider Agreement; compromise was initially difficult to achieve, alternative proposals produced by the government in

November 2001 were rejected but nevertheless worked to help bring Police Board members towards agreement, while a deadline (new police uniforms were being manufactured) helped to concentrate minds.

The new, agreed, PSNI badge contained a laurel leaf, a torch, a crown, a shamrock, a harp and scales surrounding the cross of St Patrick, all set on a six-pointed star. The greatest point of controversy surrounded the use of the crown, the shamrock and the harp with the crown as they had appeared in the old RUC badge. The Patten Report had recommended that the new badge contain no symbol connected with the British or Irish states in order to make it neutral, however this view was overridden by Secretary of State Peter Mandelson so that the new badge could include symbols which made it inclusive as opposed to neutral (Police (NI) Act 2000). As a result, the design of the new badge largely became one of horse-trading between the UUP and SDLP. In terms of the lack of controversy which now surrounds it, the badge itself could be said to be successful. Ironically, there are so many symbols on the badge that the individual components are difficult to discern, having the end effect of producing the neutral emblem originally envisaged by Patten.

What the debate over the police badge also indicates is that symbols always work in relation to one another. The very concept of 'parity of esteem' seems to suggest some sort of balancing act for the representation of the two ethno-political groups. This is more easily done in some areas than others. Royal visits have always been occasions of particular controversy in Northern Ireland because of the disputed nature of the state. For example, Elizabeth II visited Northern Ireland in 1966, a year rich with symbolism, being both the fiftieth anniversary of the Easter Rising and the Battle of the Somme, key sacred dates for nationalism and unionism respectively. On this occasion, Northern Ireland's Prime Minister hoped that the Queen would use her speech for the opening of the Queen Elizabeth II Bridge as an opportunity to endorse his policy of 'bridge building' across the community in Northern Ireland. The Queen however, did not, and her visit was marred by the controversy over the naming of the new bridge over the Lagan and two incidents when missiles were thrown at the royal cavalcade. In 1971 the Northern Ireland government was very anxious that Elizabeth II come to open Parliament as the highlight of their state's jubilee celebrations, symbolically reinacting her grandfather's actions in 1921. However, given the high level of civil disturbance, the British Home Secretary advised against it. Indeed, although the Queen paid a brief and tense one day visit to Northern Ireland for her silver jubilee in 1977 (her first visit since 1966), she was not to return to Northern Ireland until 1993.

While the peace process offered a new, improved, security context, it also created circumstances where the use of the head of state was problematic. So, for example, the opening of the new Scottish Parliament, 1 July 1999, by the Queen was not without controversy within Scotland, but such an event was impossible at the opening of the new Northern Ireland Assembly. In terms of ceremony, contemporary royal visits have taken place on a more restricted scale and have obviously been managed strategically. For instance, when Elizabeth II visited Northern Ireland in April 2000, she did so to present the (soon-to-be-disbanded) Royal Ulster Constabulary with the George Cross at Hillsborough. Politically, a visit to Northern Ireland during her golden jubilee year of 2002 had to be undertaken, but it was again relatively restricted with garden parties, a public visit to St Anne's Cathedral, Belfast (15 May 2002), and a visit to Stormont. On the visit to Stormont she was met by First Minister David Trimble (UUP) and Deputy First Minister Mark Durkan (SDLP), and members of other political parties except Sinn Féin. It is interesting that, at the same time, a story that the Queen might soon visit Dublin and that Irish President Mary McAleese might soon visit Stormont were also circulated. Both stories were an attempt to provide a context for the trip that suggested a delayed form of 'parity of esteem'. The fact that the Queen was not speaking at the Assembly had been noted by the DUP, who earlier in the year had tabled a motion at the Assembly suggesting that this would be a legitimate role for her on her visit.

Given that there has been no Assembly for much of the period after the Agreement, it is also instructive to look at the activities of local councils to see how the new political context has influenced their behaviour. With regard to flags, a range of practices are followed by district councils around Northern Ireland. These vary from the flying of the Union flag on a number of council buildings every day of the year, to flying no flags on any building or simply flying the council flag. Some councils have chosen to follow the legislation for government buildings and fly flags on designated days. There is a long history of conflict over this issue and a number of council officials interviewed would have liked legislation introduced for government buildings to have applied to council buildings as well. But legislation deriving from the Agreement has changed the context in which official flags are used. Section 75 of the Northern Ireland Act 1998 demands that a public authority, in carrying out its functions, should have 'due regard to the need to promote equality of opportunity' and should 'have regard to the desirability of promoting good relations'. Put simply, this has placed a duty upon councils to show how their policies meet equality and community relations obligations and the services they provide are available to all sections of the population equally. Additionally, fair employment legislation makes discrimination on the grounds of religious belief and political opinion unlawful both in the work place and in the provision of goods, facilities and services. This range of legalisation places local councils under some pressure with regard to their policies on flag flying. A number of councils have undertaken Equality Impact Assessments on their policies regarding flags, although as yet this process has not yielded significant policy changes. Nationalist-run councils have, as a strategy, placed greater value on the use of a local council flag, but no council has actually flown the Tricolour, despite the policy Sinn Féin advocated, in the name of parity of esteem, of flying both Union flag and Tricolour (Bryan and Gillespie, 2005). That said, Sinn Féin Councillor Alex Maskey, Lord Mayor of Belfast in 2002/3, did have both flags displayed in the mayoral office.

Another important area of the symbolic landscape of Northern Ireland, which also gives some indication of changing attitudes and identities, is the role of public events. In recent years there have been frequent debates over the funding of festivals and events such as Féile an Phobail (West Belfast Festival), Eleventh Night bonfires, the Twelfth of July and, perhaps most frequently, St Patrick's Day. For many people St Patrick's Day (17 March) represents the quintessential expression of what it means to be Irish. It is perhaps the world's most promiscuous national day, with celebrations in many parts of the world proclaiming that 'on St Patrick's Day everyone can be Irish'. St Patrick is not necessarily an anathema to unionists. Historically St Patrick has been commemorated within Protestantism in Ireland and in contemporary Northern Ireland has appeared on murals and is the subject of a number of Orange Order parades (Cronin and Adair, 2002: 191–195). In Belfast, however, where national identity, control of territory, symbolism and even the future of the state remain contested issues, the celebration of St Patrick's Day has been an arena for communal antagonism rather than one of mutual celebration. The first St Patrick's Day celebration in the city centre, in 1998, organised through the Féile an Phobail, displayed the full range of republican symbolism. Subsequent organisers of the St Patrick's Day Carnival have been more sensitive to issues of symbolism that the event has raised by, for example, attempting to utilise the flag of St Patrick in celebrations. However, organisers were not able to regain funding from Belfast City Council. Relations with the council have improved, leading to a council-funded celebration held in 2006, although not at the politically sensitive site of the City Hall. By way of contrast, in Downpatrick, the council-organised celebrations prohibit the carrying of any flag in the parade other than the St Patrick's cross or the flag of Down District Council. While this rule was objected to by republicans on the grounds that it banned their national flag, the Downpatrick celebration has prospered and grown (an estimated 20,000 people attended the Downpatrick celebration in 2005, compared to 4,500 in Belfast). The differences between the Belfast event and that organised by Downpatrick can, in part, be put down to 'ownership'. Down District Council is at the centre of arrangements for the Downpatrick event, whereas the Belfast event was originally organised, and is still closely associated with, republican orientated groups.

An example of contested symbolic space where interesting changes have been taking place is around the commemoration of the dead of the two world wars. At the beginning of the 1990s, Remembrance Day in Northern Ireland was marked publicly largely by unionist politicians and Protestant clergy, even though many members of the Catholic community had served in the forces in both world wars. In the early 1990s a number of SDLP Lord representatives began to attend Remembrance Day ceremonies in Belfast for the first time. In 1997 Alban Maginess became the first SDLP Lord mayor officially to place a wreath at the Belfast cenotaph. After significant engagement between key individuals over a number of years, Queen Elizabeth and President Mary McAleese, in September 1999, together opened a peace park at Messines in Belgium, built by groups from the North and South of Ireland in memory of all the Irish who died in the First World War. During the 1990s a new appreciation of those Irish who had fought in both world wars also developed in the Irish Republic, which served to encourage changes in Northern Ireland.

Sinn Féin representatives played no part in such events, although in 1995 Councillor Tom Hartley represented the party in Dublin at a ceremony to mark the end of the Second World War. In July 2002, however, Sinn Féin Lord Mayor of Belfast, Alex Maskey, laid a wreath at Belfast cenotaph in memory of First World War dead in a special act of remembrance. In April 2003 a cross-community service of remembrance for all those from Belfast who died in the First World War was held in St Anne's Cathedral in Belfast. Present were British crown and army representatives and republicans such as Alex Maskey. In 2004, however, Sinn Féin decided to ban its members from attending these events because they were criticised within the party as being linked to British interests. In late 2004 a number of Sinn Féin mayors organised a day of remembrance in December to remember those Irish dead in all war situations, but this event won little support.

Conclusions

In November 2004 the Scottish Parliament resolved a long-standing dispute over which flags should fly on the building at Holyrood when it was decided to fly the Saltire, the Union flag and the flag of the EU every day. While Scottish nationalists might not like the Union flag flying, the Scottish Saltire does at least provide a symbol to which nearly all Scots can show allegiance. Politics in Northern Ireland has historically had much less common ground. The 1998

Agreement simply asked participants for sensitivity in the use of symbols, suggesting that they should be used to promote mutual respect not division. The finding of such common symbolic ground, if it was associated with some political and communal consciousness, would, it was hoped, create a different political dynamic. So, for example, had a unionist and nationalist First and Deputy First Minister not only been meeting the Queen or Irish President or successful Ulster rugby or Gaelic Athletic Association (GAA) teams, but also doing so under a new flag for Northern Ireland, this would indicate a new political strategy on their part and also the possibility of a broader based civic allegiance. A sense of 'Northern Irishness' that would complement, but not exclude Britishness could be fostered. In the title of the government's 2005 policy document on community relations it would offer a *Shared Future*: 'The establishment over time of a normal, civic society, in which all individuals are considered as equals, where differences are resolved through dialogue in the public sphere, and where all people are treated impartially.'

The above examples, and others, reveal contrasting policy strategies resulting from the Agreement. Policy areas within the remit of the British government have attempted to negotiate the development of shared space (for example, Stormont, flags, the removing of crown imagery from courts and the police badge) either through direct policy and legal intervention or by indirect pressure through legislation and policy guidance. These policies have been negotiated in the midst of demands from political actors within the dominant ethnic groups, unionism and nationalism. So, for example, royal visits such as that of the Queen to recognise the role of the RUC were quite pragmatically used to try to balance the scales measuring parity of esteem, given unionist anger at the change of name to the Police Service of Northern Ireland.

Importantly, the context in which policies were being developed was not one that was conducive to any of the four major political parties promoting strategies that might develop new or shared symbolic space. While there are exceptions, mostly promoted by the SDLP and Sinn Féin (war commemoration), by far the most common strategy was to call for higher valuation to be placed upon symbols representing one or other political bloc (flags, St Patrick's Day) or strategies to appropriate particular events in specific ways (flags, St Patrick's Day and royal visits). While new emblems were developed to represent the new Assembly and the ministerial departments, the only contested symbol to be resolved through an agreed process was the emblem for the PSNI.

The Agreement has not heralded a reduction in symbolic conflict. Had the Assembly remained active it would have been interesting to see whether more imaginative symbolic strategies would have been used. We have some evidence that this can take place, with the development of new symbols for the Assembly and government departments and also the behaviour of some political parties in local government. Particularly notable were the actions of Alex Maskey described above. The holding of office offers opportunities as well as demanding different behaviour from politicians. Had David Trimble been First Minister in October 2003, would he have hosted a reception at Stormont for All Ireland GAA finalists Armagh and Tyrone, as Culture, Arts and Leisure Minister Angela Smith did? In the main, however, it has been British government ministers, and their departments, who have grappled with different strategies over symbols. Since their electoral interests are not tied to Northern Ireland, it has arguably been easier for them to do so.

From a policy perspective a range of agencies have attempted to modify the use of symbols, either by drawing upon the 'two traditions model' and 'parity of esteem' or by promoting neutral or shared space through the exclusion of symbols or the invention of new symbols. For example, the Northern Ireland Human Rights Commission has produced a draft Bill of Rights which, following on from the consociational nature of the Agreement, provides the two communities with particular recognition (Bryan, 2004), while *A Shared Future* concentrates on the shared and the neutral. Section 75 of the Northern Ireland Act 1998 and the Fair Employment and Treatment Order 1998 have provided the major legislative context for the symbolic strategies that have placed some pressure on local councils to modify policies. In the end, the pressure upon symbolic strategies has come from above rather than from within political interest groups in Northern Ireland.

Consequently, with minimal involvement of local political parties, we have seen very little evidence of the development of a new symbolic sense of Northern Irish identity, despite some evidence of people ascribing to other than unionist and nationalist identities. Rather, a range of legislative and policy developments have attempted to manage the relationship between unionism and nationalism, directed by a battery of public bodies. After an unsure start to devolution, the return of a power-sharing Northern Ireland government would place local political parties in political offices that would demand more imaginative approaches to the strategic use of symbols than has been evident in recent years. However, evidence thus far suggests that it is Westminster legislation that has most influenced changes in the symbolic landscape of Northern Ireland.

Note

1 Funding for this project was provided by the ESRC, under its devolution programme. The authors are grateful to Professor Brian Walker, Dr Gordon Gillespie and Dr John Nagle for their assistance on aspects of this chapter.

References

Brown, K. and Mac Ginty, R. (2003) 'Public attitudes towards partisan and neutral symbols in post-Agreement Northern Ireland'. *Identities: Global Structures in Culture and Power*, 10, 83–108.

Bryan, D. (2000) *Orange Parades: The Politics of Ritual Tradition and Control.* London: Pluto.

Bryan, D. (2004) 'Parading Protestants and consenting Catholics in Northern Ireland: communal conflict, consented public space, and group rights', *Chicago Journal of International Law*, 5 (1), 233–250.

Bryan, D. and Gillespie, G. (2005) *Transforming Conflict: Flags and Emblems.* Belfast: Institute of Irish Studies.

Bryan, D. and McIntosh, G. (2005) 'Symbols: sites of creation and contest in Northern Ireland', *SAIS Review*, 25 (2), 127–137.

Bryson, L. and McCartney, C. (1994) *Clashing Symbols: A Report on the Use of Flags, Anthems and Other National Symbols in Northern Ireland.* Belfast: Institute of Irish Studies.

Buckley, A. and Kenny, M. (1995) *Negotiating Identity: Rhetoric, Metaphor and Social Drama in Northern Ireland.* Washington: Smithsonian Institute Press.

Cronin, M. and Adair, D. (2002) *The Wearing of the Green: The History of St Patrick's Day.* London: Routledge.

Feldman, A. (1991) *Formations of Violence: The Narrative of the Body and Political terror in Northern Ireland.* Chicago: University of Chicago Press.

Hadden, T. and Donnelly, A. (1997) *The Legal Control of Marches in Northern Ireland.* Belfast: Community Relations Council.

Harrison, S. (1995) 'Four types of symbolic conflict', *Journal of the Royal Anthropoligical Institute (NS)*1, 255–272.

Jarman, N. (1993) 'Intersecting Belfast', in B. Bender (ed.) *Landscape: Politics and Perspectives.* Oxford: Berg, 107–183.

Jarman, N. (1997) *Material Conflicts: Parades and Visual Displays in Northern Ireland.* Oxford: Berg.

Loftus B. (1990) *Mirrors: William III and Mother Ireland.* Dundrum: Picture Press.

Loftus B. (1994) *Mirrors: Orange and Green.* Dundrum: Picture Press.

McCormick, J. and Jarman, N. (2005) 'Death of a mural', in *Journal of Material Culture*, 10 (1), 49–71.

Mac Ginty, R. and Darby, R. (2002) *Guns and Government: The Management of the Northern Ireland Peace Process.* Basingstoke: Palgrave.

Mowlam, M. (2002) *Momentum: The Struggle for Peace, Politics and the People.* London: Hodder and Stoughton.

Nic Craith, M. (2002) *Plural Identities – Singular Narratives: The Case of Northern Ireland.* Oxford: Berghahn Books.

NIO (Northern Ireland Office) (1998) *The Agreement. Agreement Reached in the Multi-Party Negotiations.* Belfast: NIO.

Patterson, H. (1999) 'Party versus order: Ulster unionism and the Flags and Emblems Act', *Contemporary British History* 13 (4), 105–129.

Rolston, B. (1991) *Politics and Painting: Murals and Conflict in Northern Ireland.* London and Toronto: Associated Universities Press.

Rolston, B. (1992) *Drawing Support 1: Murals in the North Ireland*. Belfast: Beyond the Pale Publications.

Rolston, B. (1995) *Drawing Support 2: Murals of War and Peace*. Belfast: Beyond the Pale Publications.

Rolston, B. (1999) *Drawing Support 3: Murals and Transition in the North of Ireland*. Belfast: Beyond the Pale Publications.

Santino, J. (2001) *Signs of War and Peace: Social Conflict and the Use of Public Symbols in Northern Ireland*. Basingstoke: Palgrave.

10

The changing role of women in the context of devolution

Margaret Ward

Despite the achievement of the Women's Coalition in gaining an acknowledgement of women's right to 'full and equal political participation' inserted into the Good Friday/Belfast Agreement, there has been little of the 'paradigm shift' regarding gender issues necessary if women are ever to achieve parity in terms of decision making in public and political life in Northern Ireland. Women from across the divide continue to urge that the commitment of the Agreement to ensure 'equal opportunity in all social and economic activity' must be lived up to. While these equality principles do 'transcend the binary "parity of esteem"'(Mackay and Meehan, 2003: 4), it remains more theoretical than actual, while discourses around equality and discrimination continue to focus upon religious and community affiliation. Women's inclusion within the transition process remains problematic in a number of key areas. This chapter offers a consideration of some major issues concerning gender parity and the role of women during a period of considerable political and administrative change.[1]

The period when a devolved Parliament was in existence, now fast becoming a distant memory, was too brief for definite conclusions concerning its potential for significant reform. That there were three female ministers heralded a rupture with the past in terms of women's symbolic representation. The assured performance of Bríd Rogers in particular, as Minister for Agriculture, demonstrated that women had the ability to transcend traditionally female silos of interest, while her ability to work harmoniously with Ian Paisley (her committee chair and political adversary) has been attributed in part to a female ability to work in a consensual manner (Breen, 2001).

Some commentators (Wilford, 2001; Wilford and Wilson 2000–2003) have been underwhelmed by the pace of change within the Assembly. There have been a number of studies on the performance of the 14 women MLAs and the difficulties facing those among that number who wished to promote women's interests. The lack of 'critical mass' was a definite hindrance in the development of a concerted strategy, while the level of misogyny within the chamber towards outspoken women was an additional burden for those who did not come from the unionist benches (Ward, 2000). It proved to be difficult to ensure that gender was inserted into vital policy areas. MacKay and Meehan (2003) give two pertinent examples: the first Programme for Government, which reiterated the commitment to bring about women's equality in public life, while omitting any mention of the importance of childcare in making this a reality; and an initial consideration of domestic violence, which focused on children to the exclusion of women. Women predominated in the committees concerned with health and education. Others felt pushed by their parties into taking part in these traditionally 'female' areas of policy. Some Assembly members spoke frankly to researchers of their wish to participate in other areas of decision making and expressed the hope that women would be given more prominence in initiatives like trade delegations and similar male-dominated, prestigious initiatives (Ward, 2000; Cowell-Meyers, 2003).

Given the existing political cleavages, Cowell-Meyers (2003: 10) concluded that 'gender is . . . not proving to be a particularly decisive force in the new Assembly'. However, MacKay and Meehan (2003: 7), in their wider survey of devolution, provide evidence to suggest that female Assembly members 'more often than their male counterparts' saw it as their role 'to bring public attention to unrecognised issues and to provide access for marginalised or excluded voices'. Of note is the occasion when the Assembly debated a DUP-inspired motion to prohibit the extension of the Abortion Act 1967 to Northern Ireland. Women were very active in the debate (Hansard, 2000). Joan Carson, Ulster Unionist MLA, spoke from the heart when she began her speech with the comment 'It is ironic that a man, who will never have to go through childbirth or face the personal consequences of unwanted pregnancy, is proposing the motion'. No woman spoke in favour of rejecting the Abortion Act.

Civil society access to politicians 'improved noticeably' in the post-devolution period (Mackay and Meehan, 2003: 12). The two Women's Coalition Assembly members facilitated a lobby of Stormont when a funding crisis hit the women's community and voluntary sector in March 2002. They received a sympathetic response from women from other political parties, with the result that £1 million of emergency funding from Executive Programme Funds was made available to women's groups (Taillon and McCann, 2002). In the November 2003 elections, 18 women were elected to the Assembly, raising the percentage total to 17 per cent. The Women's Coalition candidates did not retain their seats in an election which saw a polarisation of votes and large gains for the anti-Agreement DUP. An important result of the emergence of the Women's Coalition into the political scene was the 'fillip' it gave to the issue of women's under-representation in party politics, forcing parties to consider their own practice. The impact, according to *Field Day* editors, is that 'each party now claims to be woman friendly' (Crilly, Gordon, Rooney, 2002: 1480). This claim needs to be treated with some caution. In the 2003 election there were a total of 33 women candidates compared to a total of 156 men.

Research shows that public attitudes towards women in politics have become more positive since 1991, with voters looking to parties to present them with more women candidates. There is a perception that there are fewer barriers inhibiting women's political participation, compared with a decade ago, so that preferential treatment for women candidates is not popular, although half of those questioned in a survey in 2003 (Galligan and Dowds, 2004) did believe that parties should be encouraged to put forward a proportion of women candidates. In addition, the qualities people believed women brought to political life – approachability, ability to compromise, honesty and level-headedness – were the qualities identified in 'ideal' candidates, while male politicians were described as aggressive, ruthless, ambitious and crafty. Given these results, the researchers concluded that while more women were elected in the 2003 Assembly elections, the defeat of the Women's Coalition 'may be construed more as a reassertion of sectarian voting patterns rather than as a vote against women' (Galligan and Dowds, 2004: 4). The May 2005 local government elections would bear out this analysis. Women's percentage of seats increased from 19 per cent to 21.5 per cent, with Sinn Féin and the DUP again increasing their female representation. The SDLP, losing seats overall, slightly increased their total of women councillors, while the Alliance Party increased its total seats with a loss of one female seat. The single Women's Coalition candidate, while polling strongly in first preferences, lost out to a well-organised DUP campaign that benefited from the publicity given to its Westminster candidate.

The obstacle towards greater representation of women continues to be that the political parties do not stand sufficient women to make a substantial difference to the overall level of representation. The Sex Discrimination (Election of Candidates) NI Order 2002 permitting all-women shortlists in the selection process has not been implemented by any political party in Northern Ireland and, in the absence of any stronger measures of persuasion, is unlikely to be. Nevertheless, in its evaluation of the elections, the Centre for the Advancement of Women in Politics at Queen's University Belfast remained optimistic that voters had no prejudice against female candidates:

> Although the parties favour the selection of a majority of male candidates they are willing to encourage their voters to place the fewer female candidates as higher preferences on their ballot papers, the result being that 67% of all female candidates

were elected as local councillors, compared to 65% of all male candidates. (CAWP, 2005: 20)

Difficulties in redressing gender-based discrimination, in tandem with the need to ensure that public institutions be reflective of the total community of Northern Ireland, is most evident in relation to the reform of the police service, itself an area fraught with political complexity. In 1998 the Northern Ireland Affairs Committee (1997–98: para. 5), while recognising that the 'overwhelming numerical predominance of Protestant officers over Roman Catholic officers is a major problem politically and socially' also considered the necessity to ensure proper representation of women and members of ethnic minority communities. The Independent Commission that was organised under the chairmanship of Chris Patten the following year did not, however, include gender within the substantive body of proposals emanating from what became known as the Patten Report. Patten (1999: 121) recommended that an equal number of Catholics and Protestants should be drawn from the pool of qualified candidates. He argued that this proposal, while requiring an amendment to domestic legislation, was not incompatible with European legislation. He made no similar recommendation in relation to achieving an equal number of men and women in the police service. The report concluded that European legislation ruled out such a proposal 'in respect of recruitment of women'. During the period the Patten Commission was collecting evidence, the Equal Opportunities Commission advocated a gender quota be included, but this was disregarded.[2] However, while the operational side of policing was ignored in terms of gender parity, recommendation 112 of Patten urged that the staff composition of organisations and bodies responsible for policing should be representative of gender:

> Every effort should be made to ensure that the composition of the staff of the Policing Board, and the NIO Police Division (or any successor body) and the Office of the Police Ombudsman should be broadly reflective of the population of NI as a whole, particularly in terms of political/religious tradition and *gender*. (my emphasis)

The new police service came into existence on 4 November 2001 with a total of around 13,600 staff, including both police and civilian support. Section 46(1) of the Police (NI) Act 2000 allows for 50/50 Catholic/Protestant quotas in recruitment. Attention has largely remained focused on the Catholic/Protestant ratio and there is evidence that the recruitment process has not been favourable towards women. Section 48 makes provision for a gender action plan for increasing female representation in the police, in police support staff and in the staff of the Northern Ireland Policing Board (NIPB). During Competition One 7518 applications were received, and 40.9

per cent were from women. However, of the 602 who succeeded in being selected for the merit pool, only 34 per cent were women, suggesting that some part of the procedure favoured men, who formed 59.1 per cent of the initial applications but 66 per cent of the merit pool. To date, figures are unavailable on the outcome of Competition Two and Competition Three. The numbers of women within the PSNI have increased from 13 per cent of the total in 2001 to 16.5 per cent in 2004. The total numbers of women/men in full time and part-time PSNI as of 1 January 2003 were 8,171 male and 1,663 female. However, these figures do not provide a break-down of the numbers of full-time police women, as women form a large part of the part-time police reservists (NIPB, 2004). One woman has been appointed Assistant Chief Constable, together with five men. An assessment of the PSNI performance has pointed to internal problems as the numbers of women within the service increase (HMIC, 2004: 41). While female recruits went up to 34 per cent by May 2004, the Policing Board Annual Report concluded that 'With higher levels of female recruitment taking place, evidence is now starting to emerge of isolated sexist attitudes and instances of discrimination. The service is beginning to respond to these.'

A Gender Action Plan (PSNI, 2004) produced by the PSNI stated that direct recruitment had seen steadily increasing numbers of women. It concluded that if the trend continued, women could form over 26 per cent of the force by 2010. The removal of the physical competency test had seen the level of female recruits rise. The report made a number of recommendations regarding work–life balance issues intended to improve the retention rate of female officers, particularly those with families. It recommended a campaign to encourage female officers to apply to specialist units in frontline service delivery and it recommended analysis of the factors contributing towards female under-representation at senior levels of the service. The overall intention is to create a culture that is more welcoming of female officers and which challenges any bias against women. Although the Gender Action Plan made a number of positive recommendations, little or no progress has been made on implementing the Patten recommendations intended to create a culture which would be more welcoming to women. The Oversight Commissioner (2005: 117) has noted that there had been 'limited progress' on creating opportunities for part-time working and job-sharing. He stated bluntly that the PSNI had provided 'no evidence indicating progress with the implementation of this recommendation'. As regards child care, he noted that the Gender Action Plan did not specifically address the issue and that 'As at April 2005, the police service finds no basis upon which to construct a business case to progress child care arrangements' (Office of Oversight Commissioner, 2005: 118).

A major recommendation of the Patten Commission was the creation of the Northern Ireland Policing Board to replace the Police Authority for Northern Ireland. The Policing Board is intended to be independent of government and the police and consists of 19 members, ten of whom are members of the Northern Ireland Assembly, appointed according to the proportion of seats their parties hold in the Assembly. The remaining nine members are intended to be independent and are appointed by the Secretary of State for Northern Ireland. While Patten had urged gender equality in staffing levels, he omitted any such requirement regarding the operational role of the Board, stating only that the

> nine independent members be selected from a range of different fields – including business, trade unions, voluntary organisations, community groups and the legal profession – with the aim of finding a group of individuals representative of the community as a whole, with the expertise both to set policing priorities and to probe and scrutinise different areas of police performance, from management of resources to the safeguarding of human rights. (Patten Report, 1999: 17)

Echoing Patten, the Police Act 2000 (8: 1) requires the Secretary of State, who has responsibility for appointing the independent members of the Board, to ensure 'that as far as practicable, the membership of the Board is representative of the community in Northern Ireland'. The Police Act (48: 1) also requires the Policing Board to make a plan for monitoring and increasing the number of female police officers. The Committee for the Administration of Justice, in a commentary on the Policing Board (CAJ, 2003), concluded that the composition of the Board did not meet these requirements for a number of reasons. With regards to female representation 'only two out of the nineteen Board members are female, an under-representation that cannot be explained through lack of qualified female applicants'. Its report concluded that the Board's composition 'sets an unhelpful example for the PSNI and the Policing Board members themselves, who are responsible for appointing the independent members of the District Policing Partnerships and assessing measures taken to secure a representative Police Service'. There are currently two women on the Policing Board. Both are independent members appointed by the Secretary of State. The political parties did not nominate any women to the Board. An indication of the lack of awareness of gender issues can be seen in the gender-blind attitude of Jane Kennedy, then Security Minister within the Northern Ireland Office, who wrote a letter to the *Irish Times* (9 October 2001) to the effect that the appointment of the non-political members of the Board, after the political nominees were known, has 'produced a well-balanced board, which was not only a statutory requirement but is a vital element in fostering broad community confidence in the new beginning for policing', ignoring the under-representation of women.[3]

The most positive example of women's increasing role within the area of criminal justice has been on a community level. The Patten Commission recommended that District Policing Partnership Boards, made up of political and independent members, be formed in each district council area for the purpose of advising the police of local community concerns and priorities. Patten also stated that, taken as a whole, they should be broadly representative of the district in terms of religion, gender, age and cultural background. The name was subsequently changed to District Policing Partnerships (DPPs). The district councils appoint the political members and the Policing Board appoints the independent members from among the persons nominated by the district councils. The Northern Ireland Office Code (paragraphs 2 and 3) stated that 'the Independent Members appointed, together with the Elected Members, would constitute in each of Northern Ireland's 26 District Council areas a District Policing partnership composed of capable individuals who would reflect, as far as reasonably possible, the community they were chosen to serve'.

The gender and community background obtained in the DPPs have been one of the most successful recruitment processes in institutions arising out of the Agreement. That this occurred is due to the Policing Board, which developed a code of practice and appointments procedure for the appointment of more than 200 members to DPPs across Northern Ireland. The selection panels used census data to ensure that the independent DPP member appointments were representative of their communities. The report of PricewaterhouseCoopers, who were engaged as recruiters, explained the process. 4,650 enquiries led to 1,511 accepted applications. At that stage no attempt was made to strike a balance in terms of community, gender, etc. Only the merit principle was used. 739 out of the 792 applicants interviewed were judged suitable on merit for appointment, and 127 out of the 207 independent DPP members that the Board appointed were women. The report of the independent assessors (Eve, Keanie and Weir, 2003: 28) concluded that the appointment process was 'fair, robust, open and transparent. This is a model that should be used in other recruitment exercises.'

The low level of public participation by women is explained in part by the fact that 35 per cent of all public appointments are through statutory nominations, the majority of which come from political parties. That is the reason why the Policing Board female members are independent appointments. Baroness Rennie Fritchie, in her role as Commissioner for Public Appointments (CPA) for Northern Ireland signalled her dissatisfaction with this system, which gives political parties more power of patronage than is the case in the rest of the UK. The Review of Public Administration has highlighted Fritchie's concerns and indicated that the issue should be dealt with as part of the reform process (OFMDF, 2005: 99). Despite the work of the CPA in issuing codes of practice, engaging the civil service in updating its old-boy's system of 'conversations with a purpose' for public appointments and ensuring that independent assessors became part of the process, the numbers of women in public life have not increased beyond the level of 32 per cent reached in 1995 (CPA, 2004).

The remit of the CPA does not extend to appointments made by the Northern Ireland Office. In this area there has been a notable lack of effort to promote gender equality. The Parades Commission is one obvious example. The Northern Ireland European Women's Platform (n.d.), evaluating appointments to the cross-border bodies established by the British and Irish governments in December 1999 as part of the implementation of Strand 2 of the Agreement, concluded that procedures were not transparent and that no policy on achieving gender balance was evident.

Changes in the judiciary have been slow to materialise, despite the evident need to rectify the imbalance in a situation where seven out of ten of those involved in the criminal justice system are male (NISRA, 2002). Recent research from the University of Ulster (Feenan, 2005), analysing women in judicial posts and senior barristers, concluded that the number of women in top posts is considerably smaller than England and Wales and even worse when compared with other countries: 18 per cent of those holding legal office are women, compared with 24.9 per cent in England and Wales. There are 9 women and 30 men in county courts and no female high court judge.

The lack of women involved with the contentious issue of marches and parades through contested areas has been a matter of concern for many organisations. Although some women were appointed as commissioners in the early years of the Parades Commission in 1997–1999, it is notable that since the departure of Mo Mowlam, none of her successors as Secretary of State have made female appointments. The Equality Commission, after an unsuccessful representation to Secretary of State Peter Mandleson, signalled its concern:

> In our view, it is particularly important that high profile bodies, such as the Parades Commission, which deals in matters of the utmost sensitivity and political importance, is truly representative of the community. Further, we believe that where no women are represented on a body such as this, there is a very real danger that a message is put out that perpetuates the stereotype of women not being suited to the 'hard' issues. (Select Committee on Northern Ireland, 2000–1)

In November 2001 Sir George Quigley was appointed by government to consider the future of the Parades Commission. He recommended in his review that future appointments be 'reflective of gender, geography and community background' (Quigley, 2002: 115). Other recommendations made by Quigley gave the police a stronger role in adjudicating over parades. The report, unpopular amongst most political parties, has now been shelved by government.

The contribution made by women in the voluntary and community sector, both in redressing the gender deficit in decision making and in cross-community peace building, has been incalculable. Peace money from Europe provided the catalyst, with 70 per cent of groups forming since 1990. McWilliams (2002: 375) credits the Women's Information Group, formed in 1980, 'with making the women's movement in Northern Ireland an inclusive one – not only through its work across the sectarian divide but also by reaching out to working class women'. Its monthly meetings, held alternatively in Protestant and Catholic communities, are often the first time women have entered the territory of those coming from the 'other' community. While the group has provided a mechanism for cross-community contact for women, its ethos has been strictly 'bread and butter' and non-political.

Other groups have approached political issues from a strongly feminist perspective, finding common cause with women by linking local and global issues. Eight women's centres have developed within the Greater Belfast area since the 1980s, providing a range of services, from education and training, health promotion, information and advice, to full-time childcare and cross-community working (Taillon, 2000). Increasing women's understanding of local political issues, thereby encouraging greater political engagement and possible future participation, is a key challenge, and one that is being addressed by the work of Women into Politics, whose training programme 'provides women with the knowledge and skills necessary to take their place in the public domain' (Women in Politics, 2005: preface). Other organisations, such as the Women's Support Network and the Women's Resource and Development Agency, provide policy expertise and infrastructural support to a range of groups. The total membership of women's organisations is calculated at 6,000, distributed amongst 383 women's groups, 14 women's centres, 22 networks and 4 regional organisations (NIVT, 2001). While sensitive to the political differences that exist between groups, the women's sector works consciously to foster understanding as women unite around those issues they have in common. In Belfast, the centres have 'twinned' with their counterparts in the 'other' community, both in working together and in ensuring that both traditions are always represented when it comes to choosing spokespeople for different events.

As the sector becomes increasingly professional in the services that it can deliver, it has entered into partnership with the statutory sector, particularly with regards to health issues and childcare. Women who live in the most disadvantaged areas in Northern Ireland are working hard to improve the quality of life for their families and their communities; the challenge now is to ensure that their organisations are adequately resourced without compromising their essential independence. These 'new relationships' between civil society and government raise many issues, particularly regarding empowerment and representativeness (Meehan, 2003: 10). While representatives from the women's sector are active participants in local strategic partnerships, neighbourhood boards, Sure Start committees, and a myriad of other organisations requiring local input, Meehan (2003: 11) poses the question as to whether 'more symbolic representation' will come to mean 'more substantive representation'? It is too early to provide a definitive answer in a situation where women remain concerned to achieve greater levels of participation. The sector has taken on this essential and additional responsibility without receiving extra resources. This is not a sustainable policy, given limited finances, and on-going negotiations regarding the future infrastructure and funding of the women's sector include the need to core fund such work. As much of this activity involves peace-building and reconstruction, such funding would be in line with the ethos of United Nations Security Council resolution 1325 on Women, Peace and Security, which calls for the 'increased representation of women at all decision-making levels in national, regional and international institutions and mechanisms for the prevention, management and resolution of conflict'. If this were to be fully implemented, there would of course have to be greater representation of women in such key institutions as the Parades Commission and the Policing Board.

Recognition of the relationship between government and the voluntary and community sector in the delivery of policy objectives was articulated in the *Compact Between Government and the Voluntary and Community Sector in Northern Ireland* (DHSS, 1998). In *Positive Steps* (DSD, 2005: 9.8) the government acknowledged the important role of the voluntary and community sector in the development and implementation of policy: 'consultation is a key facet of a modern policy making process . . . Input from the voluntary and community sector, particularly communities of interest, assists the Government to fulfil its statutory duties'.

As section 75 of the Northern Ireland Act 1998 imposes a statutory duty upon public authorities to have 'due regard' to the need to promote equality of opportunity between persons in nine categories, which includes 'men and women, persons with dependents and persons without', the contribution of women to a participatory method of consultation has been of prime importance in ensuring that the process succeeds in its objective of mainstreaming equality in policy making. This has not, however, been a straightforward process. Joanna McMinn of the National Women's Council of Ireland believes that inadequate levels of resources 'act as a social control on women's organisations to contribute fully and effectively to the implementation of gender mainstreaming processes' (McMinn, 2002: 78). Judy Seymour, former director of the Women's Resource and Development Agency, argued strongly that 'the right to be consulted, as now enshrined within the law, is meaningless unless resources are invested in both the process and the outcome of the consultation . . . formal rights that are not supported by an investment of resources are merely symbolic rights'. In her view, mainstreaming equality was being used as a way of evading mainstreaming gender equality as women were told they were 'only one of nine groups we have to consider'. Her response was to query why '52% of the population, 1/9th of the equality agenda?' (Seymour, 2003: 21).

The controversy over the Gender Equality Strategy proposed by the Office for the First Minister and Deputy First Minister raises the question of equality legislation doing little more than embedding the status quo. The strategy of promoting 'equal opportunities', coupled with official reluctance to support affirmative action measures, has met with concerted opposition by women's organisations, as evidenced in the robust response of the Ad-Hoc Women's Policy Group (2005: 3):

> The suggested framework attempts to achieve equality between women and men through the provision of 'equal opportunities' for both sexes. This approach fails to acknowledge the factors that prevent women from being able to compete on equal terms with men and fails to consider the use of positive action measures to redress inequalities in the workplace and in public life. Its limited focus also ignores the needs of some of the most marginalised women, including migrant workers and disabled women.

Women's Aid, after engagement with government over a strategy to tackle domestic violence, has expressed concern that a 'gender neutral' policy is being adopted towards violence in intimate relationships, obscuring the root causes and impact of gender-based violence and operating to the detriment of women-specific organisations:

> Fundamental to any understanding of domestic violence must be its gendered nature. It is essential to recognise that in every class, creed and culture in the world, domestic violence is overwhelmingly perpetrated by men against women. The Northern Ireland Women's Aid Federation believes that if the definition underpinning tackling Violence at Home does not reflect this reality then strategic responses will fail. (NIWAF, 2004: 1)

The tensions between devising strategies based on 'gender' and strategies focused on the root causes of women's disadvantages have been clearly articulated in these engagements between women activists and policy makers. In the absence of a devolved institution with the power to develop strategic direction (and possessing sufficient politicians sympathetic to the argument being made by women) it is difficult to envisage a satisfactory conclusion to these exchanges. However, the UK government has signed up to international commitments in the Convention for the Elimination of Discrimination Against Women (1979) and the Beijing Declaration and Platform for Action (1995) that are concerned with the development of a national strategy for women, and women in Ireland, both North and South, are working together to ensure compliance. If women are supported and resourced to play their full part in decision making, it will go some way towards redressing the democratic deficit contingent on the lack of a devolved institution and the lack of gender parity in political and public life. It would signal a significant change in the role played by women, although their absence from substantive decision making remains.

Notes

1 Research for this paper is part of a wider study, RES–223–25–0066: 'Re-imagining women's security in societies in transition, post-conflict gender relations in Northern Ireland, South Africa and Lebanon', funded under the ESRC New Security Challenges programme.
2 This has been testified to by Evelyn Collins and Joan Smyth, former Chief Executive and Chair respectively of the former Equal Opportunities Commission.
3 Since this article was written, Peter Hain, as Secretary of State, has responded to criticism made regarding the gender composition of NIO-controlled bodies. In January 2006 he appointed three women and four men to a new Parades Commission and the Policing Board, appointed in March 2006, which currently has a total of six women and thirteen men.

References

Ad-Hoc Women's Policy Group (2005) *Gender Matters: Towards a Cross-Departmental Framework to Promote Gender Equality for Women and Men 2005–2015, A Response to Consultation*. Belfast: Women's Support Network.
Breen, S. (2001) 'Rodgers grasps NI's poisoned chalice', *Irish Times*, 21 April. Available at www.ireland.com/newspaper/ireland/2001/0421/archive01042100046. html.
CAJ (Committee on the Administration of Justice) (2003) *Commentary on the Northern Ireland Policing Board*. Belfast: CAJ.
CAWP (Centre for the Advancement of Women in Politics), Queen's University Belfast (2005) 'Modest increase: 3% rise in female councillors', *Women's News*, 153, June.
Cowell-Meyers, K. (2003) *Women Legislators in Northern Ireland: Gender and Politics in the New Legislative Assembly*, Occasional Paper No. 3. Belfast: Centre for the Advancement of Women in Politics, Queen's University Belfast.
CPA (Commissioner for Public Appointments for Northern Ireland) (2004) *Annual Report, 2003–2004*. Belfast: Office of the CPA.
Crilly, A., Gordon, H. and Rooney, E. (2002), 'Women in the North of Ireland,

1969–2000' in *The Field Day Anthology of Irish Writing*, Vol. V. Cork: Cork University Press.

DHSS (Department of Health and Social Services) (1998) *Building Real Partnership: Compact between Government and the Voluntary and Community Sector in Northern Ireland*. Belfast: DHSS.

DSD (Department of Social Development) (2005) *Positive Steps: The Government Response to 'Investing Together': Report of the Task Force on Resourcing the Voluntary and Community Sector*. Belfast: DSD.

Eve, J., Keanie, J. and Weir, P. (2003) *Northern Ireland DPPs: Appointment of Independent Members: Report of Impartial Assessors*. Available at www.district-policing.com/impartial_report.doc.

Feenan, D. (2005) 'Applications by Women for Silk and Judicial Office in Northern Ireland', reported by *BBC News*, 22 June.

Galligan, Y. and Dowds, L. (2004) 'Women's Hour?' *Research Update*, 26, February, Life and Times Survey. Available at www.ark.ac.uk.

Hansard (2000) (Northern Ireland), *Official Report*, Northern Ireland Assembly, Vol 5.

HMIC (HM Inspectorate of Constabulary) (2004) *Baseline Assessment of the Police Service of Northern Ireland*. London: HMIC.

Mackay, F. and Meehan, E. (2003) 'Women and devolution in Northern Ireland, Scotland and Wales', paper delivered to Irish Association Seminar, Mount Herbert Hotel, Dublin.

McMinn, J. (2002) 'Gender Mainstreaming in Ireland' in *Make it Happen: Effective Mainstreaming in Ireland and the UK*, conference report of the Gender Mainstreaming in UK and Ireland Structural Funds Conference, Swansea, Wales.

McWilliams, M. (2002) 'Women and political activism in Northern Ireland, 1960–93' in *The Field Day Anthology of Irish Writing*, Vol. V. Cork: Cork University Press.

Meehan, E. (2003) *From Government to Governance, Civic Participation and 'New Politics'; the Context of Potential Opportunities for the Better Representation of Women*, Occasional Paper (5). Belfast: Centre for the Advancement of Women in Politics, Queen's University of Belfast.

NIPB (Northern Ireland Policing Board) (2004) *Annual Report*. Belfast: NIPB.

NISRA (Northern Ireland Statistics and Research Agency) (2002) *Gender and the NI Criminal Justice System*. Belfast: NISRA.

NIVT (Northern Ireland Voluntary Trust) (2001) *Where To From Here – A New Paradigm for the Women's Sector in Northern Ireland*. Belfast: NIVT.

NIWAF (Northern Ireland Women's Aid Federation) (2004) *Annual Report, 2003/4*. Belfast: NIWAF.

Northern Ireland Affairs Committee (1997–98), Third Report, 'Composition, Recruitment and Training of the RUC' in *Report and Proceedings of the Committee*, Vol. 1. London: The Stationery Office.

Northern Ireland Women's European Platform (n.d.) *Alternative Report to the UK Questionnaire Response of Progress of the Platform for Action and the Outcome of the 23rd Session of the General Assembly*. Available at www.unece.org/oes/gender/documents/question/Alternativerep/NorthernIreland-niwep.

OFMDFM (Office of First Minister and Deputy First Minister) (2005) *The Review of Public Administration in Northern Ireland: The Further Consultation*. Belfast: OFMDFM.

OOC (Office of the Oversight Commissioner) (2005) *Overseeing the Proposed Revisions for the Policing Services of Northern Ireland*, 9 June, Report (13). Belfast: OOC.

Patten Report (1999) *A New Beginning: Policing in Northern Ireland. The Report of the Independent Commission on Policing in Northern Ireland.* Belfast: HMSO.

PSNI (Police Service for Northern Ireland) (2004) *Gender Action Plan: Dismantling Barriers to Reflect the Community We Serve.* Belfast: PSNI.

Quigley, Sir G. (2002) *Review of the Parades Commission.* Belfast: Northern Ireland Office.

Select Committee on Northern Ireland (2000–1) *Appendices to Minutes of Evidence*, Appendix 12.

Seymour, J. (2003) 'Making waves', *Scope*, February.

Taillon, R. (2000) *The Social and Economic Impact of Women's Centres in Greater Belfast.* Belfast: Women's Support Network.

Taillon, R. and McCann, M. (2002) *An Assessment of the Impact of the Loss of Services Provided by WSN and other Women's Organisations in NI*, Report for OFMDFM. Belfast: Women's Support Network.

Ward, M. (2000) *The Northern Ireland Assembly and Women – Assessing the Gender Deficit.* Belfast: Democratic Dialogue.

Wilford, R. (2001) 'Northern Ireland one year on: a discursive narrative', Transitions to Devolution Conference, Cardiff.

Wilford, R. and Wilson, R. (2000–2003) *Quarterly Monitoring Reports on Devolution in Northern Ireland.* Available at www.ucl.ac.uk/constitution-unit.

Women into Politics (2005) *Annual Report 2004–2005.* Belfast: Women into Politics.

11
Equality and human rights since the Agreement

Brice Dickson and Robert Osborne[1]

Equality issues

Introduction and context

One of the central policy issues during the past 30 years of the 'Troubles' has been that of ending discrimination and providing for equality of opportunity. However, the 'equality agenda', as it can be termed, has undergone significant changes since the outbreak of the political disturbances, and further major institutional, legal and other reforms have resulted from the 1998 Belfast Agreement.

The issues which were to the fore towards the end of the 1960s derived from the demands of the civil rights movement for 'one man one vote' in local elections, the ending of the gerrymandering of local government electoral areas, and an end to discrimination in employment and public sector housing allocations. Whyte's (1983) careful analysis of these 1960s claims remains the best judgement of their validity. He found convincing evidence of unfairness in some areas but less convincing evidence in others. As the civil rights protests slid into violent confrontations on the streets, reforms in many areas, instigated by the British government, ensured that the franchise and access to public housing were reformed and many services were removed from local government and centralised with new merit or needs-based allocation procedures. Fairness in employment, however, remained untouched in terms of public policy.

The suspension of the Stormont Parliament in 1972 was followed by the setting up of a review group, chaired by Conservative MP, William van Straubenzee. Reporting in 1973 the group recommended policy intervention to eliminate employment discrimination but, in so doing, rejected employment quotas. The Fair Employment Act 1976 outlawed religious discrimination, created a regulatory body, the Fair Employment Agency (FEA), provided a mechanism for the investigation of individual complaints and

equipped the FEA with investigatory powers to help secure equality of opportunity in employment.[2] The FEA at this time was notable for undertaking a
large number of investigations, especially in the public sector. The investigation of the Northern Ireland Civil Service in 1983 proved particularly important as it prompted the organisation to take the provision of fairness seriously
and, eventually, provided a template for the rest of the public sector to
improve practices.

Nevertheless, dissatisfaction with the pace of change led to a significant
strengthening of the legislation in 1989, following calls from the Standing
Advisory Commission on Human Rights (SACHR),[3] with the FEA replaced
by the Fair Employment Commission (FEC), the specific outlawing of indirect discrimination and the creation of a new tribunal system to hear individual
complaints. The reformed legislation provided for compulsory religious monitoring for those employing over 10 employees, monitoring for recruitment
and those leaving for employers with larger numbers of employees and all
public sector employers, and regular reviews of all employment practices to be
reported to the FEC. Most importantly, however, several forms of affirmative
action were now possible, while the overall commitment to the 'merit principle' was maintained. Alongside the capacity for employers to use 'welcoming
statements' and to undertake outreach activities with respect to under-repre-
sented groups, new provisions provided for the setting of employment goals
and timetables for the reduction of the scale of under-representation. Basing
the analysis on catchment comparisons with existing employment profiles, the
FEC could reach voluntary agreements with employers or use powers to
enforce their adoption.

Alongside this explicit fair employment intervention, again largely as a
response to calls from SACHR, the government began to introduce provisions for ensuring that equality provisions were inserted in the policy-making
process. The initiative, known as Policy Appraisal and Fair Treatment (PAFT),
was developed in the early 1990s, but an early evaluation sponsored by the
SACHR (Osborne et al, 1996) suggested that it was only being patchily
implemented by the public sector. However, the PAFT initiative was important for clearly broadening out equality concerns to include gender, race/eth-
nicity, disability, sexual orientation and age, as well as religion and political
opinion.

By the time of the Belfast Agreement of 1998, a further review of fair
employment and related interventions had been undertaken by SACHR
(1997). Responding to this report, the direct rule government indicated in
a White Paper (1998) that it proposed to put PAFT on a statutory basis
and to integrate existing equality bodies into a single equality commission.
These provisions were subsequently included in the Belfast Agreement

(NIO, 1998). Both were legislated for in the Northern Ireland Act of the same year. Finally, from the perspective of this chapter, the review of policing undertaken through the Patten Report (1999), created under the Agreement, and its recommendations relating to the institution of matched 50:50 (Catholics:non-Catholics) recruitment, represents a major development in equality policy.

Since 1998 Agreement the most important equality developments have related to:

- the creation of a single agency – the Equality Commission;
- the implementation of the mainstreaming equality provisions (section 75 of the Northern Ireland Act);
- the review of progress on fair employment;
- the operation of the 'quota' system for recruitment into the Police Service of Northern Ireland (PSNI).

Creating a single Equality Commission

The creation of a single Equality Commission[4] took place in the context of considerable opposition to the concept from the voluntary and community sector, who feared the domination of fair employment over other equality areas.[5] To assist in the movement towards a single body, a working party sought to address the structure of the new body and some of its priorities (ECNI, 1999). Some of the recommendations were relevant but were, to some extent, overtaken by the pace of developments. One important issue raised by the group related to the extent to which board members of the Equality Commission should be appointed on the basis of their expertise in particular areas or not (disability, gender etc.). The recommendation was that this should not be the case but that each board member should be the custodian of the whole equality agenda and that appropriate training be provided. This was a crucial recommendation that was followed in practice. True, some commissioners developed particular interests in parts of the agenda but, in the main, all commissioners regarded themselves as contributing to the whole range of the Commission's responsibilities. The working group also recommended the retention of separate directorates within the Commission's staff to cover each of the equality responsibilities in the first instance, but that this should move towards a generic structure 'within 12 months.' This proved more contentious, not least because of the much larger group of staff responsible for fair employment but also because of the arguments made internally and externally to the Commission in relation to development work associated with race and disability and the new section 75 responsibilities.

The early years of the Commission were also influenced by split-site oper-ations and significantly underestimated the difficulties of creating new prac-tices in the Commission from those contrasting 'ways of doing things' from the different equality bodies. One area of particular difficulty related to the contrasting ways of dealing with individual complaints of discrimination. Where the Equal Opportunities Commission (EOC) had largely worked with external lawyers, the FEC had developed in-house expertise but a more wide-spread practice of supporting meritorious cases. The initial adoption of the EOC outsourcing legal model, together with supporting a high proportion of cases, resulted in the accumulation of substantial external legal fees, despite having an in-house legal capacity. Nevertheless, although taking longer than might have been anticipated, the Commission became a fairly cohesive body by the end of its first five-year phase.

Implementing section 75

To many concerned with achieving greater equality in Northern Ireland, the mainstreaming equality provisions of section 75 represented potentially the most significant post-Agreement/devolution initiative. The provision of the two statutory provisions – to have 'due regard' to promoting equal-ity of opportunity in relation to the same groups identified under the PAFT initiative, and 'regard' to the promotion of good relations (on the basis of religion, political opinion and race) in developing policy – seemed to offer a major opportunity to satisfy those who believed that mainstreaming equality considerations in the policy process offered the necessary comple-ment to anti-discrimination legislation in the achievement of greater social equality.

How can we judge what has taken place with implementation? It has been suggested that the processes involved in implementing section 75 are bureau-cratic and rely on excessive consultation. Moreover, and perhaps more fun-damentally, it has been suggested that section 75 may confuse two different ideas. By relying on consultation, section 75 incorporates ideas derived from 'community governance' – simply, involving the public in policy for-mulation – together with the desire to achieve greater equality. Coupled with the absence of sanctions (relying on name and shame and, in some circum-stances a reference to the Secretary of State), the contrast with fair employ-ment could not be greater.

The first few annual reports from the Equality Commission on the imple-mentation of section 75 (ECNI, 2003, 2004) reveal a diligent but generally unambitious approach from the public services (Osborne, 2003; Osborne and Shuttleworth, 2004; Osborne, 2005). It is worth noting, however, that

McCrudden (2004) has suggested that this conclusion may be premature and that there is more evidence of successful implementation than this analysis allows. It is undoubtedly the case that those advocacy groups associated with sexual orientation, in particular, have seen the advent of section 75 as providing the first input given to policy making from their perspective. While most equality schemes were scheduled for review in the 2005–6 period, with the Equality Commission reviewing section 75 in the same period, at the time of writing there seems little evidence of a campaign for reforming and strengthening section 75.

Fair employment

As indicated, the issue of religious equality in the labour market has been a dominant theme in public policy intervention over the past quarter of a century. An attempt to assess the effectiveness of these interventions in achieving greater equality has been undertaken in a book edited by Osborne and Shuttleworth (2004). This analysis examined the current patterns in the labour market as revealed from monitoring returns, patterns of contemporary social mobility compared with the 1970s, and a review of patterns of educational attainment and interactions with the labour market. These assessments revealed the marked improvement of Catholics in employment, both in terms of the private and especially the public sector, but there were some areas of emerging Protestant under-representation. Contemporary patterns of social mobility were no longer independently influenced by religion, as was the case in the 1970s, and the patterns of educational attainment showed Catholics broadly matching Protestants at the top end of achievement but still slightly trailing Protestant at the lower end of attainment. The analysis also examined the important ways that the labour market is being restructured in response to global pressures. Finally, the review included an assessment of the effectiveness of affirmative action agreements between the FEC and employers. The analysis, which while noting the data-related caveats, provided convincing evidence that the use of affirmative action agreements had helped in the process of creating more balanced workforces. Overall, the assessment suggested that much of the blatant disadvantage in the labour market experienced by Catholics when measured in the early 1970s was being substantially reduced. Moreover, it was also observed that Protestant under-representation is now becoming apparent in some professional and managerial occupations, especially in the public sector. However, the long-standing migration of Protestant undergraduates to study and the limited extent to which they return to live in Northern Ireland after graduation has been argued to underpin this development.

Recruitment into the PSNI

One of the most politically contentious issues which emerged after the Belfast Agreement was the Patten Commission's recommendations over policing. While many aspects of the review produced political controversy, most notably the abolition of the RUC and its replacement by the PSNI, a continuing source of political difficulty stemmed from the government's acceptance of the recommendation for recruitment into the PSNI to be on the basis of 50:50 recruitment. This quota system breached existing fair employment legislation and required that legislation to be amended. There is no doubt that the operation of this mechanism for recruitment has caused great difficulty for Protestants/unionists. Many of those who supported fair employment also experienced some difficulties with this form of positive discrimination. However, the prize of securing a better representation of Catholics, (alongside moves to increase the representation of women and black and ethnic minority groups), led the Equality Commission amongst others to offer consistently its support to the new recruitment process.

Table 11.1 shows the results of the 50:50 recruitment exercises as of August 2005. It is worth noting that the 50:50 quota system incorporates a minimum attainment level as measured through a standard test. In terms of applicants, it can be seen that the ratio of Catholics amongst applicants has been consistently just above the one-third mark. With 50:50 recruitment, this produces a marked difference in the success rate of Catholics and non-Catholics (predominantly Protestants). Protestant success rates (those appointed as a proportion of applicants) are approximately half those of Catholics. This provides the 'hard' evidence of the operation of the quota system. Indeed, under the unamended fair employment legislation, this evidence would have been sufficient to reach a preliminary judgement of religious bias and to precipitate an investigation by the FEC. Since unsuccessful applicants, who have satisfied all other criteria, are informed that they are being turned down on a religion/community background basis and that the substantial majority of those receiving this communication are Protestants, this helps explain the hostility towards the recruitment process from that community.

Nevertheless, with just over 18 per cent of police officers now being recorded as Catholic (as of 1 July 2005), together with the data in Table 11.1, there is now evidence of change. At the time of writing, however, it seems to be the case that Sinn Féin is trying to shift the debate about the composition of the PSNI from religion/community background, the basis of fair employment legislation for almost 30 years, to a push to achieve equality on the basis of political opinion. Specifically, having Catholics in the PSNI is not adequate

Table 11.1. Recruiting to the PSNI, 2001–5

Advert date	Applicants	No. of Catholics	% Catholics	Catholics appointed	Catholic success rate	No. of non-Catholics	% non-Catholics	Non-Catholics appointed	Non-Catholic success rate
03/01	7,518	2,615	34.8	153	5.9	4,936	65.2	152	3.1
09/01	4,915	1,890	38.5	98	5.2	3,018	61.5	98	3.2
03/02	4,674	1,640	35.1	83	5.1	3,034	64.9	83	2.7
09/02	4,410	1,481	33.6	201	13.6	2,894	66.4	201	6.9
03/03	6,044	2,189	36.2	149	6.8	3,836	63.8	150	3.9
09/03	5,419	1,909	35.2	148	7.8	3,497	64.8	150	4.3
03/04	4,977	1,710	34.4	125	7.3	3,265	65.6	131	4.0
09/04	5,695	1,986	34.9	Appointments ongoing	Appointments ongoing	3,709	65.1	Appointments ongoing	Appointments ongoing
03/05	6,110	2,065	33.8	Appointments ongoing	Appointments ongoing	4,045	66.2	Appointments ongoing	Appointments ongoing

Note: Figures do not include civilian staff of the PSNI.

Source: PSNI and Equality Commission; success rates calculated by Osborne.

from the Sinn Féin perspective. 'Equality' in this view is about getting recognition of those associated with republicanism into the PSNI in order to make it acceptable to the republican movement. There must be considerable disquiet about an attempt to put politics into policing in such an overt manner, and subverting the whole thrust of fair employment objectives at a time when the Secretary of State for Northern Ireland, Peter Hain, has argued that policing should be 'freed from the political debate'(www.news.bbc.co.uk, 10 September 2005).

Human rights issues

Human rights in the Agreement

The Belfast (Good Friday) Agreement of 1998 is suffused with references to human rights: a category of social goods which was also very much at the core of the New Labour manifesto which won that party the UK general election a year earlier (Harvey and Livingstone, 1999). Labour promised to 'bring rights home' by incorporating into the law of all parts of the country the protections guaranteed by the European Convention on Human Rights, a treaty which had been binding on the government at an international level, though not in domestic courts, since 1953. The new government also vowed to put human rights at the centre of its foreign policy.

Among the commitments made by the British government in the Belfast Agreement were to create a Northern Ireland Human Rights Commission (NIHRC) (with powers greater than those enjoyed by the previous SACHR); to complete the incorporation of the European Convention on Human Rights into Northern Ireland law; to protect civil, political, social, economic and cultural rights; and to consider actively signing the Council of Europe Charter for Regional or Minority Languages. In the multi-party agreement accompanying the inter-governmental agreement of that day, the Northern Ireland political parties affirmed their commitment to (among other rights) the right to pursue democratically national and political aspirations, the right to seek constitutional change by peaceful and legitimate means, the right to equal opportunity in all social and economic activity (regardless of class, creed, disability, gender or ethnicity), the right to freedom from sectarian harassment and the right of women to full and equal political participation.

There was no actual commitment on the part of the British government to enact a Bill of Rights for Northern Ireland, nor on the part of the political parties to work towards the creation of such a Bill, but the NIHRC was to be tasked with advising the government on what scope there was for supplementing the European Convention on Human Rights, drawing as appropriate on international instruments and experience, and reflecting the particular circumstances of Northern Ireland, the principle of mutual respect for the identity and ethos of both communities, and the principle of parity of esteem. Any such supplementary rights, together with the European Convention on Human Rights, were to constitute a Bill of Rights for Northern Ireland. Everyone agreed that the Northern Ireland Assembly and public bodies in Northern Ireland should not be allowed to infringe the European Convention on Human Rights 'or any Bill of Rights for Northern Ireland supplementing it'.

It is easy for governments and other political players to commit to certain ideals and to setting up advisory institutions, but it is a great deal harder for them to deliver on those commitments in a way which makes a real difference to people's lives. Some might argue that the Belfast Agreement oversold the concept of human rights by not being specific enough as to which particular rights would be better protected as a result of the Agreement or in what manner those protections would be guaranteed. As well as making no commitment to a Bill of Rights, the Agreement did not promise the abolition of 'emergency' arrest and search powers, juryless 'Diplock' courts, plastic bullets or discriminatory security vetting. Nor did it say that improperly investigated killings would be reinvestigated in line with international standards, that the new police service would be trained in human rights, that an element on human rights would be included in the secondary school curriculum or that those who are marginalised in Northern Ireland (who tend to be the elderly, the poor, the unemployed, the homeless and people with disabilities) would have greater rights regarding health, their standard of living, work, shelter and access to employment and services. Perhaps those who bought into the Agreement because of its references to human rights were content with the vagueness of its provisions in this respect, but the consequence has been confusion and contestation. Certainly the British government was quick to sign up to the *principle* of greater human rights guarantees in Northern Ireland but has been slow to translate that principle into practice.

The Agreement's lack of detail in two crucial areas was, however, soon remedied by two impressive follow-up reports. One was the report of the Independent Commission on Policing (Patten Report, 1999), the other was the report of the Criminal Justice Review (2000). Each of these placed the protection of human rights at the forefront of the recommended reforms. The British government immediately lent its support to the reports' conclusions (it was in any case closely involved in drafting the criminal justice report) and in due course oversight commissioners were appointed to provide reassurance to the public that the recommendations were indeed being implemented.

The Human Rights Commission and the Human Rights Act

The NIHRC produced a draft Bill of Rights for Northern Ireland in September 2001 (NIHRC, 2001) but this document did not meet with anything like the government backing accorded to the policing and criminal justice reports. The government seemed unhappy at the prospect of Northern Ireland acquiring a comprehensive Bill of Rights – one which protected social, economic and environmental rights as well as more traditional civil and political rights – given that the rest of the UK would not be enjoying such protections. Why, it asked, should people in Belfast have more rights than people in Birmingham? Various political parties, and even some human rights non-governmental organisations, focused on criticising the Commission's draft Bill of Rights (because it did not give them all they had asked for during the pre-consultation period) rather than on acknowledging the draft to be one of the most progressive human rights documents proposed anywhere in the world. The Committee on the Administration of Justice (CAJ), for example, complained that the Bill did not go far enough to protect group rights or social and economic rights, yet the CAJ's own draft Bill of Rights went nowhere near as far in those areas, nor in the areas of women's rights, victims' rights and non-discrimination rights (CAJ, 1996). Particular opprobrium was heaped on the Commission for daring to suggest that the fair employment laws in Northern Ireland could be tweaked to ensure not just that job applicants and employees have their *perceived* community background recorded, but also their *actual* community background. The whole theoretical basis of the document was even queried (McCrudden, 2001). Some nationalists seemed unsure whether the rights they wanted as a minority group should also be guaranteed to unionists as a majority group, even though the international standards (not to say the Belfast Agreement) on this seem quite clear, namely that, in a society where minority/majority status shifts depending on the geography of the territory, both groups should be accorded the same rights in all places. The Commission's amended draft Bill of Rights, published after considering responses to the earlier draft, fared little better (NIHRC, 2003, 2004a).

Meanwhile the Human Rights Act 1998 had come fully into force throughout the UK in October 2000. This fulfilled the government's manifesto pledge to domesticate the European Convention. There were predictions in some camps that the judges in Northern Ireland would not be of a mind to apply the Act with any vigour. In fact the 'training' which judges received on the Act was first class and the jurisprudence of the Northern Irish courts in the following five years bears witness to the fact that judges in Northern Ireland were just as active in applying the Act as their counterparts in Great Britain (Dickson, 2004). Litigants in Northern Ireland, many of them supported financially by the NIHRC (NIHRC, 2000–4), have repeatedly urged local judges to push forward the boundaries of human rights guarantees and in several instances the judges have complied. Throughout the UK only one High Court decision declaring a piece of Westminster legislation to be incompatible with the European Convention has not been appealed to a higher court. That was a decision taken by the High Court in Belfast (*In re McR*, 2002).

The Human Rights Act, more than the Belfast Agreement or the Northern Ireland Act 1998, has had the signal effect of alerting every public authority in Northern Ireland to the need to operate strictly in accordance with the European Convention on Human Rights. The Human Rights Commission responded to scores of consultation papers issued by these authorities by reminding them of the Convention's requirements, especially those enshrined in article 6 (the right to a fair hearing), article 8 (the right to respect for one's private and family life, home and correspondence) and article 14 (the right to freedom from discrimination). The Commission also succeeded in linking with the Department of Education in Northern Ireland to produce extensive teaching materials for post-primary schools on what a Bill of Rights could mean for Northern Ireland (NIHRC, 2004b) and it conducted detailed investigations into juvenile justice centres (NIHRC, 2002) and into the conditions under which female prisoners are held (NIHRC, 2005). Its reports played a significant role in persuading the Northern Ireland Office to introduce reforms in both those fields.

Human rights and politics

The fact remains, however, that there are many controversial issues in Northern Ireland which cannot be determined by resorting to human rights standards, at any rate not standards which have to date been accepted internationally. Human rights standards governing the nature of, and the timetable for, the decommissioning of weapons and the demilitarisation of society have not yet been drafted anywhere in the world. The early-release scheme for prisoners, the proposed amnesty for 'on the runs', the suggestion that victims of the troubles should be accorded 'the right to truth', even the consociational framework of the power-sharing arrangements set out in the Agreement and the Northern Ireland Act 1998 – none of these can be validly sustained by reference to human rights norms as no such norms have yet been invented for those spheres. Indeed, existing human rights norms would weigh heavily *against* the realisation of some of these ideas. Granting an amnesty to human rights abusers, for example, if the abuse has been a serious one, is contrary to international human rights law. But these are the matters which have monopolised political debate in Northern Ireland over the last few years. Politicians and non-governmental organisations (NGO) who address these issues by using the rhetoric of human rights would do better to deploy a more honest discourse.

The one area which traditional human rights activists have been loathe to analyse in human rights terms has been that of criminality, particularly crimes of violence committed by or in the name of paramilitary organisations (Knox and Monaghan, 2002; Feenan, 2002). 'Punishment attacks', drug-dealing, racketeering, fuel-smuggling and armed robberies still abounded in Northern Ireland seven years after the Good Friday Agreement (IMC, 2004–5), but very few political or NGO commentators have condemned such behaviour as human rights violations. Yet that is exactly what they are: people's rights to life, to be free from torture or inhuman or degrading treatment or punishment, to respect for their private and family life and home, and to enjoyment of their own possessions, are all in play when these crimes are committed, and it is pedantic, if not positively misleading, to describe them in any other way. To some human rights lawyers and human rights NGOs they may not constitute breaches of *human rights law*, which, deriving as it does from international treaties, is considered by some to be binding only on nation states and their emanations, but to everyone else they are certainly breaches of *human rights*. Human rights lawyers need to remember that do not own the term human rights: it is a concept which predates their lawyering and which deserves to be invoked whenever the values implicit in the social goods it represents are under threat by anyone at any time (Alston, 2005; McEvoy, 2001).

New Commissioners have recently been appointed to the NIHRC, the government announced that it planned to dismantle the 'emergency' laws in Northern Ireland by August 2007, the IRA has indicated that it has ceased all activities and the DUP seems more amenable than ever before to engage on human rights issues. In addition, the system for appointing judges is being reformed, the prosecution service is being modernised (albeit slowly), freedom of information legislation has come into force and the rights of gay and lesbians people, and of transgendered people, have been increased.

But there are less hopeful signs too: the government has still not granted the Human Rights Commission additional powers to enable it to be more effective, the Prime Minister and Home Secretary want to tamper with the Human Rights Act throughout the UK as part of the 'war against terrorism', a new Inquiries Act has severely undermined the ability of tribunals of inquiry to get to the truth of official malpractice, loyalist paramilitaries continue to kill, maim and intimidate, and the prospects of the unionist parties agreeing to a comprehensive Bill of Rights such as is favoured by the nationalist parties seem as remote as ever. The Police Service, moreover, while adopting policies and codes of practice and subjecting itself to oversight mechanisms which are second to none in human rights terms, still comes under fire, literally as well as metaphorically when it attempts to control riots or to police rerouted parades.

As so often, the picture regarding human rights is rosier than it was but not as bright as it could be. Many demands are made in the area but often they are unspecific and absolutist, not recognising that the rights of individuals need to take second place to those of society as a whole (as the European Convention expressly acknowledges). Work on human rights needs to be depoliticised as much as possible, but it seems that this is a long way from being a reality in Northern Ireland.

Conclusion

From this brief review of the major areas of equality and human rights it is clear that in several respects further progress is still required. Positive developments in fair employment over the past two decades need to be matched across the rest of the equality field and aspects of the human rights agenda have yet to be addressed. A lack of any sense of urgency regarding the creation of single equality legislation, first promised in the Northern Ireland Executive's first Programme for Government, and with respect to the introduction of a Bill of Rights for Northern Ireland, highlights the need for the government to give priority to these matters. There is much to be achieved if Northern Ireland is to be a beacon of excellence in these fields.

Notes

1 The authors were, respectively, members of the Northern Ireland Human Rights Commission (1999–2005) and the Equality Commission of Northern Ireland (1999–2004). The views expressed are theirs alone and do not necessarily represent the views of the two Commissions.

2 Alongside fair employment legislation, sex discrimination and equal pay legislation were introduced in the 1970s (with the associated creation of the Equal Opportunities Commission and disability and race discrimination legislation (and the Commission for Racial Equality) in the 1990s.

3 The Standing Advisory Commission on Human Rights was created under the Northern Ireland Constitution Act 1973 with a remit of advising the Secretary of State for Northern Ireland on the adequacy and effectiveness of law preventing discrimination on the ground of religious belief or political opinion.

4 The bodies grouped into the new Equality Commission were the Equal Opportunities Commission, the Fair Employment Commission, the Commission for Racial Equality and the Disability Council.
5 These groups were also critical of the proposal as it did not simultaneously plan to produce a single Equality Act to replace each piece of anti-discrimination legislation.

References

Alston, P. (ed.) (2005) *Non-State Actors and Human Rights*. Oxford: Oxford University Press.

CAJ (Committee on the Administration of Justice) (1996) *A Bill of Rights for Northern Ireland* (updated version of the draft Bill of Rights contained in CAJ Pamphlet 17, *Making Rights Count*). Belfast: CAJ

Criminal Justice Reveiw (2000) *Report of the Review of the Criminal Justice System in Northern Ireland*. London and Belfast: Northern Ireland Office.

Dickson, B. (2004) 'Northern Ireland' in A. Lester and D. Pannick (eds) *Human Rights Law and Practice* 2nd edition. London: LexisNexis Butterworths.

ECNI (Election Commission for Northern Ireland) (1999) *Report of the Equality Commission Working Group*. Belfast: ECNI.

ECNI (Equality Commission for Northern Ireland) (2003) *Full Report on the Implementation of the Section 75 Equality and Good Relations Duties by Public Authorities, 1 January 2000–31 March 2002*. Belfast: ECNI

ECNI (Equality Commission for Northern Ireland) (2004) *Report of the Implementation of the Section 75 Statutory Duties, 1 April 2002–31 March 2003*. Belfast: ECNI.

Feenan, D. (2002) (ed.) *Informal Criminal Justice*. Aldershot: Ashgate Publishing.

Harvey, C and Livingstone, S. (1999) 'Human rights and the Northern Ireland peace process', *European Human Rights Law Review*, 162.

IMC (Independent Monitoring Commission) (2004–5) *First, Third, Fourth and Fifth Reports of the Independent Monitoring Commission*. Belfast: IMC.

In re McR (2002). The High Court's decision in *In re McR*, reported at [2002] NIQB 58.

Knox, C. and Monaghan, R. (2002) *Informal Justice in Divided Societies: Northern Ireland and South Africa*. Basingstoke: Palgrave Macmillan.

McCrudden, C. (2001) 'Not the way forward: some comments on the Northern Ireland Human Rights Commission's consultation document', *Northern Ireland Legal Quarterly*, 52, 372.

McCrudden, C. (2004) *Mainstreaming Equality in Northern Ireland 1998–2004: A Review of Issues Concerning the Operation of the Equality Duty in Section 75 of the Northern Ireland Act 1998*, mimeo.

McEvoy, K. (2001) 'Human rights, humanitarian interventions and paramilitary activities in Northern Ireland' in Colin Harvey (ed.) *Human Rights, Equality and Democratic Renewal in Northern Ireland*. Oxford: Hart Publishing.

NIHRC (Northern Ireland Human Rights Commission) (2000–4) *Annual Reports of the Northern Ireland Human Rights Commission*, (sections on 'Casework'). Belfast: NIHRC.

NIHRC (Northern Ireland Human Rights Commission) (2001) *Making a Bill of Rights for Northern Ireland*. Belfast: NIHRC.

NIHRC (Northern Ireland Human Rights Commission) (2002) *In Our Care: Promoting the Rights of Children in Custody*. Belfast: NIHRC.

NIHRC (Northern Ireland Human Rights Commission) (2003) *Summary of Submissions on a Bill of Rights*. Belfast: NIHRC.

NIHRC (Northern Ireland Human Rights Commission) (2004a) *Progressing a Bill of Rights for Northern Ireland*. Belfast: NIHRC.

NIHRC (Northern Ireland Human Rights Commission) (2004b) *Bill of Rights in Schools. A Resource for Post-primary Schools*. Belfast: NIHRC.

NIHRC (Northern Ireland Human Rights Commission) (2005) *The Hurt Inside: The Imprisonment of Women and Girls in Northern Ireland*. Belfast: NIHRC.

NIO (Northern Ireland Office) (1998) *The Agreement. Agreement Reached in the Multi-party Negotiations*. Belfast: NIO.

Osborne, R.D. (2003) 'Progessing the equality agenda in Northern Ireland', *Journal of Social Policy*, 32(3) 339–360.

Osborne, R.D. (2005) 'Equality in higher education in Northern Ireland', *Higher Education Quarterly*, 50(2) 138–152.

Osborne, R.D. Cormack, R.J., Gallagher, A.M. and Shortall, S. (1996) 'The implementation of the policy appraisal and fair treatment guidelines in Northern Ireland', in E. McLaughlin and P. Quirk (eds) *Policy Aspects of Employment Equality in Northern Ireland*. Belfast: SACHR.

Osborne, R.D. and Shuttleworth I. (eds) (2004) *Fair Employment in Northern Ireland: A Generation On*. Belfast: Blackstaff.

Patten Report (1999) *A New Beginning: Policing in Northern Ireland. The Report of the Independent Commission on Policing for Northern Ireland*. Belfast: HMSO.

White Paper (1998) *Partnership for Equality*, CM380. Belfast: The Stationery Office.

Whyte, J. (1983) 'How much discrimination was there under Unionist governments, 1920–1968?' in T. Gallagher and J. O'Connell (eds) *Contemporary Irish Studies*. Manchester: Manchester University Press.

12

Inside Stormont: the Assembly and the Executive

Rick Wilford

Introduction

The experience of devolution in Northern Ireland,[1] unlike that in Scotland and Wales, *has* resembled an event rather than a process, such that the 108 MLAs[2] enjoyed only a parliamentary half-life during the first devolved mandate. While devolution was an opportunity for locally elected politicians to work cooperatively for the common weal, its arrested development following the prolonged delay in transferring powers limited the capacity of ministers and MLAs to 'make a difference' to the lives of its inhabitants.

These were not the only constraints: another was the composition of the Executive Committee. A testament to the maximal inclusiveness of its consociational design, this four-party voluntary coalition[3] – unlike those struck in Edinburgh and initially in Cardiff – was not an agreed arrangement among more or less willing partners, but a confected grand coalition that, from its outset, resembled a loveless marriage.[4] It encompassed the staunch loyalism of the DUP, the unapologetic republicanism of Sinn Féin, together with the ostensibly more forgiving unionism of the UUP and the pragmatic nationalism of the SDLP.

This was a potentially fissile combination, not least because of the inherent strains within the UUP.[5] A number of its MLAs remained hostile to the Agreement, while the rest were at best ambivalent about the inclusion of Sinn Féin within the Executive without complete and verifiable decommissioning by the IRA. Furthermore, the DUP's decision to take the two ministerial seats to which it was entitled but to boycott meetings, the Assembly excepted, of the primary institutions in all three 'strands' of the Agreement, namely the Executive, the North/South Ministerial Council (NSMC) and the British–Irish Council (BIC), impeded the outworking of the devolved institutions, as did its decision to rotate the ministerial roles among its MLAs.[6]

While there were 'key' decisions that required agreement among ministers,[7] there was no entrenchment of the convention of collective responsibility within the Executive: rather, the Northern Ireland Act 1998 which implemented the Agreement vested ministerial responsibility in individual ministers rather than the 'cabinet' as a whole. This meant that the governing parties could each treat their departments as party fiefdoms and, if they so chose, to act simultaneously as both government and opposition: the best of all possible worlds.

In short, the Executive lacked cohesion: in the words of one coalition expert, 'The Executive Committee looks little more than a holding company for a collection of ministers with different party affiliations than a collective decision-making body' (Laver, 2000). However, a number of obligations, including that to propose annual Programmes for Government and, of course, budgetary allocations to the devolved departments, did supply some 'glue' to its operation by requiring unanimity around the cabinet table, even if two ministers were not physically present. The 'pledge of office' and the ministerial code of conduct provided some necessary additional adhesive, but it was not sufficient to overcome the simmering and occasionally eruptive mistrust among the governing parties. This did not mean however, that it was a 'do-nothing' administration but rather a 'did-less than might otherwise be hoped' one.

The mesh of constraints

The achievements of devolution were, perhaps, rather modest but they are noteworthy given that there were additional constraints that affected the activities of the Assembly and the Executive. For reasons of space these might be summarised by observing that the Assembly's first term was, to coin a phrase, 'parliamentary life, but not quite as we know it'.

For instance, unlike at Westminster or, more aptly, Edinburgh and Cardiff, the numerical strength of the four Executive parties, which together took 90 of the 108 Assembly seats, meant that there was no official 'opposition' in the chamber, in the sense of an alternative government-in-waiting. While participation in the Executive was voluntary, the fact that each of the parties entitled to 'cabinet' seats chose to exercise their ministerial options meant that they not only dominated proceedings in the chamber, but also within the Assembly's committees, both statutory and standing.[8]

Like the ministers, the committee chairs and deputy chairs were nominated via the d'Hondt procedure and the composition of each committee, though they varied in size, was broadly proportional to party strengths in the chamber.[9] This placed the smaller and minor parties at a disadvantage *vis-à-vis* the MLAs in the Executive-forming parties. Committee agendas, especially those of the statutory committees, were structured largely by Executive business and the in-built majorities enjoyed by the four main parties meant, all other things being equal, that a generally constructive, though not uncritical, mood prevailed between ministers and their party colleagues in committee.[10]

The relationship between the statutory committees and their associated departments was especially complex given the former's manifold roles. The statutory committees are hybrid creations – in Westminster terms, part select and part standing committees. Like select committees, they held the devolved departments to account by scrutinising their policies, administration and expenditure, and, like standing committees they took the committee stage of all primary legislation.[11] They were also able to pursue freely chosen enquiries into aspects of public policy and to bring forward their own legislative proposals. This was a potentially heavy load, made more burdensome by their role in policy development and consultation with respect to their associated departments: the combined weight of these responsibilities at times led to committee overload, which slowed the legislative and policy process.[12]

Moreover, committees appeared generally reluctant to employ sub-committees[13] as a means of spreading the load while, more broadly, their agenda management was not aided by their preferred operating style. The statutory committees opted for evidence sessions with witnesses who trailed dutifully into Parliament Buildings to appear before them. Indeed, unlike in Scotland and Wales where a more peripatetic style was evident, the committees led a largely sedentary existence, seldom practising outreach to the wider community by taking evidence off-site.[14]

While such procedural and operational problems are remediable, this is less the case with the behavioural disposition of MLAs. In a divided society the premium on party (for which read communal) loyalty is paramount, such that the bonds between MLAs and ministers belonging to the same party are especially strong. This has the effect of inhibiting the exercise of independent-mindedness among 'backbench' members who felt obliged to defend 'their' respective ministers. The UUP aside, intra-party dissent was rare, much less so than, for instance, at Westminster.

To summarise, there were *structural* constraints on the activities of both the Executive and the Assembly committees arising from the consociational template. Its rigidities, including inclusive power sharing, the proportionality principle and the unanimity rule in relation to key decisions, were enshrined in the Agreement and, though perhaps cumbersome, were deemed necessary by its architects to facilitate both the appearance and the substance of good government. Moreover, the statutory requirement on MLAs to designate themselves as either unionist, nationalist or 'other', hardly assisted in encouraging them to think outside a communal box, notably when sectarian violence erupted within the wider community: on such occasions the Assembly chamber was more an echo chamber of, rather than a sounding board for, the differing and conflicting traditions.

There were also *operational* constraints, occasioned in large measure by the wide remit of the statutory committees, the breadth of which, though not fully exploited, did tend to qualify their efficiency.[15] Moreover, a majority of MLAs were also elected representatives in other tiers of political life. Sixty were local councillors, there were a dozen MPs, one of whom was also a Member of the European Parliament (MEP) and there were two peers in the chamber. Some, including the First and Deputy First Ministers, held a dual mandate, and others sought to manage a triple mandate during either the whole or part of the first Assembly. Such 'double-jobbing' meant that most MLAs had to spread their energies across at least two spheres of representation, rather than maintaining a single-minded focus on the Assembly. The not infrequent clashes between Assembly business, especially on committee days, and local council meetings did cause hiccups in proceedings. Occasionally, for instance, committee meetings were rendered inquorate as members left to travel to attend meetings in their district councils.[16]

The dual mandate problem, singular to Northern Ireland in the devolved UK, was explicable in part because of the uncertainties surrounding the robustness of devolution. Potential MLA candidates may well have been reluctant to seek nomination, given doubts about the durability of the institutions, and for most parties, including the four largest, local councils were an obvious recruiting ground. This had the advantage of drawing upon individuals who had both representative and committee experience, albeit within the narrowly circumscribed field of local government. The disadvantage was that only a handful of MLAs had legislative experience and none who were nominated to the Executive Committee had cut their ministerial teeth.

This dearth of expertise was, of course, inescapable. The democratic deficit created by direct rule meant that opportunities to acquire skills appropriate to the performance of executive and legislative roles were limited.[17] Equally, direct rule had enabled a policy deficit to develop within local parties which, for a political generation, had contended with two dominant issues – the constitution and security – to the relative neglect of other matters. The salience of those two issues had not only generated the habit of adversarialism among those elected to the Assembly, it had also bred a culture of mutual mistrust among ideological opponents harbouring mutually exclusive national projects.

In the context of Executive power-sharing, trust, if not withheld entirely, had to be hard-won: it was certainly not a given. While David Trimble acknowledged that those with a past could have a future in a democratic, devolved and plural Northern Ireland, and republicans seemed persuaded, at least initially, that some unionists were, if reluctantly, content 'to have a *taig* about the place', there was an undeniably brittle quality to the new political institutions. The several attempts to exclude Sinn Féin from the Executive, the four suspensions of the Assembly, the resignation of David Trimble, the subsequent difficulties involved in electing Trimble and Mark Durkan as First and Deputy First Minister respectively in November 2001, and the limited period during which the institutions across all three strands of the Agreement were operating concurrently, were proof positive of that fragility.

In such inauspicious circumstances it is somewhat remarkable that the first devolved administration made any legislative and policy progress. Moreover, that it did so in a more or less joined-up manner is particularly noteworthy.

Assembly activities

Between the onset of devolution in December 1999 and the final suspension of the first Assembly in October 2002, a total of 27 Bills had been considered by committees and had completed all their stages, while a further 22 Executive Bills were at various stages of the legislative process when direct rule was reintroduced. In relation to secondary legislation, the committees scrutinised more than 600 statutory rules, considered a total of 214 public consultations launched by their target departments, associated agencies or non-departmental public bodies, and had undertaken the scrutiny of 123 policy development matters on their own initiative, supplementing those referred to the committees by the departments. In addition, there were 43 inquiries initiated by the ten statutory committees, the (standing) Committee of the Centre (CoC) and the (standing) Public Accounts Committee, the latter of which was responsible for 19 of them.

Both standing and statutory committees had the power to initiate legislation, as did MLAs by way of a Private Member's Bill (PMB). However, neither the committees nor the backbenchers were active in proposing legislation. Only one Committee Bill was introduced during the first mandate and just two PMBs, one of which was superseded by Office of First Minister and Deputy First Minister (OFMDFM).[18] Such reticence arose in part because it was not until 1 April 2002 – just over six months, including recesses, before the final suspension – that a panel of parliamentary draftsmen was established by the Bills Office to provide specialist drafting services to support PMBs and Committee Bills. This resource constraint, together with the compelling weight of Executive business, combined to limit the extent to which both members and committees exploited the legislative opportunity afforded them.

More positively, the requirement that *all* committee reports were to be laid before and debated in the chamber ensured that the committees were integrated fully into the life of the Assembly, which assisted in joining up the business of the legislature. Moreover, certain of the procedures adopted by the committees promoted greater coordination of their activities. For instance, the Finance and Personnel Committee (FPC) collated and summarised the responses of all of the statutory committees to the spending plans of their associated departments and was thereby enabled to recommend a number of changes to the scrutiny of the budgetary process. In addition, committees routinely sought inputs from others where a Bill was perceived to cross departmental boundaries, and, on occasion, statutory committees held joint evidence-taking sessions for the same reason. This level of joined-up cooperation was such that the parties, with the exception of the DUP, decided to establish a non-statutory 'liaison committee' to act as a source of inter-committee advice, designed to effect greater efficiency in their work.

The inter-committee linkages were one index of 'joined-upness': another was the generally workmanlike ethos within the committees. Though there were exceptions, notably the early phase of the CoC[19] and occasions when committee members broke ranks to support 'their' minister rather than their committee, in general the committees did seek to operate on an agreed, consensual basis rather than dividing routinely along party lines. Though such an operating style may have been contrived, there was nevertheless a sense among members that such unity that could be achieved was a particular asset in dealing with ministers and departmental officials. Even the standing Business Committee that met weekly under the chairmanship of the Assembly's Speaker, Lord Alderdice, and consisting of the party whips, only rarely resorted to a vote to resolve differences over the planning of the Assembly's plenary business.[20]

Thus, while the chamber did at times resemble a bear-pit, an air of, if merely studied, decorum tended to prevail in the committee rooms. As for the chamber itself, the Assembly met normally on two days per week and held a total of 158 plenary sessions during devolution.[21] Besides debates, whether on Executive, committee or members' business, oral questions were put weekly, normally to three ministers for half-an-hour each, and tended to be at their liveliest when the Sinn Féin ministers appeared at the despatch box: these occasions were regarded by anti-Agreement unionists as opportunities to engage both in republican-baiting and attempts to ring-fence the moral high ground.

As well as being the arena in which abortive attempts to exclude Sinn Féin ministers from the Executive and for (failed) votes of no confidence in both

David Trimble and Martin McGuinness, again moved by anti-Agreement unionists, the chamber also witnessed a number of fractious debates which, given the unresolved matters of paramilitary decommissioning and criminality, is unsurprising. A focus on such acrimonious exchanges should not, however, obscure the constructive debates that took place, especially in relation to the key task of holding the Executive to account. Members did work to effect in this regard, not least in relation to the scrutiny of the budget process. Led by members of the FPC, the Assembly did succeed in extending the time available to scrutinise draft budgetary allocations and in improving the quality of relevant financial and economic information for members. That said, there were lacunae in the budgetary process that exercised MLAs, not least in relation to the Executive Programme Funds (EPF) expressly designed to assist the achievement of joined-up government (see below).

Earlier, we noted the volume of legislation dealt with by the Assembly. However, this gives no indication of its significance nor of the success members and committees had in amending the legislation. There are a number of observations to be made in respect of legislative matters. Only a minority of Executive Bills (11 of the 27 which received the Royal Assent) were sent to the relevant committees for pre-introductory consultation before the first legislative stage. The low rate of such consultation arose largely because a number of those Bills were inherited from the outgoing direct rule regime and work on them was well advanced at departmental level, such that it precluded the opportunity for pre-introductory consultation. The situation did improve: of the 22 Bills in the pipeline when direct rule was reintroduced in October 2002, almost three-quarters (16) had been subject to pre-introductory consultation, 14 of them in the form of a draft Bill submitted to the relevant committee. This demonstrated a near-routine improvement to the legislative process and one that further strengthened the partnership between the Executive and the Assembly's committees. Data from the Assembly's Bills Office indicates that committees were more successful than individual members in having amendments to Bills agreed by the Assembly: 76 per cent of committee amendments were agreed compared to 25 per cent of those tabled by MLAs (NIA, 2004: 35).

The value of an agreed committee view in relation to legislative amendment appears to have been internalised by members. While some amendments were relatively minor, others were more significant. For instance, and against robust arguments by the Health Minister, the Health, Social Services and Public Safety Committee secured the Assembly's agreement to delay the ending of general practice fundholding for 12 months until an agreed alternative arrangement was secured. A second example of a committee flexing its muscles occurred when the Environment Committee opposed key clauses in the Local Government Best Value Bill. Supported in the chamber, the

Committee's opposition succeeded in greatly simplifying and amending the Department's preferred legislative proposals: the first occasion that a committee had successfully opposed the major parts of an Executive Bill.

In relation to committee inquiries, there were 24 conducted by the statutory committees and the CoC, and a further 19 by the Public Accounts Committee (PAC). Data from the Committee Office (NIA 2004: 17) shows that 62 per cent of key recommendations arising from inquiries by the statutory committees and the CoC were either implemented or accepted by the relevant departments, though process-related recommendations showed the highest rate of success, i.e. were either accepted or implemented, while those relating to legislation were the least successful. The PAC secured a 95 per cent success rate, albeit that most of its recommendations were process rather than policy-related. In general, the committees were, however, somewhat lax in having established procedures to follow up and monitor the fate of their recommendations: only about half of committee inquiry reports had formal follow-up procedures in place.

Some of the key achievements arising from committee inquiries included:

- Following a PAC report, the overhaul of fraud policy in the Department of Enterprise, Trade and Investment following a major fraud in the Local Enterprise Development Unit.
- The shaping of the role and remit of the Children's Commissioner following the CoC's report into the OFMDFM's proposal to create the office. The bulk of the Committee's recommendations were accepted, including strengthening the Commissioner's investigative powers and his power to bring, intervene in or assist in legal proceedings.
- Changes in policy to tackle homelessness, arising from an inquiry by the Committee for Social Development. The implemented recommendations included the development of a preventative strategy and measures designed to deal with homelessness among under 18 year-olds.

As mentioned earlier, the committees played a key role in developing a more accountable budget process. The FPC's consolidated recommendation to allow more time for the scrutiny of, and consultation over, the process was successful and led to the introduction of 'departmental position reports' furnished to each committee prior to the consideration of draft budget proposals by the Executive Committee. These reports extended the consultation period by up to four weeks, and enabled the committees to consult with key stakeholders in the wider community, to scrutinise more thoroughly draft budget proposals, and ensured greater transparency in the process by providing more detailed information for consideration by the committees.

Among other things, this improved process of consultation and scrutiny meant that committees and departments could gain common cause in lobbying for increased resources. One such instance of committee and departmental cooperation was the Health Committee's role in supporting the department's case for Executive Programme Fund support for capital spending on a new regional cancer centre. The Committee secured the Assembly's endorsement of the bid and £60 million was committed by the Executive in the 2003–4 budget, enabling the centre to be completed in 2005. Another example was the recommendation by the Education Committee that the department, led by Martin McGuinness (Sinn Féin), should bid for EPF monies to improve accommodation facilities in small rural schools. The recommendation was accepted and a successful bid of £6 million was submitted to the EPF.

A further demonstration of the joined-up partnership that could exist between a department and its associated committee was the close liaison between the Department for Agriculture and Rural Development and its Committee during the foot and mouth crisis. The Committee, chaired by the DUP leader, Ian Paisley, and the minister, Brid Rodgers SDLP, met weekly in the spring and early summer of 2001 so that the Committee was kept fully abreast of the evolving situation. This proved to be a successful working relationship, with the minister commended repeatedly for her prompt and effective response to the crisis as it unfolded.

There were, though, occasions when ministers and committees could not agree and divided along party lines. One such occasion arose over the Health Minister's (Bairbre de Brún, Sinn Féin), decision to site Belfast's maternity provision at a hospital in her republican/nationalist-dominated west Belfast constituency rather than one in neighbouring south Belfast where unionists held three seats and Sinn Féin none. The Committee voted in favour of the latter, as did the Assembly, although de Brún's party colleagues (and the committee chair, Joe Hendron, SDLP) rowed in behind her decision, proving themselves party animals rather than committee creatures. This was also the case in respect of the decision to defer the ending of general practice fundholding. Sinn Féin MLAs, including those on the Health Committee, rallied to the minister's cause both in the committee room and on the floor of the chamber. Similarly, the SDLP's members of the Higher Education Committee, having agreed a report on student financial support, then baulked when 'their' minister, Sean Farren, opposed certain of its recommendations and chose to back him rather than the Committee during the subsequent Assembly debate.

Before turning to the Executive Committee, two points can be noted: one in relation to inter-committee relations and another between the committees and their associated departments and ministers. In respect of the former, it is justifiable to claim the existence of a fledgling committee *system* within the Assembly. The pooling of information among and between committees, especially in respect of legislative proposals, several instances of joint evidence-taking sessions and the decision to establish a liaison committee, represented a concerted and coordinated effort to achieve the joined-up scrutiny of the Executive on both an intra- and inter-committee basis. Improvements to the process of scrutinising both legislative and budget proposals were tangible evidence of the seriousness with which MLAs treated their parliamentary roles. Though there were occasions when MLAs abandoned their committee identity in favour of their party, they were relatively infrequent, as were divided committee reports: consensus relatively quickly became the standard practice in committee.

There were, however, accountability gaps, especially in the early stages of the Assembly's existence, including pre-legislative consultation and scrutiny of the budget, in the latter case caused largely by the time pressure under which committees were expected to operate. For instance, when the first draft budget proposals were circulated to the statutory committees, two (Health and Social Development) were unable to make their views known to FPC in the time available.

There were two other accountability gaps worthy of note. The first concerns the (standing) CoC. Charged to scrutinise the OFMDFM, its remit was limited to approximately half of the responsibilities discharged by the Office. The First and Deputy First Ministers had taken the view that the 'external' functions of the OFMDFM, including those relating to Strands 2 and 3, respectively the North–South and East–West aspects of the Agreement, should be reported to plenary meetings of the Assembly rather than the Committee. Thus, the opportunity for the more forensic scrutiny afforded by cross-questioning in committee was denied to the CoC in relation to a significant bundle of the Office's responsibilities. Moreover, until standing orders were changed in January 2001, the CoC had to seek the permission of the Assembly to scrutinise legislation proposed by the OFMDFM. The change meant that henceforth the Committee would automatically have both primary and secondary legislation referred to it, thereby putting it on a par with the statutory committees.

The lacuna in respect of North–South matters also affected the statutory committees in general. The normal mode of reporting on both the plenary and sectoral business of the NSMC was that the relevant ministers made a statement on the floor of the Assembly and then took questions. This procedure restricted the extent to which the affairs of the NSMC were subject to the level of scrutiny available at committee and was a particular irritant for anti-Agreement unionists who were hostile towards what they termed dismissively as 'North–Southery'.

The Executive Committee

From the outset, the Executive was beset by operational problems. To catalogue them is to summon up the political equivalent of *coitus interruptus*. A first suspension just 72 days after the transfer of powers, the DUP boycott and its later decision to rotate its two ministries, David Trimble's refusal to authorise the attendance of the two Sinn Féin ministers to meetings of the NSMC, Sinn Féin's retaliatory boycott of the BIC, Trimble's resignation, the temporary appointment of Sir Reg Empey UUP as acting First Minister, and three further suspensions, together demonstrated that implementing devolution was fitful and as, if not more, problematic than negotiating the Agreement.

There was much unfinished business in the wake of Good Friday in 1998, including the shape and size of the Executive. In fact, the party composition of the Executive was a direct outcome of its size, i.e. the number of departments – ten – agreed essentially between the UUP and the SDLP in the latter part of 1998. Given the creation of the OFMDFM, the decision to establish another ten departments owed little if anything to administrative reasoning and much to political arithmetic: in short, there was a trade-off. The UUP wanted to minimise the number of both ministries and cross-border bodies, whereas the SDLP (and Sinn Féin) sought to maximise them. The bargain became ten departments (plus the OFMDFM) in return for the 12 North–South bodies suggested in the text of the Agreement. Given the application of d'Hondt to determine Executive seats this yielded a symmetrical 'cabinet' of six unionist and six nationalist ministers: size was everything. However, as subsequent events demonstrated, parity of numbers was no guarantee of parity of esteem.

Reconfiguring the six departments inherited from the direct rule administration proved a protracted, untidy and somewhat improvised affair that was not concluded until February 1999. Agreeing the large and imperfectly formed Executive in functional rather than more imaginative thematic terms was the prelude to the process of agreeing the Programme for Government (PfG). In the content of the policy deficit referred to earlier and the capacity and, in some cases, the readiness of certain ministers to regard their departments as petty fiefdoms, this was a doubly complex task given the doctrinal gulf that existed among the parties on many social, educational, economic and cultural matters. It made the effort to achieve a set of cross-cutting, joined-up policies even more challenging.

There was no doubting the aspirations of Trimble and Mallon as far as the Executive was concerned, especially in regard to its responsibility in devising and implementing the annually reviewed PfG.[22] Described by David Trimble as part multi-party manifesto and part Queen's Speech, the first (and second) Programme was entitled 'Making a Difference', encapsulating the ambition to exert positive change: in the words of Seamus Mallon SDLP, 'it is a defining moment in the life of our institutions. Let us not waste the opportunity we have been given to write our own script and truly serve the people'.[23] It was a vaulting ambition and, given the requirement that the PfG had to be agreed by the Executive, an ostensibly shared one, notwithstanding the DUP's absence from round-table discussions.

The PfGs, glue for a strained and unstable 'cabinet', were organised around five strategic and thematic priorities, incorporating initially more than 250 explicit 'actions' directed towards their attainment, many of which included discrete quantitative targets.[24] Space precludes discussion of the documents, but what is worth noting was the conscious attempt to promote cross-departmental and joined-up government. This holistic approach, wholly consistent with the 'Blairite' agenda for modernising government, was given an added dimension with the innovation of the Executive Programme Funds (EPFs) which were designed to encourage cross-cutting work.

The resources dedicated to the five EPFs,[25] which dovetailed with the PfG's priorities, were withheld from the departmental budget allocations: departments were invited to bid for them preferably, though not exclusively, on a cross-departmental basis, with final decisions taken within the Executive. In the event, the majority of bids in the first tranche had, in the Finance Minister's words 'a mono-departmental focus', belying much of the intent of the EPF initiative. Moreover, there was a clamour for the funds: £372 million was made available over three years, but the first bidding round produced 139 bids totalling over £581 million, 62 of which were funded at a cost of £141 million.

The PfGs, and the associated budgets, seemed to indicate the ability of the ministers to act in concert, since both had to be agreed within the Executive. This implies, correctly, that a *modus operandi* was devised to deal with the problems caused by the DUP's semi-detached status. On occasion, officials from the party's two departments (Regional Development and Social Development) attended the Executive on behalf of their respective ministers to put the views of each department, while at the same time the ministers themselves did not hesitate to make those views known to the Finance Minister directly, not least during the budgetary process. The other ministers did, in effect, accommodate the DUP's ministers by holding bilateral meetings with them so as not to compromise the interests served by the DUP's departments – but only up to a point.

When devolution was first restored in May 2000, the DUP announced that it would henceforth rotate its departments among its MLAs, that its ministers could not be regarded as being bound by the ministerial code of conduct, and that they would 'uncover and reveal what is going on at the heart of government'.[26] In response the other ministers agreed on a number of retaliatory actions, including the non-circulation of Executive Committee papers to them, other than those relating to the DUP's own departments. In that respect, the Executive could be regarded as an expression of chopped-up rather than joined-up government. Moreover, ministerial unanimity over the PfGs and successive budgets was sometimes as apparent as it was real. On several occasions the DUP and Sinn Féin sought to amend both on the floor of the Assembly, suggesting that Executive 'agreement' was on occasion an aspiration rather than a reality.

In total the Executive held just 58 meetings (all boycotted by the DUP) over the 30 turbulent months of its existence, five of which were dedicated to the foot and mouth epidemic – hardly an impressive work rate. Nor were ministers unduly distracted by committee work. Only two ministerial sub-committees were established, one tasked to oversee the review of public administration and the other to oversee the activities of the Strategic Investment Board created to steer the 'reform and reinvestment' initiative unveiled by the Prime Minister and Chancellor of the Exchequer in May 2002.[27] There was, in effect, no cabinet 'system' as such, certainly nothing akin to the sub-structure of ministerial committees common in Cardiff and Edinburgh and, for that matter, London and Dublin.

There were, however, a number of significant policy initiatives taken by the Executive. These included the review of public administration, the creation of a Children's Commissioner (modelled on the Welsh initiative), the development of new strategies including for public health, regional development, transport and the agricultural sector, free nursing care (though not, as in Scotland, personal care) for the elderly, free public transport for pensioners, a more progressive scheme of student finance (although not as generous as that in Scotland) and the negotiation of the reform and reinvestment strategy (see below).

Two key decisions, the abolition of school league tables and, more controversially, the ending of the transfer test (the '11 plus') were taken unilaterally by the Education Minister, Martin McGuinness, the latter just before the final suspension in October 2002. Whatever its motive, the decision epitomised the capacity of ministers to go on solo-runs if they so chose. There was no agreed replacement model of post-primary education within either the Assembly or the Executive, so that the minister's summary announcement made a mockery of the ambition to join up decision making.

There were other issues that divided the parties, not least over the matter of public finance. The reform and reinvestment initiative included a new loan facility negotiated with the Treasury, earmarked to tackle a long overdue overhaul of Northern Ireland's infrastructure. However, in order to repay the loan the Executive had to find new means of raising resources to supplement those allocated under the Barnett Formula on which it was almost wholly reliant. Limited almost exclusively to the rates as its major income stream, and driven by the UK Treasury, the Executive set both a rates review in train and a review of the options for introducing water service charges, necessary because, since privatisation in Britain, water services are not factored into the Barnett Formula. These, like the private finance initiative, were issues that divided the parties, but any serious rupture was avoided with the final suspension. This meant that the new rates and water charging regimes became matters for the Northern Ireland Office, thereby relieving the Executive from taking highly unpopular decisions and avoiding further straining its cohesion.

Conclusion

Should devolution be restored, the second mandate will differ from the first in a number of respects. The Comprehensive Agreement of December 2004 and the Joint Declaration of May 2003 each signal a set of measures designed to ensure the implementation in full of the 1998 Agreement.[28] The IRA's announcement in July 2005, and the subsequent acts of decommissioning in September, seem to indicate, to all intents and purposes, that the 'long war' is finally over. If the end of its paramilitary activities is borne out, and there is a corresponding end to the IRA's alleged criminal activities, then the way is paved to the implementation of the planned reforms, and devolution will be placed on a more stable footing.

The proposed changes – which affect the process of Executive formation, procedures designed to achieve collective responsibility and measures to enhance the scrutiny of the Executive, as well as the removal of Westminster's suspensory power – could engineer a more durable political arrangement and create a context within which mutual mistrust begins to dissipate. However, without an underpinning improvement in community relations, such an arrangement will be based on weak foundations.

Successive attitudinal surveys have demonstrated that the initial and broadly shared perception that the Agreement would yield equal benefits for both unionist and nationalist communities has faded, as the former increasingly understood it to have brought disproportionate advantages to the latter.[29] Notwithstanding that all legislation and policy was and will remain subject to equality, rights and rural-proofing, and that 'new targeting social need' (the major policy for tackling poverty and social exclusion) will be maintained, the failure by the Assembly and the Executive to agree a concerted community relations policy was the most conspicuous area of neglect during the devolved period.[30]

Like much else, the community relations initiative has been taken forward by the Northern Ireland Office which, since October 2002, has adopted a proactive stance on a range of policy matters. Thus, should devolution be restored in either 2006 or 2007 on the basis of a revised consociational model as set out in the Comprehensive Agreement of December 2004, a new Executive – derived from a freshly elected Assembly with, in all likelihood, a DUP First and Sinn Féin Deputy First Minister – would inherit a set of policy commitments bequeathed by British ministers.[31] This legacy would, in the shorter run, create a new context of constraints that local politicians will have to negotiate in order to 'make a difference' which, after all, is the *raison d'être* of devolution. That 'difference' will, however, have to include behavioural changes among local politicians; that, in turn, will rest on the progressive development of inter-communal trust at both elite and popular levels *before* devolution can be restored.

Notes

1 For a documentary record of the outworking of devolution since November 1999, see the monitoring reports available at www.ucl.ac.uk/constitution-unit/ nations. In addition, the State of the Nations series published between 2000 and 2005 by Imprint Academic provides analyses of the devolution project throughout the UK. On Northern Ireland, see Wilford and Wilson (2000, 2003 and 2005) and Wilson and Wilford (2001 and 2004).

2 Six MLAs, elected by means of PR-STV (proportional representation by the single transferable vote), were returned from each of Northern Ireland's 18 Westminster constituencies. The respective party strengths following the first Assembly election were: UUP 28, SDLP 24, DUP 20, Sinn Féin 18, Alliance Party 6, UKUP 5, Progressive Unionist Party 2, Women's Coalition 2, Independents (all unionist) 3. UKUP subsequently imploded, with four of its members forming the Northern Ireland Unionist Party (NIUP), while the three Independents coalesced into the United Unionist Assembly Party.

3 The coalition was voluntary in the sense that none of the parties was obliged to nominate members of the Executive. Note the attempt to form a shadow Executive before the transfer of powers, when the UUP, the DUP and the Alliance Party refused to nominate ministers. See *Official Report* 15 July 1999. Also, note the active contemplation of going into opposition rather than government by both the UUP and the SDLP prior to the second Assembly election in November 2003.

4 Inclusion within the Executive was governed by the application of the d'Hondt rule to the number of MLAs returned for each party. The adoption of d'Hondt as the means of Executive formation meant that the parties had every incentive to maximise turnout and votes within their respective and almost wholly mutually exclusive electorates, and none to encourage voters to bolster a pro-Agreement vote by expressing a preference for a pro-Agreement candidate from the 'other' tradition. The Assembly election in 1998 was in effect a first order contest: it pitched unionist candidates against one another along a pro and anti-Agreement axis, nationalists and republicans competed over a more or less assertive unification project and, of course, unionists and nationalists fought to secure the overall majority of votes and seats. While there was a pro-Agreement majority within the Assembly (80 MLAs to 28 MLAs), successful anti-Agreement unionist candidates secured marginally more first-preference votes at the election than their pro-Agreement unionist counterparts, even discounting the votes secured by successful UUP candidates who were opposed to the Agreement (see Mitchell, 2001).

5 Among unionist MLAs, the ostensible majority of pro-Agreement members (30:28) flattered to deceive. A number of UUP MLAs had voted against the Agreement at the referendum in May 1998 and one, Peter Weir, subsequently defected to the DUP, while another, Pauline Armitage, aligned herself with the anti-Agreement bloc following her suspension from the UUP. She subsequently joined the UK Unionist Party on whose ticket she contested the second Assembly election in November 2003.

6 The DUP rotated its ministers on two occasions, substituting Gregory Campbell and Maurice Morrow for, respectively, Peter Robinson (Regional Development) and Nigel Dodds (Social Development) in July 2000 and reverting to the original duo in November 2001.

7 The unanimity rule, intrinsic to consociationalism, applied to the draft budget proposals and the draft Programmes for Government. In addition, key decisions – which were designated in the text of the Agreement – were subject to cross-community consent within the Assembly. These also included the election on a joint ticket of the First and Deputy First Ministers, the election of the Assembly's Presiding Officer (Speaker) and the Assembly's standing orders. There were two tests of cross-community consent: parallel consent and a weighted majority. However, the election of the First and Deputy First Ministers was subject only to the first of these.

8 There were also ad hoc committees established at the request of the Secretary of State as consultative bodies in relation to 'reserved matters'. In total, nine ad hoc committees met during devolution, and two during the pre-devolution period. See the Committee page at www.niassembly.gov.uk.

9 Each of the statutory committees was 11-strong, the standing Committee of the Centre had 17 members and the other standing committees – Audit, Procedure, Standards and Privileges, Public Accounts and Business – varied from 5 to 13 members. The Assembly Commission, like the Business Committee, had 6 members.

10 The Agreement stipulated that committee chairs could not be drawn from the same party as that of the relevant minister. This provision enabled a working, joined-up partnership to evolve between the relevant incumbents.

11 The committees also scrutinised secondary legislation (statutory instruments).

12 One index of committee overload was that 26 of all Bills (53 per cent) were the subject of 'period extensions'. That is, the committees asked for additional time to scrutinise the provisions in the Bills, either because of the pressure of other work and/or the complexity of the proposals.

13 Only three created sub-committees, each of which was temporary. Two standing committees, the Committee of the Centre and the Procedure Committee established sub-committees. The former addressed EU Affairs, while the latter created two: one on Legislative Review and the other on Parliamentary Questions. Enterprise, Trade and Investment was the sole statutory committee to create a sub-committee, which focused on the Giant's Causeway as part of its Tourism inquiry.

14 Of more than a thousand committee meetings held during the first Assembly, there were only 78 visits by committees to venues elsewhere, including 28 which were held outside Northern Ireland, although eight venues across Northern Ireland were identified by the Assembly Commission as suitable locations for holding committee meetings. (NIA, 2002: 13). In the latter stages of the Assembly's term one committee, Enterprise, Trade and Investment, did experiment with 'conferencing' during its inquiry into the tourism industry as an alternative to the rather humdrum evidence sessions. This may act as a committee template if devolution is restored.

15 The efficiency of the committees was also hampered by the incidence of overlapping memberships. Excluding the 12 ministers, 2 junior ministers (in the OFMDFM), the UKUP's and all bar one of the NIUP's MLAs, the Speaker, and both John Taylor (Lord Kilclooney) and Gerry Adams who declined committee places, there were 87 members available to serve on the Assembly's 10 statutory, 6 standing and, eventually, 9 ad hoc committees. Some 20 MLAs sat on just one committee, but 67 served on two or more.

16 In light of this difficulty, the Procedure Committee proposed that the quorum for committees be reduced from five to three. See Procedure Committee Minutes, 27 February 2002.

17 The NIO did provide a training programme for the MLAs during the 'shadow' pre-devolution period, but attendance at its sessions was patchy.

18 The one Committee Bill was introduced by the standing Standards and Privileges Committee. It provided for the creation of the Assembly Ombudsman for Northern Ireland. The first PMB, introduced by the Women's Coalition, sought to create the Children's Commissioner but it was superseded by proposals brought forward by the OFMDFM. The second PMB, the Agriculture (Amendment) Bill, was tabled by Billy Armstrong (UUP): it sought, for tax purposes, to designate all horses as agricultural animals. There were three further PMBs in the wings at the time of suspension in October 2002.

19 Under its first chairman, Gregory Campbell (DUP), the Committee made little headway. Campbell refused to recognise the legitimacy, or even the presence, of the Sinn Féin members and the early meetings lasted only a few minutes and ended in some disarray. The situation improved when Campbell was succeeded by his party colleague, Edwin Poots, and a more pragmatic style was adopted.

20 There were six members of the Commission, including its chair, Lord Alderdice (Speaker), charged to provide and maintain the property, services and staff

required for the purposes of the Assembly. It met on 47 occasions during devolution, and only in relation to one issue, the proposal to display lilies over the Easter period in 2001 in the Great Hall in Parliament Buildings, did it resort to a vote. This was a highly controversial proposal and subsequently an emergency meeting of the Assembly was called to debate the decision taken by the Commission. See *Official Report*, 10 April 2001.

21 In the pre-devolution period there were 19 plenary meetings of the 'shadow' Assembly and 85 committee meetings.

22 The initial PfG was delayed until the autumn of 2000 because of the first period of suspension that ended in May. In its stead the Executive produced an interim Agenda for Government in June 2000, shortly after the first restoration of devolution.

23 *Official Report*, 24 October 2000.

24 The five themes were: 'Growing as a Community'; 'Working for a Healthier People'; 'Investing in Education and Skills'; 'Securing a Competitive Economy'; and 'Developing North/South and International Relations'.

25 The five major policy areas included under the umbrella of the EPFs were: 'Social Inclusion/Community Regeneration'; 'Service Modernisation'; 'New Directions'; 'Infrastructure/Capital Renewal'; and 'Children'.

26 DUP press release, 31 May 2000.

27 See NIO press release 2 May 2002. Also see the statement to the Assembly by Trimble and Durkan, *Official Report*, 7 May 2002.

28 Both documents are available at www.nio.gov.uk.

29 See the results from successive, post-devolution Northern Ireland Life and Times Surveys available at www.ark.uk.

30 Information on the proofing of legislation and policy and on new targeting social need is available at www.ofmdfmni.gov.uk. Preliminary work on community relations policy was undertaken on behalf of the OFMDFM by Dr Jeremy Harbison during the devolved period. However, the relevant consultation paper did not appear until January 2003 and the policy and strategic framework, *A Shared Future*, was not published until March 2005. See www.ofmdfmni.gov.uk.

31 There was, of course, a second Assembly election in November 2003. Following three post-election defections from the UUP to the DUP, the balance of party strengths within the 'virtual' Assembly was: 33 DUP, 24 Sinn Féin, 24 UUP, 18 SDLP, 6 Alliance Party, and one seat each for UKUP, the Progressive Unionist Party and an Independent candidate. Had d'Hondt been triggered, the Executive would have included seven unionist and five nationalist ministers.

References

Laver, M. (2000) 'Coalitions in Northern Ireland', conference paper, Democratic Dialogue, Belfast, September.

Mitchell, P. (2001) 'Transcending an ethnic party system? The impact of consociational governance on electoral dynamics and the party system' in R. Wilford (ed.) *Aspects of the Belfast Agreement*. Oxford: Oxford University Press, 28–48.

NIA (Northern Ireland Assembly) (2002) *First Report of the Northern Ireland Assembly Commission: December 1999-March 2002.* Norwich: The Stationery Office.

NIA (Northern Ireland Assembly) (2004) *Report of the Working Group on the Review of the Effectiveness of Committees.* Belfast: NIA.

Wilford, R. and Wilson, R. (2000) 'A bare knuckle ride: Northern Ireland' in R. Hazell (ed.) *The State and the Nations: The First Year of Devolution.* Thorverton: Imprint Academic, 79–116.

Wilford, R. and Wilson, R. (2003) 'Northern Ireland: valedictory?' in R. Hazell (ed.) *The State of the Nations 2003: The Third Year of Devolution in the UK.* Thorverton: Imprint Academic, 79–118.

Wilford, R. and Wilson, R. (2005) 'Northern Ireland: while you take the high road' in A. Trench (ed.) *The Dynamics of Devolution: The State of the Nations 2005.* Thorverton: Imprint Academic, 63–90.

Wilson, R. and Wilford, R. (2001) 'Northern Ireland: endgame' in A. Trench (ed.) *The State of the Nations 2001: The Second Year of Devolution in the UK.* Thorverton: Imprint Academic, 77–106.

Wilson, R. and Wilford, R. (2004) 'Northern Ireland: renascent?' in A. Trench (ed.) *Has Devolution Made a Difference? The State of the Nations 2004.* Thorverton: Imprint Academic, 79–120.

13
The financial framework

Arthur Midwinter

The financial arrangements for devolved government in Northern Ireland largely reflect the pre-devolution block-and-formula approach which evolved following the introduction of the Barnett Formula in 1980. Since 1998 the principles underpinning its operation are set out by HM Treasury for each bi-annual Spending Review exercise, in a Statement of Funding Policy, which also applies with minor differences, to Scotland and Wales (HM Treasury, 2004).

It is an expenditure-based system, focused on agreeing changes to the existing baseline. The spending control framework for the Northern Ireland Assembly is similar to that for UK departments. Three-year budget plans, reviewed every second year, are set within an aggregate called total managed expenditure (TME). Firm three-year figures are set for spending that is discretionary and controllable by the Assembly, in a departmental expenditure limit (DEL), while other spending which is demand led is known as annually managed expenditure (AME) and subject to annual review.

Within the DEL there is an assigned budget which is, in effect, a block grant to the Assembly which can be allocated to its priorities, and a non-assigned budget which for Northern Ireland is confined to the EU PEACE programme (see Figure 13.1). Non-assigned expenditure is determined through UK policy or EU regulations. It is in effect ring-fenced for the specific purpose, as is AME. However, all other EU structural funds expenditure counts against the assigned DEL.

The spending plans for 2005–6 were for TME of £14984.5 million, composed of £8607 million in the DEL, and £6377.5 million in AME. Unlike Scotland and Wales, funding for social security benefits is devolved, and accounts for £3817.7 million of AME. These benefits operate on the same model as in Great Britain.

There are two further provisions. After Labour came to power in 1997, it introduced a requirement to set distinctive current and capital budgets as it regarded capital as being underfunded by the previous administration and wished to protect it from short-term pressures (Balls and O'Donnell, 2002).

Figure 13.1 Northern Ireland Executive (excluding the Northern Ireland Office and Northern Ireland Court Service) public expenditure regime

Assigned budget	Non-assigned budget	
Departmental expenditure determined (DEL)		Annual managed expenditure (AME)
Barnett Formula determined[a]	Non-Barnett determined	Main programme spending
Agriculture, trade and industry, employment, energy, roads and transport, housing, environment and water, fire, education, health, social security administration, public corporations and other public services. Student loans: implied subsidies and provision for bad debts Capital Receipts Initiative Trust debt remuneration[b] Fossil fuel obligation Bus fuel duty rebate		Common Agricultural Policy (CAP)
	EU PEACE programme[c]	Social security benefits[d]
		NHS and teachers' pensions
		Other AME: Certain accrual items such as capital charges for roads and the water service
		Supporting people
		Education maintenance allowwnces(EMAs)
		Certain regional rate income (RRI) self-financed Borrowing anddistrict councils – self-financed Expenditure
		Regional rates

Notes:
[a] Undifferentiated expenditure linked to changes in provision to UK government departments to Barnett Formula.
[b] Trust debt remuneration is both payments and receipts (both interest and dividends).
[c] Within the non-assigned budget, set separately in Del.
[d] These and other AME items of expenditure are determined or forecast annually.

Source: HM Treasing (2004) *Funding the Scottish Parliament, National Assembly for Wales and Northern Ireland Assembly – A statement of Funding Policy* London: HM Treasury.

The other dimension is the introduction of resource accounting and budgeting (RAB) in a staged process which moved accounting to an accurals basis. This permits government to distinguish the economic significance of capital and current expenditure, in a process of expenditure control to meet its objectives. It was fully implemented in 2003–4, and has the effect of defining current expenditure in such a way as 'to encompass the consumption of fixed assets and the cost of handling them' and of requiring capital expenditure to reflect long-term investment. This uses non-cash charges such as cost of capital and depreciation allowances.

Finally, it is necessary to note that there is also spending by the Northern Ireland Office, on law, order and protective services, and the Northern Ireland Courts Service, which are determined separately as part of the Spending Review negotiations with the Treasury, and not by the Barnett Formula. In addition, there will be expenditure carried out in Northern Ireland on reserved matters such as defence and trade and industry.

The main focus of criticism within Northern Ireland has been on the operation of the Barnett Formula for determining the assigned budget. Under this arrangement Northern Ireland receives a population-based proportion of changes in planned spending on comparable government spending in England (or England and Wales; or Great Britain as appropriate). A recent Treasury Statement reported the population of Northern Ireland as 3.42 per cent of the English population. In addition, a comparability percentage is agreed for the block services, and the Northern Ireland share is calculated by multiplying the increased funding in England by the comparability factor and then by the population factor, thereby determining the addition to the Northern Ireland baseline.

There are two related criticisms of the Barnett Formula. The first concerns its convergence property, which mathematically will deliver lower percentage increases than the UK as the historic baseline is high, and the annual increment is based on equal funding per capita. In the long run, this may lead to convergence on the UK average per capita, which would be unfair to Northern Ireland as it has above-average expenditure needs, as was recognised by the Treasury's Needs Assessment Study (HM Treasury, 1979).

Second, this shift – which has been wrongly termed a 'Barnett Squeeze' (Bell, 2000) – will reduce the degree of discretion open to the Assembly. This was summarised neatly by Richard Barnett:

> Northern Ireland has enjoyed a relatively high level of per capita public expenditure, but a result of the application of the formula means that percentage increases in Northern Ireland will be less that those in Great Britain . . . (and through time) . . . Northern Ireland will receive a smaller percentage or overall UK public expenditure. It will be conducting zero-sum budgetary politics in the

context of an overall budget which is falling relative to that for the UK as a whole. (Barnett, 1998: 151)

This theme was also followed by Wilford and Wilson (2003: 104) as the rapid growth in spending in Britain 'threatened to make the Barnett Squeeze tighter'. Similarly, Tomlinson (2002: 74) argued that the squeeze occured 'with no regard to levels of need'. Finally, Trench has used this problem to argue for greater tax powers for devolved government, commenting that:

> Finance is perhaps the single greatest unanswered question in the devolution arrangements – for all its virtues, Barnett will not work well in the coming years. Already the devolved administrations are facing a slower rate of growth in the resources available to them, as a consequence of the Barnett Squeeze. The effect of this will be to limit further their room for manoeuvre in policy terms. (Trench, 2000: 8)

These are sweeping assertions on the basis of limited empirical evidence. These criticisms were repeated in a House of Lords Report and predicted to become 'a source of tension in the devolution settlement' (House of Lords, 2002: 104).

These observations reflect a limited understanding of the public expenditure process in practice. First, it must be understood that the practice of only applying the Formula to the annual uplift largely protects the historic baseline which remains the dominant element in the new budget. Although it does not use a needs formula, the underlying assumption is that the current differential in favour of Northern Ireland is a recognition of its greater need, even though this is greater than its level of need in the Treasury study. This leaves Northern Ireland with a level of spending above the recent needs update, that is 23 percent above the UK average (Midwinter, 2002a).

Second, critics ignore the large elements of expenditure determined outside the Barnett Formula. Even within the DEL, Barnett does not apply to supplementary allocations nor interdepartmental transfers. These sums can be significant, such as the Welfare to Work programme of £200 million as part of the Investment and Reform package arising from the Belfast Agreement (HM Treasury, 2002). Post-devolution, Northern Ireland expenditure remains firmly integrated within the UK expenditure system, and has the same access to the UK resource as UK departments.

Finally, while there can be convergence in certain conditions, it can be offset or accelerated through population change. Population decline has offset convergence in Scotland's case, but accelerated it in the case of Northern Ireland, as I have shown elsewhere (Midwinter, 2004).

The key point, however, is that convergence is simply a property of the Formula under specific conditions, not a policy objective of the UK government. When the population basis of Barnett was updated in 1992, it was recognised that all three Celtic nations had higher needs, and that devolved spending would not be allowed to fall below those needs. So, while there is some evidence of a convergence trend for Northern Ireland, but not for Scotland, (HM Treasury, 1998), it is open to the devolved administrations to request a review of their needs assessment if their allocations are less than their needs. So far, none have done so.

A note by Treasury officials states that:

> There is no built-in convergence factor, convergence is simply an arithmetic feature that the percentage increase will tend to be less in those devolved administrations when baseline levels of spending per head are higher than in England, so equal increases will represent smaller percentage increases. The higher spending per head is not a result of the Barnett Formula but of historic baselines inherited from the past. (Dunn and Parkinson, 2002: 2)

This view was shared with a former Northern Ireland civil servant, who commented that the capacity of Barnett to meet needs 'depends upon the adequacy of the pre-existing baseline established by custom and usage' (Bloomfield 1996: 140).

Spending Review allocations since devolution

This section examines the budgetary allocations to Northern Ireland in the UK Spending Reviews from 1998 onwards. Spending Reviews were introduced by the Chancellor, Gordon Brown, to assist in directing resources to agreed priorities, which in Whitehall were education and health. The process remained focused on incremental changes to baselines, while promoting stability and facilitating longer-term planning. The government also established a system of end-year flexibility (EYF) which allowed resources to be carried forward rather than spent quickly on lower priorities to reduce slippage. The Spending Review in 1998 indicated a relaxation on the two-year expenditure freeze on Conservative spending plans instituted by the Chancellor in 1997. Because of the phased introduction of RAB, each Spending Review is here considered separately. That means that in 1998, the figures refer to the Northern Ireland Office (NIO), and thereafter to the budget of the Northern Ireland Assembly programmes, irrespective of whether the Northern Ireland Executive (NIE) or the NIO was in control because of suspension of devolved government.

In the first Comprehensive Spending Review in 1998, Northern Ireland's budget grew by around 4 per cent per annum, while the UK budget grew by 5.6 per cent per annum. The cash figures are set out in Table 13.1, which shows that the NIE allocations have indeed risen by consistently lower percentages than the UK as a whole. Moreover, since 2000, the budget of the NIO has been

Table 13.1. Increases in departmental expenditure limits in Spending Reviews, 1998–2004

1998		1999	2001	% change
	NIO	5,680	6,310	+11.0
	UK	168,800	200,200	+18.6
2000		2000	2003	
	NIE	5,306	6,924	+13.6
	UK	195,200	245,700	+25.9
2002		2002	2005	
	NIE	6,420	7,630	+18.8
	UK	239,710	300,990	+25.6
2004		2004	2007	
	NIE	7,004	8,296	+18.4
	UK	279,300	340,500	+21.9

Source: HM Treasury Spending Reviews 1998, 2000, 2002, 2004.

frozen in real terms, and indeed is planned to fall in real terms between 2004 and 2007, reflecting what Barnett and Hutchinson (1998: 66) have described as a 'climate of peace', allowing resources for law and order to be reduced.

As was shown earlier, however, Barnett-related spending is only one element of devolved expenditure, and there is also substantial spending by UK departments. In 2001–2, for example, AME accounted for 37.5 per cent of TME in the NIO. It is clear from past research that total identifiable spending per capita fell from 37 per cent above the UK average to 34 per cent above over the 1990s (Midwinter, 2004: 505). Over this same period, Scotland, with a declining population, improved slightly, from 17 per cent to 19 per cent. A Treasury paper covering the decade from 1985 onwards, however, found Scotland's spending per capita has fallen from 21 per cent to 19 per cent, while Northern Ireland's per capita advantage has fallen from 48 per cent to 32 per cent, indicating a long-term pattern of decline (HM Treasury, 1997: 36–39).

Identifiable expenditure is updated and refined annually by HM Treasury and covers spending incurred in specific territories in the UK, in the Public Expenditure Statistical Analysis (or PESA) report. The most recent set of statistics record a trend of relative decline in Northern Ireland's per capita advantage, from 32 per cent in 1999, to 29 per cent in 2004, although the decline occurred from 2003 only.

Although precise comparisons between the devolved administrations expenditure and the UK is not possible, the convention is for researchers to exclude the programmes for agriculture (which is largely EU driven) and social protection (which is not Barnett driven). This still includes some UK departmental spending – e.g. regional development – in the totals, but is recognised by the former Senior Economic Advisor in Scotland to be the best proxy available (McCrone, 1999). In the case of Northern Ireland, it is also necessary to exclude law and order spending, as it is not a devolved function.

On block services in Northern Ireland, this delivers spending levels of £2,879 per capita in 1999, compared with £2,179 for the UK, which converts to a relative expenditure index of 132; and spending levels of £3,892 per capita in 2004, compared with £3,161 for the UK; which records a fall in the relative index to 123. Similar calculations for Scotland score a decline in the index from 126 to 123, demonstrating the adverse impact of population growth in Northern Ireland.

Trends in spending programmes

The data above can be disaggregated into spending programmes. Table 13.2 reveals a high degree of stability in big spending programmes such as health, education and social protection, and significant reductions for pubic order, enterprise and housing. However, in cash terms, almost 50 per cent of the excess comes from two key programmes – public order and social protection – which together account for £879 per capita of the total excess, or £1,781. Both these programmes have larger excesses than education, which at £291 per capita is the largest excess within the Barnett block.

Over the period of the 1990s, my previous research has shown faster rates of decline in the per capita advantage in Barnett-related services – from 49 per cent above in 1991 to 37 per cent above in 1999 – than in identifiable public

Table 13.2. Northern Ireland per capita spending relative to UK average on major services, 1999 and 2003 (UK = 100)

	1999	2003
Public order	256	189
Enterprise	314	221
Agriculture	284	296
Transport	84	77
Environment	260	258
Housing	259	203
Health	112	109
Education	140	128
Social protection	117	122

Source: HM Treasury Public Expenditure Statistical Analyses 2005.

Table 13.3. Spending per capita growth in Northern Ireland on major services, 1999 and 2003

	1999 (£)	*2003 (£)*	*%*
Public order	664	692	+4.2
Enterprise	234	222	−5.2
Agriculture	188	258	+37.2
Transport	126	210	+66.6
Environment	224	274	+22.3
Housing	164	204	+24.3
Health	940	1,367	+45.4
Education	1,004	1,322	+31.6
Social protection	2,273	3,103	+36.5
Miscellaneous	187	293	+56.7
Total	**6,004**	**7,945**	**+32.3**

Source: HM Treasury Public Expenditure Statistical Analyses 2005.

expenditure as a whole. In short, in Northern Ireland there is evidence of convergence in expenditure as expected, enhanced by population growth.

The important point to note, however, is that the decline in relative expenditure per capita has not resulted in a squeeze on spending levels in real terms. This is because the exceptionally high rate of spending growth in nominal terms in this period, combined with low inflation, meant that in practice, the greater the so-called Barnett Squeeze, then the greater was the rate of growth in public spending in Northern Ireland. Contrary to the view that the operation of the Barnett Formula would constrain choice, in a period of spending growth it actually enhances it, even if the rate is lower than the UK average. Rapid budgetary growth allows new spending commitments to be made.

PESA (2005) reports the growth in spending per capita in real terms, as being from £5,037 in 1999 to £6,164 in 2003 (or 7.1 per cent per annum) for the UK, and from £6,628 to £7,945 (or 6.7 per cent per annum) for Northern Ireland, once estimates are converted into outturn expenditure. The gap between Northern Ireland and the UK measured as 2.5 per cent for the DEL has shrunk to 0.4 per cent. In part, this will reflect the inclusion of other spending, but it also includes supplementary allocations to the original estimates.

This was examined in a paper by Heald and McLeod (2005), who showed that between transfers, policy changes and non-Barnett additions, the DEL provision for 2002–3 rose from £5,973.2 million to £6,509 million between Spending Reviews 2002 and 2004, an increase of £536 million, so for Northern Ireland, 'non-Barnett changes were much more important in SR2002 than in Scotland and Wales'. Heald and McLeod stress 'that the

Table 13.4. Percentage increase in expenditure, 1999–2003

	NIE	*UK*
Public order	+4.2	+41.1
Enterprise	−5.2	+33.3
Agriculture	+37.2	+17.5
Transport	+66.6	+82.0
Environment	+22.3	+23.2
Housing	+24.3	+60.0
Health	+45.4	+49.0
Education	+31.6	+43.2
Social Protection	+36.5	+24.3
Miscellaneous	+56.7	+21.4
Total	**+32.3**	**+35.2**

Source: HM Treasury Public Expenditure Statistical Analyses 2005.

system is much more complex that the simple calculation of formula consequences' (Heald and McLeod, 2005: 512).

It is clear therefore, that forecasts of a Barnett Squeeze based on simplistic extrapolation of percentage increases were wide of the mark. Spending outside the Formula, changes between Spending Reviews, and differential slippage in spending make such exercises of limited relevance to devolution finance. Moreover, far from squeezing expenditure, the

> gushing of resources down the Barnett pipeline has been one of the unexpected features of the early years of devolution: the standard presumption beforehand was that resources would be in short supply. Without this expected shortage of resources, the expected political conflict over funding levels between London and the territorial capitals has so far not materialised. (Heald and McLeod, 2005: 514)

Nor has the block-and-formula approach narrowed the margins of choice. Although the parameters of growth in actual spending overall are very close in real terms, between programmes significant differences can be found, as shown in Table 13.3. Only in health and transport are Northern Ireland increases significantly high, and these programmes were both priorities across the UK (see Table 13.4). Strict comparisons of expenditure plans in the second period of devolution (i.e. post-2003) are problematic because budgetary portfolios differ between Northern Ireland and the UK. However, Table 13.5 sets out the spending plans for Northern Ireland over this period, and this shows that health continues to be an overall spending priority in the Province, despite the assumption of political control by the NIO ministers. The expenditure outturn data for 1999 to 2003, and the expenditure plans data from 2004 to 2007, shows consistent growth in expenditure in real terms, average 5.5 per cent in the first period, and around 3.5 per cent in the second. The spread of cash increases

Table 13.5. TME programme growth in Northern Ireland devolved budget, 2004–8

	2004–5 (outturn) (£m)	2007–8 (plans) (£m)	% change
Agriculture	474.4	559.7	+18.0
Culture	95.5	125.1	+31.0
Education	2,088.7	2,453.1	+17.4
Enterprise	261.0	262.4	+0.5
Health	3617.1	4,476.9	+23.8
Environment	135.3	137.4	+1.6
Regional development	1,722.5	1,892.7	+9.9
Social development	4,293.0	4,819.0	+12.3
Miscellaneous	104.1	233.6	124.4
TME	13,883.1	1,6237.4	+16.9

Source: Northern Ireland Draft Priorities and Budget 2006–8.

range from −1.25 per cent per annum to 16.65 per cent per annum in the first period, and from 0.125 per cent per annum to 7.75 per cent in the second period, which infers significant scope for political choice within the block.

Assessment

In assessing the impact of the Barnett Formula on devolution finance in Northern Ireland, it is necessary also to place the issue in the changing budgetary context. The original concerns over the Formula were driven by a perception that the convergence property of the Formula was resulting in lower percentage increases in comparison with England, and that this would squeeze the block grant and reduce the capacity of the new Assembly to meet needs. In particular, there was a commitment to a major programme of reinvestment in capital spending, as 'Ministers become even more aware of the poverty of the public infrastructure bequeathed by the long Conservative era and New Labour's initial fiscal conservatism' (Wilford and Wilson, 2003: 104). These authors saw the Barnett Formula's 'inability to provide sufficient resources to tackle Northern Ireland's infrastructure deficit' as a source of frustration for all political parties in Northern Ireland. The initial response was to argue 'against the continued use of the Barnett Formula in the next spending review (i.e. 2002)' and in favour of a needs-based formula (Tomlinson, 2002: 75). As the Spending Review progressed, this position was softened into arguing for 'Barnett Plus', i.e. additional funding beyond the Formula entitlement without necessarily reviewing the formula itself.

In his budget speech to the Assembly, Finance Minister Sean Farren estimated the need for infrastructure investment at £6 billion. Labelled the Reinvestment and Reform Initiative, it was to be partly funded initially through a new borrowing power over the next decade, and repaid in part from increased revenue from the regional rate (the equivalent of council tax in Great Britain) after the basis of the rating system had been reformed into an assessment based on capital values.

Farran repeated the Executives's concern over the impact of the Barnett Formula.

> The Barnett Formula that gives Northern Ireland its population share of any change in expenditure on a comparable English programme was the principal means of allocating resources to the Executive in the UK Spending Review 2002, covering the period to 2005–06. A formula is desirable as the basis for allocating finance to the devolved administrations. However, the Executive continues to have concerns about the fairness of the Formula because of its focus on population as the only measure of need and its viability as a funding mechanism in the longer term. These concerns have been taken up with the Treasury and the Executive will continue to press the case for review and reform of the Formula. (Farren, 2002: 65)

At the same time, a Needs and Effectiveness Evaluation exercise was launched within the Executive 'to help establish the objective level of need for key public services' (Farran, 2002: 67). There are a number of problems with this critique of Barnett in practice. First, if the level of resources being delivered through the Formula is inadequate, it is a level unprecedented in the UK's public finances. The earlier analyses showed clearly that significant real terms growth has been sustained since the introduction of devolved government. There was no Barnett-driven squeeze on spending levels. As David Heald observed, 'there was almost no public attention in Northern Ireland to the overall position necessarily involving consideration of the baseline . . . it became accepted across all the Northern Ireland parties that Northern Ireland was being treated badly by the Barnett Formula system and would benefit from a review' (Heald, 2003: 32).

Heald also noted the contrary expectation in English regions that a review would result in cutting the budgets of all the devolved administrations, and urged caution in asking the Treasury to reopen the issue. He concluded that 'Northern Ireland should not become obsessed with headline comparisons of percentage increases, taking no account of the expenditure base. There is no rational basis on which Northern Ireland should expect to match percentage increases, regardless of the base' (Heald, 2003: 95).

The first point to note is that although Barnett does not utilise a needs-based formula, the allocations it delivers are broadly reflective of relative need, in terms of the higher levels of poverty, unemployment, and morbidity in the devolved nations. This is because the baselines were negotiated through arguments over needs relative to the benchmark of English spending, even though need was not quantified as in a needs formula. The 1979 Treasury study, although relatively crude, did assess Northern Ireland needs at 31 per cent above England, and while spending was a further 5 per cent higher, 'The introduction of the Formula indicated that the Treasury accepted that the current balance of spending was sufficient to justify entrenching it through the introduction of a population formula rather than some other kind' (Thain and Wright, 1994: 306).

While a number of UK governments have acknowledged the existence of a convergence property in certain circumstances in the Formula, full convergence is not policy, and devolved administrations remain free to request a needs assessment exercise if they feel their needs are not being met.

The outcomes of such an exercise are not predictable. The Treasury study of 1977 was recognised to be imprecise, and not rigorous enough for use in resource allocation. Moreover, any needs-assessment model requires political judgements as to the selection of indicators and the weights to be applied to them. Needs assessment is not rocket science (Midwinter, 2002b).

The Treasury study was updated but not published by the Treasury in 1994, and in that exercise, Northern Ireland's needs had fallen from 31 per cent above England to 23 per cent, because of improvements in Northern Ireland's housing stock, and revision to the health indicators. In the data available at that time, Northern Ireland spending was 31 per cent above England (Midwinter 2002a). This stressed the need for caution in Northern Ireland over arguing for a needs-assessment review.

The argument made over the lack of capacity to fund the £6 billion capital expenditure package also requires qualification, because of some key differences with Great Britain, namely that water remains a publicly funded service in Northern Ireland, and that Northern Ireland rates much less from its citizens in terms of local property taxation. Action has now been taken by the NIO to increase the resources raised by these mechanisms. Water charging was introduced in 2006 and will be phased in by 2009. Industrial derating is on course for implementation by 2007. Regional rates increases will also be phased in, 19 per cent in 2006–7 and a further 6 per cent in 2007–8, at an average cost of £1 per week on average rate bills. However, the Draft Budget also noted that the combined shortfall of rates and water charges with the English average was £587 per annum in 2002–3. The NIO concluded that 'the reality therefore is that people here pay much less in local taxation, and therefore, do not pay enough towards the costs of these services' (NIO, 2005: 9).

The Draft Budget also states, however, that neither borrowing nor capital spending in the budget can fund the programme overall (NIO, 2005: 6). Nevertheless, there is more scope for prioritising capital spending within the Northern Ireland budget. The PESA statistics records capital expenditure as increasing from £598 million to £843 million per annum between 1999 and 2003, an annual increase of nearly 10 per cent. Over the same period, capital spending in Scotland rose twice as fast, from £1,458 million to £2,674 million, an annual increase of nearly 21 per cent. The UK average was 15 per cent.

Differences in the range of devolved functions and their funding make strict comparisons between the devolved administrations problematic without the necessary caveats. One study showed a decline in Northern Ireland relative spending per capita (to the UK average) from 1986 to 1991, and a flattening off for the next decade. This is contrary to the expectation that this change, and a gradual tightening up of formula bypass, would lead to clearer evidence of convergence. In part, this is because the authors mistakenly include law and order as a devolved service in Northern Ireland and also agriculture, which is largely EU driven (McLean and MacMillan, 2003). Moreover, the research period ended in 2000–1, just at the time when the nominal growth in expenditure began, which we have shown speeded up the convergence process in Northern Ireland.

McLean and McMillan conclude by arguing for the replacement of Barnett with a UK-wide needs-based formula, which the estimate would reduce Northern Ireland's block grant by around £520 per head (McLean and McMillan, 2003: 65–66). Their argument is largely that Barnett is 'unfair' to the poorer English regions, even though it does not determine their allocations, which are made by UK departmental formulae.

This misinterpretation of what constitutes devolved expenditure of how the process works in England, and their reliance on proxy data, reinforces Heald's case for caution. Only when directly comparable data over a ten-year period for devolved spending is provided by the Treasury will a rigorous appraisal of the actual impact of Barnett be possible and sensible judgements on the needs for reform be reached.

Conclusions

There is insufficient evidence to demonstrate that Northern Ireland has been disadvantaged by the application of the Barnett Formula since devolution. There is neither robust spending information, nor a robust needs formula on which to draw conclusions. There is, however, clear evidence from the PESA statistics that identifiable public expenditure has been growing significantly in real terms, with convergence towards the UK average. This has been exacerbated by the high level of nominal expenditure growth in recent years.

This convergence effect has not squeezed expenditure in real terms, nor constrained choice. Ironically, the greater the convergence effect, the greater the scope for budgetary choice, as it delivers a high level of growth in nominal expenditure.

This period of growth is coming to an end. The *Pre Budget Report* (HM Treasury, 2005) shows public spending growth falling to 1.9 per cent per annum over the following Spending Review cycle. This would reduce the nominal rate of growth, and hence the rate of convergence and thus stabilise the spending position for Northern Ireland relative to the UK.

Moreover, the present government is committed to retaining the Barnett Formula, which makes it unlikely that the Treasury will institute a review, realising that the sums of money it might save from such an exercise are small – reflecting the margins between expenditure and a 'needs assessment' (Midwinter, 2002b).

The prudent approach for Northern Ireland would be to monitor the outcome of these revenue trends over the rest of this Parliament and assess the position then. Only when a robust, convincing case that Northern Ireland is being underfunded relative to need arises should the Executive seek a needs-assessment review. At the moment, neither the academic critics of Barnett, nor the Executive's own needs evaluation and effectiveness reports make such a case. It would be a rash Finance Minister who gave up a model which largely protects historic baselines, which only applies the Formula to incremental growth, and which has delivered sustained growth in the public finances post-devolution, for a needs-assessment exercise whose outcome is uncertain, and which could reduce Northern Ireland's share of the UK budget even further.

References

Balls, E. and O'Donnell, G. (2002) *Reforming Britain's Economic and Financial Policy*. Basingstoke: Palgrave.

Barnett, R. (1998) 'Financial arrangements' in R. Wilson (ed.) *Agreeing to Disagree: A Guide to the Northern Ireland Assembly*. Belfast: The Stationery Office.

Barnett, R. and Hutchinson, G. (1998) 'Public expenditure on the eve of devolution' in *Democratic Dialogue (1998) Hard Choices: Policy Autonomy and Priority Setting in Public Expenditure*. Belfast: Northern Ireland Economic Council.

Bell, D. (2000) 'The Barnett Formula', unpublished paper, University of Stirling.

Bloomfield, K. (1996) 'Devolution – lesson from Northern Ireland', *Political Quarterly*, 67 (2), 135–140.

Dunn, R. and Parkinson, M. (2002) *Funding the Devolved Administration*. London: HM Treasury.

Farran, S. (2002) *Executive Budget: Public Expenditure Plans – 2003 to 2005–06*, report presented to Northern Ireland Assembly, 24 September.

Heald, D.A. (2003) *Funding the Northern Ireland Assembly: Assessing the Options*, Research Monograph 10. Belfast: Northern Ireland Economic Council.

Heald, D. and McLeod, A. (2005) 'Embeddedness of UK devolution finance within the public expenditure system', *Regional Studies*, 39 (4), 495–518.

HM Treasury (1979) *Needs Assessment Study – Report*. London: HM Treasury.

HM Treasury (1997) Supplementary memorandum in Treasury Committee, 'The Barnett Formula', second report of session 1997–98. London: The Stationery Office.

HM Treasury (1998) 'Barnett Formula: impact on relative public spending per capita in England, Scotland, Wales and Northern Ireland', note published in HM Treasury, *The Barnett Formula: The Government's Response to the Treasury Committee's Second Report of Session 1997–08*. London: The Stationery Office.

HM Treasury (2002) *2002 Spending Review – New Public Spending Plans 2003–06*, CM5570. London: HM Treasury.

HM Treasury (2004) *Funding the Scottish Parliament, National Assembly for Wales, and Northern Ireland Assembly – A Statement of Funding Policy*. London: HM Treasury.

HM Treasury (2005) *Pre Budget Report*. CM6701. London: HM Treasury.

House of Lords (2002) *Devolution: Inter-Institutional Relations in the United Kingdom*, 2nd Report of the Select Committee on the Constitution. London: The Stationery Office.

Midwinter, A. (2002a) '*Northern Ireland's Public Expenditure Needs – A Preliminary Assessment*', report prepared for the Research and Library Service, Northern Ireland Assembly.

Midwinter, A. (2002b) 'Territorial resource allocation in the UK: a rejoinder on needs assessment', *Regional Studies*, 35, 45–71.

Midwinter, A. (2004) 'The changing distribution of territorial public expenditure in the UK', *Regional and Federal Studies*. 14 (4), 499–512.

McCrone, G. (1999) 'Scotland's public finances from Goschen to Barnett', *Quarterly Economic Commentary*, 24 (2), 30–45.

McLean, I. and MacMillan, A. (2003) 'The distribution of public expenditure across the UK regions', *Fiscal Studies*, 24 (1), 45–71.

NIO (Northern Ireland Office) (2005) *Draft Priorities and Budget 2006–08*. Belfast: NIO.

Thain, C. and Wright, M. (1994) *The Treasury and Whitehall*. Oxford: Oxford University Press.

Tomlinson, M. (2002) 'Reconstituting social policy: the case of Northern Ireland' in R. Sykes, C. Bochel and N. Ellison (eds), *Social Policy Review 14: Developments and Debates*. Bristol: The Policy Press.

Trench, A. (2002) 'Intergovernmental relations: a year on' in A. Trench (ed.) *The State of the Nation 2000*. Thorverton: Imprint Academic.

Wilford, R. and Wilson, R. (2003) 'Northern Ireland: valedictory?' in R. Hazell (ed.) *The State of the Nations 2003*. Thorverton: Imprint Academic.

14
The Review of Public Administration

Colin Knox and Paul Carmichael

Introduction

The former Northern Ireland Minister of State, Lord Rooker, announced 'there is too much bureaucracy and red-tape in all elements of public administration in Northern Ireland, which costs a lot of money' (Rooker, 2005: 1). Such a charge could have been levelled at any part of the UK, but for Northern Ireland, ministerial attention to public services as opposed to constitutional and security issues has been unusual. In turn, the minister claimed that by early 2006 he hoped to announce a much more streamlined and coordinated system for the delivery of public services which would free up money for front-line services in hospitals and schools. The structure of public administration in the province has emerged piecemeal and parts of it, conceived as a short-term palliative (described by Bloomfield (1998) as a state of 'permanent impermanence'), remained untouched from 1973 as more pressing political issues took centre stage. With the advent of a political 'settlement' in the form of the Belfast (Good Friday) Agreement in 1998 and associated devolved government, attention turned to how public services were organised and delivered.

As the outcomes of the Review of Public Administration emerge, this chapter attempts three things. First, we consider the detail of the review process – its inception, aims and consultation processes. Second, we describe the existing system of public administration and examine the responses of the main sectors, local government, non-departmental public bodies and government agencies to proposals for change. Third, we set out the outcomes of the Review and the likely consequences for public service delivery in Northern Ireland.[1]

The Review: origins and aims

The Review of Public Administration (RPA) was launched in June 2002 and had its origins in the Programme for Government in which the (then)

Executive pledged 'to lead the most effective and accountable form of government in Northern Ireland'. The prevailing argument is that Northern Ireland has moved from a position of 'democratic deficit' to surfeit mode, with 18 Westminster MPs, 108 MLAs, 582 councillors and 3 Members of the European Parliament (MEPs), all for a population of 1.7 million people. Aside from considerations of political representation, the focus is now on ways to rationalise public service provision as the Assembly (in suspension for the fourth time[2]) struggles, without the benefit of tax-raising powers, to meet the seemingly insatiable demands for public service provision.

The terms of reference for the RPA reflect the need to restructure the administrative architecture within a devolved system of government:

> To review the existing arrangements for the accountability, administration and delivery of public services in Northern Ireland, and to bring forward options for reform which are consistent with the arrangements and principles of the Belfast Agreement, within an appropriate framework of political and financial accountability. (OFMDFM, 2005: 138)

The importance of this exercise was best described by the (then) First Minister, who argued that 'it is one of the major tasks facing the Executive and will be central to the way in which we deliver, structure and organise our public services in the future' (Trimble, 2002). In general the announcement of the Review was welcomed by local politicians, many of whom have been frustrated in their role as local councillors by what they perceive as unaccountable public officials operating under direct rule circumstances.

The scope of the Review has, however, attracted criticism in that its terms of reference exclude the 11 government departments established by the Belfast Agreement. The official position is that while it is likely to have implications for the *functions* exercised by the Executive, the *institutions* and the divisions of functions between the departments have not been part of the Review's remit, although this is rather difficult to comprehend in practice. For example, if functions such as roads and water were removed from the Department for Regional Development and relocated elsewhere, it is highly unlikely that retaining this department could be justified. The inclusion of government departments was rejected on the grounds that the Review should not be used as a way of renegotiating the Agreement 'by the back door'. The rationale was simple, albeit bizarre, from a purely administrative perspective: with devolution so precarious (and so it has proved to be), nothing could be allowed that might endanger its fragile continuance.

The Review was led by a multi-disciplinary team of officials in the Office of the Minister and Deputy First Minister, working with the advice of a team of independent experts. Some initial concerns were expressed that a Review, led by civil servants, amounted to regulatory capture by officials who would have an inherent resistance to radical changes. Characterising civil servants as 'budget maximising bureaucrats' (Dunleavy, 1991), one MLA, in a rhetorical question, remarked 'officials will have a vested interest in keeping their own administrative empires going – who has ever heard of a civil servant who has been anxious to reduce the number beneath him [*sic*] in the pyramid?' (McCartney, 2002).

The existing system of public administration

The current administrative system in Northern Ireland is a complex mosaic of bodies which have evolved in response to political circumstances since the early 1970s. These arrangements include 26 district councils with limited functional responsibilities, 11 government departments, 18 (Next Steps) executive agencies, a plethora of non-departmental public bodies (NDPBs – quangos) – among which are 5 education and library boards, 4 health and social services boards and 19 associated trusts – and the Northern Ireland Housing Executive (see Figure 14.1). Overall the Northern Ireland public sector employs over 200,000 people (including 31,000 in the civil service, 68,000 in the health service, 50,000 in education and 10,000 in local government). The assorted administrative geometry has not only created confusion in the minds of the public as to who is responsible for what service, but has also led to accusations that Northern Ireland is over-administered. Importantly, however, there is much criticism about the accountable nature of the system of public administration, not least because of the selected 'quangocrats' who oversee many of the key public services (e.g. health, education and housing). These areas also absorb the largest budget allocations, with health and personal social services accounting for around 44 per cent of expenditure on devolved public services, and education and libraries amounting to 24 per cent, from an overall expenditure of some £7.3 billion (DFP, 2005).

One example is cited by the (then) First Minister to illustrate the administrative maze:

> If one considers people who live in the Cookstown District Council area. They are in the Southern Education and Library Board area, the Northern Health and Social Services area, the western area for roads and planning, and the eastern area for water. It would be scarcely surprising if people were confused about who delivers their services. (Trimble, 2002: 402)

The public sector has also remained largely insulated from the wider UK modernising agenda, except for the odd read-across reform such as Next Steps agencies where, as an after-thought, the Northern Ireland Civil Service was encouraged to follow the Home Civil Service (Knox and McHugh, 1990;

Figure 14.1 The Northern Ireland public sector

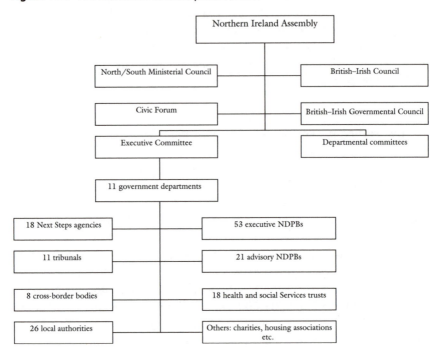

Carmichael, 2002). More recently the civil service has approved a reform strategy (*Fit for Purpose*) aimed at prioritising front-line services, building capacity and embracing diversity (OFMDFM, 2004). Such is the disjointed nature of the Northern Ireland public sector, however, that the Comptroller and Auditor General described it as 'disastrously fragmented'. Almost everybody in Great Britain that carries out any function of government, he argued, 'is duplicated on a tiny scale within Northern Ireland and that is an impediment to clarity and an enormous inefficiency' (Dowdall, 2004).

The Review of Public Administration

The original timetable for the RPA envisaged an interim report in spring 2003 and final recommendations by the end of that year. This slipped considerably. The Review team published its first consultation document in October 2003, further consultation paper in March 2005, and the outcomes were announced on 22 November 2005. The Review covers over 140 organisations within the public sector: 18 government agencies, 26 district councils and 99 public bodies, comprising 2,065 public appointees (OFMDFM, 2005). The purpose of the first consultation paper was to 'bring forward a number of important issues which influence how, and by whom, services might be provided, and to set out for discussion a number of broad models of public administration' (OFMDFM, 2003: 3).

The consultation document outlined five possible models for consideration in rethinking the structural architecture of public services. These are summarised as follows:

- *Status quo.* There would be no change to the overall structure of public administration.
- *Centralised.* All major services would be delivered directly by government departments.
- *Regional and sub-regional public bodies.* A range of public bodies, operating either regionally or sub-regionally, would deliver public services.
- *Reformed status quo with enhanced local government.* While keeping the main features of the current system, local government would be given new responsibilities.
- *Strong local government.* Major public services would be the responsibility of a smaller number of new councils.

The consultation period closed in February 2004 and 174 responses were received. The key messages from respondents were that:

- There was almost unanimous support for the need for change and a widespread demand for early action.
- Quality of public services was seen as the most important characteristic against which any new system should be measured.
- There was widespread consensus on the need for fewer public bodies, with more collaboration and less fragmentation.
- Of the five high-level models, there was a preference for either enhanced or strong local government, with fewer quangos (Pearson, 2004a).

The Review team used the feedback from the first consultation paper to engage with local political parties in the absence of a return to the Northern Ireland Assembly.

The (then) Northern Ireland Office Minister, Ian Pearson, pre-empted the launch of a second consultation paper by announcing his own views on the final reform model:

> I envisage the Assembly with departments sitting at regional level with responsibility for policy, strategic planning, setting standards and monitoring performance. At local level, larger more powerful councils could have responsibilities for

an increased range of functions . . . I will also be examining the scope for significant reductions in the number of public bodies, in particular, the administrative
structures around health and education. (Pearson, 2004b: 1)

Former Minister Pearson called for the formation of between five and eight
local councils to replace the existing 26 local authorities. The political backlash came swiftly. Local councillors viewed this proposal as an attack on local
democracy and a portent that further consultation would be a facade. Minister
Pearson sought a compromise and assured local politicians that his mind was
not yet made up.

The Review team published a final consultation document *The Review of
Public Administration in Northern Ireland: Further Consultation* in March
2005 (OFMDFM, 2005), in which the Direct Rule Minister heralded the
proposals as a 'further important step in creating a modern, citizen-centred,
high-quality system of public administration' where 'improving the quality of
public services lies at the heart of any new model' (Pearson, 2005: 1). The
final consultation based reforms on a two-tier model of public administration.
The first tier would be a regional tier encompassing the Assembly, government departments and regional authorities, the focus of which would be
policy development, setting standards and delivering regional services. The
second tier, a sub-regional tier, would encompass organisations that ideally
operate within common boundaries, to include councils, health bodies, sub-
regional bodies and delivery units of regional bodies. The model assumed
delivery at the sub-regional tier unless economies of scale (or other factors)
dictated delivery on a regional basis (see Figure 14.2).

In terms of specific sectors, three options were proposed for local government based on configurations of 7, 11 and 15 councils. These options
were as a direct result of political compromise between the minister and
political parties. The minister and the Review team favoured seven councils
as 'optimal for service delivery purposes'. This would result in local councils
with populations of between 165,000 and 390,000. The 7-council 'solution' would allow for common boundaries with regional/sub-regional services. The 15-council option originated from local politicians as a reaction
to what they perceived as the minister's attempt to cut radically the number
of district councils. This option was based on the current 18 Westminster
constituencies (with one consistuency replacing Belfast's 4 constituencies).
Civic councils[3] are proposed for the 7-council model to preserve local identity; are optional in the 11-council model; and are considered unnecessary
for 15 councils. Their suggested role is to 'consult locally, to form partnerships and to gather local views to feed into the main council's deliberations
and to undertake assigned reponsibilities on its behalf' (OFMDFM, 2005:
40, 4.33).

Figure 14.2 Two-tier model of public administration

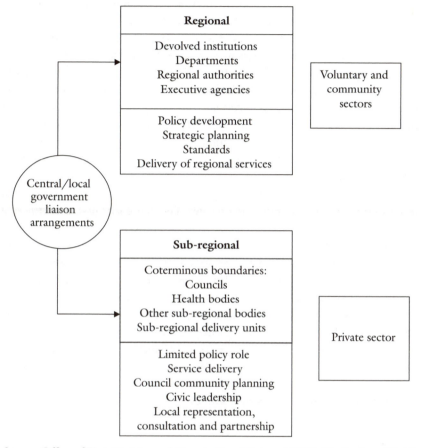

Source: Office of First Minister and Deputy First Minister (2005) *The Review of Public Administration in Northern Ireland: Further Constitution.* Belfast: OFMDFM, 22.

In the health sector, the Review team recommends the replacement of the four existing health and social services boards and 18 of the 19 trusts (the Ambulance Trust would remain), with either five or seven sub-regional health agencies. The reviewers favour five agencies, which would allow for a full range of health services (including acute hospital services); however, to benefit from co-terminous boundaries, if seven councils were agreed, they would move to seven health agencies. In addition, the existing six regional health bodies[4] would be reduced to four, and a regional forum established to advise on the development of regional services and the work of agencies. The current four health and social services councils that represent the views of consumers would be replaced by one regional body.

In education, the Department of Education would continue to be responsible for the development and implementation of education policy and strategy, monitoring standards and allocation of resources. The functions in support of education (recruitment, employment and payment of teachers, school library service, transport, admissions, raising standards) would be brought together in a new education services body, which would replace the five existing education and library boards, Council for Catholic Maintained Schools, Comhairle na Gaelscolaiochta (Irish medium schools body), Northern Ireland Council for Integrated Education and the Education Staff Commission. A second new education body would be formed to bring together existing professional support services (curriculum development, examinations and assessment, in-service training, procurement of support services).

The Review team also considered 150 quangos and executive agencies. In terms of quangos, two options are on offer. The first is that non-departmental public bodies should be abolished and their functions transferred to central or local government, the voluntary and community sectors or the private sector. The second option, favoured by the reviewers, is that public bodies should continue to exist but every effort should be made to improve their accountability. This would involve a review of all quangos, a reduction in their number and increased accountability arrangements. In terms of executive agencies, the reviewers concluded that in the absence of strong views expressed on their future, decisions should be left to a returning Executive and Assembly.

Sectoral responses to the consultation

Local government

The proposals emerging in the second consultation document are predicated on strong local government, or as the RPA described it, 'local government will have a pivotal role in the two-tier model' (OFMDFM, 2005: 29). The response from the local government sector, however, has been one of scepticism. They were unwilling to believe that the Minister was approaching the review with an open mind. Former Minister Ian Pearson had already made his preference clear for between five and eight larger, more powerful councils, and Lord Rooker, influenced by Secretary of State Peter Hain's views on Wales (with 22 unitary councils for almost twice the population of Northern Ireland), was said to back the 7-council model. Many local authorities, in a bid to preserve their own areas, have endorsed the 15-councils model, but with enhanced powers.

Much of what is proposed in the RPA consultation document is predicated on what might be described as a 'sizeism' principle (Stewart, 2003: 43), that large-scale local government is both efficient and effective. In consider-ing its own options of 7, 11 or 15 councils, the Review team make the case for seven councils based on amalgamations of existing councils as the 'optimal for service delivery'.

The RPA's arguments for its optimal solution are as follows (OFMDFM, 2005: 40, 4.32).

- It would undoubtedly provide for strong local government.
- Councils would be large, serving populations ranging from 165,000 to 390,000.
- All major service providers would operate to common boundaries (full 1:1 coterminosity), thereby providing strong collaboration for commu-nity planning and coordination of services.
- Councils would be broadly similar in size, and each would be large enough to deal on equal terms with other service providers, and to advo-cate to central government.
- The model also offers opportunities to deliver on an enhanced range of functions at a scale that would be the most efficient option.

The claim that it 'would undoubtedly provide for strong local govern-ment' is not, however, borne out by the experience of reorganisation in Great Britain. In fact, the assumption that size is associated with efficiency and/or effectiveness is far from proven. Travers et al. examined evidence from Britain and overseas and concluded:

> It does not appear possible to argue a conclusive case for a strong and one-directional link between population size and efficiency and effectiveness . . . It is not possible to say larger authorities perform, on the whole better than smaller, or smaller authorities better than larger. (Travers, Jones and Burnham, 1993: 4)

This should give the RPA team pause for thought. In the same vein, the move to unitary councils in Great Britain is described by Stewart (2003) as a period of wasted years. He explained how new councils were an amalgama-tion of previous authorities, often lacking any sense of shared identity (prophetic words for Northern Ireland). The reorganisation of local govern-ment in Great Britain in the 1990s, he claimed, increased the differences between the structure of government in the UK and the rest of Europe – 'many new councils appeared superficial, bringing together in a single author-ity, towns that in most countries in Europe would be authorities in their own right' (Stewart, 2003: 181).

The case made by the RPA team for large single-tier local authorities is simply not grounded in experience elsewhere. Stewart makes this point most succinctly:

Almost without exception there are two tiers of local government in European countries. In larger countries there are three tiers of sub-national government. The reason for the tiers is simple. Both the sense of community and the requirements of services are multileveled and do not fit a single tier . . . A two-tier system allowed different services to be delivered at different levels. The sense of community could be both local and multileveled. (Stewart, 2003: 184–185)

Not only is the RPA team opposed to the two-tier system of local government, but its proposals for civic councils, as set out, envisage them as having little more than a consultative, advocacy and civic leadership role. They will be given no functional responsibilities it appears – talking shops under any other name.

The proposals for local government in the RPA paper have several key weaknesses:

- They are predicated on the 'big is beautiful (efficient and effective)' assertion which has been discredited in other parts of the UK.
- The Local Government Commission for England estimated than in most cases, unitary authorities would have a population of 150,000–250,000 (LGCE, 1993). In Northern Ireland, the optimal model recommended by the RPA team (option 7c) shows seven councils ranging in size from 188,000 to 277,000. Yet the functional responsibilities proposed by the RPA fall far short of unitary council status in the rest of the UK, with the absence of housing, education and social services to name the most obvious.
- The proposals for civic councils, in their current format, are an attenuated form of local government amounting to little more than a consultative forum.

In short, the RPA team proposes to replace the existing 26 district councils and replace them with a smaller number of single-tier councils having a marginal increase in functions, and increased representational levels, resulting in a much more remote and disconnected tier of governance. Local authorities, in turn, driven by the limited and rather cautious aspirations of political parties, have been reluctant to push for wholesale return of functions to councils, in part a legacy of the former abuse of power and an unwillingness by councillors to place themselves in the front line of functions such as public housing. While new powers of community planning and 'well-being' have been widely welcomed by the sector, councils are worried that their proposed role as developing and coordinating local policy on service delivery between the major service providers within their boundaries will prove problematic in practice. With the limited increase in powers envisaged, councils will be seen as a minor stakeholder at the community planning table and hence their ability to hold others to account restricted. Moreover, in the minds of the electorate, a community planning role may confer on councils a responsibility for those services over which they have no direct control, but for which voters will hold them accountable.

Quangos

Although starting out with a remit to consider almost 150 non-departmental public bodies, substantive proposals for change in the health and education sectors – which are replete with quangos – reduced the effective examination to what the RPA describe as 79 'significant public bodies' including agencies (OFMDFM, 2005: 95, 7.3).[5] The RPA's preferred approach that public bodies should continue to exist but every effort be made to improve their accountability met with a mixed response. The RPA suggestion that all public bodies should be reviewed also attracted criticism in that the long-awaited proposals for change were recommending yet another review. The prevalent view, typically expressed by the local government umbrella body Northern Ireland Local Government Association (NILGA), was that 'there should be a presumption that the maximum number of powers exercised by unelected bodies should be returned to local government or the Assembly' (NILGA, 2005: 15). Where there was decision made to retain a public body, they argued, then clear lines of accountability to local government or the Assembly should be established in legislation.

The existence of quangos can be justified on at least two broad grounds (Hood, 1981):

- Government may need bodies from which it can distance itself in sensitive areas.
- There is value in having temporary organisations outside the permanent service that can be scrapped when the need for such temporary arrangements no longer exists.

In the case of the former, the Equality Commission for Northern Ireland is a good example, and the latter, the Northern Ireland Housing Executive (an organisation typically characterised as 'permanently impermanent', set up as a temporary political expedient but still in existence). Although the changed political environment has challenged the rationale for so many arms-length bodies, their integration into the public sector will prove more difficult than local politicians first envisaged. Exceptions or opt-outs quickly emerge. The Northern Ireland Housing Executive is a case in point. Its submission to the RPA notes 'the Housing Executive believes the current arrangements represent the best option for the delivery of housing services in Northern Ireland' (NIHE, 2005: 2).

Other 'candidates' for abolition/integration make a similar case. The Northern Ireland Tourist Board, for example, argues that there is a continuing need for it to exist as a strategic leader at a national level and 'this role needs to be at arms length from central government and with a strong private sector interface' (NITB, 2005: 1). The Arts Council of Northern Ireland claims that 'as efforts to build peace continue, now more than ever, there is a need for a measured independent, regional perspective' and make the case that they be retained 'as an independent but fully accountable, dynamic agency' (ACNI, 2005: 1 & 3). In the same vein the Sports Council for Northern Ireland argues for the status quo, with 'some increased political representation as the preferred option for the future development of sport' (SPNI, 2005: 5). Special pleading and the RPA's own predisposition for retention with increased accountability may lead to little more than a few trivial quangos being offered up as sacrificial lambs (e.g. Fisheries Conservancy Board, Pig Production Development Committee) but, in practice, amounting to little more than tinkering at the margins.

Agencies

The third area of the Review's remit is executive agencies. Importantly, these bodies come closest to an examination of central government departments, within which they reside. Perhaps surprisingly, none of the 18 agencies responded to either of the major consultation papers. This can be interpreted in two ways. First, there is widespread apathy among executive agencies to any changes which may take place, or second, that they are confident in the knowledge that the RPA will have limited direct impact on them. More controversially, it could be suggested that RPA civil servants are reluctant (under tacit pressure from permanent secretaries) to recommend changes which would have obvious consequences for government departments. The RPA final consultation document, supported by the fact that there were few responses on the future role and function of agencies in the first consultation, rather feebly suggests that 'decisions on the future of Executive Agencies should best be left to a returning Executive and Assembly' (OFMDFM, 2005: 100, 7.16).

The lack of attention to the detail of these bodies, some of which are major spenders, is difficult to explain. In other words, the organisations to which the RPA has paid least attention have been those most severely criticised for the management and stewardship of public funds. The Comptroller and Auditor General for Northern Ireland (C&AG), for example, was unable to form an opinion on the financial statement of the Department for Social Development (in which the Social Security Agency and Child Support Agency reside) for two consecutive years (2001–3). The Social Security Agency had estimated losses of £121 million in income support, jobseekers' allowance, disability living allowance and housing benefit, as a result of errors by officials and customers, and fraudulent benefits claims. These services have been qualified by auditors and reported on for a number of years. The C&AG similarly qualified his opinion on the Northern Ireland Child Support Agency for the ninth consecutive year, due to overpayments of maintenance by non-resident parents and inaccurate assessments of maintenance, which led to significant errors in amounts owed to non-resident parents (NIAO, 2004). As one member of the House of Commons Public Accounts Committee put it: 'every time we examine anything in Northern Ireland, it always seems to be shockingly lax' (Davidson, 2004: Q35). Deferring consideration of agencies until the restoration of devolution is inexplicable, although the RPA argues that seven executive agencies are the subject of change under other initiatives.

The outcomes

The outcomes of the RPA were announced by Secretary of State Peter Hain on 22 November 2005 and are summarised as follows.

Local government

- Twenty-six district councils are to be reduced to seven with new functional or additional responsibilities in planning, roads, physical regeneration and local economic development.
- New councils are to be given a statutory duty to develop and coordinate the delivery of community planning and the complementary power of well-being.
- The seven council boundaries (to be decided by a Local Government Boundary Commissioner) will be coterminous with other service providers (see Figure 14.3).
- Safeguards or checks and balances are to be agreed with political parties to protest minorities against domination by the majority party.
- There would be reduction in the number of councillors from 582 to a maximum of 60 councillors per council (420 in total) and the abolition of the dual mandate (councillors and MLAs).

Figure 14.3 Possible boundaries for seven new councils

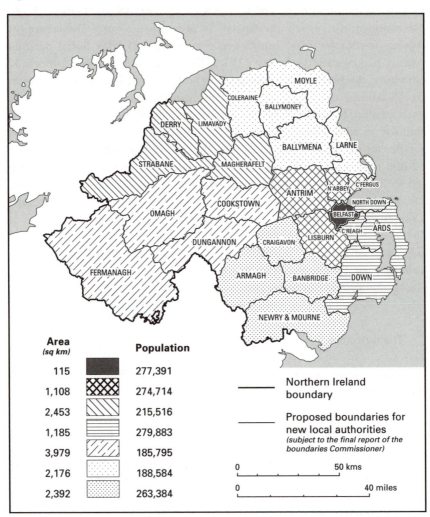

Health

Core structures in health services will reduce from 47 organisations to 18. The plans include:

- A considerably smaller government department (Department of Health, Social Services and Public Safety).
- A Strategic Health and Social Services Authority to replace the four Boards and take on functions currently with the Department.

- Eighteen trusts reduced to five by April 2007 (the Ambulance Service remains as a separate trust).
- Seven local commissioning bodies (demand-led by patients and driven by GPs and primary care professionals) taking on some roles from the four boards and some roles from the 15 Local Health and Social Care Groups, which will be abolished.
- One Patient and Client Council replacing the existing four Health and Social Services Councils.

Education

- A new Education Authority will bring together all the direct support functions currently undertaken by the Education and Library Boards and the range of other organisations funded by government (the Councils for the Curriculum Examinations and Assessment and the Regional Training Unit.
- The new Education Authority will also have responsibility for front-line support and related functions currently undertaken by the Council for Catholic Maintained Schools, the Northern Ireland Council for Integrated Education and Comhairle na Gaelscolaiochta.
- The role of boards of governors will continue much as at present.
- A new Education Advisory Forum will be established to act as a unified advisory interface between the Department and the education sector.
- Youth services will remain under the control of the Department of Education, and functions of the Youth Council for Northern Ireland will transfer to the education authority.
- The Department of Education will focus more on strategy, policy development and on translation of policy into improved outcomes at the front line.

Quangos

An announcement on quangos was not expected until the end of March 2006 but the expectation was to include the transfer of further functions to local government.

Conclusions

The RPA has been long in its gestation. Almost three and a half years after its launch, the outcomes were finally revealed. The Northern Ireland Assembly had been in suspension for over three years and its direct involvement in the Review lasted little more than three months beyond its launch. Despite the magnitude of the task and its long-term consequences for public services in Northern Ireland, local politicians will have little influence on the outcomes announced by the Secretary of State, given the unlikelihood of restoring devolution in the short term. Direct rule ministers have made it clear both by their actions and words that their tenure in Northern Ireland is not to 'mind the shop'. Local politicians revert to playing the politics of opposition. Hence the DUP has accused British ministers of shifting the Republic's borders to include nationalist councils likely to dominate in the West of the province. The SDLP complain of the total absence of local representation in super councils and the Alliance Party reject the changes because they make little sense for major services like health or for local accountability. Sinn Féin, on the other hand, the only party supporting the move to seven councils, is stressing the need to protect equality and diversity under the new arrangements – where key decisions will be taken on a cross-community basis.

The Review's claims that public administration reforms are based on 'strong local government' have been met with disbelief. The powers offered by the RPA in the outcome of the Review amount to little more than a marginal increase in their existing emasculated powers. Lord Rooker claimed the budgets of councils would double (from 4 per cent to 8 per cent of public expenditure). The RPA team, in turn, claims that the only constraint to devolving greater powers was the unwillingness of the local government sector to bid for them. Political parties have been too conservative and cautious in their demands, a legacy of past sectarian experiences in local government for some and, for others, because of a narrow and parochial view of the sector and its ability to deliver key functions. Although the changes announced in health and education will remove or integrate many of the existing non-departmental public bodies within these two functional areas, there remains a reluctance to abolish others. The RPA favours strengthening accountability and the retention of the larger quangos such as the Northern Ireland Housing Executive and Invest Northern Ireland (with budgets of £545 million and £150 million respectively). Government agencies, meanwhile, have escaped even cursory scrutiny by the RPA, so close are they to the fiefdoms of permanent secretaries who are unwilling to see their departments examined by the review. This is a serious omission, given the independent criticism which agencies have attracted in the delivery of their services. Interestingly, however, in announcing the reforms, the Secretary of State recognised that the RPA changes would have a significant impact on departmental structures and that he intended to discuss this issue with all the political parties in Northern Ireland (Hain, 2005).

Undoubtedly the RPA will rationalise structures within the public sector in Northern Ireland. Whether this will lead to savings in administrative costs (estimated by the RPA at £200 million) and result in improvements in service quality, both key claims of the RPA, is uncertain. Rationalised structures in themselves will not improve quality of provision, and as 'savings' will be redirected to front-line services, tracking these could prove difficult. As the outcomes of the Review unfold, local politicians remain observers to the most fundamental changes to the public sector in Northern Ireland for over 30 years.

Notes

1 The authors are grateful for the financial support received from the Devolution and Constitutional Change programme of the ESRC (award number L219252108).
2 There have been four periods of devolution in Northern Ireland since the Belfast (Good Friday) Agreement: 2 December 1999–11 February 2000; 30 May 2000–10 August 2001; 12 August 2001–21 September 2001; and 23 September 2001–14 October 2002.
3 Civic councils are not proposed as a 'lower tier' of local government. The Review team is keen to avoid the criticism that they replaced a unitary system of local government with a two-tier system.
4 The main regional service delivery bodies include: the Central Services Agency, the Health Promotion Agency, the Blood Transfusion Agency, the Medical Physics Agency, the Guardian Ad Litem Agency, and the Northern Ireland Ambulance Service.
5 The 79 significant public bodies were made up of 34 executive public bodies, 16 advisory public bodies, 11 tribunals and 18 Next Steps agencies.

References

ACNI (Arts Council of Northern Ireland) (2005) *Response of Arts Council of Northern Ireland to Review of Public Administration Consultation Document*. Belfast: ACNI.

Bloomfield, K. (1998) 'Central government' in K. Bloomfield and C. Carter (eds) *People and Government: Questions for Northern Ireland*. York: Joseph Rowntree Foundation.

Carmichael, P. (2002) 'The Northern Ireland civil service: characteristics and trends since 1970', *Public Administration*, 80 (1), 23–49.

Davidson, I. (2004) Oral evidence to Public Accounts Committee: Northern Ireland: the management of industrial sickness absence, *Hansard*, 28 April.

DFP (Department of Finance and Personnel) (2005) *Northern Ireland: Priorities and Budget 2005–08*. Belfast: DFP.

Dowdall, J. (2004) Select Committee on Public Accounts, *Hansard*, 23 February, Q21.

Dunleavy, P. (1991) *Bureaucracy, Democracy and Public Choice*. Hemel Hempstead: Harvester Wheatsheaf.

Hain, P. (2005) *Statement by the Secretary of State for Northern Ireland on the Outcome of the Review of Public Administration*, 22 November. Belfast: RPA.

Hood, C. (1981) 'Axeperson spare that quango' in C. Hood and M. Wright (eds) *Big Government in Hard Times*. Oxford: Martin Robertson.

Knox, C. and McHugh, M. (1990) 'Management in government: the next steps in Northern Ireland', *Administration*, 38 (3), 251–270.

LGCE (Local Government Commission for England) (1993) *Renewing Local Government in the English Shires*. London: HMSO.

McCartney, R. (2002) 'Review of public administration', *Hansard*, 24 June.

NIAO (Northern Ireland Audit Office) (2004) *Financial Audit and Reporting 2002–2003: General Report by the Comptroller and Auditor General for Northern Ireland*. Belfast: NIAO.

NIHE (Northern Ireland Housing Executive) (2005) *Response to the Review of Public Administration*. Belfast: NIHE.

NILEA (Northern Ireland Local Government Association) (2005) *Response to the Review of Public Administration*. Belfast: NILGA.

NITB (Northern Ireland Tourist Board) (2005) *Response to the Review of Public Administration*. Belfast: NITB.

OFMDFM (Office of the First Minister and Deputy First Minister) (2003) *The Review of Public Administration in Northern Ireland*. Belfast: OFMDFM.

OFMDFM (Office of the First Minister and Deputy First Minister) (2004) *Fit for Purpose: The Reform Agenda in the Northern Ireland Civil Service*. Belfast: OFMDFM.

OFMDFM (Office of the First Minister and Deputy First Minister) (2005) *The Review of Public Administration in Northern Ireland: Further Consultation*. Belfast: OFMDFM.

Pearson, I. (2004a) Speech delivered by at BMF Conference, Belfast, 29 June.

Pearson, I. (2004b) 'Improvements to quality of service key to public administration reform', 19 July. Belfast: OFMDFM.

Pearson, I. (2005) 'Foreword' in *The Review of Public Administration in Northern Ireland: Further Consultation*. Belfast: OFMDFM.

Rooker, J. (2005) 'Minister pledges to cut out red tape', Office of the First Minister and Deputy First Minister, *New Releases*, 6 July.

SCNI (Sports Council for Northern Ireland) (2005) *Response to the Review of Public Administration*. Belfast: SCNI.

Stewart, J. (2003) *Modernising British Local Government: An Assessment of Labour's Reform Programme*. Basingstoke: Palgrave.

Travers, T., Jones, G. and Burnham, J. (1993) *Impact of Population Size on Local Authority Costs and Effectiveness*. York: Joseph Rowntree Foundation.

Trimble, D. (2002) Public Administration Review, Northern Ireland Assembly, *Hansard*, 25 February.

15
The Northern Ireland economy: economic development structures

Mark Goodwin, Martin Jones and Rhys Jones

Introduction

The performance of the economy has become a critical feature of the devolved politics of Northern Ireland. This is the case across the devolved territories of the UK, for as Rhodri Morgan, the First Minister for Wales, has argued 'the most important task for any government is to create the conditions in which the economy can prosper' (*Western Mail*, 13 December 2001). In Northern Ireland, however, this task takes on a particular inflection, over and above a concern with economic prosperity for its own sake. Here it is argued that one key way of promoting lasting peace and stability is through the development of a growing and successful economy, where access to its rewards are not dependent on sectarian identity. For instance, the Northern Ireland Executive argued in its second Programme for Government that:

> We are also acutely conscious of the religious, political and racial divisions within our community and also the impact of poverty on individuals and communities . . . We are therefore committed to a society where communities pull together and inter-communal division is removed; in which people feel valued and respected and can share in growing prosperity; and in which there is equality of opportunity and justice for all. (NIE, 2002: 5)

To reinforce the importance of economic development, two of the five priorities set out for government action by the Executive in both its first and second Programmes for Government were concerned with the economy – 'Investing in education and skills' and 'securing a competitive economy'. Indeed, the themes of inclusion, fairness and economic prosperity are combined and interlinked across these and succeeding government documents, including the most recent *Northern Ireland Priorities and Budget 2005–2008*. The second Programme for Government spells out the linkages starkly, when it states that 'tackling our social division is a key requirement if we are to create the basis for a competitive economy, while economic prosperity, fairly shared, is a key requirement if we are to heal many of the social problems that we face'

(NIE, 2002: 6). It goes on to say that 'if we are to achieve a cohesive, inclusive and just society, it is essential that we create a vibrant economy to provide employment and wealth for the future' (NIE, 2002: 43).

In Northern Ireland then, the health of the economy is set out as critical, not just to achieve economic prosperity, but also to help heal social division and promote cohesion and inclusiveness. This chapter will chart the frameworks and mechanisms which the devolved Assembly put into place to promote economic development – what we label as economic governance. By this we mean factors such as infrastructure and site provision; inward investment; innovation and entrepreneurship; and training and workforce development. This is not to deny that other policy areas such as transport, education and health make a contribution to economic development, but in a chapter of this length we can only concentrate on the specific arena of economic governance. Across the chapter as a whole we will trace how, and why, the structures of economic governance were put into place after devolution, and also look at how these have developed since. We will first set out the pre-devolution structures, before going on to look at how, and why, these institutions were altered by the process of devolution. We will then analyse some of the key challenges faced by these new institutions and assess the ability of the new structures (and more importantly those working within them) to cope with such challenges. We will conclude with a brief section which asks how we might interpret these developments.[1]

Putting the post-devolution structures of economic governance into place

Northern Ireland has actually witnessed an almost complete change in the institutions which deliver economic development policy since devolution. This process of change began before devolution with the publication in 1999 of *Strategy 2010*, commissioned by the Northern Ireland Minister Adam Ingram to set out a 10-year framework for economic development. The incoming Assembly, which was established later in 1999, adopted its broad recommendations, both in terms of strategy and structure. Strategically the document argued that a more dynamic and prosperous Northern Ireland economy could be encouraged through emphasising and developing enterprise, self-reliance and a heightened international perspective via a focus on knowledge, innovation and skills. *Strategy 2010* also emphasised the fair distribution of the benefits of future economic development across the community, and argued for an emphasis on increasing the resources available for skill development and other 'soft' infrastructure rather than those spent on grants and physical infrastructure such as premises. In all these respects the document was a significant forerunner of the themes which were to appear time and time again in government documents after devolution.

In terms of structure, *Strategy 2010* set out two key principles which were to lead to huge institutional changes in the economic development landscape of Northern Ireland. One concerned the advocacy of a new single agency for economic development, and the other argued for an external forum to advise the Executive in its policy formulation. We will deal with each of these in turn. At the time of publication, and indeed at the time the Assembly was established, economic governance was centred on the Department of Economic Development (DED) within the Northern Ireland Office. The DED had responsibility for a number of agencies, including the Industrial Development Board, the Local Enterprise Development Unit, the Industrial Research and Technology Unit and the Training and Employment Agency. Between them, these agencies were responsible for providing advice and support covering inward investment grants, small business development, innovation, entrepreneurship, technological development, and training and employment services. Although comprehensive, this structure was somewhat unwieldy and *Strategy 2010* argued for the establishment of a single lead economic development agency, which

> would sharpen the direction and delivery of overall economic development policy, presenting a clearer structure to users and removing the potential for confusion in the market place. It would simplify companies' dealings with the Department [DED], and help to ensure that a clear and coherent policy message is presented to potential investors in Northern Ireland, whether indigenous or external. In addition, the integration of administrative services should yield worthwhile savings. (DED, 1999: 206)

This proposal was subsequently accepted and acted upon by the new Assembly. Interestingly, our research has revealed that those involved tend to attribute the stimulus for such change just as much to the processes of devolution as they do to the recommendations of *Strategy 2010*. As a senior civil servant commented about this reorganisation:

> We've reorganised the department . . . this is about responding to the demands of today . . . the whole paradigm of having your resources dealt with, your policy dealt with in a devolved environment is different . . . this is a devolved environment, local minister, locally accountable, he is going to be interested in knowing how policy is delivered.

Invest Northern Ireland was established in April 2002 to operate as a nondepartmental public body sponsored by the Department of Enterprise Trade and Investment, and took on the functions of the Local Enterprise Development Unit, the Industrial Development Board, and the Industrial Research and Technology Unit (INI, 2001). In addition, this new 'sole' agency incorporated the role of the Company Development Programme (formerly with the Training and Employment Agency) and the business development functions of the Northern Ireland Tourist Board.

The other key recommendation, concerning the establishment of an advisory body, was also acted upon quickly. Indeed, by the time powers were transferred to the Assembly in December 1999, the new Northern Ireland Economic Development Forum (EDF) had already been set up to make advice and recommendations on issues relating to the 'development and future competitiveness of the Northern Ireland economy'. The purpose of the forum was to ensure that the 'social partners' (trade unions, employers, community and voluntary sector, further and higher education, local government and the agricultural sector) have an effective and meaningful role in influencing the formulation and implementation of economic development policy. In setting up the EDF, Adam Ingram had put forward the following economic argument:

> There is a recognition that shared knowledge and information is becoming more significant in the competitive strategy of companies. Knowledge-based competitiveness involves not only networks forged between businesses, but between businesses, education and research institutes. These links help ensure a flow of innovative ideas and highly skilled labour. (DED, 1999)

However, our interviews uncovered a significant role for the EDF in non-economic terms. It was viewed as important in securing 'buy-in' from non-governmental agencies; as one interviewee explained 'it was a case of getting lots of different views that have been accommodated within a common forum, towards a common purpose, and again that's where EDF sits, if you like, as drawing in partners'. But equally the EDF was also seen as something which could offer a broad oversight across different government departments. As one source put it, commenting on the establishment of the EDF:

> It was [a process] that actually engaged and helped gain the buy-in of all the social partners and members and also reflects the engagement and support of all government departments. So it really is a quite unique achievement, setting a picture, setting a scene, setting a framework for action by a lot of key players.

This ability to join and link the work of different government departments became imperative after devolution, when the task of economic development was split between two new government departments, with their respective ministers and committees. The Department of Enterprise, Trade and Investment (DETI) took over most of the roles of the former Department of Economic Development (DED), and the new 'lead institution', Invest Northern Ireland (INI) is an agency of this department (see Figure 15.1). But alongside this, a new Department of Employment and Learning (DEL) was established with responsibility for higher and further education, vocational training, employment services, labour relations and training grants. The estab-

Figure 15.1 The structure of economic governance in Northern Ireland

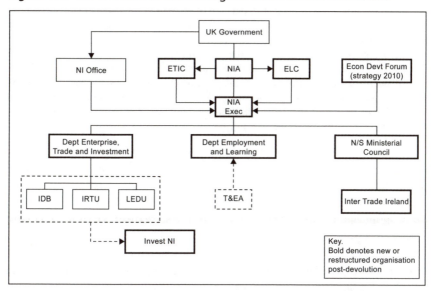

lishment of a second government department largely concerned with economic development has to be viewed in the context of the Good Friday Agreement, and the political need to create 11 departments of state to accommodate the power-sharing arrangements. Crucially, the Training and Employment Agency (T&EA), formerly a 'Next Steps' agency under the remit of the DED was immediately absorbed into the new DEL.

The rationale for this shift was also complex. The following quotes from three of those involved in the reorganisation illustrate administrative, technical and political reasons for the move:

> The T&EA was a Next Steps agency, and it was an executive agency before. When devolution came along we moved from the Department of Economic Development and became part of Higher and Further Education Training and Employment, and they shortened the name to DEL. When the department was formed, the T&EA merged with higher and further education, the post-16 stuff. So it was a fusion of higher and further education and training and employment . . . It was decided by the new ministers to bring all these things together, rather than have a small department with a big T&EA, and that's what happened, the agency was subsumed into DEL . . . There's been no change in the status of people, but what has happened as a result is better cohesion in terms of policy making, because you've got this post-16 remit together.

> You could say that if Sean Farren hadn't brought T&EA in he wouldn't really have had a department at all . . . A lot of the delivery mechanisms for education and training and learning are out there.

T&EA was the first Next Steps agency set up in Northern Ireland . . . We wound it up because numerically it is 90 per cent of the staff of this department. The theory of Next Steps agencies is that they operate at arms length from the minister on the basis of the framework document, which set up targets, reporting back to the minister quarterly and at the end of the year. But when you have a new minister who is full time, in a new devolved administration, anxious to get his hands on the levers of power and make a difference, unlike before it makes no sense to have those levers at arms length. And so the agency didn't make any sense in political terms, and in terms of creating a new dynamic cohesive department, it made no sense in terms of that either. So we reviewed the situation and we moved from Next Steps status.

What comes across strongly here is the importance of devolution in setting out a structure whereby local politicians are indeed able to 'get [their] hands on the levers of power and make a difference'. But what is also evident is the scope left to them to shape and develop such structures. One of the most significant features of the UK devolution settlement is that it is enabling rather than prescriptive. Powers are delegated to each devolved territory, but the shape and form of the new organisations which emerged to implement these powers was an open question. Indeed, the Assembly could have left the pre-devolution structures of economic governance untouched – it could have left the DED in place, along with Industrial Development Board, the Local Enterprise Development Unit and the Industrial Research and Technology Unit. As we have seen, the publication of *Strategy 2010* signalled that changes were on the way, but devolution certainly gave a huge impetus to their implementation. In other words the first major challenge faced by the devolved Assembly was to decide how to structure and organise the delivery of economic development. To deliver training policy the Assembly decided to bring back a Next Steps agency into the formal structures of government. This made sense, since without the move the new DEL would have lacked 90 per cent of its staff and would not have been 'a department at all'.

Other decisions were also fairly straightforward, such as the move to establish InterTradeIreland as one of six cross-border bodies set up under the terms of the Belfast Agreement of 1998. The body came into operation in December 1999, and its role is to exchange information and coordinate work on trade and business development between the North and the South of the island. Originally it reported to the North/South Ministerial Council, but since the suspension of the Northern Ireland Assembly in October 2002, it now reports to both governments on matters such as research, training and marketing in a cross-border context; skills, IT, telecoms and e-commerce development; North–South trade and supply chains; and a North–South equity investment programme.

If the decisions to move the T&EA back into government and set up InterTradeIreland were fairly clear cut, others were not. Indeed, devolution provides an ideal example of the way in which the state must always be viewed as a 'political process in motion' (Peck, 2001: 449). This is more than just a question of charting new institutional structures, for devolution has also ushered into play new organisational cultures and new working practices for those personnel working within the state. As Peck has reminded us, the state must also be viewed as a 'peopled organisation' (Peck, 2001: 451), and devolution has created new scenarios for the unfolding relationship between state structures and state personnel. It is to this that we now turn, by exploring some of the challenges faced by those involved in economic governance in Northern Ireland.

The challenges of economic governance under devolution

Reasons of space mean that we are not able to be extensive in our coverage of the challenges raised by devolution, so we are focusing on those faced by INI, as the new lead agency of economic governance in the province. In addition to its advocacy of a single lead agency, *Strategy 2010* had set out a vision statement which encompassed 'a fast growing, competitive, innovative, knowledge-based economy where there are plentiful opportunities and a population equipped to grasp them' (DED, 1999: 129). The question was what type of agency would be best suited to promoting such an economy. It is one thing to set out a vision, it is quite another to set up appropriate structures to implement it. In particular, a key initial challenge was whether the new lead agency should be located inside or outside government. The decision was taken to set up the new organisation at 'arms length' from the government. Sir Reg Empey, the Minister for Enterprise, Trade and Investment justified this decision as follows:

> In order to meet the challenges of the knowledge-based economy – which we must promote even more keenly – we need structures which facilitate rapid decision taking and give flexibility to respond to changing markets . . . I am convinced this cannot be easily achieved within the civil service . . . I have therefore concluded that the right model is a single economic development agency in the form of a Non-Departmental Public Body. (NIA, 2000)

Although the unstable political situation in Northern Ireland and subsequent suspension of the Assembly has meant ongoing uncertainty, INI has had to construct an operational and organisational space for itself. A key issue has been constructing a balance between the policy making and implementation, or between regulation and autonomy. One respondent put it in the following way:

> We will monitor them and keep close to them, we'll try not to be a policeman, but we'll have to be a policeman to some extent . . . Invest Northern Ireland could easily go in a direction which we haven't actually tasked them to do. But

it's up to us to ensure that the policy statement within which they work is drawn sufficiently realistically, tightly, to ensure they do what they are set up to do.

This strategy of tight control was a deliberate one, put in place by the civil service in order to rein in the new agency without suggesting outright opposition. Another interviewee suggested that:

The Department [DETI] wasn't happy about the new agency being outside the civil service. They didn't put up big opposition to it. There's ways of dealing with these things . . . a lot of processes and procedures we use would be civil service type procedures . . . we see it as the culture . . . part of the civil service.

This again draws attention to the importance of working cultures and working practices in establishing new institutions of governance. To a certain extent these will take time to emerge – as one respondent said 'we're still feeling our way' – but in order to ensure tighter control the civil servants in the DETI have moved towards a more interventionist stance. This has been explicitly recognised by those who work for INI, and as one of its employees told us:

The chief executive stands up and says 'we're not civil servants, we're a NDPB, we are business like, professional, innovative, flexible, forward thinking, fast', it doesn't matter, you see the reality, you see the language we use, and you see the speed things happen, and it's very different to that. It's right in the heart of government, NDPB, arms length, or not. It's like a division of the department.

So having deliberately set up an arms-length agency to encourage a sense of risk-taking and commercial freedom, those in political power then decided to limit its manoeuvrability. As we were told, 'the reality is that [INI] is part of the wider organisation, part of the wider system, and part of the department. *It's an organisation which has political responsibilities*' (emphasis added). A key challenge is to promote a working culture that enables staff to work efficiently and effectively within the bounds of these responsibilities. The suspension of the Assembly may have removed the more local political tensions from the immediate picture, but there are still ministerial policies and programmes to work within.

Such responsibilities of course, spread beyond single government departments, and a further challenge in the economic development arena has been to 'join up' the work and policy of several different government departments. The initial Programmes for Government made it clear that to secure a competitive economy (one of the five priorities) would entail a consideration of communications, energy, physical infrastructure and planning as well as business support and training. This would involve the DEL, the Department of the Environment, the Department of Regional Development, the Department of Finance and Personnel, and the OFMDFM as well as the Department of Trade and Investment. This has been recognised 'on the ground' – as one practitioner told us:

> What we're seeing with Invest Northern Ireland, there's a lot more engagement with other departments . . . that wouldn't have happened in the past, you'd have had DEL going out separately, they wouldn't even have come near us . . . so I see a change in that whole interconnection with the likes of DEL in terms of employ-ability. They're [the Executive are] trying to get better joined-up government, there is a sense that INI wouldn't dare go out and develop an employability ini-tiative, without engaging DEL in the planning process.

There is a strong sense that the annual Programmes for Government were designed to provide an overarching framework that could bring departments together to feed into a single strategy, but, as we were told, 'the Programme for Government [is] . . . a ten-year process, beginning to build a sense of gov-ernment instead of a sense of the . . . departments. And there's huge rivalry between departments and huge protocol.' Such rivalry has lessened slightly with the suspension of the Assembly, as the political rivalries among ministers have faded, but there are still competing demands for finance, resource and status to overcome.

Another initial challenge faced by the new DETI was to 'operationalise' the vision set out in *Strategy 2010*. This is a common task across all govern-ment departments seeking to turn visionary policy statements into practical delivery plans, but was made more difficult by the somewhat unwieldy struc-ture of the document. It runs to 264 pages and specified 62 separate recom-mendations for action. As one respondent put it:

> One of the biggest difficulties that the present DETI had with *2010* was to try and make sense of the list. There's 60 odd things to do, you can't possibly be doing that, it's much too complicated. So what they've tried to do is they've tried to sort out headings, sub-points and to prioritise the list essentially, perfectly sen-sible . . . You see the basic ideas, what people will publicly agree are the most important features of all of this, are known. Grants culture, and this and that. That's all generally agreed. It's just doing something about it.

In order to 'do something about it', the agencies of economic develop-ment have further refined their structures, strategies and working practices fol-lowing the suspension of the Assembly. *Strategy 2010* has been replaced as the key strategic document by the *Economic Vision for Northern Ireland*, published by the DETI in 2005. Although the essential 'vision' is the same – 'improving our global competitiveness through increased value-added, leading to increased market share in products and services' (DETI, 2005: 8) – this is a much slimmer and focused document, which sets out four key drivers as a means of closing the productivity gap between Northern Ireland and the rest of the UK and other European competitors. These drivers are:

- increase investment in research and development and promote innovation and creativity;
- promote and encourage enterprise;
- ensure people have the right skills for future employment opportunities;
- ensure modern infrastructure to support business and consumers.

A set of key priorities is attached to each driver. In addition, at a policy level DETI has also published a *Regional Innovation Strategy – Think/Create/Innovate*, and together with DEL has produced an *Enterprising Education Action Plan*. At a more operational level, INI has developed annual corporate plans, as has InterTradeIreland, and it has also produced an *Accelerating Entrepreneurship Strategy*. Structurally, INI has five 'local' offices, and has worked through these to collaborate with groupings of local authorities to produce regional action plans, and it also works in partnership with local enterprise agencies at the local level. Gradually these developments are helping to put the flesh on the economic governance framework created by devolution, as government departments and agencies continue to operate in the space left by the suspension of the Assembly.

Conclusion

These continuing developments remind us that we are indeed dealing with an unfolding and dynamic process following devolution. The UK's devolution settlement did not set things in stone, but rather provided a political, cultural and social space whereby each devolved territory could pursue a different set of agendas. But they also have lessons for how we might interpret the process of devolution. Many commentators have viewed devolution as a prime example of the 'hollowing out' of the nation state. According to Jessop, such 'hollowing out' occurs when the 'powers [of the nation state] are delegated upwards to supraregional or international bodies, downwards to regional or local states, or outwards to . . . cross-national alliances' (Jessop, 2002: 235). This certainly seems to capture UK devolution. However, 'hollowing out' simply refers to the delegation of powers away from the national level, and makes no claims about the organisational or institutional forms that may result from this. In other words, it refers to the beginnings of a 'process in motion', and we need other conceptual devices to help us understand how and why that process subsequently unfolds. Indeed 'hollowing out' can make no claims about the organisational and territorial forms which follow from the delegation of powers – partly because these are always open to political contestation and struggle, and partly because its analytical lens is focused at the national level. This focus means that 'hollowing out' is unable to give us much purchase on the processes of state restructuring which take place in different ways in different devolved territories.

This study of economic governance in Northern Ireland, for instance, has instead drawn our attention to the myriad processes involved in 'filling in' the state after devolution. We have seen how the power-sharing arrangements which underpinned the creation of twin government departments (DETI and DEL) were then followed by political and administrative calculations which brought the lead agency for one (T&EA) back into government, while deliberately creating a second lead agency (INI) as an 'arms-length' public-sponsored body. Just after these manoeuvres, the suspension of the Northern Ireland Assembly has temporarily removed the local political tensions which were constraining inter-departmental collaboration, and the government officials and practitioners have taken the opportunity to develop a new raft of economic development strategies. What we have under devolution is thus a complex 'qualitative process of state restructuring' rather than a simple 'quantitative process of state erosion or diminution' (Peck, 2001: 447).

We feel we can utilise the notion of 'filling in' to draw attention to the complex and contingent impacts of devolution within the various UK territories. The point to emphasise is that it is only through grappling with the notion of 'filling in' – in empirical and conceptual terms – that we can appreciate the detailed evolution of governance in particular territories and at particular scales. In this regard 'filling in' should not be conceived of in purely literal terms. It does not necessarily imply a proliferation of organisations and strategies of governance at the sub-national scale. Sub-national governments may well decide to reduce the number of organisations which operate in their territories – indeed officials and politicians in Northern Ireland decided to remove the Industrial Development Board, the Local Enterprise Development Unit and the Industrial Research and Technology Unit, and 'fill in' the administrative space that was vacated with INI. The key is to examine the relationship that exists between the 'hollowing out' of powers at the national scale, and the subsequent state restructuring which takes place at other scales. 'Filling in' can allow us to demonstrate how devolution has led to the evolution of new, or the sedimentation of old, organisations of governance, and it enables us to appreciate how different regions of the UK have adopted different scales and territories of governance (Goodwin, Jones and Jones, 2005).

The use of the concept of 'filling in', then, focuses on the manner in which power is being transferred, and on the scales it is being transferred to. Above all, 'filling in' is indeed illustrative of a state that is a 'political process in motion' (Peck, 2001: 449) allowing us to appreciate the political, cultural and social dynamics associated with the continuous 'emergence' of state organisations in the regions and territories of the UK (Jessop, 2001). Such an approach is especially suited to understanding the post-devolution development of state structures and strategies in Northern Ireland, where first power sharing and then suspension have created a complex and uncertain polity.

Note

1 The data presented here are drawn from the findings of a two-year research project on 'Constitutional change and economic governance: territories and institutions' funded by the ESRC (L219252013) as part of its Devolution and Constitutional Change programme. The discussion draws on semi-structured interviews with senior politicians, civil servants and practitioners involved in economic governance, and on a range of documentary sources including official policy papers as well as minutes and other internal records. Over 20 semi-structured interviews were undertaken between 2001 and 2002, and we sought to elicit responses from a variety of individuals involved in the economic governance of Northern Ireland. For issues of confidentiality, we are unable to name the individuals, but all quotes with respondents used in this chapter are taken from these interviews.

References

DED (Department of Economic Development) (1999) *Strategy 2010: Report by the Economic Development Strategy Review Steering Group*. Belfast: DED.

DETI (Department of Enterprise Trade and Investment) (2005) *Economic Vision for Northern Ireland*. Belfast: DETI.

Goodwin, M. Jones, M. and Jones, R. (2005) 'Devolution, constitutional change and economic development: understanding the shifting economic and political geographies of the British state', *Regional Studies*, 39, 421–436.

Jessop, B. (2001) 'Institutional re(turns) and the strategic-relational approach', *Environment and Planning A*, 33, 1213–1235.

Jessop, B. (2002) *The Future of the Capitalist State*. Cambridge: Polity.

INI (Invest Northern Ireland) (2001) *Invest Northern Ireland: Draft Corporate Plan*. Belfast: INI.

NIA (Northern Ireland Assembly) (2000) *Debate on Economic Development Agencies*. Belfast: NIA.

NIE (Northern Ireland Executive) (2002) *Programme for Government: Making a Difference 2002–2005*. Belfast: Office of the First Minister and Deputy First Minister.

Peck, J. (2001) 'Neoliberalizing states: thin policies/hard outcomes', *Progress in Human Geography*, 25, 445–455.

16

Devolution and public policy making

Michael Keating

Devolution in context

The Northern Ireland devolution settlement is an ad hoc solution to a specific problem, the communitarian conflict and the relationship of the province with the UK and the Republic of Ireland. Yet it is embedded in wider processes, in the UK and beyond. At one level it is part of the belated triumph of the Gladstonian project to convert the UK into a union of self-governing nations on quasi-federal lines. At another, it is the local manifestation of the restructuring of the state and political authority in the context of globalisation and European integration, part of the 'new regionalism' in Europe (Keating, 1998). So although as yet we have no empirical evidence on the potential and limits of devolved government in the province, we can draw on a wealth of experience elsewhere and a large body of literature in order to assess the prospects. This chapter looks at the ability of the devolved institutions to make policy and the various constraints they face. It argues from general principles and from experience in Europe and draws particularly on experience with Scottish devolution since 1999 (Keating, 2005a).

It is perhaps ironical that, after 120 years of deliberation, devolution finally came about in the UK (and much of Europe) just at a time when governments were losing their old capacity for regulation and policy making in the face of global and market forces. A cynic might argue that it is precisely because of the practical constraints on policy divergence that states are now relaxed about handing down competences to their component regions and nations. States have been losing powers, autonomy and, indeed, elements of sovereignty itself to the global trading and financial order, the market, corporations, international organisations and the EU (Camilleri and Falk, 1992; Keating, 2001; MacCormick, 1999). Their scope for autonomous policy making is limited by their insertion into dense networks of international dependency. *A fortiori*, the powers of devolved governments are constrained, since they lack even the formal status of sovereignty and are limited to powers defined in advance. They do not enjoy the classic responsibilities of stabilisation, regulation and redistribution.

Yet the very transformation of the state has meant that the classic regalian functions no longer tell us all, or even very much, about policy making and policy impact. Certainly the state remains the primary actor in the security field, but in other fields the capacity for effective intervention may lie elsewhere. There is a burgeoning literature on economic development which emphasises the renewed importance of territory and of territorially based networks of reciprocity, cooperation and competition (Storper, 1997; Scott, 1998; Cooke and Morgan, 1998). Social policy has moved from a broad interest in income maintenance and universal services towards examining the precise conditions of social inclusion and exclusion in communities. New linkages are being made among policy fields, at various spatial levels, of which the most notable example is welfare and labour market policies. In this context, there is ample scope for regional or meso-level governments to innovate and experiment, but along with the new opportunities come new constraints.

There are many versions of the new regionalism and interpretations of its implications for policy. Kenichi Ohmae (1995) in an unscholarly but influential work, paints a picture of a globalised order in which states are swept aside by dynamic and thrusting regions, competing on world markets in a Darwinian struggle for survival. This requires them to keep business costs and taxes to the minimum and leaves no space for social policy or redistribution. This is known more widely as the 'race to the bottom' scenario, promoted by neo-liberals and feared by social democrats. Another perspective sees the region as a level at which a new synthesis can be forged between economic competitiveness and social inclusion (Amin, 1999; Cooke and Morgan, 1998). Regions have an incentive to build human capital and social cooperation since, in the new era, these and not low costs and taxes are the key to success. A third view is that both of these scenarios are possible, constituting respectively a 'low road' and a 'high road' to development. Regions have scope to forge their own development projects and manage their insertion into the global and European order, albeit subject to rather severe constraints.

The devolution settlement

At first sight, the Northern Ireland settlement devolves a rather substantial range of powers. Only reserved and excepted powers are specified, with the residual powers going to the Assembly. Reserved powers can themselves be transferred over time, leaving only a core of state functions with the centre. The division of powers looks similar to that in Scotland (although Scotland only has one list of reserved powers) but the contrasting underlying philosophies can be detected in close observation, impacting on the powers and the way they are likely to work out in practice. In Scotland the UK government has devolved in order to keep the state together. This is not simply a matter of guaranteeing the borders and avoiding secession, but of maintaining the common security area, the common British market and the common welfare state. Westminster has insisted on keeping almost all taxation to itself, social security is reserved, market regulation is kept to the centre and there are provisions to prevent unfair economic competition. Policing and the criminal law are devolved because there is no worry that these powers will be used in a way that could cause complications for the centre. In Northern Ireland the preoccupations are very different. There is a weaker common market provision than in Scotland, and taxation is not excepted – tax powers were left out of the legislation only because of the insistence of Northern Ireland politicians themselves, who feared for the future of transfers from London under the Barnett Formula.[1] On the other hand, security concerns are apparent in the exception of the appointment of judges and the Director of Public Prosecutions, and a lack of trust in the local political class in the exception of local elections (in Scotland all of these are devolved). Ultimately, of course, the province has the right to secede in order to join the Republic. Beyond the precise differences in devolved competences, then, this suggests that Whitehall and Westminster are less likely to be concerned, should Northern Ireland move in its own distinct policy direction.

Another constraint absent in the Northern Ireland case is the UK political parties and their representatives. In Scotland intergovernmental relations have been conducted largely through party channels and, while there was a gradual divergence over the first term of the Scottish Parliament, New Labour in London sought to bring the Scottish party back in line. Around the time of the UK general election in 2005 a lot of pressure was put on Scottish ministers to conform to the London line on health service reform and, to some extent, education. Scottish Labour MPs have intervened on devolved matters and for a while there was the strange spectacle of a Scottish MP being Secretary of State for Health in England and pressurising his Scottish counterpart to come into line with England, where the internal market has been reintroduced and private provision encouraged. The isolation of Northern Ireland from the British party system will largely rule out this type of intervention.

The absence of taxation powers for the Assembly does not entirely constrain its ability to make policy choices, since moneys flowing through the Barnett Formula are freely disposable. Certainly, experience in Scotland shows that interest groups are constantly trying to make comparisons with

England where these serve their purposes, complaining that Scotland is losing out. Yet the impact of this is blunted by the fact that, for technical reasons, it is almost impossible to compare detailed spending priorities with England. Business in Scotland constantly complains that the national business rates are higher than in England, but this refers only to the poundage, ignoring the different valuations of property. Education spending is largely channelled through local governments as part of the block grant. In other cases there are differences in the grouping of functions and often differences in reporting conventions.[2]

On the other hand, the lack of taxation powers means that the devolved governments in the UK cannot make the critical choices about the balance among taxation and spending that is at the heart of the policy process. They are also vulnerable should the UK government choose to fund services in England through charges, as has happened with university fees and could happen in the future in health. In that case they must match the charges themselves or find the money from other services.[3]

Policy capacity and policy communities

Devolved governments tend to make policy less through authoritative legislation and more through negotiation and cooperation with other institutions and outside groups and in intergovernmental networks. It is no doubt for this reason that the overworked term 'governance' is so often applied at the regional level, as it is at the European. A term with such a vast range of meanings has little analytical value[4] but, if we take one of them and see governance as regulation and action through non-hierarchical networks of cooperation and exchange, then what we are seeing under devolution is a move away from governance to government, with the insertion of an elected tier endowed with legislative and regulatory competences. This is a difficult and often conflictual process as actors find new roles and relationships.

Devolved governments do not have as many resources as states to engage in policy development and innovation. In the UK they are descended from territorial departments whose role was to manage the periphery on behalf of the centre, and to lobby the centre for material benefit, rather than to make policy themselves. Such policy capacity as existed was often in agencies rather than ministerial departments. In Wales a decision has been made to incorporate the agencies within the Assembly Government, increasing its policy capacity but also inspired by the general anti-quango feeling. It is by no means clear that this is the best way to encourage innovation. Agencies at one remove from politicians may be freer to think creatively and to work out new ideas than ministerial departments subject to daily scrutiny. Experience in Scotland shows that the new transparency in government has made ministers risk-averse and led to a focus on short-term output measures and detailed matters of service-provision rather than longer-term policy thinking. A policy capacity diffused throughout the system may be a better way of fostering new ideas. What is important at the centre is an ability to set priorities and to allocate resources accordingly. The budgetary process in Scotland and Wales, inherited from the old offices, has not enabled this as yet. There is a more politicised process, and ministers now fight their corners within Scotland and Wales, but the centre has not yet developed ways in which to adjudicate claims. Partly this is due to the largesse that has come through the Barnett Formula in recent years. The coming squeeze on expenditure could lead to defensive behaviour on the part of departments, preventing reallocation of resources; or it could be the occasion for reinforcing strategic capacity at the centre.

The devolved governments have also lacked the range of think tanks and policy forums that have sprouted in London in recent decades. The latter have tended to range across the spectrum of the two main British parties, now jostling for position on the centre-right. The centre of political gravity in Scotland and Wales has been further to the left, but lacks the corresponding intellectual backing. Consequently, debate has often been defensive, and policy divergence has taken the form of devolved administrations not always following England all the way, rather than striking out on their own.

Party politics, however, has been a force for differentiation in Scotland, given the system of proportional representation and the need for coalition government. For the first time in the UK, a policy programme is negotiated after the elections and binds the Executive for its term in office. Beyond this, the Executive's small majority in the Scottish Parliament and the need to steer matters through the committee system has meant that the dominant party does not always get its way. The presence in the Scottish Parliament of six parties and some independents has encouraged new alignments and coalitions over individual issues. So the Labour Party was forced to retreat over university fees and, later, over personal care for the elderly by a coalition of all the other parties, including left and right. This may not be a matter of rationally considering policies and adopting the one best adapted to meet the needs. Indeed on these two issues there was a great deal of confusion and some unholy alliances. The left was for free personal care for the elderly and the abolition of university tuition fees because this represented universalism, and the right was in favour because of the benefit to the middle classes. Yet there is no doubt that distinct policies emerged, with government then forced to make the most of them. So the impossibility of getting tuition fees through the

Parliament in the near future has forced the higher education policy review on its own course (Keating, 2005b). Northern Ireland has an even more complex party system, whose lines of division do not correspond to the usual British left–right divide on economic and social policy. It is likely, then, that inter-party haggling could lead to similar forms of policy innovation and divergence.

A critical factor in the development of a policy-making system at the devolved level has been the presence, or emergence, of territorialised policy communities. Scotland and Wales have a range of types of interest group. Some are purely local, some are UK or British in scope, and some are local branches of broader groupings. In the absence of devolution these tended to constitute themselves as territorial lobbies, demanding more from the centre and able to come together in defence of territorial interests while not surrendering their own sectoral or class interests. Attitudes to devolution have varied, with trade unions and the voluntary sector in favour, since it would give them greater opportunities, while the business community has varied from outright opposition to grudging acceptance after 1998. Since then the policy communities have found adaptation difficult. Now they have to recast themselves as policy actors rather than just lobbyists, with positive ideas as well as complaints. They have to strengthen their devolved bodies and increase their own policy capacity and resources.

Devolution brings into being a political system in Scotland, which means that groups are enmeshed in more complex networks, including other groups seeking their own priorities, the Executive, parliamentary committees and other levels of government. They need to negotiate both with government and with each other. Business sought for a long time to remain aloof, privileging its relationships with London. It is more committed than in the past to regionalism and the benefits of territorial institutions for development and planning but, as its attitude in England shows, it prefers the institutional form of development agencies in which it has a guaranteed place rather than elected and politicised government. This has militated against the growth of territorial policy communities, in which interests, groups and government could engage in concerted action and negotiation around policies and priorities. Such forms of concerted action, a shadow of the old corporatist arrangements, have returned in the 1990s to small European nation states, including the Republic of Ireland, and could be a way in which devolved nations and regions could work out policies for their insertion into the new European and global order, but they have been slow in emerging. The fragmented system of representation in Northern Ireland, including the sectarian divisions, may make this even more difficult than in Scotland. On the other hand, if the consociational arrangements for power sharing and cooperation at the political level work out, then this might encourage parallel forms of concertation or corporatism among socio-economic actors.[5]

Devolution has been promoted as a laboratory for policy experiment, in which ideas pioneered in one jurisdiction can be taken up by others. There is a little evidence for this in the UK. The few examples include the idea of Children's Commissioner that was started in Wales, and the postponement of repayment of university fees in England, which was based on a Scottish precedent. The UK, however, lacks forums in which this type of policy exchange can take place on an equal basis. Whitehall is massively larger than the devolved administrations, is little interested in what they do, and spurns the idea that it might learn from them. Intergovernmental relations take the form of bilateral links between Whitehall on the one hand and Edinburgh and Cardiff on the other. The Joint Ministerial Committees, which might have developed into vibrant policy forums, have atrophied. The result is that Scotland and Wales can go their own way, as long as they do not make waves or upset the agenda in England. When they do so, as in free personal care, they are subjected to a massive campaign to discredit them and prevent them contaminating the debate in England.[6] The rejection of devolution in England leaves Scotland and Wales more isolated unless they, with Northern Ireland, can put together new networks for policy exchange and learning and create counter-poles to Whitehall. Such networks may also extend to Europe, and indeed are doing so with the growth of exchanges and partnerships. In many cases, however, European networks have limited themselves to rather formal matters and passing resolutions, or else have faded once the initial political impetus has been spent.

Policy fields

Experience in Scotland allows us to examine how policy making has worked in practice in one instance, both in policy style and in substance. Although the coexistence of Labour-dominated administrations in London and Edinburgh has limited the amount of policy variation, some distinct trends can be recognised and attributed in turn to public opinion, party competition, coalition politics, interest groups and institutional design.

Economic development has come to be a main concern of the devolved institutions, as it is in other countries, although this was not so apparent in the early days. The institutions in this case were largely inherited from the old Scottish Office days and policy has pursued a line common not only across the UK but in Europe more generally. Whereas the 1978 legislation kept reserved the economic development function, with a key role for the

Secretary of State, recent trends to decentralised regional policy made it more natural to devolve it this time. The emphasis has shifted from inward invest-ment and regional development grants and incentives towards endogenous development, entrepreneurship, skills and innovation. Emphasis is placed on the exploitation of research in universities and elsewhere, and on partnership with other levels of government and the private sector. Some have argued that, since the apparatus of Scottish Enterprise and the enterprise networks (the many agencies and partnerships at local level) already existed before, devolution has not made a difference and, indeed, that policy has now con-verged across the UK as agencies in the various parts have learned from each other (Newlands, 2003). There is a certainly an element of truth in this, although the convergence is Europe-wide rather than just in the UK. On the other hand, the issue is more prominent politically now that the opportunity has been taken to link economic development with other policy fields (notably higher education) and there is more political scrutiny. This has served to define development more broadly, as something that concerns the Executive as a whole, but the political debate has sometimes been rather ill-informed and focused on a rather old-fashioned way of looking at the field. Some com-mentators have claimed that, because regional development grants and budgets for the enterprise networks have not grown along with the overall Executive budget, development is not being prioritised, ignoring the fact that development can no longer be reduced to a specific budget and that modern thinking emphasises other matters including education, training, research and development and entrepreneurship. Political pressures have also led to major infrastructure schemes being adopted to suit the interests of the coalition parties with their local power bases.

A second critical area is that of social inclusion, which governments across the UK have declared to be a priority. There is some evidence that in Scotland this is incorporated more into the mainstream of policy, featuring regularly in legislation (Keating et al., 2003). Much of the work is intergovernmental, since it deals with the interface of the reserved social security system and devolved social services, health, education and planning. Social inclusion part-nerships have been set up across the country, some territorial and others sec-toral in scope. Yet it seems that much of the innovation that previously existed in Scotland has been lost and that the politicisation of public life has reduced the scope for the voluntary sector. Social inclusion partnerships are being incorporated into the new system for community planning, dominated by local governments rather than fostering new and innovative policy communi-ties challenging the centre. At the political level the emphasis since 2003 has been on antisocial behaviour, with a raft of populist measures following those adopted in England.

A third key area, and one in which Scotland has shown a different pattern, is public service delivery. Policy in England has increasingly emphasised selectivity, competition, choice and the involvement of the private sector in health, education and local government services generally, inspired by the principles of the New Public Management. Scotland, while going along with much of this, has a stronger attachment to universalism and public provision. This is partly a response to the different challenges facing social democracy in the two jurisdictions. In England, faced with a drift of the middle classes to private health and education, New Labour has sought to provide them with their own niche within the welfare state. In Scotland the challenge is less acute. The difference in Scotland also reflects the pattern of public opinion in Scotland, although it would be a mistake to read public policy directly from mass opinion. Rather party competition and the structure of policy communities in Scotland have sustained a consensus around these themes, drawing on public opinion and shaping it in turn. The difference was apparent in the health service from an early stage. Scotland has not reintroduced internal market elements as in England, and there are no star ratings or foundation hospitals. Scotland has placed more emphasis on local government as a service provider and less on the voluntary sector. There is an explicit commitment to comprehensive education, largely abandoned in England, and there are no school league tables in Scotland. All parties in the Scottish Parliament have rejected top-up fees for universities, and there is no move to create elite universities or concentrate all the research funding in a few institutions. Free personal care for the elderly was introduced following the recommendations of the Sutherland Commission, while being rejected in England. With the exception of free personal care, these differences are generally a matter of England diverging from Scotland rather than the other way round, preserving the basis of the post-war social democratic consensus. It is not uncontested, and there are forces within the Scottish Labour Party who want to follow the English model, as well as quite a lot of pressure from the south. In 2004 the Scottish Executive shifted its position on the use of private contractors within the NHS and private investment in education although, in contrast to England, schools are not being handed over entirely to private interests.

Policy style has also differed in Scotland. There was a great deal of consultation in the first session, in line with commitments made before devolution, although this generated a certain frustration and weariness among the consultees. Policy making is more deliberative, with less of a tendency to claim to know all the answers and more willingness to explore issues. The reasons for this are various, including the commitment at the outset of devolution to a more inclusive style, and the role of the committees in the Scottish

Parliament. Another factor is that the weakness of policy capacity in the Scottish Executive departments forces them to rely more on the broader policy networks. For the same reason there has been less centralisation, with local government and agencies in areas like health, higher education or economic development given greater scope. The resulting style sometimes comes across as a vagueness of objectives or a lack of strategic direction. It is variously praised as 'new politics' and 'stakeholder involvement', or criticised, especially from the New Labour perspective, as pandering to 'producer interests', but it is certainly distinct. This has meant that even although the policy agenda in Scotland is very similar to that in England, some issues, such as social inclusion, economic development or rural policy, have been framed rather differently and that policy linkages have been rather distinctive. For example, in securing wider access to higher education, the Scottish approach has been to work at a number of levels while seeking to learn more about the obstacles to inclusion, in contrast to the English intention to set targets and police them through a centralised 'access regulator'. The linkage between higher education institutions and economic development is being developed in a different way, although the basic idea has now come on to the regional development agenda in England.

Conclusion

A review of policy development in Scotland thus confirms the argument of the first part of this chapter. Policy making and divergence under devolution are not a matter of adopting a radically different stance on the great issues of stabilisation, regulation and redistribution where even nation states are limited in their scope. Rather it is a matter of emphasis in policy, of combining instruments in new ways, of mobilising social forces behind objectives and changing at the margin the balance between universalism and selectivity in the welfare state. These are important matters and they do respond to party politics, interest articulation and institutional differences, but do not often lend themselves to heroic initiatives. Policy communities are being reconstituted but this takes a long time and in the meantime they are vulnerable to strong pressures coming from the centre, which is possessed with such certainty about being right. Political devolution may have had the ironical effect of demobilising the active civil society that previously served as the vehicle for expression of ideas and opposition in Scotland, so reducing the vitality of debate. This is not an argument against devolution, any more than the dying down of civil society in central and eastern Europe is an argument against democracy, but it does point to the need for devolved institutions to be matched by other voices, and for institutions to be able to think creatively and contribute to policy development.

Notes

1 The original draft of the legislation contained provisions for calculating Northern Ireland taxation receipts as the basis for funding, but then added a clause allowing the Secretary of State to make whatever payments he/she chose, rendering the first clause redundant.
2 We have found, comparing spending allocations at different levels, that in one case the relevant figure will be reported as departmental expenditure limit and in the other case as annual managed expenditure. The devolved governments have no interest in these data being reported in a consistent manner, since this would make it easier for interest groups to demand parity by sector, thus undermining the discretion of the devolved institutions.
3 In the case of university fees, the Scottish Executive was able to find money in the medium term from Barnett consequentials of the decision to raise the participation rate in higher education in England to 50 per cent of the cohort. This target had already been met in Scotland.
4 For some commentators it is wider than government, encompassing all forms of regulation including the state, the market and civil society. For others it is narrower, referring to those aspects of government that rely on cooperation and self-regulation. Some commentators insist that we are moving from government to governance. Some even manage to argue all these propositions at the same time.
5 Corporatism bears strong relationship to consociationalism, the former dealing with social and economic actors and the latter with cultural, linguistic or ethnic groups, and they rely on similar assumptions and mechanisms.
6 Barely a month passes without a Westminster politician attacking free personal care in Scotland, on the ground that it is unaffordable or regressive, benefiting the middle classes. The latter argument is always ad hoc, isolating the case of free personal care; after all, if giving wealthy old people free personal care is regressive, it should follow logically that so is giving them free hospital care. In the spring of 2005 there was an extraordinary campaign in England to improve school meals, led by TV cook Jamie Oliver. No-one mentioned that the goals had already been achieved in Scotland and Wales. In a BBC radio interview, Oliver revealed that the English Department for Education and Skills had even told him not to mention Scotland (where he had got many of his ideas).

References

Amin, A. (1999) 'An institutionalist perspective on regional economic development', *International Journal of Urban and Regional Research*, 23 (2), 365–378.
Camilleri, J. and Falk, R. (1992), *The End of Sovereignty? The Politics of a Shrinking and Fragmenting World*. Aldershot: Edward Elgar.

Cooke, P. and Morgan, K. (1998) *The Associational Economy. Firms, Regions, and Innovation*. Oxford: Oxford University Press.

Keating, M. (1998) *The New Regionalism in Western Europe. Territorial Restructuring and Political Change*. Aldershot: Edward Elgar.

Keating, M. (2001) *Plurinational Democracy. Stateless Nations in a Post-Sovereignty Order*. Oxford: Oxford University Press.

Keating, M. (2005a) *The Government of Scotland. Public Policy Making after Devolution*. Edinburgh: Edinburgh University Press.

Keating, M. (2005b) 'Higher education policy in Scotland and England after devolution', *Regional and Federal Studies*, 15 (4), 423–435.

Keating M., Stevenson L., Cairney P. and Taylor K. (2003) 'Does devolution make a difference? Legislative output and policy divergence in Scotland', *Journal of Legislative Studies*, 9 (3), 110–139.

MacCormick, N. (1999) *Questioning Sovereignty. Law, State and Nation in the European Commonwealth*. Oxford: Oxford University Press.

Newlands, D. (2003) 'The economic strategy of the Scottish Parliament: policy convergence resulting from devolution or coinciding with it?', *Conference Proceedings of the Regional Studies Association Annual Conference*, November. London: Regional Studies Association.

Ohmae, K. (1995) *The End of the Nation State: The Rise of Regional Economies*. London: HarperCollins.

Scott, A. (1998) *Regions and the World Economy. The Coming Shape of Global Production, Competition, and Political Order*. Oxford; Oxford University Press.

Storper, M. (1997) *The Regional World. Territorial Development in a Global Economy*. New York and London: Guildford.

17
Stormont, Westminster and Whitehall

Oonagh Gay and James Mitchell

Introduction

The UK is a state of unions. It was created over centuries through a series of unions each leaving a distinct legacy, especially in how the components of the state relate to the centre at Westminster and in Whitehall (Mitchell, 2006). Northern Ireland's origins are found in the contested nature of one of these unions. Simultaneously inheriting the politics of the Anglo-Irish union while creating new politics, notably around devolved institutions, Northern Ireland's relations with the centre stand out as far less integrated than the centre's relations with any other component of the state. Not only has a separate party system operated in Stormont, but this was evident in the party system at Westminster. This had significant implications not only for Northern Ireland in Westminster but also in Whitehall. Though the unionists formerly had a relationship with the Conservatives at Westminster, these relations became distant, and eventually hostile to the point when it would be inconceivable that a unionist MP would be invited to serve as a minister at Westminster. Labour at Westminster has been close to some of the various constitutional nationalists but never so close that ministerial office at Westminster would be offered.

In his classic work, Sam Beer (1982) described the British system of politics as 'party government', in which strong, unified parties competed for support as the main influence on party and public policy. Each party competed for power and when elected sought to introduce its manifesto. This was mediated by policy communities in which civil servants and organised interests played a significant part. Party government provided legitimacy and sources of policy ideas. The existence of a separate party system in Northern Ireland from that of the rest of the UK has been important, especially in terms of representative democracy and accountability when direct rule has operated. Party government, in Beer's sense, hardly applied in Northern Ireland. The already delicate politics of territorial management were made more difficult with the inability to draw on representatives of Northern Ireland to contribute to its government. It is no surprise that the term 'direct rule' has been used when referring to what is referred to in Scotland and Wales as 'administrative devolution'. The claim that outsiders governed Northern Ireland was more difficult to refute than was the case in Scotland and Wales. Although a series of Secretaries of State for Wales after 1987 represented English seats in the Commons, there were junior ministers from Wales in the Welsh Office and, indeed, the prospect that Welsh MPs might become members of the government at Westminster. However, in one respect Northern Ireland government was consistently more home grown than elsewhere. The Northern Ireland Civil Service (NICS) was formally a separate civil service whereas the civil service in Scotland and Wales before and after devolution remains part of a unified British civil service. This should not be exaggerated, however, as there is evidence that the Scottish administration was fairly distinctive and the Scottish Office tended to recruit mostly amongst Scots (Mitchell 2003; Kellas 1989). Equally, the interaction between civil servants in London and Northern Ireland was considerable.

Party politics and Northern Ireland Members of Parliament

Westminster is a distant place to the Northern Ireland MP. Although the Ulster Unionists have had a long association with the Conservative Party, the importance of the unionist label has steadily declined with the decision of Enoch Powell to build a second career with the UUP in the 1980s – possibly the last example of a major Tory declaring Ulster as a political matter of prime importance. The defection of Andrew Hunter in the 2001 Parliament marked in contrast the end of a wayward political career.[1] On the Catholic side, the SDLP had an association with the Labour Party but this has grown much looser since 1979 and the politics of the province now excite little interest on the left in Britain, just as the SDLP remains untouched by New Labour packaging. At the same moment as the UUP has been eclipsed by the DUP, the SDLP has been eclipsed by Sinn Féin. The 'establishment' parties with remnants of links to the major British parties have, therefore, lost ground to the more hardline parties on either side of the key cleavage in Northern Ireland.

Moreover, the bi-partisan policy towards sustaining a 'peace process' in Northern Ireland, evident since the Anglo-Irish Agreement of 1985, has also weakened the bargaining position of Northern Ireland MPs. In January 1986, 15 unionist MPs resigned to fight by-elections to challenge the legitimacy of the Agreement, but only succeeded in losing a seat to the SDLP. This highlights the weakness of Northern Ireland MPs at Westminster who have lost

Table 17.1. Party totals at UK Parliament elections, 1997–2005

	DUP	UUP	UKUP	SDLP	Sinn Féin
1997	2	10	1	3	2
2001	5	6	–	3	4
2005	9	1	–	3	5

Source: Sessional Information Digests, House of Commons Library.

any special relationship with the two main parties there. Concessions may still be won, however, especially in a hung Parliament in which Northern Ireland MPs are pivotal. In the late 1970s when James Callaghan was Prime Minister, and again a decade later under John Major, British Prime Ministers, have had to make concessions to unionists. In 1978 the number of Northern Ireland seats in the Commons increased from 12 to 17 following a Speaker's Conference.[2] Though this increase would have been difficult to deny given population shares, parliamentary arithmetic in the Commons helped push Northern Ireland's level of representation up the government's agenda. Similarly, the UUP won assurances of a Northern Ireland select committee during the difficult months in which John Major's government struggled to ensure the passage of the Maastricht legislation.

Over the course of the 1997 and 2001 Parliaments there have been dramatic changes in the way Northern Ireland is represented, as shown in Table 17.1. Overall, representation has swung away from unionists, who hold 10 seats, down from 13. From 2005 unionism has been represented by a resurgent DUP, following significant fragmentation since 1998. The trend is likely to confirm the lack of interest shown by Northern Ireland MPs in the broader range of Westminster activities. David Trimble, leader of the UUP, was a noted parliamentarian who spoke on a range of subjects. The SDLP representatives tend to concentrate on Northern Ireland matters, and Sinn Féin bars itself from participation in Westminster politics.

The dual mandate member

The other characteristic setting Northern Ireland apart from Scotland and Wales is the extensive phenomenon of dual mandates amongst its MPs. Again, this is longstanding. Twenty-one of the 52 seats in the first Stormont Parliament in 1922 were held by MPs elected in 1918. However, dual mandates disappeared. In the post-war period, ambitious unionist politicians would seek a seat in Stormont where ministerial office, including the premiership, was in prospect. Relations between the Stormont government and unionist MPs at

Westminster was not always good. Meetings would take place between Stormont ministers and unionists MPs and there were efforts to coordinate activities. Stormont would brief MPs especially on matters of constitutional importance to Northern Ireland. In the 1950s each unionist MP liaised with a specific Stormont Ministry with the approval of the cabinet in Belfast (PRONI CAB4/701 29 November 1951).[3] Stormont ministers were concerned that unionist MPs should not cause offence in Westminster. MPs felt left out of decision making, and while the Stormont cabinet was sympathetic to the view that MPs should be brought more into consultation, the difficulties in doing so were recognised (PRONI CAB4/1103 21 October 1959). But far more important were discussions between Stormont ministers and civil servants and corresponding figures in Whitehall, especially amongst civil servants. Public policy making necessitated close contact between both governments, though each Parliament was careful not to step on the other's legislative and representative toes.

But the system which operated in the pre-1972 days of Stormont has not been adopted during Stormont's recent intermittent existence. Dual mandate has become the norm. In 2001 44 candidates in the Westminster elections were already MLAs; 12 of the 18 MPs elected were Assembly members. All four major Northern Ireland parties encourage dual mandates; MPs sit for the same seat in both legislatures without exception. In 2005 the trend intensified, with 16 seats held as a dual mandate. All nine DUP seats are held by MLAs, as are the five Sinn Féin constituencies. Two out of three SDLP seats are dual mandate, with the solitary UUP seat an exception to this feature of Ulster politics. The new SDLP leader, Mark Durkan, has followed the trend of Northern Ireland party leaders by getting elected to Westminster in 2005. However, the use of PR (STV) for Assembly elections means that they have MLAs with whom to share constituency work. It appears essential for all four party leaders to have dual mandates and also to aspire to the triple mandate of the European Parliament.

By contrast, although 15 Scots MPs were elected members of the Scottish Parliament in May 1999, after the 2001 general election no dual mandate MPs were elected in Scotland. There was a similar picture in Wales. There is no statutory ban on holding dual mandates in Scotland and Wales: it is purely as a result of the decisions of the major political parties, which do not encourage the practice. There is no evidence, however, that the Northern Ireland experience was researched before the single mandate trend elsewhere began. This is another example of the extent to which the Northern Ireland experience of half a century of living with devolution has generally been ignored in the debate on territorial politics since the1970s.

Dual mandates anchor Northern Ireland MPs as territorial representatives, keep them at the ringside of Westminster politics, but work against them spending time and effort at Westminster when devolution is in operation. They also reduce the tensions that have become apparent in Scotland and Wales, where elected representatives for different bodies become embroiled in the right to undertake constituency work and hence build a local profile (Bradbury et al., 2003). There is no equivalent in Northern Ireland to the Scottish Labour MP brooding on the sidelines while attention is focused on the Scottish Parliament. Unfortunately, the constituency work of Northern Ireland MPs remains almost completely unresearched and so only tentative conclusions can be drawn as to the effect of the dual mandate on local constituencies.

Throughout the Stormont years, Northern Ireland MPs attended Westminster but rarely built careers there. The pattern of Northern Ireland politics therefore has hardly altered for a century. Individual MPs with an Ulster background, such as Brian Mawhinney (Conservative) or Kate Hoey (Labour) may prosper in British politics, but only after adoption for a major party. It is almost unknown for a politician who has built their political career as a Northern Ireland representative to shift their horizon to a new career in the Commons encompassing British, rather than Ulster concerns. At first sight this is very curious, since it is common for MPs to 'outgrow' local politics and move on to the national stage. This route may not be open to nationalist MPs whose concerns lie on a smaller territorial stage, but one would expect more interest from unionist representatives who prize the connection with Britain.

The effects of a separate party system on Northern Ireland are well known; what has received less attention is the effect on Westminster. All representatives from this part of the UK belong to parties which consider the constitutional status of citizens the most important political issue – elevated above employment, the National Health Service, education and the environment. This makes Northern Ireland MPs appear unusual in their policy interests and reinforces the separate nature of Northern Ireland within the UK. Although Northern Ireland parties have a broad range of policies that take positions on conventional left–right issues, they are not familiar with the political vocabulary at Westminster. Moreover, their lack of experience in policy making and implementation, due to the existence of direct rule for a generation, limits their contribution.

Abstentions, facilities and allowances

The decision of Sinn Féin to engage in parliamentary politics has created another unique feature of Northern Ireland politics – the abstentionist MP.

In fact, this was a return to the position half a century before. It was only in the 1950s that nationalist MPs adopted a policy of full participation at Stormont and at Westminster. In 2005, 5 of the 18 MPs were elected on a platform of non-participation at Westminster. The non-participation is not absolute. Although Sinn Féin members take no part in proceedings, they take up their allowances and office space and use dining facilities. The election of two Sinn Féin MPs in May 1997 led to an immediate reaction from the Speaker, who ruled that those refusing to take the parliamentary oath could not have access to Commons facilities.[4] This was a riposte to the announcement by Gerry Adams and Martin McGuinness during the election campaign that they would adopt a new policy of active abstentionism involving the use of Commons facilities if elected. It was already a longstanding parliamentary rule that MPs had to take the oath to participate in proceedings and, since 1924, to receive a salary. Sinn Féin sought an immediate legal review of the Speaker's statement in the Northern Ireland courts in 1997, but was referred to the European Court of Human Rights at Strasbourg.[5] The Sinn Féin action was a rare example of a legal challenge to the Speaker, generally impossible due to the operation of Article IX of the Bill of Rights of 1689. The case indicated that the Commons was not outside the scope of the European Court of Human Rights, but the Court did declare the case inadmissible at Strasbourg in 1998 on grounds of proportionality.

As part of the orchestrated manoeuvres of the peace process, the Commons agreed a motion in December 2001 to allow MPs who had chosen not to take their seats to use the facilities and departments of the Commons and claim allowances. The motion did not provide for access to 'short money', which is intended to finance the research and staffing needs of front benchers, but the creation of a more generously funded system of Commons allowances in 2001 offered Sinn Féin substantial sums of public money amounting to over £100,000 per MP. The publication of details of MPs' expenditure on allowances in October 2004 revealed that Sinn Féin MPs were in the bottom half of the table of spenders in the Commons, slightly below the average of £118,250. The three Northern Ireland MPs who spent most in 2003–4 were all DUP, although their leader, Ian Paisley was placed at number 653 of MPs ranked by expenditure.[6]

Data for expenditure on allowances is only available from 2001–2, so it is not possible to estimate the extent to which expenditure on staff, office expenses, travel and living costs has increased since 1997–98. Northern Ireland parties also have access to short money. Figures for 2004–5 show that the UUP received the largest sum, at £101,576, with the DUP at £84, 812, and the SDLP received £58,416.[7] This compares with the £3.66 million received by the Conservatives. The allocations have roughly doubled since

1997–98. The UUP will no longer qualify for short money, since at least two Commons seats are necessary. It also lost office accommodation, which is allocated by the 'usual channels'.

Allowances were removed from Sinn Féin Assembly Members in 2004 following reports of continued paramilitary activity from the Independent Monitoring Commission. Westminster followed suit in April 2005 when a motion from the Leader of the Commons to suspend allowances for Sinn Féin MPs for one year from 1 April 2005 was passed in March 2005. Sinn Féin MPs may still use the facilities of the Commons and do make occasional appearances at Westminster.[8]

Mechanisms for scrutiny of Northern Ireland affairs at Westminster

Just as for Scotland and Wales, there is a Grand Committee to discuss Northern Ireland Affairs and a Select Committee to scrutinise the work of the Northern Ireland Office (NIO) in the province. There is also a monthly slot for Northern Ireland questions. These committees survived devolution following a review on the impact of devolution on Westminster by the Procedure Committee in 1998–99[9] but, as with Scotland, there was a reduction in the length of time for questions to 30 minutes from 1999. Despite the suspension of the Assembly, the question time period has not increased, and much of the 30 minutes is taken up by government and opposition interchange rather than a space reserved for Northern Ireland MPs.

Using the Commons Library POLIS database,[10] it is possible to analyse the type of written parliamentary questions (WPQs) being asked by Northern Ireland MPs. In the session 1997–98, 71 of the 106 WPQs were directed at the Northern Ireland Office. By 2001–02, and the advent of devolution, the overall number of WPQs had increased, but 191 of the 360 WPQs were for the NIO. The next largest category was 27 for the Ministry of Defence. By 2004–05 the activity rate had grown considerably, with the total number of WPQs at 1009, but 893 of those were again for the NIO. The next largest category was 18 for the Treasury. This indicates starkly the lack of interest in wider Great Britain matters. By contrast, Scots and Welsh MPs table WPQs across a wide spectrum of departments. Of the 2,067 WPQs from Scottish MPs in 2000–1, 189 were to the Scotland Office, with 571 to the Ministry of Defence. Scottish figures for 1997–98 totalled 924, of which 228 were to the Scottish Office. For Welsh MPs, 423 WPQs in 1997–98 were to the Welsh Office out of a total of 1,360. The total number of WPQs asked of the NIO in 2004–05 was 1,168 or 5.5 per cent of all WPQs tabled that session. This contrasts with the 164 WPQs asked of the Scotland Office or the 96 asked of the Wales Office. The behaviour of individual Northern Ireland MPs in tabling questions is considered more closely below.

The Northern Ireland Select Committee is the most important forum for Northern Ireland matters in the Commons. There was a long struggle by unionists to establish it. There was lack of enthusiasm on the part of the government for the scrutiny of NIO work and concern that its creation might be seen to entrench direct rule. The Committee came into being in 1994, when John Major depended on unionist votes to survive rebellions by anti-Europeans. The first chair was Jim Kilfedder, an independent unionist, and the Committee adopted a cautious line until 1997. Since then, it has tackled more contentious areas such as the Royal Ulster Constabulary (RUC). Harry Barnes, a member from 1997 to 2004, noted its usefulness to Northern Ireland MPs who could press for inquiries into local issues, such as the proposed aggregates tax (Barnes, 2004).

But territorial considerations do not predominate in the allocation of Select Committee places. In the 2001 Parliament, seven out of 13 places went to Labour and two to Conservatives, one of whom (Michael Mates) chaired the Committee. This was two more than normal select committees, in order to accommodate both the opposition and Northern Ireland members. The difficulties this causes are displayed in evidence from Michael Mates to the House of Lords Constitution Committee inquiry into inter-institutional relations in 2002.[11] There were only four seats for Northern Ireland MPs in 'their' Select Committee. These were carefully chosen to reflect the party balance – one SDLP, two UUP and one DUP. In the 2001 Parliament one Northern Ireland MP also secured a place on the Department for Environment Food and Rural Affairs (DEFRA) committee and one on Transport. The Committee's powers do not provide for formal joint meetings with MLAs or to exchange papers with its committees (in contrast with the treatment of the Welsh Assembly).

The remit of the Northern Ireland Committee expanded considerably once it was clear that suspension of the Assembly in October 2002 would continue and that it would have a duty to scrutinise government in Northern Ireland. It established a Sub-committee to scrutinise the work of the Northern Ireland Executive from January 2004 under the chairmanship of Labour MP Tony Clarke. All members of the main Committee are entitled to sit on the Sub-committee, which makes regular visits to Northern Ireland on Mondays to take evidence. This takes account of the weekly pattern of the Northern Ireland MPs who do not normally travel to Westminster until midweek. The Sub-committee is serviced by a clerk from the Northern Ireland Assembly, who can provide local expertise and input. The Sub-committee also makes a point of meeting outside the greater Belfast area. In 2004 more than one quarter of the meetings of the Committee and Sub-committee took place in Northern Ireland.[12] As its annual reports show, the activity rate of the Committee increased considerably in 2004 and 2005 in terms of numbers of evidence-taking sessions and reports. It tackled major issues, such as electoral fraud and the programme of reconciliation. Attendance at the Sub-committee and Committee meetings is good both from MPs based in Britain and Northern Ireland members, with the Committee itself meeting weekly in Westminster. Despite the election results in 2005, the balance of the new Committee has not changed, with two Conservative and seven Labour and four Northern Ireland members (two DUP, one UUP and one SDLP). The chairman is again a Conservative, Patrick Cormack. Overall, there has been a considerable change in personnel. Only two of the former MPs remain, Stephen Pound (Labour) and Gregory Campbell (DUP). The expertise of productive members such as Iain Luke and Bill Tynan has been lost. Such a turnover rate will mean that the Committee may take its time to find its feet.

One of the Committee's most important tasks is to highlight the continuing democratic deficit at Westminster. The reintroduction of direct rule means that legislation for Northern Ireland is passed by means of secondary legislation, which cannot be amended once presented. This applies for most legislation in excepted, reserved and transferred subject areas. The only exception is where the government decides on primary legislation, usually only as part of the peace process.[13] This procedure also applied before devolution in 1999, but since 2002 the government has processed Orders in Council for reserved and excepted matters through Parliament under the provisions of the Northern Ireland Act 2000, rather than use section 85 of the Northern Ireland Act 1998, which gave a two month period for statutory consultation. The justification is legal advice that section 85 cannot be used during the suspension of devolution. In its 2004 annual report, the Select Committee protested that the administrative convenience of the NIO was taking precedence over procedural propriety.[14]

One solution would be to include Northern Ireland within the legislative competence of Bills for Great Britain, allowing parliamentary debate on the effect of the legislation in Northern Ireland. This was urged by Harry Barnes in March 2004.[15] The government response was that this would add to pressure on legislative time and not serve the practical needs of Northern Ireland. A more fundamental stumbling block is the existence of a separate Northern Ireland statute book since 1922, which parliamentary draftsmen are anxious to preserve. The practice under Stormont was for it to pass parity legislation in areas of devolved competence and to allow Westminster to legislate in reserved areas. Including Northern Ireland within British legislation would negate the government position that direct rule is a temporary aberration. 'Sewel' type motions[16] have been rare during the existence of the Northern

Ireland Assembly; only two were passed, according to its Presiding Officer.[17] The Stormont practice was to allow Westminster to pass legislation in devolved areas by inter-executive agreement (Calvert, 1968).

Since suspension, Orders in Council in transferred areas have been used extensively to implement Executive-inspired Bills that the Northern Ireland Assembly would otherwise have processed. Twenty-two Bills have been dealt with in this way (Anthony and Morison, 2005: 187–189). But whereas the Assembly would have allocated hours of debate, these measures have been given only 2.5 hours of scrutiny by a Standing Committee on Delegated Legislation (where Northern Ireland MPs form a minority) in the Commons and then passed forthwith, without debate and usually without a vote on the floor of the Commons.[18]

Even apart from extensive use of Orders in Council, when primary legislation for Northern Ireland comes before each House, the norm is for inadequate time to be allowed. One example is the Northern Ireland (Monitoring etc.) Bill which was introduced into the House of Lords on 8 September 2003. The Bill received its remaining stages in the Lords on 15 September 2003, where government amendments were passed. It then went through all its stages in the Commons on 17 September and received Royal Assent the following day. The creation of a Monitoring Commission became urgent for the UK government as part of the complex peace process, and parliamentary scrutiny was deliberately minimal to fit in with an executive-inspired timetable. The two statutes which set election dates for the Assembly in 2003 received similar treatment.[19]

The Northern Ireland Select Committee complained about the treatment of the Police (Northern Ireland) Bill, which had been selected for pre-legislative scrutiny. The government decided to introduce the draft Bill to Parliament only 10 working days after its publication in December 2002. Its second reading in the Lords was on 16 December, and the Lords Committee stage began on 8 January 2003. When giving evidence to the Select Committee, the Minister explained that the haste was due to the need to obtain royal assent before Easter so that Assembly elections could take place in May 2003.[20] In the event, Assembly elections were postponed until later in the year. The Northern Ireland Committee commented in frustration: 'We call on the NIO to re-assess its priorities in preparing legislation, and to prepare its draft legislation in an organised manner which consistently allows for proper consultation.'[21] Where pre-legislative scrutiny has been available, parliamentary input has been significant. The draft Firearms (Northern Ireland) Order, for instance, became considerably more coherent and accurate due to Northern Ireland Select Committee involvement.[22] The committee also played a role in the draft Criminal Justice (Northern Ireland) Order 2004, which dealt with 'hate crime'.[23]

The final vehicle for scrutiny in the Commons is the Northern Ireland Grand Committee. This does not have a permanent secretariat and meets only when the usual channels decide, usually on a twice yearly basis. It is a forum for debate to which all Northern Ireland MPs belong, but in order partially to reflect the overall composition of the Commons, 25 mainland MPs are also members.[24] Its role expanded with devolution, when it was given the power under section 85 of the Northern Ireland Act 1998 to debate reserved measures to be enacted via Orders in Council. But with suspension it is now mainly confined to set-piece debates on Northern Ireland issues, although it debated two Northern Ireland draft orders in 2004–5.[25]

The House of Lords lacks any specifically territorial dimension, although ennobled former MPs from Northern Ireland have sat there, including the late Lord (Gerry) Fitt and Lord Molyneaux. Generally, the composition of the Lords has a London and southern bias.[26] Its Constitution Committee was established in 2001, but its 12 members had no direct Northern Ireland connections. Its inquiries into inter-institutional relations in 2002 and in the treatment of legislation under devolution in 2003–4 dealt almost exclusively with Scotland and Wales.[27] Following a Lords Procedure Committee report, a Northern Ireland Orders Grand Committee was established in 2003 to offer more scrutiny to Orders in Council on devolved matters.[28] Northern Ireland delegated legislation in general is much more commonly debated on the floor of the House, but votes are rare, following the convention that the Lords do not oppose Statutory Instruments.

West Lothian issues

Northern Ireland legislation is passed through both Houses by the votes of British parties that have no representation there. Northern Ireland Orders in Council are passed using the normal procedures for delegated legislation, and Acts extending only to Northern Ireland are treated as UK legislation. This preserves the existence of Westminster as the Union Parliament. The operation of the West Lothian question in Northern Ireland has to be understood in the context of the separate party system. Northern Ireland MPs vote regularly on policies which are (in theory at least) devolved to Northern Ireland. This is a more striking constitutional anomaly than in Scotland where statute is less clearly separated from British legislation. For example, in a crucial division on foundations hospitals in the Health and Social Care (Community Health and Standards) Bill in July 2003, two UUP MPs voted in favour, two against and the five DUP MPs voted in favour. Northern Ireland unionist parties do not abstain on West Lothian grounds, and may sometimes have the option of driving a bargain with the government. According to press reports, the DUP held talks with government whips over the issue of identity cards, but they voted against the Bill as a bloc in the vote on second reading in June 2005. This was insufficient to affect the result. The SDLP has a low participation rate in divisions, but this appears to be due more to the decision to spend time in other fora than a deliberate policy of abstention.

Westminster lived with the West Lothian question for half a century from 1922. Conventions were soon set out by the Speakers of both bodies about the non-desirability of parliamentary debate on matters outside the ministerial responsibility of the relevant administrations.[29] Northern Ireland MPs who took part in Westminster were invariably unionists and had no difficulty voting on British measures, provoking virtually no protest from the opposition.[30] When the situation deteriorated in the late 1960s, there was pressure for a more activist approach.[31] The advent of direct rule meant that the question remained unaddressed for a further generation. Its salience is reduced by the small size of Northern Ireland representation – with five abstentionist MPs in 2005, there are only 13 potential votes.

The parliamentary activity of Northern Ireland MPs

The type of data available on activity rates of MPs can only provide a partial picture of the range of parliamentary activities, and this takes no account of work in committees, lobbying government, or constituency work. There is no job description for an MP and no agreement as to whether time and energy are best spent on constituency casework, on select committee business, on tabling questions or voting in divisions. Data on the number of WPQs tabled and the interventions in debate run from 1997–98 and for divisions from 1999–2000. There has been a marked increase in participation rates for WPQs and debate contributions for both the unionist parties since 2001–2, presumably reflecting the electoral rivalry between the differing strands of unionism. In 2001–2 the data was as shown in Table 17.2. By 2004–5 the unionist parties were participating well above the rate of the average MP, but still below the rate of the Scottish nationalists (see Table 17.3).

As noted above, the questions have in the main been directed at the NIO rather than British policy issues. The rates of participation vary considerably among individual party members: David Trimble asked 42 WPQs in 2004–5, his colleague Lady Hermon asked 165, while Peter Robinson asked 15 and Iris Robinson 317 over the same session. SDLP activity rate is very low, but may well increase now that its elder statesmen have been replaced by younger party members.

Table 17.2. WPQs and debate contributions, averages per MP, per UUP, DUP, SDLP, SNP and PC, session 2001–2

	UUP	DUP	SDLP	SNP	PC	Average all MPs
Total WPQs	48	29	19	417	193	113
Total debate contributions	31	12	5	47	54	23

Source: House of Commons Library.

Table 17.3. WPQs and debate contributions, averages per MP, per UUP, DUP, SDLP, SNP and PC, session 2004–5

	UUP	DUP	SDLP	SNP	PC	Average all MPs
Total WPQs	88	83	20	186	53	36
Total debate contributions	12	6	3	13	12	7

Source: House of Commons Library.

Divisions data indicates moderate activity by unionist MPs. This may reflect the weekly pattern of life, as they tend to attend only midweek. The data does not take account of pairing arrangements or other reasons for non-participation in divisions. The average participation rate in all divisions in 2004–5 for all MPs was 64 per cent. The Northern Ireland MP who came closest to this rate was David Burnside, who scored 59 per cent. David Trimble had 41 per cent, the same rate achieved by the highest DUP MP, Peter Robinson. John Hume had a rate of just 1 per cent and the SDLP overall had an average of just 3 per cent. Clearly the SDLP had little interest in participating in divisions.

The 2004–5 divisions data can be compared with that for 2001–2 when the Assembly was in operation. But devolution makes little difference: the SDLP's rate of participation in divisions remains below 5 per cent, whereas some DUP members such as the Robinsons had participation rates above that of 2004–5: 51 per cent for Iris and 56 per cent for Peter. Yet it was only the latter who also held an Assembly seat. It is important not to put too much weight on the data from such a small sample of MPs. It is likely that unionist behaviour reflects long-term trends in voting behaviour since the 1970s and the imposition of direct rule. The only noticeable trend since 2001 is that the SDLP barely participates in divisions and the unionists parties' rate is below the average for a UK MP, but not appreciably so compared with the other minority parties. In 2004–5 the Scottish Nationalist Party (SNP) had a rate of 40 per cent, and Plaid Cymru (PC) scored 49 per cent (see Table 17.4).

Table 17.4. Participation in Commons divisions by session, Northern Ireland, SNP and Plaid Cymru MPs, 1999–2005

	Average participation rate (%)		
	1999–2001	*2001–5*	*2004–5*
DUP	18	38	36
Plaid Cymru	44	67	49
SNP	14	45	40
Sinn Féin	–	–	–
SDLP	3	4	3
UKUP	8	6	–
UUP	23	49	49

Source: House of Commons Divisions Database.

Policy making in a multi-tiered polity

Local government has been denuded of powers, devolution has been in suspension and London has little appreciation of local conditions in Northern Ireland. The peace process has dominated the concerns of senior politicians. Representative institutions have been inadequate in providing effective scrutiny of decision making, far less offering opportunities for serious policy debates and initiatives. But this has not amounted to a complete breakdown in public services. Schools provide education, doctors treat the sick and water runs through the taps. But the consequence of this system is that the normal interplay of organised interests, elected representatives and permanent officials has been replaced by a system in which elected representatives are marginalised. Northern Ireland is a polity in which professional and organised interests interact with a small civil service free from the degree of scrutiny and policy initiatives that usually emerge from the party political system.

In his memoirs, Richard Needham, the longest serving minister at the NIO, commented on how 'incestuous' and 'out of touch' many in the NIO were from the 'real world of Ulster' (Needham, 1999: 89). He commented that the 'overall direction of the health service was decided in Whitehall' where he had 'neither influence nor contacts' and he never once discussed the Northern Ireland health service with the Secretary of State for Health during the four years he was Minister (Needham, 1999: 99). While policy initiatives originated in London, Northern Ireland was rarely consulted. London civil servants were not obliged to consult their opposites in Northern Ireland and there was the added disincentive that doing so increased the risk of leaks (Needham, 1999: 110).

This democratic vacuum has been filled, as would be expected, by policy communities relating to various policy areas in Northern Ireland. In his comparative study of health policy in the components of the UK, Scott Greer noted that policies have histories and contexts, 'They will be filtered through policy communities that are entrenched in their jurisdiction, and politicians whose sense of their parties' situation shapes their behaviour. Politicians, too, have histories and roots; their personal and electoral constraints, the organisation and orientation of their party, and the overall party system all narrow the range of policies they can adopt' (Greer, 2004: 7). However, in Northern Ireland the role of politicians and the party system has been minimised, thus creating an unusual policy-making system which lacks the representative element normally expected in a liberal democracy. Greer characterised the Scottish health policy-making system as marked by professionalism, where health policy is 'strongly influenced by the country's impressive medical elites, while market reformers and corporate rationalisers look more English and have had their strongest bases south of the border' (Greer, 2004: 63) Northern Ireland, he maintains, is marked by 'permissive managerialism', a 'combination of minimal political activity (such as quality improvement, new public health, or acute care redesign) and an emphasis on running services with a minimum of fuss in the middle of a civil war. If these essential managerial goals are accomplished, then local health services can have considerable latitude to develop their own culture and focus on different issues' (Greer, 2004: 158) Traditionally, policy was imported from Whitehall, though sometimes after a gap of time.

A number of principles, vague and open to a variety of interpretations, guided Whitehall–Stormont relations regarding public policy during the pre-1972 Stormont years. To a considerable extent these were carried into the period of direct rule and beyond. Parity, leeway and step-by-step were principles which resulted in Whitehall departments taking the lead in public policy while permitting policy makers in Northern Ireland considerable secondary powers to interpret and implement but also to block innovation. Generous sums made available to Northern Ireland acted as a buffer to innovation. There was not the same financial nor the representative scrutinising pressures on decision makers to find alternative means of delivering or making policy that exist elsewhere.

Conclusion

Northern Ireland has operated in limbo between direct rule and devolution for more than 30 years. This had an impact on the relationship between representative institutions and decision making. So long as direct rule persisted or devolution is limited, the relationship between the public and the government is attenuated. The elected body which provides legitimacy to public policy decisions is Westminster, where the party system differs from that in Northern Ireland and has diverged further in recent times. This leaves policy making to those least influenced by public opinion and least accountable to elected representatives. Whitehall more than Westminster has a role in public policy and each is more significant than elected politicians from Northern Ireland. Northern Ireland has long experienced the West Lothian question in reverse – that is, a situation in which decisions affecting that part of the UK are unduly influenced by those from outside Northern Ireland. Sam Beer's notion of 'party government' never fully existed in Northern Ireland, but that did not mean that Westminster was unimportant but only that its functions were different from elsewhere in the UK. Its legitimising function was inevitably contested, but its role in scrutinising government as a source for policy ideas was limited as far as Northern Ireland's specific needs were concerned.

Ironically, the rise of the DUP means that Northern Ireland appears more separate within the UK than before. Northern Ireland's largest party has been less integrated into the party system and Westminster policy debates than the Ulster unionists have traditionally been. However, Northern Ireland's financial dependence on the UK Treasury means that London remains central. London's willingness to ask few questions and cause little trouble has meant that Northern Ireland has had, in mainstream public policy terms if no other, a relatively charmed experienced. However, it is doubtful whether, even in mainstream public policy terms, the relative absence of scrutiny and protection from new policy ideas has resulted in anything more than a stultifying conservatism in which elites have been protected from the kinds of pressures which have, largely for better, had considerable impact elsewhere in the UK.

Notes

1 Andrew Hunter sat as an Independent Conservative at the time of the dissolution of Parliament in April 2005.
2 The Speaker's Conference was announced following discussions with the UUP during a no-confidence debate on 23 March 1977 (Cmnd 7110). The Parliamentary Boundary Commission for Northern Ireland subsequently increased the allocation to 18 in the fourth periodic review, which came into effect in 1987 general election.
3 The matter of liaison with unionist MPs arose on a number of occasions at Stormont cabinets from 1945 until the onset of the Troubles: 20 March 1947;

29 November 1951; 7 August 1952; 24 July 1953; 8 July 1955; 26 March 1958; 21 October 1959; 4 November 1959; 17 October 1962; 5 December 1962; 31 January 1963; 28 October 1965.

4 House of Commons Debate, 14 May 1997, c35–36. See 'Decision as to the admissibility of application no. 39511/98 by Martin McGuinness against the United Kingdom'. The full background is explained in Commons Library Paper 01/116 *The Parliamentary Oath*, available at www.parliament.uk/commons/lib/research/rp2001/rp01-116.pdf.

5 For further details see House of Commons Library Research Paper 01/116 *The Parliamentary Oath*.

6 Data derived from *House of Commons; Members' Allowance Expenditure*, available at www.parliament.uk/about_commons/hocallowances/hoc_expenditure04.cfm.

7 House of Commons Operations Directorate, Department of Finance and Administration, as set out in Library Standard Note no. 1663 *Short Money* (available at www.parliament.uk/commons/lib/research/notes/snpc-01663.pdf). Short money is the colloquial term for money given to political parties represented in the Commons to assist with their parliamentary duties. It has been allocated since 1975. The amount is set by resolution of the House.

8 The Secretary of State issued a direction under 51B of the Northern Ireland Act 1998 in March 2005 for a period of 12 months. See House of Commons Library Standard Note no.1667 *Sinn Fein and Access to Commons Facilities*, available at www.parliament.uk/commons/lib/research/notes/snpc-01667.pdf.

9 HC 376, 1998–99.

10 POLIS is the Parliamentary Online Information Service, an electronic indexing system developed by the House of Commons Library for parliamentary material.

11 *Devolution: Inter-institutional Relations in the United Kingdom*, HL 146, 2001–2; evidence from Michael Mates, 3 July 2002 in HL 147, 2001–2.

12 HC 262, 2004–5.

13 There is a full explanation of the treatment of Northern Ireland legislation at Westminster, both during periods of devolution and suspension, in Anthony and Morison (2005).

14 HC 262, 2004–5.

15 House of Commons Debate, 17 March 2004 c306.

16 The Sewel Convention allows the UK Parliament to legislate for Scotland when the Scottish Parliament requests it to do so. See www.parliament.uk/commons/lib/research/notes/snpc-02084.pdf.

17 Evidence of Lord Alderdice to Richard Commission 19 September 2003. The number is challenged by Anthony and Morison (2005), with a useful discussion of the meaning of Sewel in relation to Northern Ireland.

18 The Commons Information Office Sessional Information Digest lists Northern Ireland Orders and the procedures used for their passage.

19 Northern Ireland Assembly Elections Act 2003, Northern Ireland (Elections and Periods of Suspensions) Act 2003.

20 See Library Research Paper 03/12 *The Police (Northern Ireland) Bill*.

21 HC 233, 2002–3, paragraph 11.

22 Northern Ireland Select Committee report for 2003, HC 146, 2003–4, paragraph 10.

23 HC 615, 2004–5.

24 SO no. 109 (May 2005).
25 Draft (Budget) Northern Ireland Order, debated 8 March 2005; Draft Higher Education (Northern Ireland) Order, 20 January 2005.
26 First report from the Joint Committee on House of Lords reform, HC 171, 2001–2.
27 HL 191, 2003–4.
28 Second report, Procedure Committee, HL 49, 2002–3.
29 For a detailed description, see Library Research Paper 95/95 *The West Lothian Question*, fn 46.
30 There was a rare exception in 1965 when Harold Wilson noted unionist intentions to vote against steel nationalisation in Great Britain. See House of Commons Debate, 6 May 1965, c1560–62. The West Lothian question, as it became known, came to the fore in the 1964–66 Parliament with a small Labour majority and pressure from nationalists.
31 For useful discussion of the convention in the 1960s see Callaghan (1973).

References

Anthony, G. and Morison, J. (2005) 'Here, there and (maybe) here again: the story of law making for post-1998 Northern Ireland' in R. Hazell and R. Rawlings (eds) *Devolution, Law Making and the Constitution*. London, Imprint Academic, 155–192.

Barnes, H. (2004) 'A decade of select affairs', *Fortnight*, 425, May.

Beer, S. (1982) *Modern British Politics*. London: Faber.

Bradbury, J., Gay, O., Hazell, R. and Mitchell, J. (2003) *Local Representation in a Devolved Scotland and Wales*, London: ESRC.

Callaghan, J. (1973) *A House Divided*. London: William Collins.

Calvert, H. (1968) *Constitutional Law in Northern Ireland: A Study in Regional Government*, London: Stevens & Sons Ltd.

Greer, S. (2004) *Territorial Politics and Health Policy: UK Health Policy in Comparative Perspective*. Manchester: Manchester University Press.

Kellas, J. (1989) *The Scottish Political System*. Cambridge: Cambridge University Press.

Mitchell, J. (2003) *Governing Scotland: The Invention of Administrative Devolution*. Basingstoke: Palgrave Macmillan.

Mitchell, J. (2006) 'Evolution and devolution', *Publius*, 26 (1), 1–16.

Needham, R. (1999) *Battling for Peace*. Belfast: Blackstaff Press.

18

Wider horizons: cross-border and cross-channel relations

John Coakley

Introduction

Unlike the devolution project in other parts of the UK, the experiment in Northern Ireland was a much more complex matter than seeking merely to define, or to redefine, the relationship between a regional capital and London. Instead, as the earlier chapters in this book have shown, by far the most important of the issues addressed in the Good Friday Agreement of 1998 and arising in the context of subsequent implementation difficulties were centred on relationships between communities within Northern Ireland rather than on the broader Northern Ireland–British relationship. Notwithstanding the huge importance of these domestic issues, though, there was another external relationship that played a central role in the Agreement: that with Dublin. In addition to this North–South dimension, indeed, yet another geopolitical context was thrown into the negotiating pot for good measure: links between the islands of Ireland and Great Britain.

The object of this chapter is to provide an overview of the manner in which these two relationships have changed in the years since the Agreement. This is done, in the respective cases, by sketching initially the shape that the relationship had taken by the 1990s, by looking at the provisions of the Agreement for institutionalising them, and by assessing the impact of the new arrangements – to the extent, that is, that these have been implemented. The considerably greater significance of the North–South dimension (or 'Strand 2' of the Agreement) is reflected in the rather greater amount of attention being devoted to that topic; the East–West dimension ('Strand 3' of the Agreement), though appearing to have formally equivalent weight, is considerably less important; and both are entirely overshadowed by the 'Strand 1' (domestic Northern Irish) institutions discussed in the earlier chapters of this book.

The North–South dimension

In an important sense, the North–South or 'Irish' dimension was at the core of the Northern Ireland problem, which had begun as a conflict between Ireland's North-East, which was unionist and opposed to any devolution for Ireland, and the rest of the island, which was nationalist and supported home rule (Arthur, 2000; Laffan, 1983). The manner in which the island was partitioned in 1921 left Northern Ireland with a large Catholic minority: there was little evidence of any serious effort to separate unionists from nationalists, and considerable evidence of pro-unionist bias behind the decision instead to maximise the number of Protestants who would be excluded from the southern entity, even if in frontier areas they were outnumbered locally by Catholics. Catholics amounted to 35 per cent of the population of Northern Ireland in the early decades after partition, but had increased to about 45 per cent by 2001.

Early home rule measures for Ireland had essentially proposed to establish an autonomous administration in Dublin that would exercise political control over the Irish civil service – over the network of boards and bodies up to then controlled by the Chief Secretary for Ireland. The 1921 partition scheme, by proposing separate administrations in Dublin and Belfast, implied (though it arguably did not fully require) a division of almost all these bodies into separate northern and southern branches. A few responsibilities were to be given to a weak Council of Ireland, which would bring together parliamentarians from the two new jurisdictions. But partition, as implemented, was surprisingly thorough, and by 1925 any remaining all-island institutions (such as the Council of Ireland) had been abandoned (Coakley, 2004; 2005).

There were few subsequent efforts to mitigate the negative consequences of this thorough-going partition of what had been a unified administrative structure (Kennedy, 2000; Tannam, 1999). Northern unionists generally welcomed their isolation from the poorer, Catholic south, and valued their links with Great Britain for hard material reasons as well as for emotional symbolic ones. There is little evidence that southern nationalists were too unhappy at the exclusion of a potentially troublesome unionist minority: it at least ensured that they could proceed with the twin processes of state- and nation-building unhindered by any significant domestic opposition. It is true that southern politicians roundly condemned partition, periodically called for unity forthwith, and apparently laid claim to the territory of Northern Ireland in the 1937 constitution; but this did not lead to any serious effort to resolve the matter, and southern politicians in general looked with disfavour on cooperating across the border in a way that would recognise partition. Northern Catholics are likely to have been the group most discommoded and least recognised by the new arrangements. Their collective demand for Irish unity of course went unheeded (and, in later decades, perhaps unheard), and their political prospects brightened only after this was repackaged after 1970 by the new SDLP as a more realistic demand for recognition of the Irish identity of a section of the population of Northern Ireland. This, the SDLP argued, should be attained through power sharing within Northern Ireland and an institutionalised Irish dimension (though at the time that this demand was first formulated it appeared to fall far outside the domain of political reality). But Catholic hopes suffered a setback when the power-sharing institutions of 1973–74 collapsed, taking with them the prospect of another interparliamentary Council of Ireland.

It is true that there was some structured cooperation between North and South even before the Good Friday Agreement, though this was very restricted in scope; and further forms of cooperation between local authorities, or 'cross-border partnerships', later supported by the EU Commission, eventually appeared (Tannam, 1999; Greer, 2001). But the Agreement of 1998 broke new ground in proposing all-Ireland structures that would fill at least part of a significant gap that had existed since 1921. The new structures were to be as follows:

- A North/South Ministerial Council (NSMC) which would meet in several formats: in plenary format (involving heads of government and other ministers from Dublin and Belfast), in sectoral format (involving ministers from the two sides with responsibility for specific areas), and in a residual 'institutional' format.
- A standing secretariat, comprising members of the Irish and Northern Irish civil services, to service the work of the NSMC.
- At least six 'implementation bodies' set up specifically to develop and implement policies in particular areas where cooperation between North and South made sense.
- At least six 'areas of cooperation', where the two administrations would work on matters of common interest, using existing and separate administrative structures in the two jurisdictions.

Unlike the position in 1973–74, no provision was made for a parliamentary tier, but the new Northern Ireland Assembly and its counterpart in the Republic were 'to consider developing a joint parliamentary forum, bringing together equal numbers from both institutions for discussion of matters of mutual interest and concern'. In addition, the establishment of a forum representing civil society interests was to be considered. These would include 'the social partners and other members with expertise in social, cultural, economic and other issues'.

It took some time for the new institutions to get up and running. First, the detail of the areas in which the implementation bodies would operate would have to be agreed between the parties. The Good Friday Agreement gave a deadline of 31 October 1998, but this was missed by more than six weeks, partly because of the complexity of the broad package within which this issue was embedded: other areas, such as the number and content of the departments in the new northern administration, also had to be agreed. In the end, six areas of cooperation identified in the list contained in the Good Friday Agreement were selected as ones where inter-jurisdictional cooperation could take place, but without requiring any new structures. A further three were designated as areas where new implementation bodies would be established; and the remaining three areas were dropped, to be replaced by three entirely new areas considered appropriate for the creation of implementation bodies.[1] Second, a legal basis for these decisions was needed. This was forthcoming through two new British–Irish agreements, signed on 8 March 1999. One provided for establishment of the NSMC; the other defined the areas of jurisdiction of each of the six implementation bodies and indicated how each was to be organised (DFA, 1999c; 1999d). Third, the political ground had to be cleared. All the new institutions were interlocking, and political disagreements on a range of issues, but with the decommissioning of paramilitary weapons looming particularly large, delayed a final comprehensive agreement on implementation until the very end of November 1999. Finally, on 2 December 1999, power was devolved to the new institutions in Belfast and to the North–South bodies.

Since then, the North–South dimension has operated only with some difficulty. First, there was a short-term suspension of the devolved institutions in Belfast from 11 February to 30 May 2000, which obviously prevented the NSMC from meeting (the Agreement is quite explicit in insisting that the institutions are 'interlocking and interdependent', and that 'in particular the functioning of the Assembly and the North/South Council are so closely inter-related that the success of each depends on that of the other').[2] Second, the capacity of ministers to attend NSMC meetings was compromised by political difficulties within the UUP and by hostility on the part of the DUP. On 28 October 2000 the Ulster unionists approved a proposal from David Trimble that would allow him to remain in office as First Minister but prevent Sinn Féin ministers from attending NSMC meetings, and the matter was not resolved until 6 November 2001, when the Northern Ireland Executive received a new lease of life following the first act of IRA decommissioning. DUP ministers simply refused to be involved in NSMC meetings, though in other respects filling their ministerial duties. Third, since the devolved institutions were suspended on 14 October 2002 it has not been possible for the NSMC to meet at all.

Notwithstanding these obstacles, rapid progress was made in kick-starting the new institutions. Four plenary meetings of the NSMC took place, each of them attended by most members of the southern and northern governments (the first meeting in Armagh on 13 December 1999 was a strikingly symbolic representation of this new form of cooperation).[3] In addition, 60 sectoral meetings took place. It was in these that most of the work involved in setting up the implementation bodies was carried out; in each case, the participants were the minister from the relevant area in the Republic, his or her counterpart in the Northern Ireland Executive, and a minister from the 'other' political tradition (for example, the last meeting of the NSMC in Ballycastle on 9 October 2002, focusing on the work of the Special EU Programmes Body, was attended by Tom Parlon, Minister for State at the Irish Department of Finance, Dr Sean Farren of the SDLP, Minister for Finance and Personnel in Northern Ireland, and Sir Reg Empey of the UUP, Minister for Enterprise, Trade and Investment). A further meeting in 'institutional' format took place to consider a range of structural and organisational issues.

With suspension of the institutions in October 2002, the work of the NSMC came to an abrupt end. Suspension created a new asymmetry in the pattern of implementation of the Good Friday Agreement. As part of the original Agreement, for example, the Republic had amended its constitution, not just dropping its definition of the 'national territory' as including Northern Ireland, but formally recognising partition – a change that, from a political perspective, was probably irreversible. But suspension also raised issues which were not just political. Several hundred employees of implementation bodies had now moved from secure positions within one jurisdiction or the other to what they had expected would be similarly secure positions in the North–South bodies. Winding these bodies up would both cause huge personnel difficulties and make any attempt to restart the process much more difficult. The governments responded by reaching a new understanding, confirmed in a formal exchange of notes on 19 November 2002, under the terms of which the bodies would continue on as before, but now under the more general political direction of the two governments, which would act on a 'care and maintenance' basis (HMSO, 2002). Under the terms of this arrangement, 167 formal agreements between the two governments were made in respect of the six implementation bodies and Tourism Ireland between 6 December 2002 and 13 October 2006; these covered areas ranging from budgets and board appointments to specific administrative matters.[4]

While progress on the North–South dimension has, then, been seriously compromised by political difficulties and in particular by the stalemate that

Table 18.1. North–South implementation bodies: staffing levels and budgets, 2004 (million euro)

Body	Headquarters	Staff[a]	Budget total	%NI[b]	%RI
Waterways Ireland	Enniskillen	341	45.95	15.0	85.0
SafeFood	Cork	37	8.81	29.6	70.4
InterTrade Ireland	Newry	42	13.04	33.3	66.7
Special EU Programmes Body	Belfast	44	2.93	54.8	45.2
Language Body		48	21.27	31.0	69.0
Irish Language Agency	*Dublin*	*41*	*18.69*	*25.0*	*75.0*
Ulster-Scots Agency	*Belfast*	*7*	*2.58*	*75.2*	*24.8*
Foyle, Carlingford and Irish Lights Commission		42	4.64	50.0	50.0
Loughs Agency	*Derry*	*42*	*4.64*	*50.0*	*50.0*
Lights Agency[c]	–	–	–	–
Tourism Ireland Ltd	Dublin	148	52.57	33.3	66.7
Total		702	149.21	29.5	70.5

Notes:
[a] Staffing levels refer to the position on 5 December 2004, and include temporary and seconded as well as permanent staff.
[b] The third and fourth columns of figures indicate the proportion of the budget of each body that was due from the Northern Ireland and Irish exchequers respectively.
[c] The staff and budget of the Commissioners of Irish Lights are not included in this table.

Source: Information provided by the North/South Ministerial Council secretariat.

has characterised the period since the suspension of the devolved institutions in October 2002, work has proceeded more smoothly at the administrative level. This is overseen by a permanent secretariat comprising more than two dozen civil servants seconded from the Irish and Northern Irish civil services, which is based in Armagh – a city of some symbolic significance as the traditional ecclesiastical capital of Ireland. The principal other permanent institutions are the six implementation bodies and a de facto seventh body, Tourism Ireland. The general characteristics of the bodies are described in Table 18.1, and they are discussed further below.[5]

Waterways Ireland

This body is one of the two that operates without an advisory board; it is instead run by a chief executive appointed by the NSMC. Its first task was to take over the functions of Shannon-Erne Waterway Promotions Ltd, a cross-border company established to manage the Ballinamore-Ballyconnell canal linking the Erne waterway system in Northern Ireland with the Shannon system in the Republic, following the restoration and reopening of the canal in 1994. It quickly assumed responsibility for the remainder of the country's navigable inland waterways, including the Bann in Northern Ireland and the Shannon, the Barrow and the Royal and Grand canals (both linking Dublin with the Shannon) in the South. Since it inherited a sizeable existing staff body, its number of employees is by far the largest of all of the bodies. Its domain of responsibility is essentially recreational, and is one where all-Ireland planning clearly makes sense.

SafeFood

The establishment of this body was delayed by David Trimble's refusal to authorise the participation of the relevant minister, Sinn Féin's Bairbre de Brún, in the necessary meetings, but the body was finally launched and its headquarters were officially opened in Cork on 24 November 2001. It is managed by a chief executive with the assistance both of an advisory board and of a scientific advisory committee, and it works alongside two food safety agencies within the two jurisdictions. Its responsibilities lie in the area of general promotion of food safety, including the communication of food alerts, surveillance of food-borne diseases, promotion of scientific cooperation and linkages between laboratories, and development of cost-effective facilities for specialised laboratory testing.

InterTrade Ireland

This body is managed by a chief executive and a board appointed by the NSMC. Its primary purpose it to promote economic development, especially by encouraging cross-border trade, in a context where the two economies on the island had followed very different paths and North–South trade had suffered from 80 years of partition. The body has been particularly active in developing an 'all-island business model' and in engaging in a wide range of knowledge-enhancing activities.

Special EU Programmes Body

Like Waterways Ireland, this body is managed by a chief executive without any board; and like InterTrade Ireland it has a particular interest in encouraging North–South cooperation in the economic and social fields. Its main function has been to assist in administering EU programmes with a strong cross-border component (such as INTERREG) or that are specifically designed to deal with the legacy of conflict (such as PEACE), and also to monitor and promote implementation of the 'common chapter' – the strategic framework for development, North and South, that forms part alike of the Northern Ireland Structural Funds Plan and the Republic's National Development Plan (2000–6). Its role has thus been closely tied to specific programmes with defined – and rapidly advancing – termination dates.

Language Body

The structure of the Language Body is more complex: it is divided into two agencies, each with its own chief executive, and the members of its board are similarly associated with one agency or the other. One agency was largely constructed out of an existing body in the Republic whose objective was to promote the use of the Irish (Gaelic) language, Foras na Gaeilge. The new agency continues with this mandate, but now on an all-Ireland basis, taking account of the different legal status of the language in Northern Ireland. The other agency is an entirely new one, intended to promote awareness of Ulster Scots language and culture – a surprising development, given the relatively muted efforts of linguistic revivalists in the language's home, the Scottish Lowlands, even after Scottish devolution.

Foyle, Carlingford and Irish Lights Commission

Like the Language Body, this was to have had a dual structure, with two chief executives appointed by the board, each responsible for an agency with a specific remit. One agency, the Loughs Agency, assumed responsibility for fisheries in Lough Foyle (which separates Northern Ireland from the Republic in the North-West), replacing an older cross-border body in this area (the Foyle Fisheries Commission, established in 1952). It was given similar responsibilities in respect of Carlingford Lough (on the south-eastern boundary between Northern Ireland and the Republic). But the second agency, the Lights Agency, never came into existence – or, at least, not in the form envisaged in the Agreement. An older body, the Commissioners of Irish Lights, dating from 1786 and operating under its present name since 1867, already operated autonomously in maintaining lighthouses around the whole coast of the island, and there were legal impediments to changing its status, arising in particular from the fact that lighthouse maintenance is a matter of British–Irish (rather than North–South) concern and thus subject to UK rather than Northern Ireland legislation. In the absence of a neat solution to this dilemma, the NSMC had been considering other options (including dropping this area, and creating an additional implementation body in a new area), but further progress was prevented by the suspension of devolution.

Tourism Ireland

Although the Agreement provided for only six implementation bodies, a seventh de facto body appeared. This was in the tourism sector – one of the six designated as 'areas of cooperation' under the Agreement, where it was envisaged that cooperation would take place through separate agencies in the two jurisdictions. Even before the Agreement, though, significant cross-border developments had taken place: in November 1996 a major joint marketing initiative, 'Tourism Brand Ireland', had been launched with the support of Bord Fáilte (the southern tourist agency), the Northern Ireland Tourist Board, and the Irish and British governments. Although the initiative suffered some early setbacks, the logic of cooperation was expressed in the creation of a new body, Tourism Ireland Ltd, on 11 December 2000. This operates as a limited company, with a board representing its stakeholders.

The areas of cooperation

The Agreement had also identified five other 'areas of cooperation'. Here, the rate of progress has been rather uneven. In some, such as *agriculture*, good working relationships developed across the border at ministerial and official level, and this was to be seen in particular during the crisis over the spread of foot-and-mouth disease among cattle in 2001 (in addition to infectious diseases of animals, cooperation covered the areas of cross-border rural development and the study of issues of common interest to agriculture on the two parts of the island). Progress in the area of *education* was slow, in part because the Northern Ireland minister, Sinn Féin's Martin McGuinness, was prevented for some time from attending NSMC meetings; nevertheless, discussions on mechanisms for cross-border school, youth and teacher exchange and on facilitating mobility of teachers reached an advanced stage, and an all-island centre for the education of children with autism was established in Middletown, Co. Armagh. But in these areas, and in others such as the *environment* and *health*, such progress as had been made came to a halt with the suspension of devolution in 2002: unlike the implementation bodies, which have a momentum of their own, the areas of cooperation depend critically on ministerial guidance through the NSMC. This dependence becomes particularly clear in the remaining area, *transport*: notwithstanding the overwhelming logic of island-level planning, the fact that this ministry was controlled on the northern side by the DUP meant that almost no progress was made.

The East–West dimension

If the high visibility of inter-communal conflict in Northern Ireland has tended to overshadow the earlier North–South, unionist–nationalist tension that was one of its primary causes, it has also tended to obscure the East–West, British–Irish tension that formed the context for this. The main thrust of Irish nationalism had, of course, been directed against Great Britain; and for many years after the creation of the new Irish state in 1922 Dublin's efforts to redefine its relationship with its former master appeared to be the dominant political issue. Constitutional changes between 1933 and 1936 and the adoption of a new constitution in 1937 all served to weaken the link with Great Britain, by explicitly reducing the role of the King to that of figurehead. The process was completed in 1949, when the King's few remaining functions as head of state were transferred to the Irish President, and the state left the Commonwealth. These changes may have pleased southern Irish nationalists as much as they dismayed former southern unionists; but there is little evidence that these reactions were shared by the northern sections of these two traditions. In fact, even though Irish unionism had traditionally argued for the retention of the whole island of Ireland within the UK, it is likely that by the 1940s northern unionists welcomed the intensification of the border that followed from Dublin's decision to break with the Commonwealth. On the other hand, there was no reason for northern nationalists to be particularly pleased: the reinforced border simply aggravated their sense of isolation and separation from the South.

It was, then, surprising that it was unionists who appeared most insistent in the course of the negotiations that led to the Good Friday Agreement on matching the 'Strand 2' institutions and the North/South Ministerial Council by 'Strand 3' institutions and a 'Council of the Isles'. There was a case for bringing the British–Irish relationship up as an issue, especially since the Agreement was designed to address the 'totality of relationships' on the two islands. But in an important sense unionists regarded this dimension as a mechanism to counterbalance the nationalist demand for a strong 'Strand 2', just as the demand for an Ulster–Scots agency may have derived not just from a commitment to that language but from a wish to echo the nationalist demand for an Irish language agency. In any case, agreement was reached on a complex body, the British–Irish Council (BIC), that brought together representatives not just of the two sovereign governments in Dublin and London, but also of three devolved administrations within the UK (Scotland, Wales and Northern Ireland) and three adjacent crown dependencies outside the UK (Jersey, Guernsey and the Isle of Man). The structure of the BIC is thus asymmetrical: it comprises one large and one small sovereign state, together with three autonomous regions and three tiny dependencies of the former, each with a formally equal voice; this gives it a more unbalanced structure than another such regional body, the Nordic Council (Fanning, 2005; Qvortrup and Hazell, 1998; Bogdanor, 1999; Winetrobe, 2000).

The establishment of the BIC encountered some of the same issues as the NSMC. Its looser structure meant that it did not require the same hard negotiation on points of detail as the latter body in the run-up to its going 'live'. Nevertheless, it had to be given formal legal effect (this was done by another British–Irish agreement on 8 March 1999; DFA, 1999a). It also had to wait until outstanding political difficulties in other areas were cleared up, and devolved government was reintroduced in Northern Ireland on 2 December 1999. Finally, the council met in 'summit' form (including the Prime Ministers and their counterparts) in London on 17 December 1999, and it has met in this form on eight occasions since then (in fact, it has met on the territory of seven of its eight members, with Northern Ireland as the only exception, and it continued to meet even after the suspension of devolution in Northern Ireland in October 2002). In addition, it has held 17 ministerial meetings to discuss particular sectoral issues, and more than 70 meetings of officials and conferences on topics of collective interest had taken place by the end of 2003 (BIC, 2004).[6] At its inaugural summit meeting, it was decided to proceed by allocating responsibility to particular governments on an archipelago-wide level. Thus, the British government took responsibility for the environment; the Irish for drug-related issues; the Scottish and Welsh for social inclusion; the Northern Irish for transport; and the Jersey government for the knowledge economy. The second summit (on 30 November 2001) allocated two further areas: tourism (Guernsey) and health (Isle of Man). Finally, the third summit (on 14 June 2002) agreed to yet another area, responsibility for which was assigned to Wales: minority and lesser used languages. The work of the BIC has not ignited the popular imagination, and it has singularly failed to attract the sustained involvement of the jurisdiction, Northern Ireland, that was responsible for its very creation; but a considerable volume of activity has taken place in two of the sectors of cooperation, the environment and misuse of drugs (where the British and Irish governments respectively have been taking the lead). Its work is supported administratively by civil servants in the Department of Foreign Affairs in Dublin and in the Department of Constitutional Affairs in London.

Another body that predates the BIC also links the two islands. The Agreement provided that the member institutions of the BIC 'will be encouraged to develop interparliamentary links, perhaps building on the British-Irish Interparliamentary Body'. This body has in fact existed since 1990 (see Cranmer and Roycroft, 2000; Armstrong and French, 2002). It was first suggested during Anglo-Irish talks in 1981, and its establishment was supported in the Anglo-Irish agreement of 1985 (a circumstance that caused unionists to regard it with particular suspicion). The body initially comprised 50 members drawn equally from the British and Irish parliaments, but its membership was enlarged to 68 in 2001, with the inclusion of representatives of the UK's three devolved regions (with five members each) and of Jersey, Guernsey and the Isle of Man (one each). As in the case of the BIC, Northern Ireland is currently unrepresented as such (the SDLP is represented through a Westminster representative, but unionists have held aloof). The body normally meets twice yearly, alternating between Ireland and the UK; its thirty-third plenary took place in Belfast in October 2006. Much of its substantive work is done through four committees: on political matters, European affairs, economic affairs, and environmental and social matters. Although its role has been advisory and consultative, it has been valuable in building up networks of contacts between parliamentarians in the two jurisdictions.[7]

Finally, reference should be made to yet another 'British–Irish' body that maintains a rather lower profile than the two just discussed. Two formal structures linking the two governments had pre-dated the Good Friday Agreement. First, an Anglo-Irish Intergovernmental Council had been established in 1981 to provide the British and Irish governments with a formal forum for the discussion of matters of common interest. In 1985 the Anglo-Irish Agreement established a second structure, the Anglo-Irish Intergovernmental Conference, supported by a standing secretariat made up of British and Irish civil servants and designed to give the Irish government a voice in the affairs of Northern Ireland. The Good Friday Agreement provided that these bodies would be replaced by a new British–Irish Intergovernmental Conference (BIIGC) which would have a similar remit to its predecessor, would have the same kind of standing secretariat, but would be open to participation by 'relevant' members of the Northern Ireland Executive (thus allowing for unionist representation).

The terms of reference of the BIIGC make it clear that it is concerned, like its predecessor, with matters that have not been devolved to the Northern Ireland institutions (thus, though its composition reflects the East–West axis, its focus is on the North–South one). Legal basis for the body was provided by yet another British–Irish treaty on 8 March 1999 (DFA, 1999b), and it came into formal existence at the same time as the other institutions on

2 December 1999. Its secretariat is based no longer in fortress-like conditions at Maryfield near Stormont (where the members of the old Anglo-Irish secretariat worked, and several of them lived) but in an office building in central Belfast. The first meeting of the BIIGC took place in London on 17 December 1999, and was one of only two to be held at summit level, involving the two Prime Ministers (the second was on 27 June 2005). But no further meeting took place while the devolved institutions were up and running. Following suspension, it met on 22 October 2002 and has been meeting fairly frequently since then. The importance of these formal meetings needs to be seen in the context of continuing intense ministerial and official-level contact between Dublin and London, whose significance for the management of politics in Northern Ireland should not be underestimated: the fact that the BIIGC may not hold 'regular and frequent' meetings, as provided for the in Good Friday Agreement, may simply reflect the volume of contact that takes place through other channels.

Conclusion

How, then, are we to assess progress on the North–South and East–West dimensions since the Agreement? In looking at the North–South dimension, a distinction between the political and administrative levels is important. At the administrative level, the implementation bodies are continuing with their work under the general oversight of the NSMC secretariat in Armagh. But the potential dynamism of the areas for which they are responsible is compromised by the fact that the NSMC has not been able to meet since 2002. While absence of political direction need not imply bureaucratic stagnation, it sets clear limits to the extent to which the new implementation bodies may respond in a creative and innovative way to changing circumstances. Perhaps understandably, little progress had been made in two other symbolically important areas by the time the institutions were suspended in October 2002, notwithstanding the prospects for significant institutional developments at that time. At its last plenary meeting in June 2002, the NSMC had approved the establishment of a North/South Consultative Forum of the kind for which provision had been made in the Agreement (it suggested a twice-yearly conference, alternating between North and South, comprising representatives of civil society, organised by a steering committee drawn from the Northern Ireland Civic Forum and the social partners in the Republic). It also agreed that officials from the Northern Ireland Assembly and the Republic's Parliament be invited to consider options for a joint parliamentary forum.

Whatever the promise of the 'Strand 2' institutions, then, their evolution has been stunted by continuing political difficulties. Nor are immediate prospects particularly bright. It is true that the DUP came close to full acceptance of the Agreement in December 2004, and that its policy on North–South cooperation calls for more accountability on the part of the bodies rather than their abolition (DUP, 2004).[8] But events since then may have deflected momentum towards an accommodation, and the party's ultimate position on implementation of the Agreement, and the timing of any decision to proceed, remain unclear. On the other hand, there is a possibility that other developments on the North–South front may bypass the stalemate on implementation of the Agreement. The Irish and British governments already cooperate closely in the energy sector, and ambitious island-level planning is an important component in the Irish government's thinking about the future (see Ahern, 2005). Similarly, even if, from the perspective of northern nationalists, the door to the creation of an all-Ireland parliamentary body is shut for the present, the Irish government appears to have agreed to consider arrangements to give northern representatives some kind of formal right of audience in Irish parliamentary institutions.

There was a time when moving to what is now described as 'Strand 3' would have taken us to the heart of the matter. Here, it must be conceded, the level of progress has been more consistent – but also much more modest. This may well be due to the absence of any single interest driving the process in this domain, and may also reflect another reality: that the bitter relationship between the two islands that was so dominant in the past has now been substantially overcome, making the pursuit of an institutional solution to political tension much less pressing. In this respect, in other words, it may well be the case that the small scale of explicit cooperation reflects not so much difficulties between jurisdictions as precisely the opposite: the absence of inter-jurisdictional problems at a level which requires an institutional response.

Notes

1 For the text of the agreement on 18 December 1998 which defined these areas, see NIA (1999: annex 2). (This document also outlines some of the further procedural details about North–South cooperation that had been agreed by 15 February 1999.)

2 These commitments in the 'declaration of support' at the beginning of the agreement are echoed in the section dealing with 'strand 2', which again states that 'it is understood that the North/South Ministerial Council and the Northern

Ireland Assembly are mutually inter-dependent, and that one cannot successfully function without the other'.

3 The other meetings took place on 26 September 2000 and 30 November 2001 in Dublin, and on 28 June 2002 in Armagh.

4 The texts of communiqués relating to these decisions are available at www. northsouthministerialcouncil.org/ip.htm (accessed 8 January 2007). See also NSMC, 2005.

5 Each of the bodies has a website, which can be accessed through the NSMC's website at www.northsouthministerialcouncil.org/inst.htm (accessed 8 January 2007).

6 See also the BIC website: www.britishirishcouncil.org (accessed 8 January 2007).

7 See the body's website: www.biipb.org (accessed 8 January 2007).

8 This agreement notoriously collapsed because of the DUP's insistence that the destruction of IRA weapons be photographed. The draft document, the substance of which had been agreed by the DUP, proposed only minor changes to aspects of the Good Friday agreement (in such areas as mechanisms for selection of First Minister and Deputy First Minister, ministerial accountability and functioning of the North–South and East–West institutions); see DFA (2004: annex B).

References

Ahern, B. (2005) *The Future of North-South Cooperation*, IBIS working papers, 50. Dublin: Institute for British-Irish Studies, University College Dublin.

Armstrong, E. and French, C. (2002) *Parliamentary Systems: The British-Irish Interparliamentary Body*. Edinburgh: Scottish Parliament Information Centre; also available at www.scottish.parliament.uk/business/research/pdf_res_brief/sb02–131.pdf (accessed 8 January 2007).

Arthur, P. (2000) *Special Relationships: Britain, Ireland and the Northern Ireland problem*. Belfast: Blackstaff Press.

BIC (British-Irish Council) (2004) *Report 1999–2003*. Dublin, London: British-Irish Council; also available at www.britishirishcouncil.org/work/report060704.pdf (accessed 8 January 2007).

Bogdanor, V. (1999) 'The British-Irish Council and devolution', *Government and Opposition* 34 (3), 287–298.

Coakley, J. (2004) 'Northern Ireland and the British dimension' in J. Coakley and M. Gallagher (eds), *Politics in the Republic of Ireland* 4th edition. London: Routledge, 407–429.

Coakley, J. (2005) 'The North-South relationship: implementing the agreement' in J. Coakley, B. Laffan and J. Todd (eds) *Renovation or Revolution? New Territorial Politics in Ireland and the United Kingdom*. Dublin: University College Dublin Press, 110–131.

Cranmer, F. and Roycroft, J. (2000) 'The British-Irish inter-parliamentary body: the first ten years', *The Table* 68, 11–16. Revised and updated version available at www.biipb.org/biipb/tenyears.htm (accessed 8 January 2007)

DFA (Department of Foreign Affairs) (1999a) *Agreement between the Government of Ireland and the Government of the United Kingdom of Great Britain and Northern Ireland establishing a British–Irish Council*. Available at http://www1.british-irishcouncil.org/documents/establishing.asp (accessed 8 January 2007).

DFA (Department of Foreign Affairs) (1999b) *Agreement between the Government of Ireland and the Government of the United Kingdom of Great Britain and Northern Ireland establishing a British–Irish Intergovernmental Conference*. Available at http://www.dfa.ie/home/index.aspx?id=8742 (accessed 8 January 2007).

DFA (Department of Foreign Affairs) (1999c) *Agreement between the Government of Ireland and the Government of the United Kingdom of Great Britain and Northern Ireland establishing a North/South Ministerial Council*. Available at http://www.dfa.ie/home/index.aspx?id=8739 (accessed 8 January 2007).

DFA (Department of Foreign Affairs) (1999d) *Agreement between the Government of Ireland and the Government of the United Kingdom of Great Britain and Northern Ireland establishing Implementation Bodies*. Available at http://www.dfa.ie/home/index.aspx?id=8740 (accessed 8 January 2007).

DFA (Department of Foreign Affairs) (2004) *Proposals by the British and Irish Governments for a Comprehensive Agreement in Northern Ireland*. Available at http://193.178.1.205/angloirish/documents/AIrish.pdf (accessed 8 January 2007).

DUP (Democratic Unionist Party) (2004) *North, South, East, West: Northern Ireland's Relationship with the Other Regions of the British Isles*. Belfast: DUP.

Fanning, R. (2005) 'The North-South relationship: implementing the agreement' in J. Coakley, B. Laffan and J. Todd (eds) *Renovation or Revolution? New Territorial Politics in Ireland and the United Kingdom*. Dublin: University Colllege Dublin Press, 132–146.

Greer, J. (2001) *Partnership Governance in Northern Ireland: Improving Performance*. Aldershot: Ashgate.

HMSO (2002) *Exchange of Notes between the Government of the United Kingdom of Great Britain and Northern Ireland and the Government of Ireland Concerning Certain Decisions of the North/South Ministerial Council*. London: HMSO; also available at www.northsouthministerialcouncil.org/pdf/cmnd_5708.pdf (accessed 8 January 2007).

Kennedy, M. J. (2000) *Division and Consensus: The Politics of Cross-Border Relations in Ireland, 1925–1969*. Dublin: Institute of Public Administration.

Laffan, M. (1983) *The Partition of Ireland 1911–25*. Dundalk: Dundalgan Press.

NIA (Northern Ireland Assembly) (1999) *Matters Referred by the Secretary of State: Report from the First Minister (designate) and the Deputy First Minister (designate)*. Available at www.niassembly.gov.uk/reports/nnia7.htm (accessed 8 January 2007).

NSMC (North/South Ministerial Council) (2005) *Annual report 2004*. Armagh: North/South Ministerial Council; also available at www.northsouthministerial-council.org/pdf/AnnualReport2004.pdf (accessed 8 January 2007).

Qvortrup, M. and Hazell, R. (1998) *The British-Irish Council: Nordic Lessons for the Council of the Isles*. London: Constitution Unit, University College London.

Tannam, E. (1999) *Cross-border Cooperation in the Republic of Ireland and Northern Ireland*. Basingstoke: Macmillan.

Winetrobe, B.K. (2000) *The British–Irish Council*. Edinburgh: Scottish Parliament Information Centre; also available at www.scottish.parliament.uk/business/research/pdf_res_notes/rn00–07.pdf (accessed 8 January 2007).

19
The European dimension

Lee McGowan

Introduction

Few areas of policy were more revolutionary and innovative for Northern Ireland politics and its political system under the devolution arrangements provided for under the Belfast Agreement than the interface with the EU. Yet the recognition, development and pursuit of this European dimension were some of the most notable (if overlooked or underestimated) achievements of the brief on/off devolution period from 1999 to 2002. The learning curve for both the legislature and the executive *vis-à-vis* EU politics and policy making had been a particularly steep one. It had commenced with a visit by most of the 108 newly elected MLAs to Brussels in the autumn of 1998 in an effort to address the generally low levels of knowledge among many MLAs about the workings of the EU. Within a few years the Assembly had produced one of a few, and arguably the most significant of its reports (Committee of the Centre, 2002) on institutional relations between the Northern Ireland devolved authorities and the EU. Moreover, by the time of the Assembly's suspension, substantial work had been done by a sub-committee on the benefits of a new and statutory Assembly committee devoted exclusively to European matters. The Northern Ireland Executive, likewise, had begun also after a slow start to acknowledge the significance and importance of the EU at the regional level and sought to explore and develop mechanisms by which the region could usefully tap into networks and processes at the EU level. The most striking illustration of this proactive engagement was the opening of the Office of the Northern Ireland Executive in Brussels (ONIEB).

In short, both the Assembly and the Executive rapidly adjusted to the impact of the EU on a host of salient public policy issues of direct concern to them. These ranged from agriculture and fisheries to the environment and the euro; all were becoming increasingly Europeanised (Featherstone and Radaelli, 2003). This accommodation was clearly evident, albeit to varying degrees, among elected politicians from all political parties and also found reflection among a majority of the Northern Ireland civil service departments. This chapter explores how Northern Ireland's devolved institutions responded to the European dimension and focuses principally on the organisational set-up, that is the formal structure of offices and key positions, and considers their efforts at actively engaging in EU policy formulation.[1]

Northern Ireland and the EU: an introduction

Northern Ireland's formal links with the EU commenced when this region acceded to the then European Economic Community (EEC) as a constituent part of the UK in January 1973. Given that accession occurred after the Stormont Parliament had been suspended the previous year, this meant that the region's former government and administration had never really needed to contemplate European affairs. Arguably, little changed within the main political parties and the civil service over the course of the next two decades. Northern Ireland's economic and political relationship with the EU was largely shaped and determined by the national level. Exploring relations between Northern Ireland and the EU after 1973 can be viewed from essentially four perspectives. These centre on: an economic assessment of the benefits of membership; an institutional analysis that focuses largely on civil service interaction with the Brussels machinery; party political approaches to EU integration; and finally, public attitudes towards the EU. This chapter focuses on the devolved institutions' responses to the EU. Traditionally, direct contacts between Belfast and the EU were largely the preserve of officials from the Northern Ireland government departments who dealt directly with the European Commission, for example, on the Social and Regional Development Funds, and on other matters such as the Common Agricultural Policy. These links intensified following the radical overhaul of the EU's Structural Funds in 1988 when Northern Ireland was designated as a single Objective One region.

The extent to which the European dimension featured as an issue among the locally elected politicians and political parties varied considerably. This is scarcely surprising given that they did not participate in the political direction of the Northern Ireland government departments. Indeed, the European dimension all too often appeared well down the political agenda of most of the political parties in this region, with the notable exception of both the pro-European SDLP and the Alliance Party.

In the wider public domain, interest in this European dimension has largely been negligible. Indeed, a broad apathy and indifference existed within both the two main Northern Ireland communities towards the European integration process. The levels of disinterest and dearth of knowledge have not substantially changed over the years and were aptly illustrated in the only major survey on attitudes towards and knowledge of the EU in Northern Ireland in 2004 (McGowan and O'Connor, 2004).[2] The European dimension has gone largely unnoticed also by a relatively disinterested media. Where and when the EU does surface as an issue it is all too often in connection with funding opportunities. The issue of European funding has clearly stimulated some interest and contacts in Brussels among parts of the wider civil society in Northern Ireland, but the European dimension goes much deeper than just grants.

European issues have been thus generally low key and to a large extent remained the preserve of the three Northern Ireland MEPs, and to a much lesser extent of the members of the two consultative and practically invisible EU institutions, the European Economic and Social Committee (ECOSOC) and the Committee of the Regions (CoR). True, the MEPs have buried their political differences in the past to lobby together for Northern Ireland interests in exceptional circumstances, such as the future of the Belfast shipyard, the bovine spongiform encephalopathy (BSE) crisis, and the creation of the EU's Special Support Programme for Peace and Reconciliation (PEACE I). However, the relationship between the three current MEPs (elected in June 2004) is far less amenable and how much cooperation will develop is questionable.[3] Local politicians have not always been entirely indifferent to Europe and combined in 1991 to part-sponsor the opening of a non-governmental Northern Ireland regional office in Brussels.[4] Nevertheless political interest was largely concentrated on the question of funding from Brussels, and tended to ignore most other aspects of EU membership. The introduction of devolution in 1999 (currently suspended since October 2002) changed the axis and structure of the Northern Ireland/EU relationship, especially as it provided for the creation of new regional political institutions that assumed responsibility for policy making (McGowan and Murphy, 2003).

European policy making remained under the Concordats a reserved matter for the UK government, but much of what had been traditionally regarded as a foreign office preserve increasingly featured as an integral part of the work of many of the nationally based and devolved departments. Indeed, it was estimated that between 60 and 80 per cent of the Northern Ireland Assembly's legislation (Committee of the Centre, 2002: 12) was destined to originate from Brussels European directives and regulations from Brussels, for example, on the environment or on agricultural issues, and went to the very core of the Assembly's policy interests.[5] Consequently there was a puissant European dimension to devolution in Northern Ireland and one that required urgent consideration if the region was ever seek to influence EU policy formulation, as well as raise its profile in an enlarged EU of 25 member states after May 2004.

There is little doubt that devolution in Northern Ireland certainly presented the potential for major change in governance. The 1998 Belfast Agreement created a series of new interlocking institutions, the primary ones being the Northern Ireland power-sharing Executive, the Northern Ireland Assembly, the North/South Ministerial Council and the British–Irish Council. These institutions were all affected by, and concerned with EU policy. Was this region, however, equipped and ready to meet the challenge of the European dimension? Did Northern Ireland, for example, have a set of clearly distinct policy priorities in comparison to the rest of the UK, much in the same way that Scotland does in relation to the fishing, whisky and oil industries (Wright, 2000)? Traditionally the responsibility for representing Northern Irish–EU interests at cabinet level rested with the Secretary of State for Northern Ireland, while the United Kingdom Permanent Representation (UKREP) was charged with representing such interests in Brussels. This arrangement continued under devolution, but the modified institutional environment in Northern Ireland under devolution provided greater scope for the devolved administration to foster institutional linkages with the EU and to pursue Northern Ireland-specific interests. These are explored below.

Institutional designs and the European dimension: the Executive

Overall responsibility for EU matters under devolution lies with the Office of the First Minister and Deputy First Minister (OFMDFM). Under the Agreement, the OFMDFM was charged with the responsibility for coordinating the European response, though the Department of Finance and Personnel (DFP) retained control over the most visible manifestation of a European input into Northern Ireland, the structural funds. Coordination in the OFMDFM was specifically the task of the European Policy and Coordination Unit (EPCU). Although a relatively small unit, EPCU sought to provide a central policy and coordination role in relation to EU issues. It was very much designed as a central resource for the Executive on EU matters and to ensure that Northern Ireland fulfilled its EU responsibilities while proactively developing a positive approach to participation in the EU. This involved ensuring that Northern Ireland government departments were aware of developments relevant to each of them at EU level. The Executive's Programme for Government (of February 2001), for example, explicitly included a commitment to develop strategies on Structural Funds, agriculture, competition, the internal market, environment and the single currency.

Many of these areas lie largely within the competence of one of the functional departments, but all required considerable input from the EPCU. EPCU's remit was therefore wide and its task was a formidable one, especially when it came to ensuring the incorporation of EU directives affecting devolved matters into Northern Ireland legislation and within the specified time limits. This task is particularly difficult and there have been a number of very advanced infringement (or infraction) proceedings against Northern Ireland (all related to environmental policy) for failure to implement the required directives.[6] Regular changes in EPCU staff have clearly not facilitated their job, but positively they have at least made a difference. Externally EPCU, for example, has sought to engage with the wider policy community, and this was illustrated in the discussions surrounding the drawing up of its 2004 European Strategy consultation paper (OFMDFM, 2004) and also concerted efforts to facilitate knowledge of the EU amongst the civil service through a number of specifically designed EU-awareness training courses. Arguably, the best illustration of how attitudes towards the EU had changed or been transformed into a much more proactive response in such a short time period was seen when OFMDFM organised a conference on the future of Europe in the late summer of 2002. Its intention was to feed into the deliberations of the Convention (under the chairmanship of Valery Giscard d'Estaing) established by the European heads of government at Laeken in December 2001 (Murphy and Phinnemore, 2005) to prepare the ground for a new treaty.[7] In contrast, early deliberations on the 2000 Nice Treaty had passed by unnoticed.

Unlike Scotland, Northern Ireland did not opt to appoint a minister of or for Europe. Instead the two junior ministers shared responsibility for, among a range of other policy areas, European matters. Part of their task was to convene an inter-departmental EU Policy Group, which replaced the perfunctory and moribund pre-devolution EU Steering Group, which was under the direction of the Permanent Secretary of the Department of Finance and Personnel (DFP). The new EU Policy Group lacked any formal timetable of meetings and the fact that it was convened by junior ministers may have detracted from its authority. However, the ministers were supported by EPCU and this amounted in itself to a significant organisational change in dealing with Europe. Discussion within the Northern Ireland Executive on matters European developed gradually. The first year was preoccupied with discussions on a Brussels office, and the Executive's Programme for Government gave priority to developing links with the EU institutions. EPCU was handed specific responsibility of this task and direct relations were strengthened with the opening of the Office of the Northern Ireland Executive in Brussels (ONIEB) in January 2002 – one of over 200 regional offices. The Brussels office, although technically part of the UKREP, occupied its own separate premises and reported directly to the devolved Executive in Northern Ireland. This unit had two core functions: on the one hand it operated as an early warning system for local government departments in so far as it could alert them to policy developments relevant to Northern Ireland; and on the other, sought to raise the region's profile in Brussels. Another aspect of the official remit of the office included supporting Northern Ireland officials in Brussels and ensuring a flow of good intelligence back to the Executive on EU matters.

Given the limited resources allocated to the Brussels office in terms of staffing levels and financial means (annual budget of about £500,000) the burden may be considerable. Nevertheless, if a vital aspect of devolution in the EU context is to enable Northern Ireland departments to monitor closely the evolution of policy in Brussels so as to ensure the earliest possible input into the process in the Commission, then the flow of intelligence to Belfast is vital. A small multipurpose office in Brussels may assist in this regard as a 'focal point' for Northern Irish interests. Critics may argue that the impact is marginal as Northern Ireland civil servants travel to Brussels on a weekly basis and these are reciprocated by Commission officials (mainly from the departments of Directorate General (DG) Regional Policy and DG Employment) travelling to Belfast. Yet even departments with their own long-established direct lines of contact and communication with Brussels, particularly the Department for Agriculture and Rural Development (DARD), have opted to use it. Commission officials have likewise indicated their satisfaction with these existing channels. This, in theory, should leave the office in Brussels, and the EPCU, more time to develop EU knowledge and awareness among other departments which, up to now, have had limited dealings with or interest in Brussels. Indeed, this is one of the priorities of the ONIEB and involves ensuring that all ministers initiate a review of their departments' dealings with the EU. ONIEB's existence has continued long after the suspension of devolution and its presence has led some of the departments, such as Agriculture, to place a desk officer in situ there in 2003 to monitor more carefully EU developments. This in itself is a positive sign of a more active engagement.

Another avenue that the Executive began to explore, albeit rather more tentatively, centred on links with the three Northern Irish representatives in the European Parliament, and the two representatives in both ECOSOC and CoR. Certainly in pre-devolution days there had not been any formal attempt to develop a coordinated Northern Ireland approach to European issues among these representatives. Post-devolution, the Northern Ireland Executive gained powers to shape developments and had the authority to nominate (to the UK government) individuals from Northern Ireland to serve on both

ECOSOC and CoR. Overall, progress here was disappointing. Certainly the MEPs, ECOSOC and CoR members were consulted (as part of the Committee of the Centre's EU Inquiry) and OFMDFM was envisaging the creation of a more formal and structured forum on the EU, including not just Northern Ireland's representatives in the EU institutions, but also other non-governmental actors involved in Northern Ireland–EU issues and relations. Surprisingly, and in contrast to the position in Scotland, little progress was made.

Within the Assembly responsibility for European and international issues had been assigned to a new non-statutory Committee of the Centre. In retrospect, this reality quickly became problematic as the Committee's remit was particularly broad and covered over a dozen policy areas (including also equality and human rights). It could be argued that under devolution the proper handling of EU business at a regional level is best handled by the functional departments where the EU impinges on areas of devolved competence. This has proved effective in the past, and continues to do so under devolution for DARD and also for DFP. Both those departments had long experience of handling EU business and had an accumulated expertise in and familiarity with the EU, but this was not replicated in all other departments. Indeed its absence in others presents formidable problems because such lack of familiarity and contact could be seriously damaging to Northern Ireland interests. In the Assembly, the departmental committees might have been expected to examine any EU business arising relevant to their departmental responsibilities. However, the serious lack of knowledge of the EU, its policies and mechanisms among the Assembly members became all too readily apparent. To make matters worse the very generalist nature of the composition of the Assembly's Committee of the Centre and its portfolio brief made this deficiency even more problematic.

In its defence this Committee recognised its limitations through its participation in the regular consultation process that exists between the specialist European Committees of the Scottish and Welsh Assemblies, and those of the Commons and Lords at Westminster. The Committee of the Centre moved to tackle such initial 'teething difficulties' on two fronts. First, it opted to launch its own inquiry into how relations with the EU could be improved (in October 2001) and second, created its own sub-committee on the necessity of an EU Affairs Committee (in the late spring of 2002). There was a general recognition that only a European Committee could effectively deal with the EU dimension. Moreover, the absence of a European Committee also removed a possible point of contact between the Assembly and other regional players at European level, principally the three MEPs, ECOSOC and CoR members.

It is significant that the Committee of the Centre did not contemplate any attempt to follow the practice of the Scottish Parliament's European Committee, which seeks to divert documentation to relevant committees and select mainline policy concerns for its own examination. The Committee of the Centre simply did not have sufficient resources to do so. Instead the lines established under direct rule between Northern Ireland departments and corresponding Whitehall departments to ensure the preparation of legislation to meet the requirements of EU directives would have continued, as would the general machinery for scrutiny and distribution of relevant EU documentation via London. Provision of such information was covered by the Concordat on Coordination of EU Policies agreed between the Northern Ireland Executive and the UK government.[8] But the primary onus for drafting and adopting such legislation lay with the Northern Ireland Executive and Assembly. This presented the Assembly and OFMDFM with a substantial challenge and an urgent need to prioritise certain policy areas.

Arguably the most innovative and radical of the institutions established under the Belfast Agreement was the North/South Ministerial Council (NMSC), comprising ministers from the Northern Ireland Executive and the government of the Republic of Ireland. It was designed 'to bring together those with executive responsibilities in Northern Ireland and the Irish Government, to develop consultation, co-operation and action within the island of Ireland – including through implementation on an all-island and cross-border basis – on matters of mutual interest within the competence of the administrations North and South' (Strand 2, paragraph 1). The NSMC has a specific mandate to 'consider the European dimension of relevant matters including the implementation of EU policies and proposals under consideration in the EU framework', and the Agreement requires that its views on these issues are taken into account and 'represented appropriately at relevant EU meetings'.

The NSMC is a truly fascinating creation and no clear explanation has yet emerged as to how the views of a body made up of the government of one member state and the executive of the region of another might be 'represented appropriately' at EU meetings (Strand 2, paragraph 17), nor what weight any such views might have. It certainly presents an interesting scenario for political scientists. On the one hand it was pointed out that the only possible line of communication was via the governments of the two member states, and that it was inconceivable that the NSMC could ever adopt a position at variance with that of the UK. Others see the potential of the NSMC as an opportunity for Northern Ireland to exert its own influence in Brussels by gaining access to the Council of Ministers via Dublin. Additional institutional complexity stems from the existence of six executive implementation bodies set up under the NSMC. One notably covers EU Special Programmes as they apply to both parts of the island. These currently include INTERREG III, LEADER+, EQUAL, URBAN II and most notably, the cross-border aspects of the PEACE II programme.

On an organisational level the impact of devolution on the handling of EU matters and on relations between Belfast and Brussels has certainly complicated the machinery of government.[9] The intial arrangements were clearly inadequate as a means of facilitating discussions about Northern Ireland's EU priorities. The innovations at Executive level to deal with the European dimension under devolution seem minimal, but must be regarded as first initial steps only as they adjusted to this European tier of governance. Nevertheless this brief period contained opportunities for Northern Ireland's devolved institutions to participate both informally and formally in the processes of EU policy making. But just how effectively?

Active or passive engagement? Northern Ireland's participation in EU policy making

To what extent Northern Ireland's interests found consideration in terms of EU decision making depended on three key factors: first, this region's ability to identify its own policy interests; second, its ability to have its interests supported and incorporated into the member state's European stance; and third, its ability to exert influence directly on the institutions of the EU, or on other member states or regions (Jeffery, 2000; Keating and Hooghe, 1996; Loughlin, 2001). In retrospect, Northern Ireland struggled to meet any of these objectives in 1999. In reality, a European dimension was simply neither readily apparent in the Assembly nor its Committee of the Centre. Worse, political and public debate on the EU was practically non-existent. Were the politicians able to take the initiative forward?

Understandably, politics in this region has been dominated by communal conflict and been isolated from mainstream political life in the UK (see Chapter 17). Under the rules of devolution, the Executive in Northern Ireland was an involuntary (or forced) 'coalition' of four parties, based not on any common policies or agreed platform, but on their numerical strength in the Assembly. This power-sharing Executive has been aptly described as a 'coalition government without a coalition agreement' (O'Leary, 2001). Development of policy has to come after, not before the formation of the Executive. The problem in these cases is that all the parties have diverging views on Europe. Of the four main parties that shared government, one, the SDLP, is enthusiastically pro-European integration, while the UUP is less enthusiastic, and the DUP and Sinn Féin are considerably more euro sceptical. Accordingly, the particular interests of the region in the European context are rarely analysed or debated. Despite the high-profile visit by both the First and Deputy First Ministers to Brussels in June 2000 there were hardly any major ministerial speeches on the EU. Of course, agriculture was the main exception, given the efforts of the Agriculture Minister, Bríd Rodgers (SDLP) in trying to argue the 'Northern Ireland case' in the wake of the foot-and-mouth disease and the continuing discussions over BSE and fishing stocks. But even here, policy has been largely reactive.

Should EU affairs have remained mainly matters for Westminster? No, because European issues affected many aspects of the Assembly's activities. Consequently, Northern Ireland's policy makers needed to prioritise and define their interests. This was never going to be a simple task for any given policy issue, as a joint Executive position had to be agreed among the four parties and often common ground did not and may not exist if and when devolution returns. Moreover, given prevailing party differences on the ongoing process of European integration, fundamental questions must be raised as to how this new form of Executive will ever approach the issue of Europe.

On a more positive note, devolution (with a regional Executive drawn from an elected Assembly and a popular mandate), should facilitate access to, and discussions with the institutions of EU governance. It should also in the first instance strengthen the region's position *vis-à-vis* the UK government. The formal mechanisms setting out relations between Stormont and London, and thus enabling the devolved authorities to have an input into the framing of UK policy on EU matters, were covered by the Memorandum of Understanding and the Concordats. The chosen vehicle for doing so was the Joint Ministerial Committee (JMC), which brought together the UK government and the three devolved administrations under the chairmanship of the Prime Minister, and included from Northern Ireland the First Minister and Deputy First Minister.

The JMC also exists in sectoral forms with an EU JMC chaired by the Foreign Secretary. The EU JMC, whose secretariat is provided by the UK Cabinet Office, was conceived as a means to institutionalise consultation between the UK government and the devolved institutions about European issues. While most matters may be dealt with by correspondence, it was widely anticipated that where disputes arise then meetings will take place. The JMC in this format seems almost a last court of appeal, designed for resolving disputes, rather than a routine mechanism for policy formulation. Otherwise the European Secretariat within the Cabinet Office in London has the function to co-ordinate the government's policy on EU issues across departments at both ministerial and official levels. The link to Northern Ireland departments is via the EPCU of the OFMDFM.

Of course, one other avenue of input for the region into national policy on EU matters centres on the Secretary of State for Northern Ireland. This individual remains responsible for ensuring that Northern Ireland interests in the EU arena are properly represented and considered at government level, even with devolution. To this end the Secretary of State, in organisational terms at least, under the devolution arrangements, relies very heavily on a small number of officials in the Northern Ireland Office (NIO) to inform him/her of where Northern Ireland's interest lies.

Conclusions

This chapter set out to explore the European dimension to the devolutionary arrangements established under the Belfast Agreement. It has demonstrated that the EU, given its policy competences, matters. It effectively started from the often unspoken assumption that access to EU decision making is, or ought to be, among the top priorities for any region achieving devolved status within an EU member state. Is it? How far can regions attempt to influence EU policy debates? To what extent does the Commission pay closer attention to regional offices when ultimately the member state government is the signatory to the treaties and exerts influence over the allocation of posts within the Commission?

Raising the region's profile at European level may be a legitimate concern of any regional government. There is a role to play. The question remains very much how to play it. The Belfast Agreement brought devolution to Northern Ireland as almost an incidental element of an attempt to resolve the historic conflict in this region of Europe. The European dimension was always going to prove a secondary consideration. Innovative aspects of devolution, such as the unique cross-border relations with another EU member state, were included to satisfy in part nationalist demands for an expression of Irish identity, not as radical means of promoting cooperation within the EU. Positively, the institutions established under devolution quickly appreciated and understood the impact of EU membership on a region, i.e. the substantial amount of legislation adopted at European level in areas of devolved responsibility and its importance to Northern Ireland, for example energy and agriculture and rural development, as well as issues such as equality and citizenship. The devolved bodies increasingly sought to develop a means to ensure that the region's interests were taken into account in the formulation of national policy. Towards the end of 2002 it is fair to argue that many of those in government in Northern Ireland were aware of these priorities, and the measures taken, both within the Executive and its departments, and in the Assembly, should be regarded as tentative first steps to deal with the impact of Brussels. There was and still is much to do when devolution returns.

Notes

1 The content of this chapter derives from the ESRC-funded research programme on Devolution and Constitutional Change (award project number L327 25 3047).

2 Full details of the research questionnaire used, the complete results and the statistical breakdowns are available on the Life and Times website run by ARK (Northern Ireland Social and Political Archive), which makes political and social information on Northern Ireland widely accessible (www.ark.ac.uk). Tables of results for every question broken down by age, sex and religion are available at www.ark.ac.uk/nilt/results/europe.html. The questionnaire is available in PDF format at www.ark.ac.uk/nilt/2002/quest02.html.

3 The three MEPs elected to represent Northen Ireland in June 2004 were Jim Allister (DUP), Bairbre de Brún (Sinn Féin) and Jim Nicholson (UUP).

4 This was called the Northern Ireland Centre in Europe and it sought to foster links with the EU institutions and open doors for groups visiting Brussels. Ultimately, however, it lacked the authority of an 'official' office and its Brussels office was closed in June 2000 due to lack of funding.

5 See Committee of the Centre Inquiry on European Union issues (Committee of the Centre, 2002).

6 Infringement proceedings relate specifically to the implementation of European Communities (EC) laws. The Treaty of Rome charged the European Commission with the responsibility of ensuring that all laws and rules are applied. In its guise as guardian of the treaties, the Commission can initiate infringement proceedings under article 226 against a member state for failure to do so. Most of the infringement issues relate to the free movement of goods, free movement of people and free movement of capital, as well as to decisions relating to public procurement and financial services. The Commission becomes aware of infringement by various means, as anyone residing in the EU or outside can lodge a complaint with the Commission against a member state on any issue that is deemed to be inconsistent with EC law. The Commission then decides whether to take the issue any further. If it does, the Commission in the first instance may wish to bring the infringement to an end after presenting a letter of formal notice to the member state government concerned. Approximately 1,000 such letters are generated each year. This reasoned opinion alerts the member state concerned to the details of the infringement and asks the country to comply with EC law. If the state in question declines to end the infringement or ignores the letter, the Commission can then take the case to the Court of Justice. The Treaty on European Union gave the Courts the authority to levy fines against states infringing EC law.

7 OFMDFM published the rationale and findings from this conference at www.ofmdfmni.gov.uk/futureofeurope/report.htm.

8 The Concordat (Cm 4444) stemmed from the Memorandum of Understanding (MoU) between the UK government and the devolved administrations and set

out the relationship between them in policy areas that remained specifically the preserve of the UK government. International relations and European (and, naturally, EU issues) represented one such policy area. In this instance the UK government would speak for the UK as a whole at Council meetings. In recognition of the significance of the EU dimension for the devolved administrations it was agreed to establish a Joint Ministerial Committee (JMC) as a mechanism to filter the concerns/issues of the devolved bodies into the UK position. The Concordat also allowed the creation of a European office for Northern Ireland in Brussels (ONIEB) but it had to work under and as a part of the UKREP (United Kingdom Permanent Representation).

9 Devolution produced one perhaps relatively minor but unexpected negative affect. Pre-devolution, the Northern Ireland departments were under the political headship of the Secretary of State and his junior ministers, all of whom were members of the UK government. This meant UK government papers circulated via the ministers to the Northern Ireland departments. Under devolution this is no longer the case, and as the Northern Ireland government departments are not local offices of Whitehall departments, there have been complaints that relevant information is not always reaching Belfast. Instead of being automatically available via the minister, these papers may now have to be sought via interdepartmental request.

References

Committee of the Centre, NIA (2002) *Inquiry into the Approach of the Northern Ireland Assembly and the Devolved Government on European Union Issues*, Report 02/01R. Belfast: The Stationery Office.

Feathersone, K. and Radaelli, C. (2003) *The Politics of Europeanisation*. Oxford: Oxford University Press.

Jeffery, C. (2000) 'Sub-national mobilisation and European integration', *Journal of Common Market Studies*, 38 (1), 1–23.

Keating, M. and Hooghe, L. (1996) 'By-passing the nation-state? Regions and the EU policy process' in J. Richardson (ed.) *European Union: Power and Policy-making*. London: Routledge.

Loughlin, J. (ed.) (2001) *Sub-national Democracy in the European Union: Challenges and Opportunities*. Oxford: Oxford University Press.

McGowan, L. and Murphy, M. (2003) 'Northern Ireland under devolution: facing the challenge of institutional adaptation to EU policy formulation', *Regional and Federal Studies*, 13 (1), 83–101.

McGowan, L. and O'Connor, J. (2004) 'Exploring Eurovisions: awareness and knowledge of the European Union in Northern Ireland', *Irish Political Studies*, 19 (2), 21–42.

Murphy, M.C. and Phinnemore, D. (2005) 'Northern Ireland and the future of Europe debate' in M. Holmes (ed.) *Ireland and the European Union*. Manchester: Manchester University Press.

OFMDFM (Office of First Minister and Deputy First Minister) (2004) *Taking our Place in Europe: Northern Ireland's European Strategy, 2004–8*. Belfast: OFMDFM.

O'Leary, B. (2001) 'The character of the 1998 Belfast Agreement: results and prospects' in R. Wilford (ed.) *Aspects of the Belfast Agreement*. Oxford: Oxford University Press, 49–83.

Wright, A. (2000) 'Scotland and the EU: all bark and no bite?' in A. Wright (ed.) *Scotland: the Challenge of Devolution*. Aldershot: Ashgate.

Index

Note: NI = Northern Ireland; RI = Republic of Ireland; entries refer to NI unless otherwise specified; 'n' after a page number indicates the number of a note on that page; italicised page numbers refer to tables or illustrations